The CSR International Research Compendium

Volume 1: Governance

The CSR International Research Compendium

Volume 1: Governance

Accountability | Transparency | Ethical Behaviour

Responsible Investment | Stakeholder Interests

Fair Operating Practices

Summaries of the Best Research from 2009 to 2014

Wayne Visser

Ileana Magureanu

Karina Yadav

KALEIDOSCOPE
Futures ▷▷▷▶▶

Contents

CONTENTS

Acknowledgements and Disclaimers

We would like to express our heartfelt gratitude to everyone who has volunteered their time and efforts to compile the CSR International monthly Research Digests between 2009 and 2014. Their work is greatly appreciated and we look forward to continuing to collaborate, as well as to welcome new CSR enthusiasts into our virtual research team.

Our thanks also goes to the researchers and the research organisations authoring the reports, surveys and papers compiled in the current compendium.

This is the first of a series of three volumes of the CSR International Research Compendium. It covers governance-related research sourced from publicly available research publications, which we have summarised. The research summaries originally appeared in our Research Digests, which have been produced and made available to the public since our free, knowledge sharing platform was launched in 2009.

The authors of each research publication are cited and readers are encouraged to refer to the original document to fully comprehend the findings. Each research publication also indicates which Research Digest it originally appeared in. These monthly Digests are prepared by CSR International as a voluntary service to its freely subscribed members.

The views expressed in the research summaries in this Compendium in no way reflect those of CSR International, nor does CSR International endorse or vouch for the quality or accuracy of any third party research included.

All the proceeds for the book will go to the ongoing resourcing of CSR International, a nonprofit organisation run by volunteers.

Introduction

By Wayne Visser, Founder of CSR International

When I founded CSR International in 2008 and officially launched the organisation as a social enterprise in London in March 2009, I had two main objectives:

1. To create a focal point for the community of professionals, students and enthusiasts who are deeply concerned about the world's social and environmental problems and profoundly inspired by the potential of business to contribute to the solutions; and
2. To be an incubator for CSR 2.0 inspired, knowledge-based solutions, through research-related projects and by constantly challenging the theory and practice of corporate social responsibility to be more effective.

As I look back over the past six years, I am satisfied that we have remained true to our original vision. Today, we have a database of over 7,000 members who have registered on our website or subscribed to our monthly newsletter. We also have more than 15,000 Twitter followers, and an active presence on Facebook and LinkedIn.

Through our virtual internship program, we have given over 500 CSR champions the opportunity to volunteer (usually for 3 months) to do research and publish book reviews, blogs, sustainability report profiles and other outputs on the CSR International website. Recently, we reached out to our membership to ask them about their vision for CSR in 2020. They identified 10 key trends, to be published in a research report in 2015.

CSR International has also been steadfast in promoting the concept of CSR 2.0, which I established as a new framework in 2008. CSR 2.0 strives to move beyond defensive, charitable, promotional and strategic CSR to transformative CSR, based on the principles of creativity, scalability, responsiveness, glocality and circularity. Applied research on CSR 2.0 has been written up in my books *The Age of Responsibility* (2010) and *CSR 2.0* (2014), as well as numerous journal papers and media articles.

CSR International also worked with Hexagon Consultores to develop an online CSR 2.0 Self-Assessment Diagnostic Tool, which professionals and consultants can be trained on and accredited to use with their companies and clients.

In terms of research projects, in 2010 we published *The World Guide to CSR*, an analysis and profiling of corporate sustainability and responsibility practices in 5 regions and 58 countries, bringing together the research of 87 contributors. In 2015, a sequel will be published called *The World Guide to Sustainable Enterprise*, which will cover more than 100 countries and appear in four regional volumes.

Besides all of this activity and these accomplishments, the most consistent thread – and arguably the greatest service we have provided – has been the monthly Research Digests. This continues a tradition I started in 2003 of summarising key findings from the best research, which I first did on behalf of KPMG and then for the Cambridge Institute for Sustainability Leadership.

Now, for the first time, we are bringing together all of the research summaries since 2009 into three thematic volumes: on Governance, Environment, and Society. This first volume alone profiles over 450 research publications relating to governance, from over 300 authors and over 250 organisations. I believe this will serve as an invaluable resource for CSR researchers and professionals everywhere.

I must express my heartfelt thanks and gratitude to my co-editors. Karina Yadav served as Research Associate and Managing Director at CSR International from 2011 to 2013 and Ileana Magureanu, our Research Director and compiler of this volume, has been active in the organisation since 2012. Between them, Karina and Ileana have put together almost all of the Research Digests over the past six years, so this Compendium is the fruit of their unfailing commitment and hard work.

I invite you to write to us at info@csrinternational.org and tell us if you find our Research Digests and these Compendiums useful, so that we know whether to continue and whether to update the Volumes periodically.

Cambridge, February 2015

I. ACCOUNTABILITY

1.1. The CSR Concept

1.1.1 Exploring the Nature of the Relationship Between CSR and Competitiveness

Author(s): M. Vilanova, J.M. Lozano, D. Arenas

This paper explores the nature of the relationship between corporate social responsibility (CSR) and competitiveness. CSR criteria used by financial analysts are identified and compared with company valuation methods, and the results of a multi-stakeholder dialogue on CSR and competitiveness of the European financial sector are presented.

Key findings

Although CSR is considered critical for companies as "a license to operate", it is rarely measured or evaluated because there is a lack of a common framework for both CSR and competitiveness.

- Reputation is a key driver in framing and embedding CSR in corporate strategy.
- The debate should, therefore, not be about reputation or competitiveness, but rather on how to best use reputation as a driver to embed CSR in core business processes that have a direct impact on competitiveness.
- CSR managers from companies seem to use corporate reputation as the key driver to sell and embed CSR internally in the organizations.
- In addition, labour unions, NGOs and other civil society organizations also seem to focus on corporate image and reputation as leverage to force corporate change towards implementing CSR.
- Most companies seem to adopt CSR approaches as a reactive, rather than proactive strategy, at least initially, usually after a specific reputation or image scandal or conflict.
- In that regard, practitioners from the European financial sector propose

that CSR impacts firm competitiveness mainly through the strategic reflection process, stakeholder engagement and management, and reputation, branding and accountability.

- The authors propose that propose that image and reputation make the connection between CSR and competitiveness through three management processes: (a) strategy, (b) stakeholder management and (c) accountability.
- That is, adopting a CSR strategy has an impact on identity and branding, which has a direct impact on competitiveness as it forces sustainable development in corporate vision through corporate strategy.
- Many practitioners argue that CSR will become a truly strategic business issue when the financial sector in general and financial analysts in particular broadly use CSR criteria to evaluate firms.
- Here, the authors propose that the fact that the financial sector and financial analysts define, judge and determine what variables are critical to firm competitiveness reflects one of the problems with the current management field.
- Current management practices, particularly in the field of CSR, are based on outputs rather than processes, which creates difficulties for understanding and managing the relationship between CSR and competitiveness.
- Thus, to explain the nature of the relationship between CSR and competitiveness, explanations should centre on framing and interpreting how companies manage their paradoxes, rather than the results, impacts or outputs generated from CSR policies.

Source: CSR Research Digest, July 2009 (Vol. 1, No. 7)

1.1.2 CSR and Quality: A Powerful and Untapped Connection

Author(s): BSR / American Society of Quality

BSR in partnership with the American Society of Quality have launched a report "CSR and Quality: A Powerful and Untapped Connection". The report explores in more depth the connection between CSR and quality, and opportunities for increased collaboration.

Key findings

Quality tools have been used by industry for decades to create lean operations, reduce waste, and improve efficiency, buy they have not been widely recognized in the corporate social responsibility space.

- CSR grapples with energy efficiency, supply chain metrics, supplier engagement several tiers away, reduced waste, and keeping a strong focus on customer value, which in the quality world can be viewed as old challenges put in a new context and for a new era of increasingly networked and globalized operations.
- Over a half-century ago, quality pioneers Edwards Deming and Joseph Juran encouraged organizations to ask better questions about corporate challenges and enabled companies to redesign systems for improvement.
- They started with a systems approach and then grounded quality in practical analytical tools to foster product, service, and organizational improvements.
- Today's CSR frameworks encourage businesses to ask better questions about impacts to stakeholders, society, and the environment, and they seek to develop the tools and measures needed to demonstrate improvements.
- CSR tools for quality management:
  - stakeholder engagement: existing CSR approaches and best practices for stakeholder engagement can help quality professionals collaborate and communicate with a wider range of internal and external stakeholders;
  - transparency: CSR reporting has innovated a range of standard nonfinancial reporting metrics and indicators that quality professionals can use to build more holistic models;
  - systems thinking: CSR approaches incorporate the interdependence inherent in ecosystems and can bring in important aspects of society and environment into business decision making.

Source: CSR Research Digest, September 2011 (Vol. 3, No. 9)

1.1.3 Corporate Social Responsibility: A Brand New Spirit of Capitalism?

Author(s): ICCSR

This paper aims to contribute to the current debate over whether corporate social responsibility (CSR) is either a source of radical change for corporations or a smokescreen to maintain business as usual. Authors intend to move beyond ideological debates and consider the managerial literature on CSR to assess its potential to influence corporate practices.

Key findings

Authors draw from Boltanski and Chiapello's work on the transformation of the spirit of capitalism, through an analysis of managerial literature.

- First, it is suggested that CSR, as advocated in the analysed literature, exhibits many of the characteristics of a potentially major transformation of corporate practices, defined by Boltanski and Chiapello as a new 'spirit of capitalism'.
- Secondly, authors also highlight shortcomings, which might undermine the transformative function of CSR, in the suggested strategies for implementation, while suggesting some directions for research and work on CSR implementation.
- These results also contribute to the ongoing research on transformations in capitalism.

Source: CSR Research Digest, January 2013 (Vol. 5, No. 1)

1.1.4 Report on Corporate Social Responsibility: Accountable, Transparent and Responsible Business Behaviour and Sustainable Growth

Author(s): European Parliament

The European Parliament has published a report on CSR and its impact on accountable, transparent and responsible business behaviour and sustainable growth. The report analyses the European Commission's definition of CSR as and disseminates the opinions of various Committees in regards to CSR.

Key findings

Commission and the Member States should encourage EU companies to take initiatives aimed at promoting CSR and to exchange good practices with their partners in other countries.

- There is a need for any regulatory measures to be drawn up within a robust legal framework and in line with international standards, in order to avoid disparate national interpretations and any risk of competitive advantages or disadvantages emerging at regional, national or macroregional level.
- Commission is encouraged to continue its efforts to promote CSR in relations with other countries and regions around the world; calls, in this connection, for greater efforts to make reciprocity a central tenet of trade relations.
- The development of CSR should be driven primarily through the multi-stakeholder approach assigning a leading role to businesses, which must be able to develop an approach tailored to their own specific situation; it stresses the need for targeted measures and approaches for the development of CSR among SMEs.
- Commission is called to ensure that an ambitious strategy is adopted in good time for the period after 2014.

Source: CSR Research Digest, March 2013 (Vol. 5, No. 3)

1.1.5   Corporation and Polis

Author(s): G. K. Henning

Given the problems in the business world, the article rethinks business from a perspective that is not (neo)Marxist or capitalist. This article does just that by rethinking the ideology of human freedom in business.

Key findings

This article argues that corporations are freer than humans under capitalism.

- Moreover, corporations, more so than humans, engage in free action, as Arendt defines action.

- To return to the place where human freedom is an actuality not ideology, we must understand the nature of freedom and how the present situation arose.
- From that we can then develop solutions.
- One solution posited here is that managers must treat employees as worthy of empowerment.
- This solution gives organizational behavior theory the ethical status that it has not had earlier.
- Even if the solution set out in this review is not functional, the view of business developed in this article is new and merits further examination in order that business can functional more ethically, including the treatment of people.

Source: Governance Research Digest, September 2011 (Vol. 2, No. 5)

1.1.6   The Icelandic Banking Crisis: A Reason to Rethink CSR?

Author(s): D. Sigurthorsson

This article discusses the 'Icelandic banking crisis' in relation to the notion of corporate social responsibility (CSR). It explores some conceptual arguments for the position that the Icelandic banking crisis illustrates the broad problem of the indeterminacy of the scope and content of the duties that CSR is supposed to address.

Key findings

The way the banks in question conceived of CSR, i.e. largely in terms of strategic philanthropy, was gravely inadequate.

- It concludes by proposing that the case of the Icelandic banking crisis gives us a reason to rethink CSR.

Source: Governance Research Digest, November 2012 (Vol. 3, No. 11)

1.1.7   The Casual Effect of Corporate Governance on Corporate Social Responsibility

Author(s): H. Jo and M. A. Harjoto

In this article, authors examine the empirical association between corporate governance (CG) and corporate social responsibility (CSR) engagement by investigating their causal effects. The study is conducted by employing a large and extensive US sample.

Key findings

First authors find that while the lag of CSR does not affect CG variables, the lag of CG variables positively affects firms' CSR engagement, after controlling for various firm characteristics.

- In addition, to examine the relative importance of stakeholder theory and agency theory regarding the associations among CSR, CG, and corporate financial performance (CFP), authors also examine the relation between CSR and CFP.
- After correcting for endogeneity bias, the results show that CSR engagement positively influences CFP, supporting the conflictresolution hypothesis based on stakeholder theory, but not the CSR overinvestment argument based on agency theory.
- Furthermore, firms' CSR engagement with the community, environment, diversity, and employees plays a significantly positive role in enhancing CFP.

Source: Governance Research Digest, February 2012 (Vol. 3, No. 2)

1.1.8 Sensemaking of Social Issues in Management by Authorities and CEOs

Author(s): *Y. Fassin, A. Van Rossem.*

This study explores how opinion leaders – CEOs and other authorities in the domain of social issues in management – understand and differentiate various concepts of social responsibility. Empirical material was generated via 41 interviews with top experts and CEOs of the Belgian economy and civil society.

Key findings

A process of sensemaking occurs amongst opinion leaders. Each individual opinion leader in the study constructed their own mental model of the state of CSR and corporate governance.

- Opinion leaders clearly differentiated corporate governance from both CSR and business ethics.

- They further confirmed an assertion within the academic literature that there is a close link between CSR and sustainability, but rejected the view that the terms 'business ethics' and 'CSR' are interchangeable, even if interrelations between the concepts are acknowledged.
- The Belgian respondents supported what is seen as the European (as opposed to the Anglo-Saxon) view that philanthropy is not a part of CSR.
- The clear distinction drawn between CSR, corporate governance and business ethics implies that companies cannot restrict their actions and programs to one single issue. Instead they must address the three complementary concepts simultaneously.
- One of the possible reasons for the intermingling of terms in corporate communications is the dilemma presented by contradictory demands and pressures from stakeholders, and the need to demonstrate compliance and responsiveness to these demands.
- Often companies feel obliged to mention 'causes of the moment' when responding to ratings and ranking agencies representing stakeholder interests.
- Depending on the sector of activity, the overall company's strategy, the managing director's views and the communications adviser selected, companies may opt for one of the leading concepts using a specific internal company terminology, or select one of the classical terms.
- In the relevant part of their report, companies then refer to the other related topics, such as business ethics, codes of conduct, sustainability, and other sub-domains relevant to their business.
- As a practical implication for practitioners the present analysis demonstrates that corporations cannot restrict their acts and programs in social issues in management to one single domain.
- Several complementary issues in the dimensions of management, governance, and values have to be addressed simultaneously.

Source: Social Research Digest, November 2009 (Vol. 1, No. 11)

1.1.9 Capitalism In Question: A Review of Corporate Responsibility

Author(s): Lifeworth

The Lifeworth Annual Review of 2009, Capitalism In Question, invites readers to explore what kind of economic system will be required for a sustainable enterprise economy. Using examples from the last year, the report highlights how leaders from business, government and civil society are joining that exploration.

Key Findings

In the move towards a period of potential reconfiguration of economic governance, leaders of organisations will need to better understand the issues, actors and dynamics in order to safeguard their success.

- Four key implications are identified as emerging from this need:
  - Moral consciousness: Without moral conscious-ness it will not be possible to engage usefully in processes concerning the common good.
  - Trans-functional competence: If managers develop a competence for trans-disciplinarity or trans-functionality, they can draw upon the expertise of different specialisms while rejecting knowledge claims from those disciplines that are identified as being the result of unhelpful assumptions or preoccupations.
  - Systems thinking: This can promote a focus on how to create new, self-sustaining relationships that could grow to influence and eventually transform wider systems. It may also encourage a de-centring of the firm in the mind of managers, such that issues are considered from a broader perspective, highlighting opportunities for mutual benefit as well as impediments to lasting progress.
  - Responsible political engagement: a key implication of awareness of the need to transform economic systems. The nature of a company's direct and indirect political influence is now understood as a key dimension of its CSR. In future, well established principles of stakeholder engagement, transparency and accountability that apply to other aspects of CSR should be applied to corporate lobbying.
- The report also offers some initial ideas about the implications for companies of a move towards 'capital democracy':
  - Becoming proactive in influencing the research and teaching agendas of business schools to address this agenda, including the competencies outlined above.

o Develop a policy and programme to promote responsible political engagement by the company and the associations it is part of.

o Shift strategic thinking from firm-centric stakeholder management to a democratic stakeholder engagement that seeks mutual benefit in addressing social challenges together.

o Examine the firm's governance and model of ownership, including whether both the purpose of the company can be legally defined to serve a social purpose, and whether greater levels of employee and customer ownership can be promoted.

o Become involved in initiatives that are seeking to transform economic systems, such as The Finance Lab, Corporation 20/20 and the Transforming Capitalism project of MIT.

o Working towards a shift in the Responsible Investment field from investor-determined interests in environmental, social and governance issues to Accountable Investment, where investors would have an obligation to respond to stakeholder-defined interests.

Source: CSR Research Digest, May 2010 (Vol. 2, No. 5)

1.2 The Business Case for CSR

1.2.1 Reviewing the Business Case for Corporate Social Responsibility: New Evidence and Analysis

Author(s): P. Schreck

The study complements previous empirical research on the business case for corporate social responsibility (CSR) by employing hitherto unused data on corporate social performance (CSP) and proposing statistical analyses to account for bidirectional causality between social and financial performance. By allowing for differences in the importance of single components of CSP between industries, the data in this study overcome certain limitations of the databases used in earlier studies.

Key findings

The econometrics employed offer a rigorous way of addressing the problem of endogenity due to simultaneous causality.

- Although the study's results provide no evidence that there is a generic or universal business case for CSR, they indicate that there is a strong link between single stakeholder related issues of CSR and financial performance.
- However, the analysis does not establish causality within these relationships.

Source: CSR Research Digest, October 2011 (Vol. 3, No. 10)

1.2.2 Do Lenders Value Corporate Social Responsibility? Evidence from China

Author(s): K. Ye and R. Zhang

Drawing on risk mitigation theory, this article examines whether the improvement of firms' social performance reduces debt financing costs (CDFs) in China. Both the ordinary least square (OLS) and the two-stage instrumental variable regression methods are employed in the study.

Key findings

It was found that improved corporate social responsibility (CSR) reduces the CDF when firms' CSR investment is lower than an optimal level.

- However, this relationship is reversed after the CSR investment exceeds the optimal level.
- Firms with extremely low or high CSR are subject to a higher CDF.
- The results also suggest that the optimal CSR level for small firms is higher than that for large firms.
- This study is the first to document a U-shaped relationship between CSR and CDF and also the first to investigate this relationship within an emerging market context.

Source: CSR Research Digest, January 2012 (Vol. 4, No. 1)

1.2.3 Do Actions Speak Louder than Words? The Case of Corporate Social Responsibility

Author(s): Duke University

The study by Duke University explores under what conditions CSR affects financial performance. The authors tested their theory using a market value equation and a database of 2,261 firms in 43 countries from 2002 and 2008.

Key findings

Symbolic environmental, social and governance actions have a greater positive impact on a company's market value than substantive actions.

- Symbolic actions have a higher impact on market value than substantive actions, when the company has higher CSR-based assets.
- A larger gap between symbolic and substantive actions has a higher positive impact on firm performance; and the more companies engage in both symbolic and substantive actions, the higher the value accumulates to the company.
- Symbolic actions include any ceremonial conformity or compliance: for example, a company announcing plans to form a sustainability or corporate ethics committee to provide the appearance of an action, without necessarily having any substance.
- Symbolic actions can be more generally described as "window dressing" or greenwashing – essentially anything designed to give an appearance of an action while allowing business to proceed as usual.
- Substantive actions are the real actions taken by an organization to meet certain expectations and often require changes in core practices, long-term commitments and investments in corporate culture.

Source: CSR Research Digest, August 2012 (Vol. 4, No. 8)

1.2.4 Survey on CSR and Profits

Author(s): Adam Friedman Associates

New York based Corporate and investor relations firm Adam Friedman Associates recently conducted a survey on corporate social responsibility globally. The survey of CSR executives focused on how executives within Fortune 1000 organizations develop, measure and report the results of their CSR initiatives.

Key findings

Profits and CSR are closely linked, and many businesses evaluate the relationship between these two variables when developing strategy.

- Some executives believe the CSR function may disappear altogether as corporations begin to absorb CSR into all aspects of their business and make it a part of every employee's responsibilities.
- As companies begin to assess and measure the effects their CSR programs have on the business's reputation, CSR may increase in both scope and importance.
- When evaluating motivations behind CSR policy, results signal that the primary motivation behind CSR initiatives lies in the company's reputation (88%), followed by the company's competitive positioning and social consciousness (71%).
- Significantly, profitability (38%) and pending or existing legislation (32%) were determined to be motivating factors.
- Results overwhelmingly show that respondents believe CSR is either very or extremely important to the mission of their companies (86%).
- Results suggest that internally the opinions of C-suite executives (86%) and other employees (76%) are most important when measuring the company's CSR efforts.
- Following the C-suite and board of directors, respondents said the legal (51%) and public relations (45%) departments were both involved nearly half the time when setting CSR strategies, and the sales (24%) and marketing (30%) departments were involved nearly a quarter of the time.
- In terms of external audiences, the opinions of customers (73%) and investors (69%) were the most important considerations when measuring CSR strategies.
- More than half the time, companies evaluated the company's media coverage (51%) and government feedback (52%) to assess the success of their CSR programs.
- When evaluating communication channels corporations use to disseminate information about the organization's CSR policies, respondents indicated that they most commonly use the company's website (95%) and the annual report (72%) for CSR-related communication, but more than half of respondents also indicated that they disseminate information via social media (54%) including Facebook and Twitter.
- Respondents said environmental issues were a top focus (96%),

followed by health issues (68%), educational issues (59%), human rights (55%), labor issues (50%) and an additional number cited safety (11%) as a program focus.

Source: CSR Research Digest, December 2012 (Vol. 4, No. 12)

1.2.5 Finding the Value in Environmental, Social and Governance Performance

Author(s): Deloitte

Deloitte has launched a new report that assesses both the short and long-term implications of ESG management. The report, called "Finding the Value in Environmental, Social and Governance Performance", suggests that ESG performance will continue to be a consideration in financial valuation and offers a number of reasons risks may play an increasingly important role on performance.

<u>Key findings</u>

Environmental, social and governance (ESG) performance can directly affect market valuation.

- The average investor is paying more attention to ESG information, especially related to downside risks;
- Volatility in the global business environment due to financial risks, regulatory uncertainty, extreme weather and social unrest are all more critical and persistent than previously thought;
- Today's lean supply chains are often brittle and vulnerable to disruption because supply chain managers may be too focused on efficiency; and
- The rise of social media rivals the impact of public politics and regulatory processes.
- Many ESG risks – from labor protests and safety concerns to ecosystem damage – are embedded in vast corporate supply chains, where they are getting more attention.

Source: Governance Research Digest, February 2013 (Vol. 4, No. 2)

1.2.6 "Good" Companies Launch More New Products

Author(s): X. Luo and S. Du

The study questions if CSR had any impact on the inventiveness and creativity of a company and investigates the idea by measuring the number of new products released each year. The researchers examined 128 firms from all major sectors, from 2001 to 2004.

Key findings

Companies in the top third of the CSR index are four times as inventive as those in the bottom third.

- Companies that operate in highly competitive industries or invest more in R&D achieved further advantage and greater return on investment in CSR and new products.
- Companies in the top third of the CSR index released on average 47 new products a year.
- One theory is that CSR strengthens relations with and understanding of customers, suppliers and other stakeholders created by CSR.
- The researchers speculate that competition energises organizational learning greater return among companies in industries such as air travel and automotive manufacturing, which generates a greater on CSR investments.
- The authors also found companies that pursued CSR activities and spent more on R&D than industry are more likely to launch first-of-a-kind innovations.
- Examples include Toyota's Prius and Marks & Spencer's new "teardrop"-shaped trailer, which uses 10% less fuel and produces 10% fewer carbon emissions.

Source: CSR Research Digest, July 2012 (Vol. 4, No. 7)

1.2.7 Does It Pay To Be Different? An Analysis Of The Relationship Between Corporate Social and Financial Performance

Author(s): S. Brammer, A. Millington

This study explores the relationship between corporate social performance (CSP) and corporate financial performance (CFP) within the context of a specific component of CSP: corporate charitable giving. 537 companies listed on the London Stock Exchange were used as the sample for this study. Their financial and social performance were measured over three different time periods.

Key findings

Firms with both unusually high and low corporate social performance have higher financial performance than other firms, with unusually poor social performers doing best in the short run and unusually good social performers doing best over longer time horizons.

- Firms in environmentally damaging industries such as mining, and those in consumer oriented sectors such as retailing, give significantly more heavily to charity than other firms, while firms in newer, cleaner industries such as the IT and electronic equipment sectors give significantly less.
- These differences might reflect a difference in the extent of spare financial resources, the availability of investment opportunities, or governance conditions between new and established firms, or the sensitivity of decisions relating to charitable giving to the broad social responsibilities of firms.
- The results of the study suggest that high performing firms either differentiate themselves by investing in an unexpectedly high degree of social responsibility or choose to save the resources that could have been invested in social responsibility.
- Those that give at an unexpectedly high rate differentiate themselves in the eyes of stakeholders and reap the benefits of this differentiation in improved employee motivation and increased customer and investor loyalty.
- Firms that give at an unexpectedly low rate conserve the financial resources they might have otherwise donated to charity.
- These resources can then be allocated to alternative investment projects or returned to shareholders as dividends.
- Firms that give at around the expected rate neither differentiate themselves from competitors nor conserve resources and may thus be

'stuck in the middle' in the sense that neither their social nor their financial performance is exceptional.

Source: Social Research Digest, February 2009 (Vol. 1, No. 2)

1.2.8   Business at its Best: Driving Sustainable Value Creation

Author(s): CECP / Accenture

"Business at its Best: Driving Sustainable Value Creation" is a report coauthored by CECP and Accenture which provides practical guidance from CEOs on how to implement a Sustainable Value Creation strategy. Insights were gathered based on CEO interviews and polling—as well as analysis and experience from Accenture and CECP.

<u>Key findings</u>

Sustainable Value Creation is a new mode of business that addresses fundamental societal issues by identifying new, scalable sources of competitive advantage that generate measurable profit and community benefit.

- 91% of CEO respondents faced difficulties in identifying an initial set of societal issues that link to competitive advantage, scaling the strategy across the company, measuring the societal and business performance of these initiatives or scaling down their scope to projects where the company can make an impact.
- Business at its Best is organized around five implementation imperatives for planning, managing and scaling a Sustainable Value Creation strategy.
- These imperatives are:
  o Recognize the Opportunity: Analyze the root causes of existing core business challenges to uncover underlying societal problems that, if addressed, may lead to new sources of competitive advantage.
  o Recalibrate Your Radar: Pinpoint the optimal role the company can play in helping to address those issues by expanding internal and external networks to tap into trends. Improve the company's ability to screen ideas based on need, uniqueness, strategic fit, and core competencies.
  o Research, Develop, Repeat: Plan and manage Sustainable Value

Creation initiatives as R&D projects and subject them to the same rigor as any corporate initiative, accommodating an iterative development cycle and being prepared to learn from setbacks.

- o Rewire the Organization: When bringing a project to scale, embed new governance structures, communications, incentives, and metrics across the organization to sustain new behaviors and attitudes.
- o Reinforce the Value: CEOs will need to assume leadership to ensure the entire company remains focused and motivated, and its stakeholders committed. This requires courageous conversations with employees, consumers, investors, and partners.
- Along with these five imperatives, the report presents company case studies and practical insights that businesses can use to implement the concept of Sustainable Value Creation.

Source: CSR Research Digest, July 2011 (Vol. 3, No. 7)

1.2.9 The Business Case of Being a Responsible Business

Author(s): Business in the Community

The report offers up-todate data on the business benefits of today, and predictions for what the benefits will be tomorrow. It is aimed to help organisations to understand what areas of operations they can look at to assess their societal, economic and environmental impact, how to gather support for building a responsible business, and why being a responsible business makes good business sense.

Key findings

To ensure viable and sustainable businesses in a more responsible – and low carbon – economy, we need to increase the speed and scale of change towards responsible business and operate in a more connected way.

- This means ensuring that responsible business is at the heart of all aspects of business operations and business models, and not just a preoccupation of one department.
- And it means new connections and partnerships that will help businesses take a more joined-up approach to their activities.

- Responsible business is not a trade-off between people, planet and profit – companies should be expanding the connections between societal and economic progress and looking at innovative ways to integrate responsible business practices into their core practices.
- A divide is emerging between those that embrace sustainability-driven strategy and management, and those that don't.
- These 'embracers' are the businesses that will survive and thrive and to help those currently at an earlier stage of the journey, we need to provide the proof – the argument and numbers – that show why and how responsible business practices build successful organisations, to help them define those materially relevant to them.

Source: Governance Research Digest, June 2011 (Vol. 2, No. 2)

1.2.10 When Does a Corporate Social Responsibility Initiative Provide a First Mover Advantage?

Author(s): C-A. Tetrault Sirsly, K. Lamertz

In this paper the authors assess strategic CSR initiatives and examine the conditions that might give rise to a sustainable competitive advantage in social performance. The article asks in what circumstances a firm's CSR initiative creates a first-mover advantage, and when a firm should prefer an early- or late-adopter position.

Key findings

For a CSR initiative to lead to a sustainable firstmover advantage, it must be central to the firm's mission, provide firm-specific benefits, and be made visible to external audiences.

- These strategic attributes generate internal sustainability and must be complemented to ensure external defensibility by a firm's ability to assess its environment, manage its stakeholders, and deal with social issues.
- The theory of first-mover advantage and the resource-based view of the firm are both concerned with the strategic competitive advantage of business firms in markets where the need for a sustainable economic advantage is implicit. However, today's business reality means that

firms must act strategically, not just in their traditional product and factor market domains but also in their non-market environments.

- A superior bundle of CSR capabilities is a necessary but not sufficient condition for building a first-mover advantage in CSR initiatives.
- In addition to economic benefits, CSR initiatives also lead to social benefits in the form of legitimacy and reputation both of which are classified as strategic organizational resources.
- First-mover advantage requires two essential elements: (a) the initiation of a CSR activity that is integrated into the firm's competitive strategy and (b) the development of capabilities for performing that CSR activity rooted in asymmetries between the firm's nonmarket strategic behavior and that of its competitors.
- CSR initiatives may be a source of sustainable competitive advantage in gaining economic or social benefits or both when such an initiative is strategic and supported by CSR process capabilities that advantage a focal firm over its competitors.
- The former ensures that an advantage in CSR benefits and its sustainability are supported from inside the firm, whereas the latter focuses on the importance of sustainable advantage for maintaining the CSR initiative in relation to external competitors for similar benefits.
- It is suggested that these two elements work in conjunction to support each other.
- A first-mover advantage is thus likely to accrue to a firm and generate sustainable competitive advantage when it capitalizes on asymmetries in environmental scanning, stakeholder management, and issues management to develop a strategic CSR initiative that is central to the firm mission, visible to stakeholders and with firm-specific benefits beyond those of public good.
- Variation in such advantage is likely to be observed when one or more of the attributes that make the initiative strategic fail to materialize.
- Some specific outcomes of achieving firstmover advantage include being able to establish the firm as the model or benchmark against which all others are judged, setting the industry standards, influencing the direction of environmental regulations, and reinforcing the firm's reputation to embed legitimacy in the eyes of its stakeholders.

- The distinctiveness of the CSR initiative will procure significant firm-specific benefits, of which some, such as reputation, are intangible, whereas others, such as cost reduction, are material.
- Whether it is a readily quantifiable financial advantage or a more intangible leadership advantage will depend on the nature of the CSR initiative and the stakeholders involved.

Source: CSR Research Digest, February 2009 (Vol. 1, No. 2)

1.2.11 Entrepreneurial Ecosystems Around the Globe and Early-Stage Company Growth Dynamics

Author(s): World Economic Forum, Stanford University and Ernst & Young

The World Economic Forum, in collaboration with Stanford University and Ernst & Young surveyed over 1,000 entrepreneurs from around the globe with the goal of better understanding how successful entrepreneurial companies speed access to new markets and become scalable, high-growth businesses. The report, Entrepreneurial Ecosystems Around the Globe and Early-Stage Company Growth Dynamics, features executive case studies for 43 companies from 23 different countries.

Key findings

- Entrepreneurs are key drivers of economic and social progress. Rapidly growing entrepreneurial enterprises are often viewed as important sources of innovation, productivity growth and employment (small and medium-sized enterprises account for a high percentage of all jobs in emerging economies).
- For entrepreneurs, major differences in entrepreneurial ecosystems exist from one region to the next. When entrepreneurs consider expansion opportunities beyond their country or region, there is a potential alignment issue with governments that often adopt a strong "within country/ region" focus in their entrepreneurial ecosystem policies.
- According to entrepreneurs, three areas of an entrepreneurial ecosystem are of pivotal importance – accessible markets, human capital/workforce and funding & finance. This report is the first large-scale study that systematically examines which pillars of an ecosystem

matter most to entrepreneurs when it comes to the growth of their companies. A potential alignment issue can arise between the time horizon of an entrepreneur and that of a policy-maker or politician, with the time horizon of the latter two typically following the electoral cycle.

- In most regions, only a small number of breakout companies are the main contributors to a healthy, growing early-stage company sector. There are also substantially more similarities than differences in the issues facing entrepreneurs around the globe. These similarities appear in all regions and have an impact on the major growth accelerators and growth challenges for early-stage companies.

- Large companies in the overall business ecosystem have the potential to provide important leverage for early-stage companies in their growth and development. However, there are potential pitfalls to navigate through in the relationship. The report highlights areas for productive relationships as well as areas where relationships can inhibit growth or be the source of revenue and job destruction in an early-stage company.

- Entrepreneurs themselves can play multiple important roles in the build-out of an entrepreneurial ecosystem. Using case studies from Endeavor, five important roles are illustrated – mentorship, inspiration, investment, new founders and new employees.

- Government and regulatory policies are viewed by entrepreneurs as both potential growth accelerators and growth inhibitors. The report highlights examples of case studies from different geographical regions that reflect the positive and negative impact economic policies can have on entrepreneurs. In some cases, entrepreneurs believe that government/regulatory policies aimed at supporting economic growth can actually be counterproductive to the growth of their early-stage company.

Source: CSR Research Digest, April 2014 (Vol. 6, No. 4)

1.2.12 The Good, the Generous and the Galvanic: Marketing's Role in Social Responsibility

Author(s): The Australian Market Institute

The Australian Market Institute published a paper designed to stimulate thinking and debate within organisations and the broader marketing community by highlighting key issues around social responsibility and their connection with marketing at multiple levels. In particular, The Good, the Generous and the Galvanic: Marketing's Role in Social Responsibility explores how marketers could play a more proactive role in enabling organisations to become increasingly responsible socially, environmentally and ethically while ensuring the sustainability of bottom line performance.

<u>Key findings</u>

- Marketers have influence on a number of key organisational processes which generally relate to their core marketing responsibility: management of the 4 Ps. It could be argued that in many organisations, while marketers have control of promotion and possibly place, their influence on other elements of the marketing mix, namely, pricing and product (for instance, in terms of sourcing) can be limited.
- The good looks at aspects of marketing mostly within the direct control or influence of the marketing function. In other words, decisions relating to product, pricing, promotion and distribution etc., that have the potential to create opportunities for demonstrating greater transparency in corporate behaviour and concern for the consumer, society and environment collectively leading to increased reputation, competitive advantage or brand preference.
- As part of their CSR charter, organisations can support a wide range of programs involving health, literacy/education, indigenous wellbeing, human rights, poverty alleviation, homelessness, women's emancipation, discrimination against girls, youth suicide, obesity, environment protection, pollution, alternative energy, waste disposal and so on.
- The generous focuses on what is commonly regarded as corporate social responsibility, a term that has been used loosely to represent any activity that signals an organisation's commitment to giving back to society and the community whether or not there is a direct or indirect benefit to the organisation's present or future performance.
- The underlying principle is the creation of value that can be shared by both the community and the organisation. This incremental value could be a result of a new technology, a renewed operating model, transfer of

missing skills or infrastructure, or building additional capacity; anything that allows the organisation to add value to their business model through cost reduction, assured supply, improved quality or similar benefits. At the same time, it allows the host community to become engaged in productive income-generating activity, boost its purchasing power and improve the lifestyles of its people.

- The third and final dimension, the galvanic, represents the emerging trend towards creating shared value, a concept that symbiotically links community and business self-interest, integrating corporate social responsibility into an organisation's core business model. Such an approach delivers outcomes that help less advantaged communities to build both productive and consumptive capacity i.e. to become capable producers and able consumers, while creating a spin off bottom line benefit to the business.

Source: CSR Research Digest, August 2014 (Vol. 6, No. 8)

1.2.13 Measuring and managing total impact – strengthening business decisions for business leaders

Author(s): PwC

PwC launched a report that explores why business needs total impact measurement, how to do it and the benefits of embedding it into decision making. Measuring and managing total impact – strengthening business decisions for business leaders showcases 'Total Impact Measurement & Management', the framework PwC has developed with their clients to provide the total perspective on business impact.

Key findings

- There is a need for more holistic measurement systems that take account of global mega-trends and allow management to make decisions based on a broader set of criteria than traditional management accounts.
- If the measure of business success goes beyond financials, and a value (and a cost) is calculated for the social, environmental, fiscal and economic activities of a company, business can see at a glance the impact they're making and the trade-offs between their strategies. In effect, the business can see the optimal decision for all its stakeholders.

- For example, PUMA, the Sportlifestyle company, and its parent company Kering have been pioneers in the development and reporting of an 'Environmental Profit & Loss (E P&L)'. The aim is to put a monetary value on the environmental footprint across the entire value chain (material sourcing, manufacture and disposal), which in the case of PUMA is now being applied to particular products to help consumer comparison. For example, the environmental impact of its InCycle shoe is nearly a third less than its conventional suede shoe and equivalent to €2.95, or 3% of the retail price.
- SHE Transmission is currently building a new 400-kilovolt transmission line in Scotland. At present there is no approach to help assess the value of the full range of impacts, including consent conditions, of a new transmission line. Through the use of our TIMM framework, PwC has worked with SHE Transmission to develop a range of methods to measure and value all material social, economic, environmental and fiscal impacts in the UK resulting from the construction of the transmission line.

Source: CSR Research Digest, August 2014 (Vol. 6, No. 8)

1.2.14 Corporate Foundations – A Global Perspective

Author(s): Corporate Citizenship

Corporate Citizenship released a report that explores models of delivery; benefits to business, foundation and society; and how corporate foundations are adapting to today's business environment. The report, Corporate Foundations – A Global Perspective considers the role and approach of corporate foundations around the world, through in-depth interviews with a range of corporate foundations in UK, USA, India, Scandinavia, Europe and Asia.

Key findings

While corporate foundations globally are as idiosyncratic – in terms of the reasons behind their existence, what they give to and how - the research also shows similarities in many of the characteristics, challenges and experiences across the different region.

- The nature of the corporate foundation is changing away from a pure altruistic grant giver to a more strategic business tool.
- An increasing number of foundations are moving away from the traditional grant giving model towards a more focused and hands on approach, which in some cases draws on the expertise and knowledge of the funding company to solve key social issues.

Source: CSR Research Digest, September 2014 (Vol. 6, No. 9)

1.2.15 A New Vision of Value

Author(s): KPMG International

KPMG International published a global report that identifies three key drivers that are that are closing the gap between corporate and societal value creation: new regulations and standards; the growing influence of stakeholders; and changing market dynamics driven by economic, social and environmental megaforces. The report, A New Vision of Value contains case studies which illustrate how new regulations, stakeholder action and market dynamics could affect the earnings of three model businesses: a gold mine in South Africa, a brewery in India and a plastics plant in the US.

Key findings

The disconnect between corporate value and societal value is disappearing.

- Firstly, the effects of negative externalities such as pollution, carbon emissions and ecosystem damage are becoming impossible to ignore as population growth and wealth growth drive consumption ever higher. An example of this is the extreme level of air pollution in many Chinese cities, which a senior Chinese scientist has described as being "at an unbearable stage".
- Secondly, public awareness and understanding of corporate externalities is growing as more information becomes available and that information, thanks to digital connectivity, spreads more widely and rapidly than ever before.
- Thirdly, a number of factors are at work that are internalizing corporate externalities at a rapid rate. Companies are finding that by increasing their positive externalities and decreasing the negative they can actually grow revenues, cut costs and reduce risk.

- These drivers of internalization include greater levels of regulation, which can offer financial incentives for companies to create positive externalities or impose direct costs on them for their negative externalities.

- Actions taken by stakeholders such as workers, communities, NGOs and consumers over negative corporate externalities are also becoming more frequent, high profile and impactful.

- Such actions can have direct implications for cash flows and risk and as a result are driving more companies to look closer at their externalities and how they can be managed better.

- Market dynamics, such as changing operating environments, resource pressures and market disruptions are also bringing new opportunities and risks related to externalities.

- These drivers of internalization have always existed. What is different today is that companies are seeing a rapid acceleration and intensification of these drivers on multiple fronts.

- This trend means that companies in all sectors are finding that their externalities have increasing implications for theircorporate value creation.

Source: CSR Research Digest, September 2014 (Vol. 6, No. 9)

1.2.16 Corporate social responsibility: beyond financials

Author(s): Grant Thornton

Grant Thornton launched its 2014 International Business Report that looks at how companies are making their operations more sustainable and what role they feel integrated reporting can play. The report, Corporate Social Responsibility: beyond financials draws on more than 2,500 interviews with business leaders in 34 economies.

Key findings

Businesses are being driven towards more socially and environmentally sustainable practices not simply by brand building or altruism, but because it makes good financial sense.

- An increasing number of companies report on sustainability while a majority now view integrated reporting as best practice.

- The top driver towards more sustainable business practices globally is cost management, cited by two thirds of respondents (67%), up from 56% in 2011. It is a particularly dominant driver in Latin America (77%, up from 68% in 2011) and North America (76%, up from 45%). The second biggest driver is client/consumer demand (64%), followed by 'because it is the right thing to do' (62%).
- At present just under one third (31%) of firms globally report on sustainability initiatives, either combined with financial reports or separately. However, a further quarter (26%) plan to begin reporting externally on sustainability matters in the next five years. And overall, 57% agree that reporting on non-financial matters, such as sustainability, should be combined with financial reporting.
- Initiatives
- Vast majority of businesses are involved with local charities, either through donating time, money or products/services
- Businesses are working to reduce their environmental impact, with increasing numbers calculating the carbon footprint of their operations.

Source: CSR Research Digest, September 2014 (Vol. 6, No. 9)

1.2.17 Combining Profit and Purpose

Author(s): Coca-Cola Enterprises (CCE) in partnership with Cranfield's Doughty Centre for Corporate Responsibility and The Financial Times' FT Remark (FT)

Coca-Cola Enterprises (CCE) partnered with Cranfield's Doughty Centre for Corporate Responsibility and The Financial Times' FT Remark (FT) to conduct research on the future of sustainability. The resulting study, 'Combining profit and purpose: A new dialogue on the role of business in society' explores what is the purpose and responsibility of business, now and in the future and is based on the views of 50 CEOs[1] and almost 150 MBA and MSc students and recent graduates across Europe.

Key findings

- 88% of current CEOs and 90% of future leaders* surveyed believe businesses should have a social purpose.
- However, only 19% of future leaders think businesses already have a clear social purpose, compared to 86% of CEOs

- CEOs and future leaders hold different beliefs on the biggest barriers to businesses adopting a social purpose, with current leaders citing external factors such as government and regulation , while future leaders believe current management attitudes play a larger role
- Both current and future leaders agree that a business' profit and the ability to provide shareholder value are the best barometers of business success today. However, the groups disagree on how that may change in the future.
- While the overwhelming majority of current CEOs feel that profitability and shareholder value will remain key in the future (94% and 88%, respectively), the findings suggest future leaders have higher expectations of the role business should play, claiming that societal and environmental impact (80%), innovation (61%) and development of future talent (57%) will be more important indicators of business success in the years to come.
- The two groups also differ in opinion about the barriers to businesses combining social purpose with profit. Two-thirds of CEOs (66%) view external factors such as government and regulation as the main barrier, while the majority of future leaders cite internal factors, such as current management attitudes (55%).
- There are believed to be many rewards for businesses that prioritize social purpose; more than three quarters of CEOs (78%) say it offers relevance to the next generation of customers and employees, and 70% claim it actually ensures business survival. Future leaders identified the key returns as more engaged employees (54%) and increased innovation (53%), while increased trust in business is also seen as a key benefit.

Source: CSR Research Digest, October 2014 (Vol. 6, No. 10)

1.2.18 Doing Business 2015: Going Beyond Efficiency

Author(s): *World Bank Group*

The World Bank Group issued its 12th flagship publication, in a series of annual reports measuring the regulations that enhance business activity and those that constrain it. Doing Business 2015: Going Beyond Efficiency presents quantitative indicators on business regulations and the protection of property rights that can be compared across 189 economies—from

Afghanistan to Zimbabwe—and over time and also measures regulations affecting 11 areas of the life of a business, ten of which are included in this year's report (starting a business, dealing with construction permits, getting electricity, registering property, getting credit, protecting minority investors, paying taxes, trading across borders, enforcing contracts and resolving insolvency).

<u>Key findings</u>

Entrepreneurs in 123 economies saw improvements in their local regulatory framework last year.

- Between June 2013 and June 2014, the report, which measures 189 economies worldwide, documented 230 business reforms, with 145 reforms aimed at reducing the complexity and cost of complying with business regulation, and 85 reforms aimed at strengthening legal institutions – with Sub-Saharan Africa accounting for the largest number of such reforms.
- Tajikistan, Benin, Togo, Côte d'Ivoire, Senegal, Trinidad and Tobago, the Democratic Republic of Congo, Azerbaijan, Ireland and the United Arab Emirates are among the economies that improved the most in 2013/2014 in areas tracked by Doing Business. Together, these 10 top improvers implemented 40 regulatory reforms making it easier to do business.
- Sub-Saharan Africa accounts for 5 of the 10 top improvers in 2013/14. The region also accounts for the largest number of regulatory reforms making it easier to do business in the past year—75 of the 230 worldwide. More than 70% of its economies carried out at least one such reform.
- For the first time this year, Doing Business collected data for 2 cities in 11 economies with more than 100 million inhabitants. The economies are: Bangladesh, Brazil, China, India, Indonesia, Japan, Mexico, Nigeria, Pakistan, the Russian Federation, and the United States. The added city enables a subnational comparison and benchmarking against other large cities. Differences between cities are more common in indicators measuring the steps, time and cost to complete a standardized transaction where local agencies play a larger role, finds the report.
- Case studies highlighting good practices in 8 of the areas measured by Doing Business indicator sets are featured in the report: the growing

efficiency of company registries in starting a business; zoning and urban planning in dealing with construction permits; measuring quality of land administration in registering property; importance of registries in getting credit; going beyond related-party transactions in protecting minority investors; trends before and after the financial crisis in paying taxes; judicial efficiency supporting freedom of contract in enforcing contracts; and measuring strength of insolvency laws in resolving insolvency.

- The report this year expands the data in three of the 10 topics covered, with further plans to expand on five topics in next year's report. The Doing Business rankings are now based on a distance to the frontier measure. Each economy from the 189 economies measured is evaluated based on how close their business regulations are to the best global practices. A higher score indicates a more efficient business environment and stronger legal institutions.

Source: CSR Research Digest, November 2014 (Vol. 6, No. 11)

1.2.19 Tomorrow's relationships: unlocking value

Author(s): Tomorrow's Company, CIMA, KPMG and Linklaters

Tomorrow's Company, CIMA, KPMG and Linklaters produced a report that explores the importance of relationships in business and how they help organisations create value, sustainability and good governance. The report, Tomorrow's relationships: unlocking value makes the point that it's important to understand the business value that our relationships create, and the need to ensure that those relationships are aligned to this value creation and characterised by mutual support.

Key findings

'Good' relationships are not necessarily effective relationships. Neither is satisfaction a good measure of whether a relationship is an effective one.

- There is a tendency to assess the quality of a relationship on the basis of how 'satisfied' someone is with the relationship. However, a relationship where one or both parties is satisfied is not necessarily a relationship that is helping both parties to achieve their goals, even if they are compatible.

- It is better to focus on the effectiveness of a relationship in that it satisfies both parties' goals. Happiness, or satisfaction, is a beneficial but not essential side effect.
- Relationships are all about creating an environment in which everybody can thrive – which is all about behaviour.
- Treating the other party to the relationship as a means to one's own ends is not the route to building an effective relationship and such a short-term view is ultimately destructive in the long term.
- It is only through treating the other party as an end in their own right that a mutually beneficial relationship is created.
- Much of the available data uses the term 'stakeholder' reflecting common use.
- There are four aspects to creating effective relationships:
  o identifying key relationships,
  o tuning in to relationships,
  o measuring the effectiveness of relationships and
  o reporting on the effectiveness of relationships.
- Embedding a relational approach starts with the board treating relationships with the same importance as any other business-critical issue. Relationships are being developed everyday by everyone in the organisation. A board cannot be involved in all of them or seek to manage them.
- The key role of the board is to:
  o set the tone from the top
  o discuss relationships on a regular basis as part of the board agenda
  o foster the right environment to ensure that all the relationships which are important to its long-term business success are identified and being nurtured and valued by everyone
  o assure themselves that the necessary systems are in place to monitor, measure and report on the effectiveness of relationships

Source: CSR Research Digest, November 2014 (Vol. 6, No. 11)

1.2.20 Social Value Business Guide

Author(s): Strandberg Consulting

Strandberg Consulting issued a guide that identifies ways to build social value creation into your company's business model. It is drawn from a more comprehensive list of social sustainability opportunities. The Social Value Business Guide helps managers understand four emerging opportunities to create strong social value from your business investments and tap into the business benefits: Community hiring, Living wage, Social buying and Social innovation.

<u>Key findings</u>

By adding a social value component to HR and procurement, business can create direct and immediate community benefits – and help to reduce poverty, boost the local economy, foster social inclusion and enhance social cohesion.

- Community hiring is a deliberate human resource strategy to fill job positions by hiring people from groups who face employment barriers whether they are youth, Aboriginal people, people with disabilities, new Canadians, people recovering from addictions, or are re-entering the workforce or are otherwise long-term unemployed.
- A living wage is an hourly wage that enables employees and their families to meet their basic needs such as food, clothing, shelter, transportation and childcare. It sets a higher test than the legal minimum wage, reflecting what earners in a family need to earn based on the actual costs of living in a specific community.
- Social buying is purchasing goods and services from social enterprises – business ventures owned by non-profit organizations that sell goods and services to generate income and achieve social aims such as employment development and workforce integration for people with employment.
- Social innovation is defined as an "initiative, product, process or program that profoundly changes the basic routines, resource and authority flows or beliefs of any social system (e.g. individuals, organizations, neighbourhoods, communities, whole societies)."
- Social innovation is when companies re-engineer their business models, products, services, structures, systems, processes or relationships to generate profits and new value propositions in tandem with social outcomes.

- Social innovation businesses use design thinking, rapid prototyping, innovation labs and open innovation platforms to harness unique corporate assets (such as their entrepreneurial skills, business acumen, resources and ability to scale) to create solutions to complex societal issues, in ways that contribute to business success.

Source: CSR Research Digest, December 2014 (Vol. 6, No. 12)

1.2.21 Profit with Purpose Businesses

Author(s): Social Impact Investment Taskforce

Social Impact Investment Taskforce's Mission Alignment Working Group published a report that sets out the three pillars of a new social business model: 1) Intent: committing to a social purpose, 2) Duties: creating duties for directors and officers to strive for and deliver the social purpose and 3) Reporting: measuring and reporting on social impact – both directly on the intended social purpose and being transparent more broadly. The Profit-with-purpose Business report draws on legal innovations in various countries, including the Benefit Corporation model from the United States and market mechanisms such as the B Lab accreditation system. The report includes a full draft of legislation for countries wishing to adopt the new model.

Key findings

A growing number of for-profit companies are going more social, to focus on creating positive impact, and reporting on their progress in achieving it.

- Entrepreneurs create a new style of business: fully profit-distributing, and with a long-term commitment to prioritise, deliver and report on their social impact. These are profit-with-purpose businesses.
- Profit-with-purpose businesses form part of the wider group of 'impact-driven organisations'
- They are flanked by non-profits and social and solidarity enterprises on one side, and on the other side, 'businesses-seeking-impact' which set significant outcomes objectives but do not lock in their mission.

Source: CSR Research Digest, December 2014 (Vol. 6, No. 12)

1.2.22 Extracting with Purpose

Author(s): The Shared Value Initiative and FSG

Shared Value Initiative and FSG launched a report that highlights how companies in the oil and gas as well as mining and minerals fields can create shared value by pursuing opportunities that tie business success to the prosperity of host communities and countries, often working in collaboration with governments, multilateral institutions, nonprofit organizations, and even competitors. The study, Extracting with Purpose provides a pathway for the extractives sector to deliver positive social outcomes by tying business success to the prosperity of host communities and countries.

Key findings

Creating shared value in the extractives sectors is not a new concept, but current practices fall short of potential, and few companies have overarching shared value strategies.

- Even among the more enlightened companies, project execution is inconsistent.
- Companies need to change the existing mindset that sees projects in local communities only as a cost to the business. Rather, companies can start from the premise that there is real business value in solving societal needs. Otherwise, there is an immense opportunity lost – for both extractives companies and society.
- There are four critical challenges that impede the development of shared value strategies in the extractives sectors. Finding opportunities and implementing shared value strategies consistently hinges on commitment from companies and other stakeholders to overcoming these challenges via:
- Removing Internal Barriers: Companies have built-in organizational barriers that prevent shared value creation. These barriers manifest themselves in limited understanding of societal issues across the business and a lack of skills to address these issues, a perceived lack of rigor and measurement in social engagement functions, and incentive structures that do not reward strong performance against societal measures. To counter these barriers, companies can make operational changes, including integrating business and social

functions, aligning societal and business reporting processes, and creating incentives for measurable improvements in host communities.

- Measuring the Opportunity: Companies do not size shared value opportunities accurately and underestimate the business benefits of shared value. The full upside of the opportunity is not captured, and the full costs of not investing in shared value strategies – e.g., paying a premium for local content or employing an expatriate workforce – are not measured. Approaches that capture the full financial impact, including both benefits and costs, of potential interventions can expose their materiality and thus justify more shared value activity.

- Embracing Collaboration: Collaboration often is seen as difficult, impractical, time-consuming, and at odds with reputational objectives. But the scale and range of the societal challenges that companies must tackle to create shared value requires collaboration with a wide range of partners – even other extractives companies. Collaboration can make the difference between token actions with little impact and measurable societal change.

- Aligning with Government: Local, regional, and national governments can promote shared value effectively, but they often do not. While companies cannot and should not replace government, they can strengthen their own ability to create shared value by helping to build local, regional, and national capacity for effective governance.

Source: CSR Research Digest, November 2014 (Vol. 6, No. 11)

1.3 CSR Implementation

1.3.1 Embedding Corporate Responsibility Report

Author(s): Ethical Corporation

Ethical Corporation has released a new report into how to embed corporate responsibility into different parts of the company. The report includes a practical guide covering tips for corporate responsibility implementation in departments including procurement, HR, communications and marketing, finance and accounting, and facilities, logistics and operations. Guidance is also provided on methods for engaging external stakeholders and designing department-specific corporate responsibility metrics.

Key findings

Companies which have successfully embed responsible practices into their operations recognize that a number of basic steps must be met, including the incorporation of corporate ethics and a focused strategy to develop sustainable practices in the company's legal structure.

- Senior management should be engaged as early as possible and CR champions at the top of the company should be sought.
- For global companies operating in different countries and cultures, regional relevance to employees is crucial. Developing a 'one size fits all' approach will be considerably less effective.
- It is beneficial to spell out how corporate responsibility programmes and a sustainability agenda benefit employees.
- Successful practitioners recommend moving on from risk avoidance to taking advantage of the opportunities presented by corporate responsibility.
- By decentralizing corporate responsibility activities, corporate responsibility professionals can access the diverse skills set required for a successful corporate approach to responsible business.
- Respondents (a range of CSR professionals and executives from multinational companies) were asked which topics they feel they will need to know more about in order to succeed in their jobs:

Knowledge areas CR professionals need to develop	
Performance measurement and reporting	13%
CR reporting	11%
Partnerships and collaboration	10%
Community engagement	9%
Assessing environmental and CR risk	7%
Internal marketing and employee engagement	6%
Rebuilding corporate reputation	6%
Managing supply chains	5%
External marketing and consumer engagement	5%
Energy efficiency	4%
Water ethics and stewardship	4%
Compliance with legislation	4%

Dealing with climate change	4%
Anti-corruption and business ethics	4%
Gender diversity in the workplace	3%
Resource efficiency and waste	2%
Biodiversity	2%

- 46% of respondents have a CSR team of between two and four people.
- Nearly half (46%) have recently experienced a budget reduction.
- A small team and budget makes it even more pertinent that other departments be accountable for implementing corporate responsibility practices.
- The survey findings revealed a distinct disparity between CR departments' budgets, with 48% falling under £5,000 and 24% over £30,000.
- Only 32% of respondents to the survey have a company-wide framework for monitoring social or corporate responsibility impacts per department.

Source: Governance Research Digest, December 2009 (Vol. 1, No. 12)

1.3.2 Influence and Advocacy for CSR in the Healthcare Sector

Author(s): Article 13

Responsible business experts, Article 13, have released the latest in a series of case studies which offer examples of CSR implementation in different industry sectors. This case study of BMJ Group provides an overview of the drivers prompting the company to implement a more detailed CSR programme, as well as the actions taken and the next steps.

<u>Key findings</u>

The main drivers in encouraging the company's actions were: recruitment and retention of talented staff, and developing skills at all levels within the business.

- Additional drivers included:
  - o promoting work/ life balance;
  - o building relationships with charitable organisations and local stakeholders;

- o attracting customers;
- o adding value to client/supplier relationships;
- o enhancing the BMJ brand and profile;
- o improving workplace diversity;
- o reducing environmental impact while saving money.
- BMJ Group took the following steps, seen as crucial to the future success of the business and company, as part of their CSR implementation programme:
  - o Ensure compliance with all relevant environmental legislation.
  - o Adopt best practice and encourage members and suppliers to do the same.
  - o Set environmental objectives and appoint a senior member of staff to carry out regular reviews of environmental performance, to ensure maintenance and where possible, continuous improvement.
  - o Maximise energy efficiency, using the best available techniques not entailing excessive cost, and explore renewable energy sources.
  - o Minimise waste and promote re-use and recycling, avoiding the use of disposables wherever practicable.
  - o Adopt an environmentally sound transport policy, setting targets to reduce staff travel, especially by car and air.
  - o Encourage the use of public transport and walking for local travel where time constraints allow.
  - o Encourage the use of cycling where practicable.
  - o Encourage the use of electronic communications, including video conferencing as alternatives to meetings. The travel authorisation form requires employees to confirm that video conferencing has been considered as an alternative.
  - o Avoid the use of building materials from unsustainable sources, giving preference to timber and wood products from responsibly managed forests.
  - o Reduce the use of paper stationery but, when used, maximise the use of recycled and sustainably produced stationery.
  - o Require similar environmental standards from suppliers.

Source: Governance Research Digest, December 2009 (Vol. 1, No. 12)

1.3.3 Responsibility in Paradise? The Adoption of CSR Tools by Companies Domiciled in Tax Havens

Author(s): L. Preuss

This paper addresses the lacuna where in contrast to the recent rise to economic importance of offshore finance centres (OFCs), the topic of taxation has so far created little interest among scholars of corporate social responsibility. Applying a range of influential normative theories of ethics, it first offers an ethical evaluation of tax havens, then the paper examines what use large firms that are headquartered in two OFCs— Bermuda and the Cayman Islands—make of formal CSR tools.

Key findings

The emerging duplicity in tax haven-based companies professing social responsibility highlights once more the political nature of CSR, where at least some firms and/or industries can successfully limit government power to enact regulation as well as shape the discourse around CSR.

- The study of CSR in OFC-based firms thus calls into question the usefulness of the often quoted definition of CSR as going beyond the law.

Source: CSR Research Digest, October 2012 (Vol. 4, No. 10)

1.3.4 Beyond The Game: Perceptions and Practices of CSR in the Professional Sport Industry

Author(s): H. Sheth, K.M. Babiak

This study employs a mixed methods approach to investigate the perception and practice of CSR in professional sport. The survey and interviews explore how sports executives define CSR and what priorities sports teams have regarding their CSR activities. 237 respondents were drawn from US football, basketball, baseball and ice hockey teams.

Key findings

Professional sports executives view CSR as a strategic imperative for their business.

- Sports executives indicated that a number of factors influenced the practice of their CSR including; philanthropy (altruistic giving), an emphasis on the local community, partnerships, and ethical concerns.

- Nearly all respondents felt that their CSR-related activities held a strong philanthropic component.
- This philanthropy may be strategic as well as altruistic, since engagement with a community in this way may encourage new fans to the team. These, in turn, represent potential new purchasing opportunities.
- Thus, having a community-focused CSR approach was also deemed important. In part this is due to the fact that sports teams tend to identify with a particular city or region, and often have a significant economic impact on that area.
- Respondents perceive the agents and beneficiaries of their CSR practices as both internal and external stakeholders: employees, athletes, fans, customers, corporate sponsors, and local communities.
- The strategic use of a sports team's resources was another priority for sports executives.
- Respondents claimed that teams do not donate funds or in-kind products for just any reason. Rather, they attempt to use a strategic approach to ensure that their socially responsible activities positively impact other areas of their business, as well as the local community.
- Respondents also suggested that teams use players as vehicles to help the community, thereby using their strategic assets – financial and non-financial – to meet the goals of CSR.
- The authors suggest that sports teams are in a unique position to make a significant impact through CSR given their unique resources.
- These unique resources include: brand recognition, ability to evoke passion in fans, fan identification with team, celebrity cache, sports facilities, corporate sponsors, expertise, and ability to convene non-traditional partners.
- Maintenance of "proper" partnerships for the betterment of the entire community and its networks was also cited as a CSR priority.
- Many respondents stated that CSR was important because teams needed to be a "partner" to address social issues facing communities in which teams operate.
- A number of respondents discussed the importance of being a role

model as an organization or a leader in the community.

- The wide scrutiny to which professional sport is open as a result of increasing media coverage means that teams feel it makes sense for them to serve as role models for their communities.
- Such public displays of social responsibility may motivate other organizations to follow suit.
- Some respondents felt that their ethical responsibility went above and beyond merely following the law.

Source: CSR Research Digest, January 2010 (Vol. 2, No. 1)

1.3.5 Socially Responsible Small and Medium Enterprises (SMEs): A Guide for Integrating Social Responsibility

Author(s): UNDP Romania

This guidebook aims to increase awareness on social responsibility in Romanian SMEs, engaging entrepreneurs and managers in applying sustainable principles. It was developed as part of the project 'Strengthening the capacity of Romanian companies to develop social partnerships – Corporate Social Responsibility (CSR)', by UNDP Romania.

Key findings

Today, businesses of all sizes have an important role in society, connected to economic, social, human, technological, and environmental development.

- The content of the guidebook is organized in two parts: the first part centers on the background of CSR - definition, global trends, and case studies for SMEs within the Romanian and European context.
- And the second part focuses on implementing CSR - practical foundations, specific areas and expected actions related to responsible entrepreneurship.
- It also provides a four-step model for integrating social responsibility.
- As part of the project, along with this guidebook, two others will be developed as pillar-guidebooks - focusing on case studies, instruments and tools - and a fourth one will act as an umbrella guidebook presenting the overview on the Romanian CSR model, its implementation and case studies of Romanian SMEs.

Source: CSR Research Digest, April 2012 (Vol. 4, No. 4)

1.3.6   Corporate Social Responsibility and Firm Size

Author(s): K. Udayasankar

This paper examines the different economic motivations of firms with varying combinations of visibility, resource access and scale of operations. It is proposed the largest and smallest firms are most motivated to participate in CSR, although the motivational bases will be different. Medium-sized firms are the least motivated to engage in CSR.

Key findings

Firm attributes					
Size	*Visibility*	*Resources*	*Scale of Operations*	*CSR Participation*	*MF*
Small	Low	Low	Small	High	A
	High	Low	Small	High	B
	Low	Low	Large	Mod/High	C
	Low	High	Small	Moderate	D
	Low	High	Large	Low	E
	High	High	Small	Mod/High	F
	High	Low	Large	High	G
Large	High	High	Large	High	H

MF: Motivating Factors

- A: Basis for differentiation, and access to resources. Firms likely to seek visibility in order to enhance access to resources.
- B: Basis for differentiation, and access to resources. Firms also under scrutiny of various stakeholders.
- C: Low-cost means of access to resources, essential to gain from cost-leadership based on scale of operations. Firms may also seek visibility.
- D: Basis for differentiation strategy. Firms however not likely to be under much scrutiny, and are also pressure-resistant.
- E: Least motivation, given lesser visibility and higher pressure-resistance due to resources access and scale of operations.
- F: Firm under scrutiny of stakeholders. But firms may be pressure-resistant given resource access. Supports differentiation strategy.
- G: Low cost means of access required to gain from large scale of operations. In addition, the firm is highly visible.

- H: Firms perceived as visible, and able to commit resources to CSR. Non-participation likely to be detrimental, even though firms may be moderately pressure-resistant.

Source: CSR Research Digest, January 2009 (Vol. 1, No. 1)

1.3.7   Moving to Next Generation Corporate Citizenship

Author(s): Center for Corporate Citizenship Germany

This report, "Moving to Next Generation Corporate Citizenship" examines how companies are progressing along the developmental stages of corporate citizenship, both from the outside in and the inside out. The authors look at the development of corporate citizenship in companies as they face a new operating environment where the public's regard for business is low but its expectations are high regarding the role of business in addressing society's problems.

Key findings

Leading-edge firms make the link between business and society in their strategies, plans, and value chains from sourcing through to products and services.

- The essence of their methods: 1) look outside-in to define the issues that are "material" to the firm and to society and 2) consider, from the inside out, how to address them authentically and distinctly.
- Gathering intelligence on social, political, cultural, and environmental issues that bear on the business was once the realm of public affairs departments. Now the scanning and calibration of this kind of information is the work of top executives, board members, and operating managers.
- The reasons for their sharpened focus on the many issues at the intersection of business and society are twofold: These issues pose potential risks and portend significant opportunities.
- Increasingly, what drives social innovation is shared leadership whereby top executives work in partnership with multiple stakeholders and leaders at every level of the organization step up to the challenge.
- Interestingly, a study of several companies advancing their citizenship agendas found that middle managers could be the catalysts for change.

- European firms are far more likely than American ones to issue social and environmental reports and to have them verified by external auditors.
- Firms like Dow Chemical, IBM, Interface Carpets, and Wal-Mart, have made the link between social/environmental issues and their business in their strategies, plans, and supply chain through to products and services.
- The strategic intent in these firms is not simply to go about business responsibly and sustainably, it is to make a responsible and sustainable business out of addressing the world's social and environmental needs.
- Some see a sixth stage of corporate citizenship developing, whereby firms respond to global social, political-economic, and environmental threats and opportunities by establishing "extraorganizational" forms, such as partnerships with other businesses, governments, and civil society.
- This phase raises questions about the "business of business" in different kinds of socioeconomies and invites a new line of inquiry into the respective roles of private enterprise and the public sector in the next stage of corporate citizenship.

Source: CSR Research Digest, September 2009 (Vol. 1, No. 9)

1.3.8   Does Ownership Form Matter for CSR?

Author(s): M-D. P. Lee

This study examines whether a firm's ownership form has any influence on its social performance and offers an alternative perspective on thinking about the relationship between the two. It focuses on the environmental performance of public, private and joint venture firms. The data informing the study is taken from a panel of 118 facilities from the US Toxic Release Inventory, a database of corporate pollution management practices, from 1991-2003.

Key findings

Although public corporations are often criticized as poor managers of pollution, the findings show that they have acted more responsibly than private corporations.

- The findings show that public corporations also perform better than joint-venture firms.
- The determining factor is identified not as the ownership form, per se, but differences in the corporations' social accountability structure.
- Because of the more diversified and exposed ownership structure, public corporations are often embedded in interdependent relations with actors who possess strong social and environmental interests.
- Their dependence on external actors for critical resources also makes them more vulnerable to external influences.
- As a result of these factors, the difference in the structure of ownership entails a significant difference in the degree of the social accountability of organizations.
- Ownership form also shapes an organization's exposure and vulnerability to social pressure by altering the organization's social accountability structure.
- Further, this study shows that the social accountability structure of a firm has a significant influence on the firm's environmental performance.
- Instead of manipulating incentives, environmental policies can shape accountability structure by disclosing more information and empowering social movement actors through partnership.

Source: CSR Research Digest, May 2010 (Vol. 2, No. 5)

1.3.9 Criteria For Responsible Business Practice in SMEs: An Exploratory Case of UK Fair Trade Organisations

Author(s): G. Moore, R. Slack, J. Gibbon.

This paper develops a set of 16 criteria for responsible business practices (RBP) in small and medium-sized enterprises (SMEs). These criteria (which include factors such as the existence of a code of conduct, ethics committee, and production of a social report) are applied to a selection of UK Fair Trade organisations in order to assess their applicability to UK Fair Trade organisations and SMEs as a whole.

Key findings

14 of the 16 RBP criteria were found to be present in at least one or more of the Fair Trade organisations that formed the sample. For the authors this suggests that the criteria form a firm basis for future investigative work.

- With the broad aim of Fair Trade being to influence the mainstream, RBP disclosure and practice might be seen to be part of what a Fair Trade organization should be doing.
- However, there is insufficient evidence to suggest that currently Fair Trade's ability to influence the mainstream is undermined by deficiencies in practice.
- Fair Trade's emphasis on RBP relations with suppliers is one of the most powerful influences on mainstream business's own comparable practices.
- There was an apparent under-disclosure of RBP activity compared with actual levels of RBP performance.
- Fair Trade organisations could make more use of their websites to accurately reflect their responsible business practices, where limited resources permit.
- While previous studies have suggested that SMEs' responsible business practices tend to remain somewhat hidden, a collective SME group (or network), such as Fair Trade organisations, has the potential to offer a more noticeable and transformative approach.
- This could lead to a common RBP message, but in order for this message and practice to be seen and adopted by others it would require communication and wide disclosure.
- A similar approach could be advanced for industry specific or local groupings of SMEs to promote RBP as a group.
- Dissemination of good practice amongst Fair Trade SMEs is not, in general, taking place to the extent that might be expected.

Source: Governance Research Digest, December 2009 (Vol. 1, No. 12)

1.3.10 Future Business – The Four Mega-Trends that every company needs to prepare for

Author(s): Corporate Citizenship

Corporate Citizenship, part of The Good Business Group, released a report mapping out the trends believed to mould the next decade of business practise. As well as outlining how businesses are likely to react to challenges to come, the "Future Business – The Four Mega-Trends that every company needs to prepare for" report provides techniques and tools for businesses to use when preparing for predicted changes in their working landscape.

Key findings

In ten to twenty years four mega-trends are going to shape the future operating environment for companies.

- Megatrend one, 'Crunch' will target the rising pressure on key resources such as food, water and energy. As a result, businesses in the 2020s will need to sustainably manage scarce resources to ensure long-term success.
- Megatrend two, 'Fragment', generated by current power structures diffusely distributed between citizens, not-for-profits, governments and corporations, will determine companies to work with more varied organisations and plan for uncertainty
- Megatrend three, 'Connect', triggered by the accelerating growth of online communication, will force businesses to respond to challenges such as channel overload, data leaks and security
- Megatrend four, 'Rebalance', driven by the increasing importance of emerging markets, will produce a structural shift in the world economy and companies, from multinational to multilocal. As a result, businesses will adapt by tightly tailoring their products and brands to local circumstances.
- Although certain areas of a business may be better suited to meet the challenges that arise from a particular megatrend, it is likely that these challenges will merge and overlap meaning collaboration between departments is needed to ensure success.
- Two tools suggested by Corporate Citizenship to plan ahead are Horizon Scanning or Scenario Scanning.

Source: Governance Research Digest, April 2013 (Vol. 4, No. 4)

1.3.11 Corporate Citizenship Report

Author(s): Boston College Center for Corporate Citizenship

Boston College's Center for Corporate Citizenship has released its 2009 State of Corporate Citizenship Report. The findings in the report are based on responses from 756 small, medium and large US businesses. An online survey was conducted in June 2009.

Key findings

54% of business leaders participating in the study felt that corporate citizenship efforts are even more important during a recession.

- The majority of US companies are not making major changes in their corporate citizenship practices.
- Among those that are, 38% reduced philanthropy/giving, 27% increased layoffs, and 19% reduced R&D for sustainable products.
- Based on current economic conditions, 15% of companies are increasing R&D for new sustainable products; 11% are increasing corporate citizenship marketing and communications; and 10% are increasing local and/or domestic sourcing or manufacturing, according to the report.
- The findings also show that executives believe business should have a greater role in solving problems in health care, product safety, education, and climate change, but dismiss the need for greater regulatory oversight by the federal government.
- Only 34% of executives who responded to the survey say greater regulatory oversight by the federal government is an important part of solving the current economic crisis and creating a more stable economy.
- Reputation was cited by 70% of respondents as a driver for corporate citizenship, tied for the top spot with "it fits our company traditions and values."
- The report also reveals significant expansion of environmental sustainability efforts (greening of products, services and operations), and increasing integration of corporate citizenship into the business strategy, with 75% of CEOs leading the agenda and 40% of all

companies (65% for large companies) with a team or individual assigned to work on corporate citizenship issues.

- In 45% of companies employees were compensated for ideas benefitting the bottom line and the environment or community, compared to 37% in 2007.
- The top three areas of corporate citizenship rated most important continue to be: operating with ethical business practices (91%), treating employees well (81%), and managing and reporting company finances accurately (76%).
- Companies increased employee support in their workplace with 60% backing work/life balance practices for all employees, compared with 46% in 2007.

Source: Social Research Digest, October 2009 (Vol. 1, No. 10)

1.3.12 Striving for Legitimacy through Corporate Social Responsibility: Insights from Oil Companies

Author(s): S. Du and E. T. Vieira Jr.

Adopting a case study methodology, this research examines the characteristics of CSR strategies and CSR communication tactics of six oil companies. The research analysed their 2011–2012 web site content.

Key findings

All six companies engaged in CSR activities addressing the needs of various stakeholders and had cross-sector partnerships.

- CSR information on these companies' web sites was easily accessible, often involving the use of multimedia technologies and sometimes social media platforms.
- Furthermore, to boost the credibility of their CSR messages, these companies utilized a variety of tactics, such as factual arguments and two-sided messages.
- In sum, this research unveils the interconnectedness among business strategy, CSR practices, and CSR communication in oil companies' attempt to gain legitimacy in an environment of controversy.

Source: CSR Research Digest, December 2012 (Vol. 4, No. 12)

1.3.13 Redefining Materiality II: Why it Matters, Who's Involved, and What It Means for Corporate Leaders and Boards

Author(s): AccountAbility

AccountAbility released a comprehensive report examining the growing importance of non-financial factors on corporate performance, disclosure, and valuation. Redefining Materiality II describes the landscape of various global materiality initiatives and provides a framework for corporate leaders and boards to enhance the definition and management of non-financial materiality.

Key findings

The corporate lens through which material issues are identified is expanding from strictly financial to other sustainability issues affecting human, social, natural, intellectual, and built environment capitals.

- Traditionally, materiality has been defined through the lens of financial reporting. Now, there's a powerful and growing movement to apply a more expansive definition that includes disclosure of the risks and opportunities posed by sustainability issues such as climate change, human rights, and board accountability.
- In addition to the substantive issues affecting environmental, social, and governance (ESG) domains, other features of this new materiality framework include: longer time horizons in which to gauge impacts on corporate performance, greater uncertainty concerning outcomes, and the views of a wider group of stakeholders who impact, and are impacted by, corporate behavior.
- To remain competitive, firms need to develop new perspectives and processes on materiality that include the ability to:
- Discern which issues are most material to the company, its stakeholders, industry, and the wider operating environment. This is especially important because the materiality of sustainability issues continues to oscillate, with their impacts occurring over different time frames;
- Develop appropriate mechanisms and processes that enable continual learning and assessment of material priorities, and how performance improvements can occur;

- Manage materiality, based on these insights, in ways that anchor sustainability issues at the heart of a company's operating system;
- Disclose on a timely and transparent basis both progress and impacts of sustainability commitments within a wider context where they actually are felt. Taken together, this means CEOs, senior managers, and boards need to gear up for a wider, more sophisticated, and—in some cases—mandatory framework for corporate disclosure.

Source: CSR Research Digest, May 2014 (Vol. 6, No. 5)

1.4 Country Trends in CSR

1.4.1 A Comparative Study of CSR in Bangladesh and Pakistan

Author(s): M.A. Naeem, R. Welford

This paper measures the sensitivity to corporate social responsibility amongst businesses operating in Bangladesh and Pakistan through a review of written policies of both listed local firms and multinational corporations operating there. 46 Bangladeshi companies (out of 100) and 83 Pakistani companies (out of a further 100) completed the questionnaire, which was disseminated by mail.

Key findings

There is a considerable difference between local and multinational firms in terms of having written policies on the four areas of CSR in both countries.

- In Bangladesh, on average, 79.5% of multinational companies (MNCs) surveyed have written policies on the four areas (labour standards, environmental protection, human rights and anti-corruption) in contrast to 31.25% of listed local companies.
- Similarly, 79.2% of MNCs have written policies in contrast to 35.6% of listed local companies in Pakistan.
- A significant difference was observed in having written policies in the area of environmental protection and anti-corruption.
- A large number of MNCs (81.8%) have written policies on each of these two elements in contrast to a small number of listed local companies – 33.3% and 16.7% respectively – operating in Bangladesh.

- Similarly, a large number of MNCs operating in Pakistan also have written policies on environmental protection and anti-corruption – 100% and 83.3% – compared with 45.7% and 20.3% of listed companies having policies on the two areas respectively.
- A large number of listed local firms in the two countries – 68.75% in Bangladesh and 64.4% in Pakistan – do not have written policies on the four CSR areas.
- However, the listed local firms that do have written policies have attached more attention to two areas of CSR, namely labour standards and protection of environment.
- In Bangladesh, 45.8% of the listed local firms have written policies on labour standards while environmental protection is incorporated into written policies by 33.3% of firms.
- In Pakistan, labour standards and environmental protection have been included into written polices by 59.5% and 45.7% of firms respectively.
- A large number of MNCs in Bangladesh, 77.3% as compared against 54.2% of those of in Pakistan, have written policies on human rights protection.
- Except for the area of environmental protection, there is no significant difference in written policies of MNCs of the two countries.
- In Pakistan, 100% of MNCs have written policies on environmental protection in comparison to 81.8% of those in Bangladesh.

Source: CSR Research Digest, May 2009 (Vol. 1, No. 5)

1.4.2   CSR For Developing Country Multinational Corporations

Author(s): P. Gugler, J.Y.J. Shi.

This article explores the conceptual and practical gap existing between the developed and developing countries in relation to CSR, or the North-South 'CSR Divide'. In doing so, the authors use an analysis of possible impacts on SME and MNE competitiveness in developing countries.

Key findings

The majority of CSR standards are now developed by large MNEs from the North, based on the social and environment conditions of their home countries.

- The focus of issues and standards tend to reflect the concerns and priorities of consumers in the North regardless of the relevance or importance of those issues in developing countries.
- The governments or firms from the South have limited participation in the "rule-making" process, such as the development of ISO 26000.
- The current situation ignores the reality that CSR practices are diverse and reflective of the national, regional as well as local context, based on variance in legal regimes, institutional structure, social and cultural attitudes, natural endowment of production factors and environmental conditions.
- 'Competitive' CSR risks instigating a race to create CSR standards, which will reduce efficiency given the costs spent in complying with a proliferated network of CSR measures which may entail either duplication, inconsistent or even contradictory requirements.
- While consensus will be difficult to reach, the South has to actively participate in CSR standards and policy making processes.
- This requires cooperation from the North, which should be responsible in managing the cost and risk of CSR initiatives between businesses along the supply chain.
- In a highly competitive market, companies that take the steps necessary to truly address labour and human rights issues find themselves undermined by less scrupulous competitors.
- If governments can work together to establish common standards and rules that takes into account CSR issues that all business should comply with, large corporations will find little chance to accentuate the imbalance of power and resource disparities intrinsically attached to large MNEs and small firms, and mitigate the less competitive positions of MNEs from the South being late comer to the field.

Source: CSR Research Digest, August 2009 (Vol. 1, No. 8)

1.4.3   Does CSR Matter in Asian Emerging Markets?

Author(s): Y-L. Cheung, W. Tan, H-J.Ahn, Z. Zhang.

This study addresses the question of whether corporate social responsibility (CSR) matters in Asian emerging markets. Based on CSR scores compiled by Credit Lyonnais Securities (Asia), the authors assess the

CSR performance of major Asian firms over a period of three years, from 2001 to 2004.

Key findings

There is a positive and significant relationship between CSR and market valuation among Asian firms.

- During the three year study period, the only Asian emerging market (AEM) in which there was no improvement in CSR performance was Malaysia.
- The market is seen to reward firms that are socially responsible and also those that show improvement in CSR performance.
- In addition to market valuation, investors are also concerned with whether better CSR performance will translate to higher stock return.
- A positive change in CSR is significantly associated with a higher buy-and-hold market-adjusted return. The market rewards firms for improvement in CSR.
- CSR can have both negative and positive effects on firms. This depends on the structure of the market that determines the interplay between social costs and benefits.
- Asian capital markets could play a significant role in promoting CSR.
- Investor education is also crucial in CSR development. Investors should be educated to not only invest in firms for short term profits but also in firms that are committed to sustainability and responsible business practices that could generate long-term profits.

Source: CSR Research Digest, September 2009 (Vol. 1, No. 9)

1.4.4   Corporate Governance Country Ranking

Author(s): Governance Metrics International

Corporate governance research and ratings firm Governance Metrics International (GMI) has released a set of country rankings based on overall quality of corporate governance. The rankings are based on data from 4,207 companies in 45 countries. 565 of the companies are from emerging markets. The ratings scale runs from 1.0 to 10.0, with 10.0 being the highest possible score.

Key findings

The highest ranking market was Ireland with a score of 7.44, followed by the UK (7.36), Canada (7.35), Australia (7.32) and the US (7.18).

- South Africa ranked the highest amongst the companies from emerging markets with a score of 6.49.
- The average overall rating for all emerging markets companies covered by GMI was 4.09.
- Singapore's average rating of 5.07 ranked number one among the Asian markets.
- Within the Latin American region, Brazilian companies ranked the highest with an average overall rating of 4.01.
- The lowest ranked countries worldwide included China (3.01), Mexico (2.48) and Chile (1.96).
- China's low ranking was largely due to the fact that 82% of the companies covered by GMI have a non-independent board. Disclosure levels are also still far below standard.
- Despite being the world's second largest economy, Japan had a low average rating of 3.32.
- This may be explained by the fact that 96% of Japanese companies rated by GMI have a majority of non-executive directors on their boards. 45% have no independent directors at all and 30% comprise executive directors only.
- The average rating for Israel was only 3.88, largely due to non-independent boards, with only one of the 16 companies rated by GMI having an independent Chairman (most are nominated by the majority owner or an executive).
- Disclosure in Israel is also below standard, particularly on remuneration issues.
- Israel's low ranking is particularly noteworthy since index compiler MSCI Barra announced earlier this year that Israel would be moving from emerging market to developed market status in 2010.
- GMI also looked at the average number of red flags assigned to companies in each market.
- GMI uses red flags to highlight particularly problematic governance developments that have the potential to impair valuation.

- These include: accounting irregularities, significant related-party transactions, limitations concerning shareholder rights, significant litigation and criminal investigations, among other things.
- The country with the highest ratio of red flags was Turkey, with an average of 2.73 per company.
- Russia and China were next, with an average of 2.08 and 2.05, respectively, followed by Chile (1.83) and Hong Kong (1.78).
- UK companies fared the best in this analysis with an average of only 0.27 flags per company.
- The average for all companies covered by GMI worldwide was 1.0 flag per company.

Source: Governance Research Digest, October 2009 (Vol. 1, No. 10)

1.4.5   Vietnam Corporate Governance Scorecard

Author(s): International Finance Corporation and the Global Corporate Governance Forum in collaboration with The State Securities Commission of Vietnam

IFC's Vietnam Corporate Governance Project and the Global Corporate Governance Forum (GCGF) produced the third Corporate Governance Scorecard monitoring CG standards and practices in Vietnamese companies. Vietnam's 100 largest publicly listed companies, representing more than 80% of the combined market capitalization on the Hanoi (HNX) and Ho Chi Minh (HOSE) stock exchanges, were assessed against five areas recognized by the OECD as keys to good corporate governance.

<u>Key findings</u>

All CG scores were below 60%, with an average score across all companies of 42.5% Company disclosure declined, particularly in regard to board and SB activities.

- Area D, Disclosure and Transparency, declined by 3.1% compared to 2010's results. Reported information was generally lighter and more superficial than previously observed. Also, information related to stakeholders was noticeably poorer.
- Area C, the Role of Stakeholders, comparatively declined by a significant 6.7% against 2010's results. In difficult economic times companies

seemed to not consider, not do as much previously or not report on activities regarding employees, the environment, the community and in relation to working conditions, health and safety.

- Furthermore in 2011, the SSC was more active in monitoring and enforcing regulations and announcing violations to the market. As a result, more negative information about companies was available and regulatory challenges to related party transactions and to financial statement information were evident.

- Some 25 companies, new to the Scorecard 2012, underperformed against the average score, particularly in Area D, Disclosure and Transparency and Area E, the Responsibilities of the Board. These companies' average CG score was 38.7%, against the overall average of 42.5% for all 100 companies and less than the average CG score of 43.8% for the remaining 75 companies reviewed last year.

- Some 22 of the 25 companies were newly listed and they seemed ill-prepared for the responsibilities that come with listing, particularly an awareness of corporate governance practices, adherence to stricter reporting requirements and understanding and fulfilling expected board responsibilities.

Source: Governance Research Digest, February 2013 (Vol. 4, No. 2)

1.4.6   Asian Corporate Governance Briefing

Author(s): ACGA

ACGA gave a briefing on recent developments in corporate governance in Asia, looking at factors impeding reform in North Asia and promoting improvements in Southeast Asia. The presentation, "New Developments in Corporate Governance Reform in Asia: Northern Chills, Southern Warmth" summarised the state of play in several major Asian economies and the impact of culture and custom on modern notions of corporate governance.

Key findings

CG scores for most Asian markets have been quite unstable regarding corporate governance rules and practices.

- CG scores are better for rules relating to the timeliness and frequency of financial reporting, disclosure of director share transactions, disclosure of substantial ownership stakes (5% and above) and whether audit committees are mandatory.

- CG scores are worse for non-financial reporting, voting by poll, legal remedies for shareholders, definitions of independent director, quality of CG Codes, and preemption rights.
- Japan, Korea and Taiwan share certain cultural, legal and political similarities that, in combination, impede and undermine fundamental corporate governance reform.
- Hierarchical and relatively more closed corporate cultures.
- An ongoing battle between regulators, conservative business interests and legal scholars over company law / board reforms.
- Weak governments that lack consensus on corporate governance reform and show little leadership.

Source: Governance Research Digest, March 2013 (Vol. 4, No. 3)

1.4.7 Maala Index 2011

Author(s): Maala

Maala unveiled the results of its 2011 CSR Index at the Tel Aviv Stock Exchange in June. Eighty-five leading companies participated in the Index, representing 60% of the business sector's output.

Key findings

The 2011 Maala Index reveals a continuing upswing in the adoption of CSR principles by Israel's most prominent companies, with 12 new participating companies in 2011 and 15 more set to join in 2012.

- 62% of manufacturers have set goals for waste reduction, water and electricity conservation.
- 94% of participating companies are addressing environmental issues.
- Among participating companies, 7% of employees are from the Arab sector, while only 1.1% employ people with disabilities.
- 84% of the companies educate their employees about sexual harassment in the workplace.
- Among 40% of companies, less than 1/3 of the board of directors is composed of independent board members, as per government recommendations.

- Only 12% of board members are women.
- 76% of top income earners at the companies are men.
- Only 24 out of the 85 companies ranked publish corporate social and environmental responsibility reports.

Source: CSR Research Digest, July 2011 (Vol. 3, No. 7)

1.4.8 Compendium of Public CSR Policies in the EU 2011

Author(s): European Commission

The newly updated Compendium of public policies on corporate social responsibility (CSR) in the EU offers a snapshot of CSR activity in EU countries. The Compendium is richly illustrated with examples and includes an index of initiatives by country and links to relevant national websites.

Key findings

Given the highly complex nature and adaptability of CSR, governments all over Europe strive to harness its potential for public policy goals, as can be seen in the variety of CSR-supporting policy frameworks.

- Grouped by themes the Compendium covers the full range of today's issues, including:
  - human rights;
  - reporting and disclosure;
  - climate change;
  - issues affecting small businesses;
  - socially-responsible investment;
  - education;
  - public procurement.
- The Compendium also covers the different kinds of tools used by national governments to encourage CSR:
  - legislation;
  - economic and financial incentives;
  - awareness-raising;
  - multi-stakeholder engagement;
  - "hybrid" instruments (a combination of the above).

Source: CSR Research Digest, July 2011 (Vol. 3, No. 7)

1.4.9 Convergence versus Divergence of CSR in Developing Countries: An Embedded Multi- Layered Institutional Lens

Author(s): D. Jamali and B. Neville

The paper capitalizes on an institutional perspective to analyze corporate social responsibility (CSR) orientations in the Lebanese context. Specifically, this paper compiles a new theoretical framework drawing on a multi-level model of institutional flows by Scott and the explicit/implicit CSR model by Matten and Moon.

Key findings

The findings highlight the usefulness of the compiled multi-layered institutional framework and the varied nuances and profound insights it offers in analyzing CSR in context.

- They also suggest that a cosmetic level of global convergence in explicit CSR may materialize in light of mimetic isomorphic pressures, but that the path dependence hypothesis is indeed salient in light of national history trajectories and socio-political configurations.
- The findings correspond most closely to patterns of CSR crossvergence, combining elements of both convergence and divergence, and reflecting in complex hybridized CSR expressions.

Source: CSR Research Digest, September 2011 (Vol. 3, No. 9)

1.4.10 The Effect of Ownership Structure on Corporate Social Responsibility: Empirical Evidence from Korea

Author(s): W. Y. Oh, Y. K. Chang and A. Martynov

The article examines the effects of ownership on the firms' corporate social responsibility (CSR). A sample of 118 large Korean firms is used for the study.

Key findings

Authors hypothesize that different types of shareholders will have distinct motivations toward the firm's CSR engagement.

- Authors break down ownership into different groups of shareholders: institutional, managerial, and foreign ownerships.

- Results indicate a significant, positive relationship between CSR ratings and ownership by institutions and foreign investors.
- In contrast, shareholding by top managers is negatively associated with firm's CSR rating while outside director ownership is not significant.
- Article concludes that different owners have differential impacts on the firm's CSR engagement.

Source: CSR Research Digest, January 2012 (Vol. 4, No. 1)

1.4.11   State of CSR in Australia Annual Review 2011/2012

Author(s): ACCSR

The State of CSR in Australia is ACCSR's ongoing study of the CSR capabilities and performance of Australian organisations. ACCSR reports annually on the results of this research, which is one the biggest ongoing survey of CSR practice and performance in Australia.

Key findings

Australian companies and organisations are missing out on creating new products, services and markets because they fail to take advantage of opportunities for innovation provided by their CSR programs

- CSR in Australia is still driven by the traditional perception that its value lies in enhancing reputation, reducing risk and facilitating regulatory compliance.
- Respondents rated 'helping to obtain better access to new markets' as 9th out of 13 drivers of CSR in their organisation – far below strengthening brand and managing community expectations about the impacts of their business.
- The 'main game' for CSR in Australia this year was responding to Australia's new carbon pricing regime, with one quarter of respondents nominating 'carbon/carbon tax' as the issue that will be highest priority for their organisation in 2012.
- Managing regulatory impacts was chosen from a pre-set list as a high or very high priority for 2012 by more than two thirds of respondents, while other carbon price–related priorities were 'addressing the impact of the carbon pricing scheme', 'reducing/eliminating negative environmental impacts' and 'managing the impact of climate change on

our organisation'.

Source: CSR Research Digest, May 2012 (Vol. 4, No. 5)

1.4.12 Corporate Social Responsibility and Government in Western Europe and Northeast Asia from a National Governance Systems Perspective

Author(s): ICCSR

This paper explores the relationship between corporate social responsibility (CSR) and government. It relies on the national governance systems literature, under whose rubric is included 'national business systems' and the 'varieties of capitalism' to fame the discussion.

Key findings

Given the rising importance of CSR, authors demonstrate that there is a varied role that the governments can play in order to promote CSR in accordance with the wider national governance systems.

- Whilst CSR – often viewed as self-regulation – and government reflect no obvious relationship for many, by following the CSR practices in Western Europe and Northeast Asia (Japan, South Korea, and China), historically and dynamically, we identify six types of CSR government relations:
  - namely, not only CSR as self-government,
  - but also CSR as endorsed by,
  - facilitated by,
  - in partnership with, and
  - mandated by, and
  - as an alternative form of government.

Source: CSR Research Digest, June 2012 (Vol. 4, No. 6)

1.4.13 CSR and the National Institutional Context: The Case of South Korea

Author(s): C. H. Kim, K. Amaeshi, S. Harris and C.-J. Suh

This study follows recent studies in employing institutional theory to explore the specific pressures and factors that lead CSR practices to differ between countries, and how they lead to those differences. The study is a detailed qualitative analysis of CSR practice in South Korea, a country with very different value and governance systems from the US and UK where contemporary CSR evolved.

Key findings

- Contrary to simplistic expectations, Korea shows a concern for short-termism more than for sustainability; and a normative more than a strategic orientation in its CSR, where CSR lies at a crossroads between implicit and explicit CSR behavior.
- The practices reflect many Korean institutional factors, but not in simple and direct ways.
- Institutional factors interact in intricate ways to create complex and dynamic pressures for CSR practice.
- CSR research needs to consider these interactions and dynamic processes with care and institutional theory can help provide a sufficiently intricate research framework.

Source: CSR Research Digest, November 2012 (Vol. 4, No. 11)

1.4.14 State of CSR in Australia and New Zealand Annual Review 2012/2013

Author(s): Australian Centre for Corporate Social Responsibility (ACCSR)

Australian Centre for Corporate Social Responsibility (ACCSR) released this year's edition of their ongoing study of the CSR capabilities and performance of Australian organizations. The "State of CSR in Australia and New Zealand Annual Review 2012/2013" focused on leadership in CSR.

Key findings

CSR practitioners doubt the quality of leadership in their organizations.

- When asked how companies displayed CSR leadership, respondents were cited examples of bold, visionary sustainability actions, programs, targets and initiatives from large-sized and prominent companies like Marks & Spencer, Westpac, Rio Tinto, NAB and Unilever.
- In contrast, when asked to share their own organizational experiences

of CSR leadership, responses commonly related to traditional CSR elements like community investment and philanthropy. The third highest response overall was that the respondent's company had not displayed any CSR leadership at all.

- Respondents rated the most effective tactics they used to overcome obstacles to CSR success. Those which were both widely-used and effective were linking CSR strategy to business strategy, increasing stakeholder engagement and enlisting senior management support.

- Tactics that are effective but less commonly used identifying CSR champions, setting operational indicators or targets and implementing CSR related key performance indicators for staff. The full report outlines a range of CSR tactics that work.

- For the fifth year running, a lack of organizational support was rated the greatest obstacle to CSR success. This ongoing challenge has implications for CSR leadership due to the inter-relationship between both issues.

Source: CSR Research Digest, April 2013 (Vol. 5, No. 4)

1.4.15 "My Country's Future": A Culture-Centered Interrogation of Corporate Social Responsibility in India

Author(s): R. Mitra

The article focuses on the Indian context and critically examines mainstream CSR discourse from the perspective of the culture-centered approach (CCA). Next, author outlines a CCA-inspired CSR framework that allows corporate responsibility to be re-claimed and re-framed by subaltern communities of interest.

Key findings

Companies operating in emerging economy nations routinely couch their corporate social responsibility (CSR) work in nation-building terms.

- Accordingly, five main themes of CSR stand out:
  o nation-building façade;
  o underlying neoliberal logics;
  o CSR as voluntary;
  o CSR as synergetic;

o   and a clear urban bias.
- Author identifies such resistive openings via interrogations of culture (oft-cited Gandhian ethics), structure (State policy, organizational strategy, and global/local flows), and agency (subaltern reframing of institutional responsibility, engagement with alternative modes of agency, and deconstructive vigilance).

Source: Governance Research Digest, March 2012 (Vol. 3, No. 3)

1.4.16   ASEAN Corporate Governance Scorecard

Author(s): The Asian Development Bank (ADB) in partnership with the ASEAN Capital Markets Forum

The Asian Development Bank (ADB) in partnership with the ASEAN Capital Markets Forum have jointly developed an ASEAN methodology of corporate governance assessment using a scorecard system that is based on international best practices and that encourages publicly listed companies to go beyond national legislation requirements. Their inaugural report is a compilation of corporate governance assessments of publicly listed companies in six ASEAN countries—Indonesia, Malaysia, the Philippines, Singapore, Thailand, and Viet Nam—using the Scorecard to improve corporate governance in the region collectively and to brand ASEAN as an asset class.

Key findings

Building consensus across countries with different levels of economic and regulatory development, different types of legal architecture, and different corporate governance cultures requires participants to focus on the bigger picture of regional integration and needs a body to lead and coordinate these efforts.

- Some compromises may be necessary to get agreement, but the agreement should not be based on the lowest common denominator.
- The corporate governance experts engaged should not only be technical experts, but must also enjoy the confidence of the regulators. Ideally, all participating countries should be represented during the development stage. This encourages a deliberative process that considers the unique

characteristics of each country's corporate governance legal architecture and culture.

- During the final development stages and before the publicly listed companies (PLCs) are assessed, the private sector i.e., companies that will be the subject of the assessment, should be sufficiently engaged and the Scorecard should be adequately disclosed and distributed.

- During the assessment stage, even after the experts have agreed on the content of the Scorecard and even when the questions are objective and require "yes" and "no" responses, differences of interpretation are unavoidable.

- To mitigate and minimize the differences, two steps are required: first, a detailed guidance note for the assessors, and second, a robust peer review process after the initial assessment.

- During the peer review, differences of opinion should be discussed and debated.

- Although decisions have to be made by the majority, they should be based on sound justification.

- For future implementation, four recommendations can be considered to keep the momentum of the initiative and take it to the next level:
  - assessment using the Scorecard should be a continuous process, which will require several iterations before the Scorecard becomes selfsustaining;
  - different countries should lead the initiative by rotation;
  - while assessment and ranking has its own value, especially given that good corporate governance practices increase shareholder value at least in the medium term, opportunities for synergy with other regional capital market initiatives should also be explored; and
  - the ASEAN Scorecard can also be a reference point for the development of national corporate governance frameworks

Source: Governance Research Digest, October 2013 (Vol. 4, No. 10)

1.4.17 Middle Eastern Executives Study

Author(s): Sustainability Advisory Group

Sustainability Advisory Group has conducted the second survey exploring executive views on corporate social responsibility and sustainability in

Middle East. Over 150 respondents from the Yemen, Saudi Arabia, Jordan, Oman, Qatar, Bahrain, Egypt and the UAE were surveyed covering both public and private sector organisations.

Key findings

Regional businesses are increasingly recognizing that Corporate Social Responsibility (CSR) is a business imperative rather than a philanthropic add-on, and a large number of executives now agree that properly conceived and managed CSR will result in a wide range of benefits including business reputation, innovation and growth.

- Over 90% of respondents expressed the opinion that credible CSR programmes can enable companies to build and maintain a strong reputation.
- Over 80% asserted that CSR can attract new customers and foster innovation.
- And over 70% believed that CSR can help capture new markets and market share
- 65% believe 'minimizing negative and maximizing positive impacts' is the most appropriate definition of CSR (up almost 10% points on last year)
- 65% no not think community investment is an adequate definition of CSR (up from 53% last year)
- Less than 8% view community investment to be the core definition (down from 17% last year)
- 30-50% respondents believe issues of:
  - climate change
  - waste management
  - ecological health
  - energy conservation
  - access to resources and
  - green buildings
- are not really addressed by or considered applicable to their business.
- Although over half of the respondents claimed that they have a clearly articulated CSR strategy signed off at the highest level, these numbers go down dramatically when it comes to systematic management of the agenda.

- For instance, only 14% of the responding organisations have formal CSR-related KPIs in place and 11% consider CSR performance as part of their bonus schemes.

Source: CSR Research Digest, August 2010 (Vol. 2, No. 8)

1.4.18 Governance of State-owned Enterprises in the Baltic States

Author(s): Baltic Institute of Corporate Governance

This publication intends to build a more profound understanding of how governance works in the Baltic States, and to develop suggestions for how to implement world class standards in the Baltic region. It looks at four interlinked aspects of State-owned Enterprises (SOEs) governance: public perceptions; individual SOE rankings; an examination of board structures; and an analysis of the legal and institutional framework.

Key findings

There is considerable public dissatisfaction with SOE governance and SOE performance in the Baltic region.

- The issue of SOE governance and SOE performance has the potential to become politically inflammatory if a scandal or financial duress should emerge.
- Governance practices pose both an economic and a political risk.
- One can clearly identify SOEs that are leaders and SOEs that are not.
- The leaders are rapidly approaching worldclass standards of governance.
- These SOEs show that modern and professional governance practices are possible in the Baltics. They should serve as models for other SOEs in the region.
- Unfortunately, many SOEs are still far removed from good practice, much less best practice.
- The report identifies both areas of strength and areas of weakness where governance practices could improve.
- All SOEs will benefit from a governance improvement plan and a concerted governance improvement effort.

- The state itself will likely reap significant benefits in terms of the efficiency and effectiveness of its SOE oversight.
- In some cases financial reporting is comparable to world class practice.
- However, in most SOEs the control environment is compromised by the absence of a direct reporting relationship between the internal auditor and independent board members or an independent audit committee.
- Audit committees are either missing, or are constituted only to comply with formal requirements.
- Civil servant board members are stretched beyond what can be reasonably expected of them, leaving the state's capacity for oversight dangerously weak.
- Many boards are fiefdoms of ministries or political parties leaving SOEs vulnerable to political influence.

Source: Governance Research Digest, July 2012 (Vol. 3, No. 7)

1.4.19 Corporate Social Responsibility of the Most Highly Reputed European and North American Firms

Author(s): Ladislao Luna Sotorrío, José Luis Fernández Sánchez.

This paper analyses the main differences in the social responsibility efforts of the 40 most highly rated European and US firms from 2003 and 2004. In addition, the authors investigate whether the motives behind corporate social behaviour differ depending on the region or country of the firm.

Key findings

Previous research on the explicatory factors of CSR has tended to focus on the UK and US.

- Little research has examined whether the CSR principles used are matched by similar initiatives in different countries.
- The research uses a set of indicators to measure the corporate effort/responsiveness in economic, social and environmental responsibility, as well as an aggregate indicator of sustainability.
- There are a number of very different CSR constructions, some of which are local or national although many are international.
- The differences that can be appreciated among them are sometimes marked in the divergence in CSR practices through countries.

- Institutions other than the market are often necessary to ensure that corporations are responsible to the interests of social actors beside themselves.
- Thus, the institutions of each country or region are the forces that put pressure on firms to adopt similar CSR constructions to those adopted by other societies in the same context.
- In general, CSR is more active in Europe than in the US or Canada, and mainly in Northern European countries such as Sweden, Finland, the UK, Switzerland and Holland. These countries ranked top in Accountability's National Corporate Responsibility Index (NCRI-2005).
- On the whole, the European companies present higher frequency of social responsiveness in most of the elements which compose social responsibility than the North American companies.
- In particular, European companies surpass North American companies in all elements of responsibility with customers and employees.
- The most frequently reported activities generally relate to information about policies, objectives or company actions, such as environmental management systems.
- Less frequently reported information is usually sensitive information related to economic or reputational risk.
- The existence of decreasing returns in the social effort of the firm has been detected: the larger the firm, the greater the social responsibility effort, although there is an optimum value beyond which companies reduce their effort in social responsibility.
- For North American companies, the generation of value has greater power in explaining CSR behaviour with customers than for European firms.
- However, in explaining CSR behaviour regarding environment, firm size (in order to achieve legitimacy) has more power for the North American firms that for European companies.
- Regarding environmental responsibility, the economic motive of value generation (to achieve stronger financial performance) has more power for European than North American firms.

Source: Social Research Digest, January 2009 (Vol. 1, No. 1)

1.4.20 Responsible Enterprise Report

Author(s): Lifeworth

This year's edition of Lifeworth's annual review includes a report on some of the characteristics of Asian forms of responsible enterprise and finance. The Eastern Turn is described in terms of the shifting locus of responsible enterprise challenges and the origin of responsible enterprise ideas and initiatives that arise due to the growing power of the Middle East and Asia.

Key findings

Diverse Asian approaches to responsible enterprise will increasingly affect business practices around the globe.

- During 2008, Lifeworth conducted a survey of its 4,000 subscribers, asking about their view of the future of research needs on responsible business. Respondents considered that the most important regions for future research are in Asia.
- Research findings indicate that environmental awareness exists in Asia, and connections can be made to consumer behaviour, thus constituting a local business case to address sustainability issues within Asia.
- The speed of economic development, as well as changes in traditional political systems and cultural norms, has contributed to a growth in corruption across Asia – a key responsible enterprise challenge.
- Estimates suggest that sometime in 2008 the number of middle class people in Asia exceeded that in the West. A middle class has the power to be more discerning consumers, creating a direct driver of responsible enterprise.
- A range of Asian responsible enterprise challenges are arising due to the operations of Asian firms other parts of Asia and around the world. For instance, although Chinese investment in Africa is helping finance new infrastructure, it raises concerns about corrupt payments, and the knock on effects on effective and accountable governance.
- A study of CEOs found that Asian respondents placed higher importance on their social responsibilities than those from other regions.
- Asia is now the second largest GRI reporting region, with an exceptionally high rate of sustainability reporting in Japan.

- Of the twenty Asian countries with companies reporting to GRI standards, twelve began reporting in the last four years (Cambodia, Indonesia, Israel, Jordan, Pakistan, Palestine, Philippines, Saudi Arabia, Singapore, Thailand, Turkey and UAE). Reporting levels in Asia in 2008 were up 133% on the previous year.
- In general, the Eastern Turn in responsible enterprise is being encouraged by government policies. In 2008, Asian governments regularly announced new policies and regulations to promote change, from a new environmental tax in China to a new child labour free product label in India.
- The relative distribution of environmental management system certifications around the world is another indicator of the pursuit of responsible enterprise in different countries.
- By the end of 2007 there were 71,458 ISO14001 certifications in the Far East. That was 46% of certifications worldwide, up from 42% in 2005 and making it the leading region for total certifications.
- A plethora of responsible enterprise institutes have emerged across Asia. Qatar CSR and CSR ASEAN were born in 2008, following the previous year when CSR Centre Bangladesh, CSR Kuwait and CSR Bahrain were established. CSR ASEAN is important given its international reach and connection with government.

Source: CSR Research Digest, July 2009 (Vol. 1, No. 7)

1.4.21 Responsible and Inclusive Business in Myanmar

Author(s): CSR Asia

CSR Asia produced a research report that provides practical guidance and recommendations for organisations, enabling them to operate in a way that contributes to the sustainable development of Myanmar while protecting businesses from financial, legal and reputational risks. The 'Responsible and Inclusive Business in Myanmar' report developed a framework that enables companies to define a responsible and inclusive business strategy for operating in Myanmar and it provides guidance on how to conduct business in a way that protects the organisation from reputational, financial or legal risks, and contributes to the sustainable development of the country.

Key findings

The model consists of the following three components: 1. Responsibility: An analysis of Myanmar and contribution of business to the country's future development; 2. Inclusivity: Incorporation of low-income populations into corporate operations and value chains to reduce poverty; 3. Strategy: Development of a comprehensive strategy to facilitate responsibility and inclusivity.

- Based on the underlying approach that argues responsible companies contribute to Myanmar's development, six capitals that provide opportunities for business contributions are assessed. These include the economical, political, legal, technological, social and environmental capital.
- This report provides guidance for companies aiming to enter Myanmar and operate in a responsible and inclusive way and includes the following recommendations:
- Get the basics right: Be transparent and accountable, put CSR policies and procedures in place and understand the business environment
- Engage with your stakeholders: Know who your key stakeholders are and what they think
- Compensate for incomplete regulation frameworks: Know what is going on, get legal advice and engage with governments and other important institutions
- Consider both risks and responsibilities: Do not rush in, make a business plan and map out contributions to the six capitals outlined in this report
- Create new inclusive business models: Identify inclusive business opportunities, achieve co- creation, commit for the long-term, look for partnerships and manage expectations
- Although businesses are facing a difficult environment, it is possible to invest and operate in a way that supports the responsible and inclusive development of Myanmar and offers prosperous business opportunities.

Source: CSR Research Digest, March 2014 (Vol. 6, No. 3)

1.4.22 STING Corporate Accountability Index in Sri Lanka

Author(s): Sting Consultants

STING Consultants published their annual Corporate Accountability Index that assesses Sri Lankan companies across six key areas which constitute the necessary components for holistic and integrated corporate accountability: Corporate values, Stakeholder engagement, Identifying impacts, risks and opportunities, Policy coverage, Management and governance, Measurement and disclosure. The 2014 STING Corporate Accountability Index features 67 companies, including listed, private and state-owned entities categorised into broad bands based on the scores achieved (Platinum 75-100, Gold 60-74.9, Silver 50-59.9, Bronze 40-49.9).

Key findings

Forty companies achieved scores above the minimum cut off point for classification (40%), which implies that at least 27 companies of those who are featured have yet to fully realise the significance of sustainable business operations for long-term success.

- Progress in implementing strategic responsibilities amongst many of the featured organisations has remained very slow since the initial Corporate Accountability Index was published in 2010.
- In the past year or so, there have been many examples globally – and more alarmingly, in Sri Lanka – of corporations that have in one way or another failed to consider critical aspects that are of importance to their stakeholders. This, in turn, has significantly affected their reputations, bottom lines and ability to continue operations in the long term.
- The average score of 47.18 achieved by companies in the Corporate Accountability Index represents a drop from 49.4 in 2012 – and this is a worrying sign, given that businesses are now at a critical juncture, in terms of establishing their sustainability.
- Of the 67 entities featured this year, training in key areas were mentioned by the following number of companies: corporate values – 17; environmental policies – 22; workplace standards and practices – 21; human rights policies – 20; and social aspects, bribery and corruption and codes of ethics in particular – 26.

- Albeit slowly, companies are also beginning to establish systems to manage social and environmental impacts. This is reflected in the rise of the number of CSR and sustainability committees in the companies featured in the 2014 index. Of the entities listed, 27 now have committees that are responsible for social and/or environmental aspects, compared to 13 featured in the 2012 index.

Source: CSR Research Digest, March 2014 (Vol. 6, No. 3)

1.4.23 The State of Corporate Social Responsibility in Australia and New Zealand

Author(s): Australian Centre for Corporate Social Responsibility (ACCSR), in conjunction with Deakin University

The Australian Centre for Corporate Social Responsibility (ACCSR), in conjunction with Deakin University released its seventh annual research study into CSR capabilities and practices in Australia (and one of the largest in the world). The State of Corporate Social Responsibility in Australia and New Zealand Annual Review analyses the level of social responsibility that organisations across all sectors demonstrate when implementing their policy and practices.

Key findings

The advent of the International Integrated Reporting Committee's Integrated Reporting Framework and the new Global Reporting Initiative fourth generation (G4) guidelines have prompted organisations to reassess whether, how and why they report.

- Most organisations stick with reporting or start reporting. However, 20% plan to change the way they report. The changes will entail adopting new reporting frameworks, increasing stakeholder engagement for reporting, improving data and experimenting with new formats
- The most popular and useful framework for respondents is GRI G3/G3.1, which has largely defined sustainability reporting practice.
- People working in CSR continue to have very diverse disciplinary backgrounds, with around a quarter having a business qualification, a quarter qualified in social sciences and humanities, with environmental

studies, engineering, science, law, marketing and economics making up another 40%. Other backgrounds include journalism, information technology, architecture, health sciences and education.

- The top scoring organisations, relative to their CSR capabilities (stakeholder engagement, stakeholder dialogue, integrating stakeholder values, social accountability), are: ABC, ARUP*, GHD*, Melbourne Water*, National Australia Bank*, Newmont Mining Corporation*, PwC Australia*, Rio Tinto*, The University of Queensland, Main Roads Western Australia

Source: CSR Research Digest, July 2014 (Vol. 6, No. 7)

1.5   Policies and Strategies

1.5.1   CSR Orientation, Goals and Behaviour: A Study of Small Business Owners

Author(s): B.K. Burton, M. Goldsby.

In this study, the authors examine how corporate social responsibility orientation relates to the behaviours and goals of company managers. 401 small business owners in the American Midwest took part in the study.

Key findings

Small business owners, in effect, translate their attitudes into behavior fairly directly.

- Those businesses who place more emphasis on the economic domain concentrate on economic stakeholders and profit-related goals; those who place more emphasis on non-economic domains concentrate more on non-economic stakeholders and community-related goals.
- Small business owners tend to be oriented more toward CSR than many of the other populations studied (including most samples of managers, students, and the public).
- The amount of importance placed on the economic dimension by owners is related positively to the time they spend focusing on economic stakeholder groups.
- The amount of importance placed on the legal dimension by owners is

related positively to the time they spend focusing on legal stakeholder groups.

- The amount of importance placed on the ethical dimension by owners is related positively to the time they spend focusing on ethical stakeholder groups.
- The amount of importance placed on the discretionary dimension by owners is related positively to the time they spend focusing on discretionary stakeholder groups.
- The amount of importance placed on the economic dimension is related positively to the importance placed on profit-related goals.
- The amount of importance placed on the noneconomic dimensions will be related positively to the importance placed on community-related goals.
- The number of employees in a firm has no effect on the relationship between importance placed on CSR domains and percentage of time devoted to stakeholder groups in those domains.
- The annual sales of a firm has no effect on the relationship between importance placed on CSR domains and percentage of time devoted to stakeholder groups in those domains.
- Small business owners see trade-offs between economic and non-economic dimensions and between legal responsibilities and discretionary opportunities (which they associated with responding to ethical norms).

Source: CSR Research Digest, April 2009 (Vol. 1, No. 4)

1.5.2 Beyond Credibility of Doing Business in China: Strategies for Improving Corporate Citizenship of Foreign Multinational Enterprises in China

Author(s): M.L-L. Lam

This study examines the perceptions of Chinese executives concerning CSR in their Chinese subsidiaries of foreign MNEs. 11 Chinese executives from nine multinational enterprises (MNEs) were interviewed in 2006. Ten were middle managers and one held a senior management position.

Key findings

Chinese subsidiaries have not yet seen their responsibilities beyond their legal requirements and their immediate stakeholders, and there is a significant gap between headquarters' and subsidiaries' attitudes towards CSR.

- The corporate socially responsible actions of Chinese subsidiaries are mainly driven by the fulfillment of the requirements of Chinese laws and their economic return and efficiency objectives of Chinese subsidiaries.
- Seven interviewees from five American MNEs perceived that their companies' corporate social programmes were superficial public relationships in China and were not proud of their MNEs' practices.
- Seven interviewees who were working for five "good" American MNEs, could not comprehend how their areas of sales and marketing relate to the values of CSR. They perceived that corporate social programmes should be done by their human resources department or a few high-ranking staff members.
- The values of corporate social responsibilities were not integrated with their functional strategies, performance appraisal, and reward structures.
- As a result, many Chinese employees often demand financial incentives to devise and deliver CSR initiatives.
- Eleven of the study's interviewees perceived that their subsidiaries had to deal with problems, such as the specific Chinese business culture, problems of intellectual property rights, problems of internal due process, and lack of government support in the process of being engaged in a wider scope of corporate social responsibility.
- Many perceived that the difficulties of adopting corporate social responsibility were their busy work schedule and specific Chinese culture.
- It is important for MNEs to move their Chinese subsidiaries from the elementary stage of CSR implementation to the advanced stage if they want to develop sustainable competitive advantage in the Chinese market by narrowing the gap between the headquarters' attitude and their Chinese subsidiaries' attitude toward corporate social responsibility.

- Managers at headquarters and subsidiaries need to develop new skills and knowledge to diffuse the concept of social responsibility and sustainable development across different functional areas in their Chinese subsidiaries.
- MNEs, which are in the advanced stage of corporate citizenship in their home countries, must invest in the social capital that facilitates the transfer of comprehensive corporate social responsibility programmes.
- These social capital entities are personnel transfer between their headquarters and their Chinese subsidiaries; low turnover of expatriates in the Chinese subsidiaries; shared visions and goals about corporate social responsible practices; accommodation of local Chinese culture and concerns of local staff; and increased trust between Chinese employees and employers in the intra-corporate networks.
- Many Chinese executives are willing to learn corporate socially response programs if these programmes can strengthen their managerial and organization skills, which increase their competitiveness in the global market economy.

Source: CSR Research Digest, May 2009 (Vol. 1, No. 5)

1.5.3 Management Perceptions of the Impact of CSR on Organisational Performance in Emerging Economies: The Case of Dubai

Author(s): B. Rettab, A.B. Brik, K. Mellahi.

Although a number of studies have shown that corporate social responsibility (CSR) activities often lead to greater organisational performance in western developed economies, researchers are yet to examine the strategic value of CSR in emerging economies. Using survey data from 280 firms operating in Dubai, this study examines the link between CSR activities and organizational performance.

Key findings

There is a positive relationship between CSR and financial performance for companies in Dubai.

- In fast developing regions in emerging economies, where most of the emphasis is on economic growth and competitiveness, CSR is given low priority.

- Although it is likely that some firms may engage in CSR activities largely on moral grounds, providing evidence of a positive link between CSR and financial performance may help firms enact CSR initiatives.

- The results of this study raise doubts about the validity of the assertion that, as a result of the absence of strong institutional support for CSR, and presence of weak and ineffectual laws to guard against unethical practices, firms in emerging economies do not capture rents from their CSR activities.

- The results also show that CSR initiatives have a positive association with employee commitment. This is understandable because firms that are engaged in CSR activities generally tend to have fairer HR practices, and are highly regarded by their employees.

- Further, a positive relationship was found between CSR and corporate reputation, as, perhaps because of the small size of Dubai, firms are able to make their CSR initiatives visible.

- CSR is currently being heavily promoted by a number of institutional bodies such as the Dubai Chamber of Commerce, which has a dedicated CSR and ethics centre (Centre for Responsible Business), which enables firms engaged in CSR activities to celebrate their success and boost their corporate image and competitiveness.

Source: CSR Research Digest, September 2009 (Vol. 1, No. 9)

1.5.4 Responsible Entrepreneurship in Developing Countries: Understanding the Realities and Complexities

Author(s): F. Azmat, R. Samaratunge

This paper explores the reasons for the less than optimal level of social responsibility demonstrated by some small-scale individual entrepreneurs (SIEs) in developing countries. The authors examine the influence of a number of contextual factors including: business environment; cultural traditions; socio-economic conditions; and both international and domestic pressures on business practices. They offer some suggestions as to the reasons for the lack of responsible entrepreneurship of SIEs and signpost important implications for promoting sustainable business practices.

Key findings

CSR in industrialized nations does not reflect the way SIEs operate in developing nations.

- While some SIEs are managing to forge a responsible orientation despite situational restrictions, the number engaged in socially irresponsible business practices is on the rise.
- Corruption: while there have been significant efforts to combat corruption in developing countries, it remains the most corrosive problem with far-reaching implications threatening economic and social development.
- Patron-client relationships characterized by close intermeshing of economic and political connections present opportunities for granting benefits to and redistributing resources towards favoured groups.
- These problems are often exacerbated by weak enforcement of sanctions and the poor functioning of the judiciary and legal system.
- Pervasive corruption has led to a number of related actions, such as lack of rule of law, government ineffectiveness, and a lack of accountability that in turn undermine regulatory quality, thus creating a vicious circle of poor governance.
- Due to the lack of a strong and effective judiciary, enforcing contracts is problematic. This can lead to, amongst other challenges, severe environmental degradation.
- Sanctions, which play an important role in encouraging the enforcement of regulation and underpin compliance, are not effectively implemented as private entrepreneurs are able to circumvent them through irregular, illegal payments.
- The limited and unsteady income achieved by SIEs not only limits their commitment to social responsibility but is one of the reasons for their focus on short-term rather than long-term profitability.
- Consumers in developing countries are not generally aware of their fundamental rights, and businesses, including SIEs, are ignorant of the importance of mutual trust and a committed relationship with their customers. As a result, consumer rights are frequently abused.
- This can take the form of: unsatisfactory goods and services; price hikes; lack of necessary information for consumers to make informed decisions; deceptive advertising; power abuse; little after-sales service;

and very little concern for environmental protection.

- The adoption of responsible practices by some SIEs despite the difficult context might be explained by their religious beliefs and ethical values.
- Informal rules are often the norm in developing countries. These undermine legal obligations. This is as applicable for formal business as for the public sector.
- International drivers such as donor agencies and MNCs (multinational corporations) have an important role to play in improving CSR in developing nations.
- While several organizations have advocated various reforms, none have offered a path, assistance or suggestions to devise relevant accountability measures. Prescriptions were superficial with little consideration given to the unique contextual factors of developing countries.
- MNCs have the opportunity to be a role model by complying with the standards of their home country, obeying the laws and setting examples for local companies.
- Unfortunately, MNCs often adopt double standards of CSR in developing countries, depending on their level of economic development.
- There is considerable scope for involving civil society to enhance rights of public participation and create awareness about socially responsible business practices and customers rights.

Source: CSR Research Digest, February 2010 (Vol. 2, No. 2)

1.5.5 Leadership in a Rapidly Changing World: How Business Leaders are Reframing Success

Author(s): Ashridge Business School and IBLF

The joint report by Ashridge Business School and IBLF identifies a range of examples where helping addressing major societal challenges goes hand-inhand with successful business practice. It is based on a series of indepth interviews with senior executives such as Sir Stuart Rose, former CEO and Executive Chairman of Marks & Spencer, Neville Isdell, former Chairman & CEO of The Coca Cola Company and others.

<u>Key findings</u>

Business leaders are increasingly aligning their core business to serve not only customers, but also the interests of wider society.

- More business leaders are paying attention to social and environmental issues that have conventionally been the territory of political leaders and NGO activists.
- Senior executives increasingly recognise that 'smart', 'inclusive' and 'responsible' business growth is fundamental long-term value creation.
- Not only do business leaders need to lead significant cultural change within their businesses, but they now need to increasingly work with others to play a leadership role beyond conventional business boundaries.
- Senior executives now need to develop skills in areas that have not previously been a conventional part of the business leader's repertoire
- To achieve this, executives must lead significant cultural change.
- They must also play a leadership role beyond conventional business boundaries and engage with increasingly diverse stakeholders.
- Younger people in the organisation often 'get' the sustainability agenda and it is often the people at the top who are slower to change.
- It is the CEO's job to keep up the drumbeat and unleash the energy and power of the organization.
- It is crucial for business leaders to set ambitious targets and to be prepared to put their heads above the parapet.
- Despite the risks, they must set a course of action and stick to it.
- It is critically important for businesses to build trust with consumers and society by acting with integrity and delivering value to society.

Source: CSR Research Digest, July 2012 (Vol. 4, No. 7)

1.5.6 The Conference Board CEO Challenge 2012: Risky Business – Focusing on Innovation and Talent in a Volatile World

Author(s): Conference Board

The Conference Board CEO Challenge survey has asked CEOs, presidents, and chairmen from across the globe to identify their most critical challenges. This year's survey features a somewhat revised set of 10 overall challenges and a more in-depth strategy section to better reflect today's business environment.

Key findings

The race to innovate, the war for talent, "black swans" and bad debts, and the hunt for new markets—all driven by an increasing drumbeat of regulation and oversight—define today's global business environment.

- When this combination of risk, regulation, uncertainty, and complexity is mixed with the need for speed and an overwhelming flow of information and data (not all of it reliable), it makes for risky business and an intense set of unique leadership challenges for CEOs in every region of the world.
- The five top challenges—Innovation, Human Capital, Global Political/Economic Risk, Government Regulation, and Global Expansion—show a balance between concerns related to the macro business environment (of which business leaders have limited or no control individually) and company-specific challenges that are driven by management action and require a well-executed business strategy.

Source: Governance Research Digest, April 2012 (Vol. 3, No. 4)

1.5.7   Developing Economies Leadership Report

Author(s): Boston Consulting Group

A report examining the emergence of global leaders from developing economies has recently been released by Boston Consulting Group. The report looks at how these companies have reached these positions of leadership and presents a list of the top 100 challengers for 2009.

Key findings

New entrants to the BCG 100 New Global			
Company	*Country*	*Company*	*Country*
Carnago Corrêa Group	Brazil	Wilmar International	Indonesia
Falabella	Chile	Agility	Kuwait

ChemChina	China	Mexichem	Mexico
Dalian Machine Tool Group	China	Evraz Group	Russia
Sinosteel	China	Sisterna	Russia
Suntech Power	China	Dubai World	UAE
Gedeon Richter	Hungary	Emaar Properties	UAE
Tata Chemicals	India	Emirates Airlines	UAE
United Spirits	India	Etisalat	UAE
Vedanta Resources	India		

- The 2009 BCG 100 new global challengers represent a highly diverse group. Companies are based in fourteen rapidly developing economies: Argentina, Brazil, Chile, China, Hungary, India, Indonesia, Kuwait, Malaysia, Mexico, Russia, Thailand, Turkey and the UAE.
- 36 Chinese companies make it onto this year's list, followed by 20 from India, 14 from Brazil, seven from Mexico and six from Russia.
- The United Arab Emirates and Kuwait have companies on the list for the first time, reflecting the rapid globalisation of service and development companies based in these countries.
- Natural resources and metallurgy is the sector with the most number of companies on the list (20). This is followed by food and beverage companies (13) and automotive and component suppliers (10).

Source: Social Research Digest, April 2009 (Vol. 1, No. 4)

1.5.8 Perceptions on Social Responsibility: The Entrepreneurial Vision

Author(s): R.T. Peterson, M. Jun.

This article outlines the results of an inquiry into the nature of entrepreneurial commitment to social responsibility as a business philosophy. The empirical findings were generated via questionnaires issued to 100 professors of entrepreneurship and/or small business management from 100 US colleges and universities. Each professor received 15 copies of the questionnaire along with the request to issue them to colleagues with whom they had a business consulting relationship and who were entrepreneurs. The total number of usable responses was 482.

Key findings

Generally, there was an expressed dedication to the philosophy of social responsibility amongst the responding entrepreneurs. They cited a firm inclination towards serving the listing of stakeholders.

- However, it is not clear whether these inclinations are the result of altruism, efforts to comply with the law or the demands of important stakeholders.
- Specific issues of interest to the respondents were consumer welfare, public health and safety, employee welfare, moral values, religious values and combating drug usage.
- Despite evidence from previous studies suggesting differences in the characteristics, attitudes and behaviours among entrepreneurs, respondents in this study displayed considerable similarity in their assessment of the issues.
- This may be the result of their ongoing experiences in operating their businesses, their fundamental values and philosophies of life, their exposure to media coverage related to social responsibility, or to other factors.
- The data indicated that stated dedication to social responsibility concept is directly related to age. Older individuals indicate that they are more devoted to this philosophy than are their younger counterparts.
- With the passage of time, senior entrepreneurs have the opportunity to examine the mission and role of their companies and consider their interactions with various stakeholders.
- This experience may generate insights and attitudes that transcend the mere earning of profits and that focus more on the environment and its needs.
- Furthermore, some senior entrepreneurs have previously been able to satisfy their primary needs and are now in a position to concentrate on higher-order needs that are closely allied with social responsibility.

- Income was found to be directly related to expressed social responsibility. Those respondents with higher income levels report larger social responsibility assessments.
- Once high incomes are obtained, entrepreneurs may feel that they are in a position to contribute to others outside the firm and to attempt to enhance the status of their environment.
- Gender was not found to be related to expressed social responsibility commitment.
- The study found that the level of education was directly related to stated dedication to social responsibility. Those who are engaged in formal education initiatives are exposed to a number of issues, concepts and philosophies that may not confront those with more limited access to education.
- There was a direct association between degree of religious commitment and stated dedication to the social responsibility concept. This may result from the extent to which the majority of religions and spiritual movements speak out in promoting societal wellbeing.
- The data did not reveal a relationship between commitment to the profit motive and social responsibility. The perspective may be that profits are the major objective of the firm and that social responsibility is secondary, or at least not correlated with success in the marketplace.

Source: Social Research Digest, December 2009 (Vol. 1, No. 12)

1.5.9   Business Trends 2013 Report

Author(s): Deloitte

Deloitte released a report outlining eight trends expected to be crucial strategic drivers for global business. This inaugural "Business Trends 2013" report is intended to help executives bolster strategic planning efforts, become more interconnected with customers and stakeholders and find opportunities for innovation and growth.

Key findings

The eight business trends for 2013 are:

- The Rewired Customer: The flexibility of the human brain ("neuroplasticity") enables and is driving rapid and substantial shifts in consumer behavior and smart companies will find ways to anticipate and capitalize on these shifts

- The Scale Paradox: The disruptive power of analytics is helping small companies be more insightful and large companies be more agile, upending conventional wisdom about how small and large companies compete
- Reengineering Business Intelligence: Companies are embedding social data into core strategic decisions and leveraging this data in novel and impactful ways
- Partnerships for the Future: Recent shifts in economic and social forces are driving government and business to collaborate in new ways
- The Responsible Enterprise: Companies are recognizing the advantages that come from embedding environmental, social and governance (ESG) factors into their core business activities
- Manufacturing Beyond China: China has long been the default choice for offshore manufacturing, but several converging trends are causing companies to consider alternative locations
- Emerging Market Talent Strategies: Global talent strategies are evolving as BRIC economies begin to mature and new emerging markets evolve into major contenders on the global stage
- Building on the BRICs: Brazil, Russia, India and China have been effective stepping stones for multinationals from developed nations, but seven new emerging markets provide fresh opportunity.

Source: CSR Research Digest, September 2013 (Vol. 5, No. 9)

1.5.10 What CEOs Really Think about Sustainability

Author(s): Verdantix

In a survey by Verdantix, instead of asking CEOs if they personally view sustainability as important for business, the analysis firm asked sustainability leaders how they think their CEOs perceive sustainability. Verdantix interviewed 250 sustainability decision makers at firms with revenues of over $250 million, across 13 countries and 21 industries.

Key findings

More than one third (38%) of corporate sustainability leaders say their CEOs take a longterm perspective on sustainability.

- There are stark differences in the governance of sustainability between firms where the CEO is still grappling with the concept and firms where the CEO is better informed.
- Some 12% of sustainability leaders say sustainability is a new concept for their CEOs, while 21% of CEOs believe sustainability affects quarterly performance.
- Just under a third (31%) of those interviewed say that, for their CEOs, sustainability describes their organizations' medium-term performance on non-financial metrics such as energy, environment and social responsibility.
- The study also found that 62% of companies surveyed have an environment, health and safety director at headquarter level, but sustainability program management offices vary in size.
- While 95% of firms have a sustainability program management office at headquarter level, 46% of these have more than five employees and 49% have less than five.
- Fifty-seven percent of sustainability leaders report directly to the CEO; 72% report to a different executive officer.

Source: CSR Research Digest, December 2012 (Vol. 4, No. 12)

1.5.11   CEO Study on Sustainability 2013

Author(s): UN Global Compact and Accenture

UN Global Compact and Accenture conducted a survey of 1,000 CEOs across 103 countries and 27 industries examining business leaders' views on the pathway towards a sustainable economy. 'The UN Global Compact-Accenture CEO Study on Sustainability 2013' is the largest study of CEOs on sustainability to date.

Key findings

33% of CEOs report that business is making sufficient efforts to address global sustainability challenges.

- 32% of CEOs believe that the global economy is on track to meet the demands of a growing population
- 83% of CEOs believe that government policymaking and regulation will be critical to progress

- 38% believe they can accurately quantify the value of their sustainability initiatives
- 37% see the lack of a link to business value as a barrier to accelerating progress
- Insights from CEOs, supported by analysis from Accenture's High-Performance Business research, have identified seven themes that are enabling leading companies to achieve both value creation and impact on global sustainability challenges
    1. Realism & context: Understanding the scale of the challenge—and the opportunity
    2. Growth & differentiation: Turning sustainability to advantage and value creation
    3. Value & performance: "What gets measured gets managed"
    4. Technology & innovation: New models for success
    5. Partnerships & collaboration: New challenges, new solutions
    6. Engagement & dialogue: Broadening the conversation
    7. Advocacy & leadership:Shaping future systems.

Source: CSR Research Digest, October 2013 (Vol. 5, No. 10)

1.5.12 A Practice Guide for Authentic Leadership toward Sustainability

Author(s): C. Baan, P. Long and D. Pearlman

The report presents nine personal leadership capacities that authentic leaders find essential in their work when facilitating large-scale, complex, transformational change in organisations and communities. Furthermore, it suggests practices (ranging from contemplative and spiritual to physical, engaging head, heart and hands) that help in developing your personal leadership capacities.

Key findings

Planning processes of complex and transformational change, call for collaboration among stakeholders and for highly skilled facilitative leaders who are committed to the development of self, others and society.

- This study explores the 'interior state' of facilitative leaders as a high leverage point in moving society towards sustainability.

- Authors identify nine personal capacities that enable leaders to facilitate collaboration in Strategic Sustainable Development:
  (1) Being Present,
  (2) Whole Self-Awareness,
  (3) Suspension & Letting Go,
  (4) Compassion,
  (5) Intention Aligned with Higher Purpose,
  (6) Whole System Awareness,
  (7) Personal Power,
  (8) Sense of Humour, and
  (9) Holding Dualities and Paradoxes.
- Authors identify a range of personal and collective practices that help develop these personal capacities.
- It is proposed these capacities are the foundation for a more holistic and authentic facilitation approach applied to strategic sustainable development.

Source: CSR Research Digest, May 2012 (Vol. 4, No. 5)

1.5.13 Global Executive Study

Author(s): MIT Sloan Management Review / Boston Consulting Group

MIT Sloan Management Review and Boston Consulting Group have released its second annual Sustainability & Innovation Global Executive Study. The study examines two distinct camps of companies: "embracers" — those who place sustainability high on their agenda — and "cautious adopters," who have yet to focus on more than energy cost savings, material efficiency, and risk mitigation.

Key findings

Embracers place sustainability high on their agenda, and cautious adopters have yet to focus on sustainability measures besides energy energy cost savings, material efficiency and risk mitigation.

- Nearly three times as many embracers (66%) as cautious adopters (23%) said that their organization's sustainability actions and decisions have increased their profits.
- Embracers are significantly more confident about their competitive

position than nonembracers are, with 70% of embracers saying that their organizations outperform industry peers.

- Only 53% of cautious adopters described themselves as outperformers, and 14% admitted to lagging behind peers—more than twice the percentage of embracers who made the same claim (6%).
- The report found that improved brand reputation is the biggest benefit of addressing sustainability, cited by nearly half of respondents.
- Automotive is seen as the industry for which sustainability is most critical now: 80% of executives said sustainability-related strategies are necessary to be competitive in the auto sector.
- But only 29% of respondents thought sustainability strategies are currently necessary for the media and entertainment industry. Another 51% said they will be necessary in the future.

Source: CSR Research Digest, March 2011 (Vol. 3, No. 3)

1.5.14 UNGC-Accenture Industry CEO Study

Author(s): UNGC / Accenture

A new research study published by the United Nations Global Compact and Accenture shows major differences in perceptions of sustainability between CEOs in different industry sectors. The study is based on a survey of 766 CEOs worldwide, initially conducted for the joint report, A New Era of Sustainability, published in 2010.

Key findings

Upon closer examination, significant differences appear at the industry level: 100% of automotive CEOs and 100% of executives heading large consumer goods companies, see sustainability as critical to their success.

- CEOs in the banking sector, which has not traditionally focused on sustainability, also see these issues as a strategic priority: 68% regard sustainability as "very important" to their future success, and 63% report that their company is integrating sustainability "much more" than five years ago.
- Conversely, only 22% of CEOs in the communications sector perceive sustainability to be a "very important" factor in shaping their future success, the lowest in any of the seven industries.

- However, research suggests that even in this sector, sustainability may be growing in importance, with 70% of CEOs seeing the potential for revenue growth and cost reduction as a primary motivation for taking
- action on sustainability – the highest figure across the seven sectors.
- The industry analysis shows that some sectors may be ahead of the pack when it comes to integrating sustainability into core business.
- Eighty percent of utilities CEOs, for example, report their company has embedded metrics to track sustainability performance, ahead of the cross-industry average of 64%.
- Similarly, 83% of CEOs in the energy sector and 81% of those in infrastructure say their company measures both positive and negative impacts of their activities on sustainability outcomes, a finding which suggests sustainability performance management capabilities are beginning to take root in leading industries.
- Nevertheless, performance gaps remain between CEOs' ambition and execution.
- Ninety-five percent of automotive executives, for example, believe that companies should invest in enhanced training of managers to integrate sustainability into strategy and operations, but just 52% report that their company already does so.

Source: CSR Research Digest, June 2011 (Vol. 3, No. 6)

1.5.15 Opinion Survey: Small Business Owner Opinions on Access to Credit and Proposals to Boost the Economy

Author(s): American Sustainable Business Council / Main Street Alliance / Small Business Majority

A report, based on a national survey of 500 small business owners, was released by the American Sustainable Business Council, Main Street Alliance and Small Business Majority. Researchers used a random sample of small business owners obtained from Harris Interactive, with additional samples from InfoUSA.

Key findings

Small business owners say their main concern is weak customer demand, not regulations. 34% cited weak customer demand as the most important problem for their business, while only 14% named government regulations.

- In fact, when asked what would do the most to create jobs, small business owners' top response was eliminating incentives to move jobs overseas.
- The top response was eliminating incentives to move jobs overseas at 24%; reducing regulation was fifth at 10%.
- Small business owners see government standards as an important tool to level the playing field with big business.
- 78% believe some standards are important to protect small businesses from unfair competition, and 76% believe regulations on the books should be enforced.
- In addition to protecting small businesses the vast majority of owners view regulations as a necessary component of a modern economy.
- 93% agree their business can live with some regulation if it is fair, manageable and reasonable.
- Small business owners express strong support for specific rules and standards.
- 78% support rules to prevent health insurance companies from increasing rates excessively, 84% support food safety standards, 80% support product safety standards and 80% support disclosure and regulation of toxic materials.
- Small business owners support clean energy policies.
- 79% support ensuring clean air and water, and 61% support moving the country towards energy efficiency and clean energy.
- Small businesses believe in streamlining government processes.
- 73% of respondents believe we should allow for one-stop electronic filing of government paperwork.

Source: CSR Research Digest, February 2012 (Vol. 4, No. 2)

1.5.16 Breakthrough: Business Leaders, Market Revolutions

Author(s): Volans

A new market intelligence report calls on business leaders to help drive 'breakthrough' innovation, as part of a coming revolution in global markets.

The Volans team interviewed 120 leaders (ranging from the CEOs of some of the world's largest companies through to innovators determined to disrupt just such companies), representing multiple sectors and geographies.

Key findings

Our current resource crunch coupled with ongoing population growth means that life will become increasingly turbulent – "Extreme is the new normal," as New Scientist has put it.

- We must do things differently, but government leadership has been conspicuous by its absence, as illustrated by the failure of last year's Rio+20 summit.
- Against such a backdrop, business has an increasingly crucial role to play in creating a world fit for the 9 billion people predicted for 2050.
- The report outlines the context in which business operates today and suggests three possible scenarios for the future:
  o Breakdown – where business misunderstands the complexity of global challenges and resists change;
  o Change-As-Usual – where earnest efforts are made, but the overall outcome is little more than a set of patches on the existing, dysfunctional system;
  o Breakthrough – where business dares to create ambitious ventures with innovators, entrepreneurs, intrapreneurs, investors and policy makers, helping drive disruptive change into markets and political systems.

Source: CSR Research Digest, March 2013 (Vol. 5, No. 3)

1.5.17 Advancing from the core – Profile of the practice 2013

Author(s): The Center for Corporate Citizenship

The Center for Corporate Citizenship produced a report that explores how the environmental, social, and governance (ESG) dimensions of business—corporate citizenship—are managed today. The 'Advancing from the core – Profile of the practice 2013' report analyzes corporate citizenship strategies, operational structures, and business practices of 231 companies.

Key findings

The management of corporate citizenship is advancing and continues to be formalized and integrated into business.

- Above-average industry performers are more likely to have a formal corporate citizenship department, a program led at the executive level, and higher budgets for corporate citizenship and charitable giving.
- Executives are leading corporate citizenship efforts more frequently.
- Fifty-eight percent of the companies now have an executive at the head of corporate citizenship, compared to 33% reported in 2010.
- Nearly one-third of corporate citizenship leaders are within one level of the chief executive.
- In 2013, 97% of companies reported having an operating budget dedicated to corporate citizenship. In 2010, 81% of companies reported devoting financial resources to corporate citizenship.
- Thirty percent of companies reported an annual corporate citizenship budget of at least $1 million in 2013, a 25% increase from 2010. These budgets are exclusive of philanthropic giving.
- Corporate citizenship continues to become an established practice in business. Increased chief executive engagement and more professional development suggest this positive trend as well.

Source: CSR Research Digest, February 2014 (Vol. 6, No. 2)

1.5.18 Looking beyond the checkbox

Author(s): CIMA and St Paul's Institute

CIMA and St Paul's Institute published an event summary report that explored developments in regulatory frameworks, how leading organisations can work towards embedding good practice, use sustainability strategies, and create a culture that is beyond checkbox compliance. The research report, Looking beyond the checkbox, highlights discussions that explored how good corporate governance depends on the right questions being asked, and addressed, within the context of a values-based approach to organisational culture.

Key findings

There's a whole range of resources that are becoming increasingly scarce and more costly that a lot of businesses existence depends upon – water is a great example of this.

- These aren't just topics that address the needs of certain stakeholders, these issues are absolutely fundamental to the existence of organisations that operate in a global world today.
- Those organisations that can grasp this agenda most effectively are those businesses that are going to be most successful.
- So it's no longer 'tick box', the sustainability agenda responding to this is about creating business models for the long term. It's not about choice; organisations that want to be successful have to do this.
- The reporting needs to reflect the underlying business processes and that's where many organisations fall down. They may make broad statements in their reporting about value creation beyond the financial but actually the way decisions are made by the business, particularly at a senior level, might be focused much more exclusively around core financial concepts.
- Compliance and regulation are necessary – but they are by no means sufficient. The real power is about unlocking the beauty of doing something you feel is worthwhile while you're on this planet and spending most of your time at work and really leveraging that, because a company is nothing more than a group of human beings.

Source: CSR Research Digest, October 2014 (Vol. 6, No. 10)

1.5.19 Towards Dynamic Governance 2014

Author(s): Heidrick & Struggles

Heidrick & Struggles published their long-standing European-wide Corporate Governance Report that analyses the board composition and habits of Europe's top 400 publicly listed companies. 'Towards Dynamic Governance 2014' sets out a new charter for governance based on the firm's work with high-performing boards and the proprietary biennial research on European board behaviours which it has undertaken for the past 15 years.

Key findings

Governance must undergo a shift from box-ticking compliance to a leadership imperative that is capable of enabling and empowering business performance.

- Deep Business Knowledge – It is critical that board members understand the commercial DNA of the company and that chairmen and boards possess deep insights into the business. The report reveals that one in five boards in Europe still combine the role of CEO and Chairman, holding management to account becomes a challenge in such circumstances.

- Diversity of Thought – Boards need to contain a range of personalities, characters, skills and backgrounds if they are to function successfully. Encouragingly, boards are becoming more international in their mix with non-national directors making up 30% of the director pool in Europe. Yet, female representation is still lacking — Europe's worst performers are Poland and Portugal with 40% and 30% respectively of company boards without any female directors.

- Engaged Leadership – The best chairmen work hard on team dynamics; this requires a sophisticated understanding of people. A total of 93% of survey respondents identified the leadership styles of the Chairman as an important contributor to board effectiveness. Of particular concern however, only 76% of respondents thought their own Chairman was doing a satisfactory job in this respect.

- Strategic alignment and execution – Boards must use their knowledge and experience to help executives develop robust and sustainable strategies. Given the length of service, with one in five directors on European boards being in the role for more than nine years, it is crucial that board experience is kept current.

- Capacity to adapt – Boards must do more to create the conditions within which innovation and adaptation can thrive. While 80% of respondents agree that innovation and adaptability are important, only 63% felt the performance of their own boards was satisfactory in this area.

- Leadership talent – Talented people lie at the heart of dynamic governance and drive the boardroom's transformation agenda. Fully 92% of respondents agree that top talent performance and engagement in succession planning are important yet only 55% believe it is being satisfactorily delivered by their board.

Source: Governance Research Digest, March 2014 (Vol. 5, No. 3)

1.5.20 Risk Management and Corporate Governance

Author(s): OECD

OECD released its sixth peer review of the OECD Principles of Corporate Governance which analyses the corporate governance framework and practices relating to corporate risk management, in the private sector and in state-owned enterprises. The review, Risk Management and Corporate Governance covers 26 jurisdictions and is based on a general survey of all participating jurisdictions in December 2012, as well as an in-depth review of corporate risk management in Norway, Singapore and Switzerland.

Key findings

While risk-taking is a fundamental driving force in business and entrepreneurship, the cost of risk management failures is still often underestimated, both externally and internally, including the cost in terms of management time needed to rectify the situation.

- Corporate governance should therefore ensure that risks are understood, managed, and, when appropriate, communicated.
- Following the financial crisis, many companies have started to pay more attention to risk management. This is, however, seldom reflected in changes to formal procedures, except in the financial sector and in companies that have suffered serious risk management failure in the recent past.
- Most companies consider that risk management should remain the responsibility of line managers. Responding to public and/or shareholder pressures, some company boards, especially in widely-held companies, have started to review their incentive structures, including through the reduction of potential incentives for excessive risk-taking, notably stock options for top executives.
- Listed company boards need to be provided with incentive structures that appropriately reward business success, as well as awareness and management of risk.

- Existing risk governance standards for listed companies still focus largely on internal control and audit functions, and primarily financial risk, rather than on (ex ante) identification and comprehensive management of risk.

- Corporate governance standards should place sufficient emphasis on ex ante identification of risks. Attention should be paid to both financial and non-financial risks, and risk management should encompass both strategic and operational risks.

- Currently, risk governance standards tend to be very high-level, limiting their practical usefulness, and/or focus largely on financial institutions.

- There is scope to make risk governance standards more operational, without narrowing their flexibility to apply them to different companies and situations. Experiences from the financial sector can be valuable, even if not necessarily transferable to the non-financial sector.

- Outsourcing- and supplier-related risks, for example, deserve attention in both the financial and the nonfinancial sector.

- It is not always clear that boards place sufficient emphasis on potentially "catastrophic" risks, even if these do not appear very likely to materialise.

- More guidance may be provided on managing the risks that deserve particular attention, such as risks that will potentially have large negative impacts on investors, stakeholders, taxpayers, or the environment. Boards should be aware of the shortcomings of risk management models that rely on questionable probability assumptions.

Source: Governance Research Digest, September 2014 (Vol. 5, No. 9)

1.6   Respect for the Rule of Law

1.6.1   Assessing Vulnerability of Selected Sectors Under Environmental Tax Reform

Author(s): J. Fitzgerald, M. Keeney, S. Scott

This paper examines the vulnerability of various subsectors of the manufacturing industry to environmental tax reforms. The authors look at the price setting power of these sub-sectors using historical data.

Key findings

The basic metals sector revealed the least pricing power and therefore the greatest vulnerability. The non-metallic minerals sector revealed most pricing power.

- The results revealed that the world price, proxied by the US price, was less of a constraint than the EU price, proxied by the German price.
- Thus, international competitiveness fears are reduced not just where there is good potential for adapting technology but also if application of environmental tax reform is EU-wide.
- The chemicals sector could be vulnerable under an environmental tax regime (ETR) in certain countries, namely in the Netherlands and in Ireland, which showed clear signs of taking the US price.
- The influence of the German price in Sweden, the UK and also in Ireland suggests that the sector is a price taker on the 'EU market'. However if ETR were applied on an EU-wide basis, it would affect EU 'competing' countries in a consistent manner, reducing vulnerability.
- In the food, beverages and tobacco sector, there does not appear to be broad vulnerability to environmental tax reform if applied at EU level. The UK provides an example of where both domestic costs and the foreign (German) prices are significant so that the sector is subject to competitive pressures with respect to European prices, while also responding to domestic cost developments.
- For non-metallic mineral products, this sector is not highly traded and the US (world) price, when used to represent the foreign price, is nowhere significant in explaining movements in the sector's output price. If the sector responds to any foreign price, it is likely to respond to the European price.
- To the extent that the external price is at all significant, the fact of it being the German price indicates that a carbon-energy tax applied EU-wide would not create significant competitive disadvantage, given that the rest of the EU would face a similar tax.
- Within the paper and paper products sector, this highly traded sector is

a price taker. However, with minor exceptions in Germany and the Netherlands where the US price is partially influential, the effect on competitiveness would be reduced if ETR applied across all of the EU.

- There is a signifcant degree of market power on the part of firms in the wood and wood products sector, and an ability to absorb at least some of the incidence of any environmental taxes.

- Where an environmental tax regime is introduced on an EU-wide basis, there would be little effect on the competitiveness of domestic output. All firms supplying the EU market would be affected in a consistent manner.

- For the basic metals sector, consistent application of environmental tax reform across the EU could temper the effect on competitiveness, although the sector would be vulnerable under a carbon tax nonetheless.

Source: Environmental Research Digest, June 2009 (Vol. 1, No. 6)

1.6.2 Environmental Compliance: The Good, The Bad and The Super-Green

Author(s): J.J. Wu

This paper uses primary data to examine why some firms violate regulatory standards on water pollution, solid waste, toxic and hazardous waste, and hazardous air emissions, while others overcomply with them. 689 companies in Oregon, USA, took part in the survey. Participating companies represented the food manufacturing, timber products, computer and electronic products, construction, road haulage and accommodation industry sectors.

Key findings

One of the leading factors that drives companies to exceed environmental regulations are the values of senior management.

- A facility is more likely to over-comply with environmental regulations if its upper management believes that it has a moral responsibility for resource conservation and environmental protection, and that environmental management is good for business in the long term.

- Thus, programs that foster upper management's environmental values and beliefs may lead to more environmental overcompliance.

- Competitive market forces such as improving environmental performance, investing in cleaner products to differentiate from competitors and taking environmental steps to reduce employee turnover and increase productivity also help to reduce violations.

- If a company sees costs and risks like high upfront investments, high day-to-day costs and uncertain future benefits associated with environmental practices, it is more likely to violate regulations.

- Companies with annual revenue of less than $5 million and publicly-traded companies are more likely to violate regulations than larger and privately owned companies.

- Facilities that offer services direct to consumers or make products sold direct to consumers are also less likely to violate regulations.

- Pressure from consumers, investors and interest groups, though, has no statistically significant impact on company actions.

- Risks of downtime, delivery interruptions, and uncertain future benefits were cited as a barrier to environmental management.

- Some facilities cited a lack of knowledgeable staff as a barrier to adopting environmentally friendly processes, practices, or products.

- This suggests that training employees for environmental management and providing educational courses and materials at a reduced cost may reduce environmental violations and increase overcompliance.

- Such an educational program would be particularly desirable when it contains a large portion of public goods and targets small and medium sized firms that lack the capacity for environmental management

Source: Environmental Research Digest, September 2009 (Vol. 1, No. 9)

1.6.3 Corporate Environmental Citizenship Variation in Developing Countries

Author(s): S. Özen, F. Küskü.

This study focuses on why some companies in developing countries go beyond environmental regulations when implementing their corporate environmental and social responsibilities or citizenship behaviour. The authors develop a conceptual framework to explain three institutional factors: companies' market orientations, industrial characteristics, and corporate identities. The study also discusses the policy and managerial implications of the proposed framework.

Key findings

Three main forms of corporate environmental citizenship (CEC) were apparent: regulative adoption to avoid punishment, normative adoption to obtain social approval, and cognitive adoption to reduce uncertainty.

- Within this framework, CEC adoption patterns of companies within developing countries vary according to their market orientation, industry concentrations and organizational identities.
- Companies from developing countries that are oriented towards markets in developed countries would be expected to demonstrate higher CEC adoption than inward-oriented companies.
- Developing country companies that operate in highly concentrated industries would be expected to demonstrate higher levels of CEC adoption than companies operating in low-concentrated industries. This is largely due to the lower level of (or emerging) customer expectations for CEC behaviour in developing countries.
- Missionary organizations (those which aim to contribute to the modernization of their nation in addition to their own economic goals) within developing countries would demonstrate higher levels of CEC adoption that non-missionary organizations (those that are indifferent to the ideological goals of modernization).
- The framework proposed in this study is considered more appropriate for those developing countries where developmental state tradition and centre-periphery dichotomy are more prevalent.
- This means that the framework may work better in countries that have state-dependent or state-coordinated business systems, such as South Korea, Thailand, Turkey, the Middle East and Eastern Europe.
- The authors highlight reputational advantages and the avoidance of targeted campaigns by environmental organizations as key benefits for companies who address CEC.

Source: Environmental Research Digest, November 2009 (Vol. 1, No. 11)

1.6.4 Evaluation And Reliability Of The Organic Certification System: Perceptions By Farmers In Latin America

Author(s): F. Albersmeier, H. Schulze, A. Spiller

Organic certification systems are now used worldwide. If these standards are unable to meet their promises, their reliability will be called into question and trust in organic produce will fade. This paper offers a critical review of their reliability from the point of view of organic farmers. 149 Brazilian and Costa Rican farmers took part in either face-to-face interviews, guided telephone or web surveys between November 2007 and January 2008.

Key findings

Acceptance (overall evaluation) of the organic scheme is higher and less controversial in Latin America than in Europe.

- An increase in farmers' conviction that the certification system is reliable ensures their diligence in working to the organic certification standard.
- As well as ensuring that the costs of the system are accurately communicated, benefits should also be highlighted. These include a better relationship with buyers and lower managerial and bureaucratic costs.
- Although it has no significant influence on the perceived reliability of the certification system, fraud remains an important issue.
- For example, 41.6% of the farmers taking part in this study believe the number of 'black sheep' in the organic farming sector will rise, and 20.8% partly agree with this perception.
- Most respondents are aware that cheating generally occurs. However, they are still unaware of the consequences (for export) connected with fraud. Such discussions appear to be limited to developed countries.
- Besides the perceived usefulness of the certification system, the reputation of the certification bodies, which includes the skills and thoroughness of their auditors, enhances perceptions of the system's reliability.
- However, there is evidence of variations in the level of audit quality or thoroughness. Better training and further education of auditors, as well

as the development of an audit quality control system, seem necessary to prevent the threat of weak auditing procedures in organic certification and therefore a loss of reliability.

- External variables can also enforce the reliability of the scheme. Buyers and farmers' associations in particular can perform a social monitoring function.
- Since public authorities in Latin America seem to possess a rather weak position in this discussion, more emphasis may be placed on the function of private institutions as control bodies. There is therefore significant potential for industrial self-regulation.

Source: Environmental Research Digest, December 2009 (Vol. 1, No. 12)

1.6.5 The Costs and Benefits of Mandatory Greenhouse Gas Reporting

Author(s): Aldersgate Group / Christian Aid / The Co-operative / WWF

The report published in partnership by the Aldersgate Group, Christian Aid, The Co-operative and WWF disputes the findings of the Department for Environment, Food and Rural Affairs (Defra) impact assessment. This paper analyses the assumptions made and steps taken in the IA to arrive at the costs and benefits presented by Defra for option 3.

Key findings

Overall, the report found, Defra's IA has taken a fairly narrow focus when looking at benefits, rarely taking into account wider social and environmental benefits that arise.

- The rebuttal assessment, modeled after the Defra IA, finds that when analyzing the impact scenario of mandatory greenhouse gas reporting by large companies, Defra overestimates the total costs by up to $7.5 billion (£4.6 billion) and underestimates the benefits by up to $1.6 billion (£980 million).
- The findings show that mandatory carbon reporting would be good for business and play an important part in the transition to a lowcarbon economy.

- The best companies are already measuring and managing their carbon as a matter of best practice, and it's time the laggards were made to do so as well.
- Voluntary carbon reporting has played its part but now it's time for mandatory carbon reporting to be brought in to really drive efficiency savings and drive down greenhouse gas emissions.

Source: Environmental Research Digest, August 2011 (Vol. 2, No. 4)

1.6.6   The Determinants of Regulatory Compliance: An Analysis of Insider Trading Disclosures in Italy

Author(s): E. Bajo, M. Bigelli, D. Hillier, B. Petracci.

This paper investigates the determinants of regulatory compliance in corporate organisations in Italy. The data informing this study consists of 5,853 trades reported on 748 filings sent to the Italian Exchange during 2003. These come from 146 listed companies.

Key findings

Corporate insiders in Italy very rarely report their full trading activity. In the sample used in this study, only 58 out of 195 insiders reported their activities.

- More insiders were wholly non-compliant than either fully or partially compliant.
- Chief executives seem particularly negligent in their reporting with 50% of the group completely non-compliant.
- Family firms are widespread in Italy. In this study 125 of the companies were controlled by families. 50.6% of the shares traded by insiders are disclosed in family firms relative to a lower 39.5% in non-family firms.
- Chairmen of family firms are also more likely to disclose trades than chairmen of non-family firms.
- Family firms and firms with a high separation of ownership from control (the ownershipcontrol wedge) are more likely to comply with disclosure regulations.
- Managers in family firms are more likely to have a longer term orientation with a stronger focus on wider stakeholders than

professional managers, whose objectives span only the length of their employment contract.

- The family firm effect is independent of the ownership level, suggesting that corporate ethos is an important factor for whether a firm is diligent in complying with regulation.
- The degree of compliance to insider trading disclosure regulation significantly increases for higher levels of ownership-control concentration.
- The greater the ownership-control wedge, the more that controlling shareholders may consider insider trading activity to be an unattractive source of pecuniary gain, compared to other, more lucrative forms of expropriation.
- Compliance does not appear to be affected by either firm-level characteristics such as size or market to book ratio.
- Board structure innovations such as separating the role of chairman and chief executive or hiring more non-executive directors have no effect on the propensity of a firm to comply with regulation.
- Visible actions relating to good governance (publishing the company's internal dealing code, early adoption of the code, a lower threshold for disclosure, and the introduction of a blackout trading period) also do not have any explanatory power.

Source: Governance Research Digest, October 2009 (Vol. 1, No. 10)

1.6.7 Development of Corporate Governance Regulations: The Case of an Emerging Economy

Author(s): J. Siddiqui

This paper investigates the development of corporate governance regulations in emerging economies, using Bangladesh as a case study. The author examines the type of corporate governance reform that Bangladesh has adopted, and looks at what sort of models are conducive to the country's current state of economic, legal and socio-political environment. The paper investigates the role of different actors – professional bodies, regulators and the private sector itself - in this changing business environment.

Key findings

The Anglo-American shareholder model of corporate governance, based on agency-based notions of market efficiency, will not be entirely suitable for Bangladesh. Nevertheless, this is the model Bangladesh adopts at present.

- This is because the Bangladesh corporate and economic environment is characterized by high ownership concentration, primitive capital markets, high government dependence on international financial agencies (IFAs), easy availability of bank credit and subsequent default culture, and poor labour conditions.
- Instead, the presence of representatives of banks and workers, as suggested by a stakeholder model, could contribute to better loan recovery and improvement of working conditions.
- The adoption of the stakeholder model may be even more appropriate against the backdrop of the ongoing financial crisis, which, in its second phase, is likely to impact most severely on developing economies like Bangladesh as exports and remittances suffer.
- The financial crisis may also exacerbate unemployment, result in even lower payments for labourers, and result in a worsening bad debts situation for banks. These factors provide further justification for the adoption of a stakeholder model, where the interests of employees and banks would be protected through the presence of their representatives on the board.
- The process of development of corporate governance regulations in Bangladesh is characterized by the absence of self-regulation by the professional bodies, a dominant presence of donor-driven private-sector regulations and the adoption of private-sector regulations by government-funded regulators.
- The private-sector think tanks that have taken responsibility for developing corporate governance regulations do not have any regulatory or statutory authority. However, their projects are funded by donor agencies and, as a result, they have significant influence on the regulators.

Source: Governance Research Digest, October 2009 (Vol. 1, No. 10)

1.6.8   Development of Norms Through Compliance Disclosure

Author(s): B. Fasterling

The article introduces compliance disclosure regimes to business ethics research. Compliance disclosure is a relatively recent regulatory technique whereby companies are obliged to disclose the extent to which they comply with codes, 'best practice standards' or other extra-legal texts containing norms or prospective norms.

Key findings

Such 'compliance disclosure' obligations are often presented as flexible regulatory alternatives to substantive, command-and-control regulation.

- However, based on a report on experiences of existing compliance disclosure obligations, this article will identify major weaknesses that prevent them from becoming effective mechanisms to discipline a certain type of behaviour.
- It will be argued that regulatory recourse to compliance disclosure obligations is nonetheless worthwhile if we view them as mechanisms that can initiate a dialogue about norm interpretation, application and norm desirability.
- From this perspective, compliance disclosure obligations serve less to discipline companies by making corporate practices transparent, and more to trigger a process of norm development, in which the law, companies and their stakeholders interact.
- This article provides an illustration of how mandatory disclosure, if it is restricted to a unilateral communication process, may produce no effective results (or even prove counterproductive), whilst highlighting the alternative potential of disclosure as an initiator of dialogue, supported by laws, geared towards the development and refinement of norms applicable to business in a global context and the values they promote.

Source: Governance Research Digest, February 2012 (Vol. 3, No. 2)

1.6.9   EU Roadmap on Corporate Governance

Author(s): European Commission

The European Commission has recently released a roadmap concerning corporate governance. The "Enhancing the EU corporate governance framework" initiative falls under the Action Plan on European Company

Law and Corporate Governance adopted by the Commission on 12 December 2012 and highlights shortcomings in the past years and examines alternatives to improve corporate governance.

Key findings

This initiative aims at improving the functioning of the 'comply or explain' approach within the EU corporate governance framework and at enhancing the quality of corporate governance explanations provided by companies departing from corporate governance codes provisions.

- It should provide investors with better information in order to assess whether the deviations from best corporate governance practices are justified.
- The initiative will build on existing rules in the field of corporate governance.
- In the absence of EU action, the quality of 'comply or explain' is likely to improve only in a few Member States which take measures in that field.
- In addition, Member States are likely to adopt different requirement, resulting in divergent application of the 'comply or explain' approach across the EU.
- Detailed guidance would ensure a greater level of uniformity, but could leave less flexibility for Member States.
- A less detailed approach could have the advantage of ensuring an appropriate balance between the need of uniformity and the need of flexibility.

Source: Governance Research Digest, February 2013 (Vol. 4, No. 2)

1.6.10   CG Consultative Paper

Author(s): Security and Exchange Board of India (SEBI)

Security and Exchange Board of India (SEBI) issued a consultative paper on review of corporate governance norms in India. The regulator also pitched for aligning rules relating to listed entities along with the proposed Companies Bill that is awaiting Parliament's approval.

Key findings

SEBI has proposed separating the CMD position in a company mainly to avoid concentration of power with one person.

- The paper suggested that the appointment of independent directors should be only by minority shareholders, such directors should be formally trained to be on company boards and they should also be regularly evaluated for their performance.
- The regulator also suggested that all independent directors should go through a compulsory training session, followed by an exam, both under National Institute of Securities Markets (NISM), a training body under SEBI.
- However, it has not stipulated any exemptions even for reputed independent directors in the country, who, with years of experience and a solid track record, may not be willing to take such tests, a corporate lawyer pointed out.
- SEBI is also aiming to change Clause 49 of the listing agreement between companies and stock exchanges to align it with the proposed Companies Bill.

Source: Governance Research Digest, February 2013 (Vol. 4, No. 2)

1.6.11 Green Tax Index

Author(s): KPMG

KPMG launched The Green Tax Index providing insight into how countries are using taxes to influence corporate sustainability. It aims to encourage companies to explore the opportunities of green tax incentives, and to reduce exposure to green tax penalties.

Key findings

The US ranks No. 1 among 21 countries most actively using the tax code to influence sustainable corporate activity, reflecting the country's federal tax incentives for energy efficiency, renewable energy and green buildings.

- Japan, the UK, France, South Korea and China are also among the leading countries using tax as a tool to drive corporate sustainability, according to the index.
- Key policy areas explored in the index include energy efficiency, water efficiency, carbon emissions, green innovations and green building.
- Japan, for example, ranks No. 1 in promoting tax incentives for green vehicle production, while the US tops the rankings for its renewable

energy tax incentives. The result: more electric and alternative fuel cars coming out of Japan and strong growth in the US renewable sector.

- The KPMG index identified more than 200 individual tax incentives and penalties of relevance to corporate sustainability. At least 30 of these have been introduced since January 2011.
- Japan is ranked second overall but, in contrast to the US, scores higher on green tax penalties than it does on incentives.
- The UK ranks third and has a green tax approach balanced between penalties and incentives. The UK scores most highly in the area of carbon and climate change.
- France occupies fourth place in the overall ranking with a green tax policy more heavily weighted toward penalties than incentives.
- South Korea ranks fifth, and like the US, has a green tax system weighted toward incentives rather than penalties. South Korea leads the ranking for "green innovation" which suggests that South Korea is especially active in using its tax code to encourage green research and development.

Source: Governance Research Digest, April 2013 (Vol. 4, No. 4)

1.6.12 Indian Green Accounting Framework

Author(s): National Statistical Organization, the Ministry of Statistics and Programme Implementation Government of India

The National Statistical Organization, the Ministry of Statistics and Programme Implementation Government of India produced a framework of what would ideally be needed for a comprehensive set of green national accounts. The framework uses existing data and studies to discuss the green accounting methodology, valuation techniques, and feasibility of compilation of various sectoral accounting tables.

<u>Key findings</u>

National governments and international agencies ought to go beyond even green national accounts, by reclassifying certain classes of goods and services and adding others that are currently missing.

- National accounts should ideally be so constructed that they permit citizens in their private capacity and as government officials to sift evidence in ways that inform their ethical perspectives.
- Adjusting for population, the coin on the basis of which economic evaluation should be conducted is a comprehensive notion of wealth (adjusted for the distribution of wealth in the economy), not gross domestic product (GDP).
- Wealth is the social value of an economy's stock of capital assets, comprising (i) reproducible capital (commonly known as "manufactured capital": roads,ports, cables, buildings, machinery, equipment, and so forth), (ii) human capital (population size and composition, education, health), and (iii) natural capital (ecosystems, land, sub-soil resources, and so on).
- Wealth per capita tracks intergenerational wellbeing averaged across the generations exactly: the former increases over a period of time if and only if the latter increases over that same period of time. This equivalence forms the basis for what may be called sustainability analysis.

Source: Governance Research Digest, July 2013 (Vol. 4, No. 7)

1.6.13 Rule of Law Index

Author(s): World Justice Project

World Justice Project delivered an innovative quantitative assessment tool designed by the World Justice Project offering a detailed and comprehensive picture of the extent to which countries adhere to the rule of law in practice. The report, 'Rule of Law Index' provides original data regarding a variety of dimensions of the rule of law, enabling the assessment of a nation's adherence to the rule of law in practice, identify a nation's strengths and weaknesses in comparison to similarly situated countries, and track changes over time.

Key findings

Countries in Western Europe and North America tend to outperform most other countries in all dimensions.

- These countries are characterized by relatively low levels of corruption, open and accountable governments, and effective criminal justice systems.
- The greatest weakness in Western Europe and North America appears to be related to the accessibility of the civil justice system, especially for marginalized segments of the population.
- Denmark is the world leader in two dimensions— government accountability and criminal justice—and places in the top 10 in all dimensions.
- The East Asia and Pacific (EAP) region is one of the most diverse and complex regions in the world. Taken as a whole, the EAP region falls in the upper half of the global rankings in most categories.
- China scores well on public safety, ranking thirty-second overall and fourth among its income peers. The criminal justice system is relatively effective, but compromised by political interference and violations of due process of law.
- Overall, the Middle East and North Africa region receives middling scores for most factors, although the Arab Spring has put several countries on the road towards establishing governments which are more open and accountable, and functioning systems of checks and balances.

Source: Social Research Digest, December 2013 (Vol. 4, No. 12)

1.6.14 The Sorry State of Corporate Taxes

Author(s): *Citizens for Tax Justice (CTJ) and the Institute on Taxation and Economic Policy (ITEP)*

Citizens for Tax Justice (CTJ) and the Institute on Taxation and Economic Policy (ITEP) published a study examining five years' worth of data on federal income taxes paid by 288 corporations–every Fortune 500 company that was profitable each year of the study and provided sufficient, reliable information in their financial reports to allow calculation of their effective U.S. and foreign tax rates. The report, The Sorry State of Corporate Taxes outlines a set of sensible reform options that could help revitalize the corporate tax, including ending the indefinite deferral of taxes in foreign profits and tax breaks for executive stock options.

Key findings

111 of the companies enjoyed at least one year in which their federal income tax was zero or less.

- 26 companies, including Boeing, General Electric, Priceline.com and Verizon, enjoyed negative income tax rates over the entire five-year period, despite combined pre-tax profits of $170 billion.
- Of the 125 multinational companies in this sample, two-thirds paid a lower U.S. tax rate than the rate they paid to foreign governments on their foreign profits. On average, their foreign effective tax rate was 12% larger than their U.S. effective rate.
- The total amount of federal income tax subsidies enjoyed by the 288 profitable corporations over the five years was $362 billion.
- Wells Fargo tops the list of corporations receiving the most in tax subsidies, getting more than $21 billion in tax breaks from the U.S. treasury from 2008 through 2012.
- Pepco Holdings had the lowest effective tax rate of all the companies in the study, at negative 33% over the five year period.
- Industry tax rates varied widely, from a low of 2.9% for utilities to a high of 29.6% for healthcare companies.
- Some companies within sectors fare worse than others. For example Time Warner Cable paid 3.9% over five years, while its competitor Comcast paid 24%.
- More than half of the federal corporate tax subsidies received by the companies in the study went to four industries: financial services, utilities, telecommunications, and oil, gas & pipelines.

Source: CSR Research Digest, June 2014 (Vol. 6, No. 6)

1.6.15 State of Compliance 2013 report

Author(s): PwC

PwC published their third annual survey designed to give corporate compliance officers the benchmarking data they need to understand common industry practices today, and to plan for more effective and more efficient compliance operations in the future. The State of Compliance 2013 report aims to give leaders of the compliance function a comprehensive view into how their peers staff and structure their organizations; the scope of their responsibilities, the risks they target, the processes they use to manage their compliance programs, how they work with others outside the compliance function, the resources at their disposal, and much more.

<u>Key findings</u>

While the demand to improve compliance programs is on the rise, there is still plenty of room for organizations to evolve their programs.

- Formal reporting of the corporate compliance function to the legal department continues to be relatively high compared to other areas of the business (and is higher in the US than the UK), but it has slowly declined over the past three years.
- As the importance of compliance becomes more evident to business leaders, we are seeing an upswing in the number of organizations in which the CCO reports formally to the CEO.
- This reporting structure is more likely to occur in UK-based companies, but we are seeing this trend emerge within US companies as well (28% of US CCOs in 2013 vs. 20% in 2012).
- This is a positive trend overall, as it brings the compliance function clearly onto the C-suite agenda.
- While 42% of respondents said their central compliance functions have more than five people, a slightly higher percentage (45%) indicated there are more than five people working in compliance outside the centralized function. While CCOs are involved in many risk areas; increasingly ownership of those risks resides with the business.
- Compliance committees are dominated by traditional corporate functions, including legal (77%), compliance (76%), and internal audit (61%).
- There is only limited participation from operations or business units, where many compliance risks reside (e.g. only 23% of respondents indicated that the sales and marketing function, which faces bribery and corruption risks, is represented on compliance committees).

Source: Governance Research Digest, February 2014 (Vol. 5, No. 2)

1.6.16 Cost of Compliance Survey 2014

Author(s): Thomson Reuters

Thomson Reuters issued its annual Cost of Compliance survey that provides insight into the experiences and expectations of compliance professionals. This global report is driven by a great level of industry participation and is intended to help regulated firms with future planning, resourcing and focus.

Key findings

More than half of compliance professionals expect their personal liability to increase in 2014 with 17% expecting a significant increase.

- Two-thirds of respondents expect the cost of senior compliance to increase in 2014 with over a fifth (21%) expecting costs to rise significantly.
- In parallel, nearly two-thirds thought that the total compliance team budget would increase in 2014 and a fifth (20%) thought that the budget would be significantly more in 2014.
- Over a third of firms globally spend at least a whole working day every week tracking and analyzing regulatory change.
- The number of compliance teams spending more than 10 hours a week tracking and analyzing regulatory developments has nearly doubled in both the U.S. (13% in 2013 and 25% in 2014) and the Middle East (8% in 2013 and 18% in 2014).
- Globally, compliance functions again reported spending very little time liaising with the internal audit function, a persistently repeated finding which is a growing cause of concern.
- Compliance teams in Asia spend more time consulting other control functions than those in other jurisdictions.
- Across the board, there was a significant increase in the time spent consulting with other functions (legal function: 8% in 2013 and 16% in 2014; internal audit function: 4% in 2013, 11% in 2014; risk function: 2% in 2013, 15% in 2014).

Source: Governance Research Digest, March 2014 (Vol. 5, No. 3)

1.6.17 FTSEcrecy: the culture of concealment throughout the FTSE

Author(s): Christian Aid

Christian Aid released a report that reveals an information void which threatens investors, customers and government regulators, because it leaves them without the facts they need to make good decisions about FTSE100 companies. The report entitled "FTSEcrecy: the culture of concealment throughout the FTSE", warns that the secrecy surrounding thousands of subsidiaries created in tax havens by leading UK companies has created a black hole at the heart of London's FTSE100.

Key findings

Secrecy is not the exception but the norm, even among the biggest companies listed on the London Stock Exchange.

- 14% of the FTSE 100 subsidiaries outside the UK are based in highly secretive jurisdictions. All sectors of the FTSE 100 companies have subsidiaries in such places.
- Investment and finance (37%), banks (28%) and mining (19%) have the highest percentage of subsidiaries in highly secretive jurisdictions.
- Mining (46%), oil and gas (40%), insurance (30%), banks (27%), and media (25%) are the sectors that show the largest proportion of subsidiaries in nontransparent jurisdictions for which no data at all is available.
- Data on turnover, assets, employees or shareholders' funds could only be accessed at no cost for 26% of all FTSE subsidiaries. For the remaining 74%, either data was not available (21% of all subsidiaries) or data was available but could only be accessed after payment of a fee (53% of all subsidiaries).
- In 35 of the FTSE 100 companies, the percentage of subsidiaries for which data can be obtained at no cost is lower than 10%.
- According to a secrecy score that takes into consideration both the location of all subsidiaries and the level of control of those subsidiaries by FTSE 100 companies, mining, oil and gas, travel and leisure, banks, and engineering are the top five most opaque sectors of the FTSE 100.
- The report recommends that the UK and other governments require all companies to report their accounts on a public country-by-country basis, requiring them to publish data such as profits made and taxes paid separately for each country in which they operate. Such a rolling back of secrecy would help governments to ensure that companies are paying the right amount of tax.
- FTSEcrecy also calls for all jurisdictions to require all companies registered in their territory to submit annual statutory accounts, including audited balance sheets, profit and loss accounts, cash flow statements and directors' report or annual returns. Governments should enforce the requirements.
- Further recommendations are that companies' statutory accounts should be publicly accessible at no cost and that governments in Europe

and G20 countries should establish public registers of the real (or 'beneficial') owners of companies, foundations and trusts.

Source: Governance Research Digest, June 2014 (Vol. 5, No. 6)

1.6.18 Giving with one hand and taking with the other – Europe's role in tax-related capital flight from developing countries

Author(s): European Network on Debt and Development

Civil society organisations (CSOs) in 13 European countries, coordinated by the European Network on Debt and Development, have come together to produce a report that examines the tax-related capital flight policies in their respective countries; the actions taken by their national governments to tackle money laundering and tax avoidance and evasion; and attitudes towards EU laws that could help solve the problem. The report, Giving with one hand and taking with the other – Europe's role in tax-related capital flight from developing countries, highlights the efforts, and the shortcomings, of European leaders on this issue, and proposes ways forward.

Key findings

There is a significant discrepancy between tough political rhetoric from the governments surveyed and their actions. This is having a particularly damaging impact on developing countries.

- Tax-related capital flight is a major problem the world over, particularly for the poorest people, who are unfairly losing billions of euros every year as a result of this practice.
- In Europe, the loss of income caused by tax evasion and avoidance is estimated to be around €1 trillion per year. When it comes to the world's developing countries, conservative estimates report that these countries lose between €660 and €870 billion each year through illicit financial flows, mainly in the form of tax evasion by multinational corporations.
- All governments surveyed are failing to demand sufficient levels of tax transparency from companies as no government has implemented full

country-by-country financial reporting requirements for multi-national companies.

- The majority of governments surveyed are reluctant to establish public access to information on the beneficial owners of companies, trusts or foundations in their jurisdictions.
- Data to monitor the information that governments are exchanging with each other on tax matters is rarely publicly accessible. And findings from this report indicate that countries from the global south are barely participating in this form of information exchange.
- None of the governments surveyed support the equal inclusion of developing countries in policy making in this area in practice. All the governments surveyed support the European Union (EU) position, which is that the Organisation for Economic Co-operation and Development (OECD) should be the leading decision-making forum. This is despite concerns about the OECD's legitimacy for this task and the lack of decision-making power in this area for governments in the global south.

Source: Governance Research Digest, June 2014 (Vol. 5, No. 6)

1.6.19 Multinational corporations, stateless income and tax havens

Author(s): Association of Chartered Certified Accountants (ACCA)

The Association of Chartered Certified Accountants (ACCA) released a report that provides evidence to show that the corporate income tax system is not 'broken' and that the corporate income tax base is not being eroded. The report, Multinational corporations, stateless income and tax havens offers a critique of the stateless income doctrine and the interaction between tax havens and multinational corporations.

Key findings

It is not clear that tampering with the tried and tested norms of corporate income tax to (possibly) generate more corporate income tax revenue while reducing the corporate income tax collected in foreign economies, and possibly reducing investment at home, employment at home and consumption at home, is good policy.

- The corporate income tax system is not broken. It is true that some multinational corporations do not pay as much tax in their host economies as their consumers and voters in those economies might expect. Yet this does not necessarily imply any wrongdoing on the part of those corporations.
- Multinational corporations are fully compliant with the law of the land in those economies where they operate and the governments of those economies have been unwilling to change the international income tax norms and tax architecture.
- The stateless income doctrine may be used as a catalyst for re-writing the corporate income tax system. In the same way that an old tax is a good tax, so an old tax system is likely to be a good tax system.

Source: Governance Research Digest, July 2014 (Vol. 5, No. 7)

1.6.20 The Changing Role of Criminal Law in Controlling Corporate Behavior

Author(s): RAND Corporation

The RAND Corp. launched a study that looks at the government's increasing use of criminal law to control corporate conduct and explores how companies are avoiding criminal trials. 'The Changing Role of Criminal Law in Controlling Corporate Behavior' report had three primary goals: (1) trace the development of the application of criminal law to corporate activities, (2) identify and analyze empirical trends with respect to the use of criminal law in this context, and (3) use this research to develop guidance for policymakers in this area.

Key findings

Corporate leaders perceive that criminal sanctions are being imposed more than ever. But in reality there has been a decrease in the number of corporations prosecuted and convicted during the past decade.

- However, the perceptions aren't totally wrong. The decrease in the number of firms convicted coincides with a striking increase in the number of DPAs and NPAs [deferred prosecution and nonprosecution agreements] reached by prosecutors with firms suspected of criminal behavior.

- Large firms were more likely than smaller ones to experience prosecutions and convictions.
- Regarding security and commodity-related offenses, the United States appears to pursue civil sanctions more often than criminal. But not so for antitrust issues. It says more criminal "prosecutions for antitrust matters appear to take place than civil suits.
- Given that so many investigations are settled even before the formal filing of criminal charges, there is little or no judicial oversight over prosecutorial decision-making and case resolution, no formal fact-finding and no development of the law.
- And corporations now face pressure to investigate and develop cases against individual wrongdoers.
- The result has been a kind of privatization of corporate criminal law.
- Suggestions:
- Prosecutors should act "sparingly" in cases that lack clear criminal intent.
- Judges should review DPAs and NPAs to "allow third parties to air objections," provide transparency and reassure the public that justice was being served.
- Prosecutors should consider substituting civil sanctions for criminal ones. "In many cases, civil sanctions that include formal fact-finding might function as well as or better than criminal sanctions

Source: Governance Research Digest, November 2014 (Vol. 5, No. 11)

1.6.21 Whistleblowing in Europe: Legal Protections for whistleblowers in the EU

Author(s): Transparency International

Transparency International issued an overall assessment of the adequacy of whistleblower protection laws of 27 member countries of the European Union (EU). 'Whistleblowing in Europe: Legal Protections for whistleblowers in the EU' also looks at a range of political, social and other factors that promote or discourage whistleblowing in the workplace, and that enable or inhibit the enactment of whistleblower laws in EU countries.

Key findings

Despite the well-documented value of whistleblowers in exposing and preventing corruption, only four European Union (EU) countries have legal frameworks for whistleblower protection that are considered to be advanced: Luxembourg, Romania, Slovenia and the United Kingdom (UK).

- Of the other 23 EU countries, 16 have partial legal protections for employees who come forward to report wrongdoing. The remaining seven countries have either very limited or no legal frameworks.
- Moreover, many whistleblower provisions that are currently in place contain loopholes and exceptions.
- The result is that employees who believe they are protected from retaliation could discover, after they blow the whistle, that they actually have no legal recourse.
- Without sufficient legal protections and reliable avenues to report wrongdoing, employees throughout Europe face being fired, demoted or harassed if they expose corruption and other crimes.
- With would-be whistleblowers inhibited from coming forward, taxpayer money, public property, environmental resources and lives themselves are at risk.
- Encouragingly, several EU countries in recent years have taken steps to strengthen whistleblower rights, including Austria, Belgium, Denmark, France, Hungary, Italy, Luxembourg, Malta, Romania and Slovenia.
- Countries that have issued proposals or have announced plans for proposed laws include Finland, Greece, Ireland, the Netherlands and Slovakia.
- Despite these signs of progress, much remains to be done toward ensuring that whistleblowers in the EU receive the protections they deserve under European and international standards.
- Political will is lacking in many countries. More whistleblower laws would be in place today had government leaders followed through on their commitments to pass and enforce them.

Source: Governance Research Digest, January 2014 (Vol. 5, No. 1)

1.6.22   Waste Crime Report 2011-2012

Author(s): Environment Agency

The Environment Agency's first evidence-based report reveals the latest developments in waste crime prosecutions. Environment Agency's National Environmental Crime Team carried out a close monitoring of current waste disposal practices made by waste contractors.

Key findings

Waste crime prosecutions have increased threefold, as businesses are urged to report suspicious waste management operators.

- The number of illegal waste sites detected by the watchdog has almost doubled to 1,175.
- The increase in the number of sites being detected was primarily the result of the launch last year of a new dedicated £5m Illegal Waste Sites Taskforce, which has closed more than 750 large-scale illegal waste sites and successfully prosecuted 335 individuals and companies for waste-related offences last year.
- 16 people were handed custodial sentences for commiting waste crimes last year, while the total fines increased by nearly £800,000 to £1.7m.

Source: Environmental Research Digest, September 2012 (Vol. 3, No. 9)

1.6.23 Climate Change Litigation Report

Author(s): DB Climate Change Advisors

A report Growth of US Climate Change Litigation: Trends & Consequences was recently released by DB Climate Change Advisors (DBCCA). The paper summarizes the current state of play with climate litigation in the US, and assesses the range of likely outcomes.

Key findings

Without federal legislation regulating greenhouse gas (GHG) emissions, litigation is on the rise in the U.S. with the number of climate change lawsuit filings doubling between 2006 and 2007, and set to triple 2009 levels this year.

- The largest increase in litigation has been challenges to federal action, specifically industry challenges to proposed EPA efforts to regulate greenhouse gas emissions, according to researchers.

- From 2001 to date, 24% of total climate change-related cases were filed by environmental groups aiming to prevent or restrict the permitting of coal-fired power plants, with about 37 states joining, or stating their intent to join, either side of the litigation.
- DBCCA expects the number of climate change related court cases to continue growing for the foreseeable future.
- Industry groups are specifically targeting three Obama-era U.S. Environmental Protection Agency regulations: the December 2009 finding that greenhouses cases endanger human health and welfare, fuel efficiency standards for cars and light trucks in April, and rules released in May to curb emissions by factories and power plants, reports The New York Times.
- The report also notes that the Chamber of Commerce, the National Association of Manufacturers, the American Iron and Steel Institute and the American Chemistry Council, and others had filed multiple lawsuits in the United States Court of Appeals for the District of Columbia, according to the article.
- In August, the U.S. Chamber of Commerce filed a lawsuit that challenges EPA's 2009 endangerment finding, which is the foundation for the agency's ruling on limiting emissions from power plants, factories and other heavy emitters.
- In February, several industry groups, conservative think tanks, lawmakers and three states filed 16 court challenges against EPA's endangerment finding.

Source: CSR Research Digest, December 2010 (Vol. 2, No. 12)

1.6.24 Dirty Money, Dirty Water: Keeping Polluters and Other Campaign Donors from Influencing North Carolina Judicial Elections

Author(s): Center for American Progress

Center for American Progress released a report that follows this year's North Carolina high court election, which saw an unprecedented $4 million in campaign contributions—dramatically more than any election in the past decade. The report, Dirty Money, Dirty Water: Keeping Polluters and Other Campaign Donors from Influencing North Carolina Judicial Elections, also highlights the influence of lawyers and corporate polluters, who also spent big in the 2014 North Carolina Supreme Court race, and underscores the need for state legislators to restore a public financing system to keep corporations and attorneys from trying to curry favor through judicial campaign cash.

Key findings

The report found a troubling correlation between North Carolina judicial campaign contributions and the success rates of law firms that donate money.

- The report also raises concerns about corporate influence in more recent judicial races, including that of Duke Energy, the country's largest power company.
- Since 2012, the company has given hundreds of thousands of dollars to groups such as the Republican State Leadership Committee—by far the biggest spender in the two most recent elections for the North Carolina Supreme Court—which ran ads to elect conservative justices to the bench.
- Meanwhile, Duke Energy has billions of dollars at stake in North Carolina courts, with lawsuits over its responsibility to keep toxic coal ash out of the state's drinking water.
- The report urges North Carolina legislators to restore reforms "that keep corporations from flooding the state supreme court with dirty money.

Source: Environmental Research Digest, December 2014 (Vol. 5, No. 12)

1.7   Respect for International Norms of Behaviour

1.7.1   An Assessment of the Contribution of the UN Global Compact to CSR Strategy

Author(s): H. Runhaar, H. Lafferty

Only a few empirical evaluations of the contribution of the Global Compact (GC) to CSR strategies have been conducted, and few have taken into consideration differences in company performance within and between different industry sectors. This paper aims to partly fill this knowledge gap by a case study examination of three frontrunner companies in the telecommunications industry. The Global Compact is only one of the many initiatives that telecommunications companies employ in shaping, implementing, and reporting about their CSR strategies, and that its role is at most modest.

Key findings

- There are two important reasons for the minimal role of the GC in the case study companies' CSR strategies:
- Many of the CSR issues that these companies deal with are industry specific and are hence addressed in specific networks;
- The GC principles are perceived as minimum requirements that do not provide many incentives to the three case study companies to perform better.
- The authors feel that the GC could be of more value to companies with less finely articulated CSR strategies. They identify four possible ways in which the GC can be used in CSR strategy development and implementation:
  - Adoption of the normative guidelines;
  - Participatory learning in GC-based local networks;
  - Structured partnerships with other companies or stakeholders for implementing specific aspects of CSR;
  - A pro-active attitude to reporting and communicating CSR.
- While the authors feel that the contribution of the GC to CSR strategy in the telecommunications industry is limited, they feel it could provide more value if it more explicitly aimed at stimulating frontrunner companies to perform better.

Source: CSR Research Digest, March 2009 (Vol. 1, No. 3)

1.7.2   Analysis of Policy Author(s)s made by large EU Companies to Internationally Recognised CSR Guidelines and Principles

Author(s): European Commission

European Commission carried out a survey of the public CSR statements of 200 randomly selected large European companies. The "Analysis of Policy Author(s)s made by large EU Companies to Internationally Recognised CSR Guidelines and Principles" took into account UN Global Compact, the Organisation for Economic Co-operation and Development Guidelines, ISO 26000, the Universal Declaration of Human Rights, The UN Guiding Principles on Business and Human Rights, and the International Labor Organization's Multinational Enterprises and Social Policy (ILO MNE) Declaration.

Key findings

The UN Global Compact and the Global Reporting Initiative, with 32% and 31% respectively, are the most commonly referenced instruments, followed by the Universal Declaration of Human Rights and the Instruments of the International Labour Organisation.

- 68% of the sample companies make reference to "corporate social responsibility" or an equivalent term, and 40% refer to at least one internationally recognised CSR instrument.
- 33% of the sample companies meet the European Commission's call to refer to at least one of the following: UN Global Compact, OECD Guidelines for Multinational Enterprises, or ISO 26000.
- 2% of the sample companies meet the European Commission's call to refer to the ILO MNE Declaration.
- 3% of the sample companies refer to the UN Guiding Principles on Business and Human Rights, which the European Commission expects all enterprises to implement with regard to the corporate responsibility to respect human rights.
- Very large companies in the sample (those with over 10.000 employees) are about 3 times more likely to refer to internationally recognised CSR instruments than companies with between 1.000 and 10.000 employees.
- Danish, Spanish and Swedish sample companies refer to internationally recognized CSR instruments more often than the average EU sample company. Dutch, French and Italian companies were about average for the sample, and Czech, German, Polish and UK companies in the sample refer to CSR instruments less frequently that than the average.

Source: CSR Research Digest, April 2013 (Vol. 5, No. 4)

1.7.3 The Contribution of Environmental and Social Standards Towards Ensuring Legitimacy in Supply Chain Governance

Author(s): *M. Mueller, V. Gomes de Santos, S. Seuring.*

This paper aims to strengthen the legitimacy of those social and environmental standards which are most effective in helping companies to meet their CSR objectives. The authors discuss four different standards – ISO 14001, SA 8000, Forest Stewardship Council and Fair Labour Association) – and examine how they impose legitimacy on the companies implementing them.

Key findings

For each standard, deficits are apparent, particularly when considering the supply chain.

- While standards are passed upstream in the supply chain, this seems to be done on a practical basis, while the normative implications and stakeholder requirements might not be integrated into the standard at all.
- ISO 14001 and SA 8000 are the most popular standards, likely due to the support of large, well-known companies.
- In some cases – e.g. sustainable forestry - similar standards with less stringent compliance requirements have diffused more widely.
- Such actions can make it more difficult for CSR to gain credibility through environmental and social standards. Legitimate instruments may become discredited.
- In order to ameliorate legitimacy of such standards among stakeholders, it is important to improve the transparency of the certification results.

Source: CSR Research Digest, February 2010 (Vol. 2, No. 2)

1.7.4 SMEs and Global Compact Implementation

Author(s): *Danish Ministry of Foreign Affairs/UNDP*

The Danish Ministry of Foreign Affairs, working with the UNDP, has released a set of ten case studies detailing how Danish SMEs are implementing Global Compact principles in their operations. The case studies cover a wide range of industry sectors from food to jewellery, and each addresses several of the Global Compact Principles.

Key findings

Company	Challenges	Advice
Rice Ltd. (gift articles)	How to provide agreeable conditions for village home workers.	Organise efforts through dialogue, SA8000 and Global Compact.
Eurotex Apparel Ltd. (textiles) with Save The Children.	How to handle child labour in Bangladesh responsibly.	Participate in partnerships with specialist organizations and other businesses.
JUAL Ltd. (roof accessories)	How to ensure Chinese subsidiaries and suppliers live up to Danish working standards.	Create small success stories; build on success with continuous improvements.
Butler's Choice Ltd. (food)	How to work with suppliers to raise environmental standards.	Promote corporate responsibility built on strong convictions; build long-term trust with suppliers.
Pilgrim Ltd. (jewelllery)	How to inspire suppliers to improve working environment and labour standards.	Use networks and dialogue; focus on partnerships and real improvements rather than control.
Katvig plc. (children's clothing)	How can a small enterprise promote acceptable environmental standards to large suppliers?	Don't think you have to invent everything yourself; use networks and existing labeling schemes.
Ingemann Foods Ltd. (food)	How to ensure small-scale developing nation farmers qualify to be part of the company supply	Integrate CSR into the company business model; build long-term relationships with

	chain.	suppliers.
Orana Ltd. (fruit)	How to link business development and CSR in partnerships in India.	Select partners carefully and be patient; build long-term partnerships.
Henning Larsen Architects (architecture)	How to work strategically with environmental improvements and energy efficiency in construction projects.	Start where you have the most influence; share experiences with other businesses.
Emunio plc. (syringes)	How to implement Global Compact principles strategically with partner in Tanzania.	Actively involve staff; put policies in writing; update documentation of progress continuously.

Source: Governance Research Digest, October 2009 (Vol. 1, No. 10)

1.7.5   Code Certification Statements

Author(s): IBE

This Briefing explores how companies use certification statements as a part of their ethics programme, using the results of an IBE survey. It examines the uses and drivers for certification statements as well as providing examples of companies' certification statements.

Key findings

- IBE research of 17 FTSE100 companies (2012) found that the three most common uses of certification statements were:
  - o   to confirm receipt of the code of ethics;
  - o   to obtain acknowledgement from employees that they have read and understood the code of ethics;
  - o   or that they have abided by, or will abide by, the code of ethics.
- Other uses include obtaining confirmation from employees that they have reported any breaches of the code that they have been aware of.
- For one company, management were required to certify that they had discussed the code with their team and informed them of the availability of the hotline for raising employee concerns.

- Companies may ask their entire workforce to sign a certification statement for the code or only specific groups.
- The small IBE survey found that 71% of companies surveyed require employees; 82% require managers and 94% require senior managers to sign one.
- Asking employees and management to sign certification statements is one way that a company can demonstrate the importance of the code of ethics and its commitment to live up to the values contained within it.
- The data on the number of employees that have signed a certification statement can be collected by the ethics office and reported upwards internally e.g. to a board committee responsible for ethics as part of the regular update on code certification, training, communication etc.
- It may also be reported to other departments such as compliance, risk, or legal as it is integral to internal control and risk management systems and may be part of "adequate procedures" compliance under the UK Bribery Act.

Source: Governance Research Digest, April 2012 (Vol. 3, No. 4)

1.7.6   2010 Global Compact Annual Review

Author(s): UN Global Compact

An annual survey was completed anonymously by more than 1,200 companies participating in the Global Compact, the UN corporate responsibility initiative, and forms the basis of the 2010 Global Compact Annual Review. All 6,000+ companies participating in the Global Compact were invited to take the survey, which was conducted in multiple languages in November and December 2010.

Key findings

Companies' implementation of environmental policies and actions improved in 2010, with large corporations continuing to show better performance than small and medium-sized enterprises.

- Despite progress by SMEs, company size has a significant impact on how likely firms are to set environmental policies.
- But on environmental actions, the performance gap between large and small companies narrowed in the past year.

- Publicly-traded companies show markedly higher implementation rates those that are privately held, in nearly all environmental areas.
- Companies reported higher rates of environmental policy implementation in 2010 compared to 2009, and the increase was more marked than the slight upward trend from 2008 to 2009.
- There were significant increases in triple bottomline, production, and sustainable consumption policies.
- The most common environmental policy was sustainable consumption, with a participation rate of 71%.
- Companies in the survey also took key environmental actions at higher rates in 2010 than in 2009 – especially in the areas of management systems (+15%), life-cycle assessment (+6%) and reporting greenhouse gas emissions (+5%).
- But the survey found that only a minority of companies are taking steps around water footprinting – even among the largest companies.
- And only half of the largest companies are taking steps on life-cycle assessment and ecodesign.
- More than 70% of all respondents indicate the active involvement of their chief executives in policy and strategy development.
- This reflects the growing relevance of sustainability issues to business performance.
- Nearly 60% of all publicly traded companies report active involvement of their boards of directors.
- Regarding supply chain implementation of sustainability principles, 65% of companies report some measure of supplier involvement, with 12% requiring their suppliers to be Global Compact participants.
- Likewise, 79% of companies spread their commitment to the Global Compact principles to their subsidiaries, with nearly half of those (44%) creating separate sustainability functions at the subsidiary level.

Source: CSR Research Digest, July 2011 (Vol. 3, No. 7)

1.7.7 The European UN Global Compact Companies towards Rio +20 and Beyond: A Best Practices Collection

Author(s): UN Global Compact

UN Global Compact Local Networks Europe released the report to showcase 100 best practice examples. It showcases cases across 20 countries that are implementing sustainable development initiatives and programs to help advance the Rio+20 agenda.

Key findings

Work with others to meet the real demands and basic needs of the rural population in developing countries.

- Users will be able to adopt advanced techniques for utilizing power, with an active and more sustainable management of energy consumption.
- Mobilized a number of its specialists to develop sustainable solutions in the fields of energy, mobility, security, health and sustainable finance.
- Achieving corporate success in respect to moral values and satisfying the ethical, legal, environmental and social expectations of society to the company.
- Eco-efficiency close to core business activities and increasing fuel prices mean that this policy is not "nice to do" category any longer, but rather "must to do".
- If you want to remain a viable global player for the future, you also have to be a part of the solution to today's problems.
- Promoting the health and enhancing the wellbeing of workers is as vital as protecting their safety.
- No responsible development without responsible purchasing.
- Respect human rights, which in essence means to manage the risk of damaging human rights with a view to avoiding it.

Source: CSR Research Digest, August 2012 (Vol. 4, No. 8)

1.7.8 Beyond Compliance – Below Expectations? CSR in the Context of International Development

Author(s): R. Barkemeyer

In this paper, the results of an empirical analysis of a set of 416 descriptive case studies published by corporate members of the UN Global Compact are presented. The analysis illustrates which kinds of projects are deemed appropriate as best practice examples among Compact members, and therefore indicate the direction, in which predominantly voluntary and business-led CSR might at best be evolving.

Key findings

Contemporary CSR initiatives may not be suitable for tackling some of the most pressing development challenges.

- Only certain topics are commonly addressed (environmental issues, for example) while a number of issues such as anti-corruption measures or labour rights are underrepresented.
- Despite the successful efforts to attract small and medium enterprises as well as Southern companies, large Northern companies continue to play a key role in the Global Compact.
- If the Compact is to effectively engage multinational corporations (MNCs) in development through their CSR activities, it will have to be ensured that sufficient communication channels exist between these companies and the intended beneficiaries in the South.
- In this regard, the recent decision to decentralize the Compact structure and to strengthen the country networks can be seen as counterproductive, since MNCs are now more embedded in the network of their countries of origin, than in the networks of those countries in which their operations take place.
- The vast majority of case stories address issues tackled in the companies' home countries.
- Given the link between the Compact and the UN Millennium Development Goals (MDGs), and the pronounced role of leadership within the network, a proactive role of the private sector in international development would presuppose a more international perspective of the Northern companies.
- In terms of both the reporting of best practice examples and the countries of impact that are addressed, the case stories are mainly limited to a small number of sub-centres in the South, such as India, China, South Africa and Brazil.
- The question emerges as to how those countries that are playing only a marginal role in international trade can be reached by predominantly voluntary, market-based instruments, or whether measures such as the Compact rather contribute towards a further 'South-South divide'.

- The majority of case stories focus on policyrelated activities. The institutional embedding of sustainability issues is clearly important; however, this can only be an intermediary goal on the way towards actual performance improvement.

- From the sample of case stories by EU-based companies, it becomes evident that only a few development issues are addressed through specific activities, whereas the majority of development-related projects focus on policy or strategy formulation and the implementation of management systems.

- The paper concludes that rather than systematically addressing and internalizing all principles, companies pick and choose among the principles and corporate activities they want to deal with.

Source: Social Research Digest, July 2009 (Vol. 1, No. 7)

1.7.9 Perceptions and practice of King III in South African Companies

Author(s): The Institute of Directors in Southern Africa and the Albert Luthuli Centre for Responsible Leadership, University of Pretoria

The Institute of Directors in Southern Africa and the Albert Luthuli Centre for Responsible Leadership of University of Pretoria published a study whose aim was to investigate how various South African companies perceive the recommendations on corporate governance as set out in the King Report on Corporate Governance in South Africa 2009 (King III), to what extent these recommendations have been applied and what the effects of the application of these recommendations have been on various aspects of the companies' business practices. In order to meet the central research objective, a web-based questionnaire was sent to the IoDSA membership database consisting of 5221 members and 183 responses were received from JSE-listed companies, non-profit organisations, private equity organisations, state owned enterprises and other companies such as unlisted public companies, regulating bodies, subsidiaries of listed companies and multinationals.

Key findings

The successive King Codes have, according to respondents, added value to both the respondents' respective organisations and to the economy of South Africa on the whole.

- The majority of respondents (65%) indicated that King III has added value to their company. Only four percent of respondents were of the opinion that their company has not experienced a value add from the application of King III. Thirty one percent of respondents provided a neutral response to this question.
- On average, the highest number of respondents (46%) chose the demonstration of commitment to corporate governance to external stakeholders as their primary reason for applying King III.
- Twenty percent of respondents rated the need for improved efficiency and effectiveness within the organisation as their number one reason for applying King III which makes this the second highest frequency of primary reasons why companies choose to apply King III.
- As the second most important reason for applying King III, the desire of the board to enhance confidence in the organisation's performance through application of King III was the most frequently selected option (24%).
- The second most frequently selected choice was the need for improved efficiency and effectiveness within the organisation as the second most important reason for applying King III.
- Other high ranking reasons included the improvement of efficiency and effectiveness within the organisation and the board seeking application as a means to enhance confidence in the performance of the organisation.
- In general, respondents felt that King III had mostly positive effects on board deliberations and decision making in the following respects:
  o Enhanced leadership by the board in providing strategy and direction;
  o The exercising of control and monitoring of management which enabled the board to discharge its accountability;
  o The delegation of authority enabling the board to function effectively and efficiently while retaining adequate control;

o An appropriate board composition which resulted in increased effectiveness and efficiency, and;

o Enhanced confidence in the quality of its decisions.

Source: Governance Research Digest, October 2013 (Vol. 4, No. 10)

1.7.10 Smallholders: Costs and Challenges of Small-Farmer Certification

Author(s): *World Growth*

The World Growth Palm Oil Green Development campaign and World Growth NGO released a report that provides insight into the costs and challenges of small-farmer certification. This "Smallholders: Costs and Challenges of Small-Farmer Certification" Report focuses on case studies from France, Indonesia, Malaysia and South East Asia.

Key findings

The campaign to require smallholders to be certified as RSPO-compliant breaches the UN mandated and Rio Earth Summit adopted consensus that sustainability should go hand in hand with action to raise living standards.

- Retailers in France rallied against palm oil in order to promote their own private-label products over established food products that rely on palm oil for receipt consistency demanded by consumers.
- RSPO certification is an expensive process and it is beyond the means of most small holders due to a lack of capital and technical expertise.
- Insufficient economies of scale make the certification economically viable option for large farm operations.
- WWF has initiated a campaign to promote RSPO certified palm oil in India in an attempt to reduce the attractiveness of imported palm oil.
- India's main priority to acquire affordable palm oil is to feed poor population and not embrace expensive certification standards, which raise the price of food.
- The root of the problem is that RSPO system does not add value to smallholder farmers and it adversely affects their viability.
- In Malaysia a system has been developed by the government to encourage 'Good Agricultural Practices' (GAP) amongst small farmers.

- Malaysian Sustainable Palm Oil (MSPO) standard is currently being developed, based on input from local stakeholders such as Malaysia small farmers.
- The result of this campaign is the reduction in the amount of land used for production.

Source: Social Research Digest, May 2013 (Vol. 4, No. 5)

1.7.11 UN Global Compact 2014-2016 Strategy

Author(s): UN Global Compact

The UN Global Compact released its 2014-2016 strategy, which lays out how the initiative will work to make corporate sustainability a transformative force in achieving a shared, secure and sustainable future. Developed by the management and staff of the Global Compact with support from Deloitte, the strategy was released after 18 months of consultation with a range of key stakeholders including the Global Compact Board, Government Group and Local Networks.

Key findings

Over the next three years, the Global Compact aims to achieve scale and transformation, while maintaining quality and impact, by focusing on four priorities: participant engagement; Local Networks, a global portfolio of issues, and responsible business in support of UN goals and issues.

- The Global Compact's participant engagement strategy emphasizes reaching 13,000 business participants by 2016, while focusing on enhanced levels of reporting and transparency among participants.
- Local Networks serve an essential role in rooting the UN Global Compact within different national contexts – and their distinct economic, cultural and linguistic needs.
- The Global Compact seeks to empower networks by setting standards and equipping them to facilitate transformative actions and solutions that impact the Post-2015 Development Agenda, and support widespread advances in corporate sustainability performance.
- The Global Compact's global portfolio of issues – covering human rights, labour standards, environment and anti-corruption – has been at the forefront of engaging companies and driving implementation of the

ten principles. Its array of issue platforms, working groups, specialised workstreams, and collaboration with sister initiatives will be highlighted as premier opportunities for business to advance corporate sustainability.

- The Global Compact will seek to improve the quality and quantity of partnerships by its participants to advance UN goals, to enhance the UN system's capacity to partner more effectively with the private sector, and to illustrate ways that the Business Engagement Architecture can contribute to the Post-2015 Development Agenda.

Source: CSR Research Digest, April 2014 (Vol. 6, No. 4)

1.8   Rankings, Ratings and Indices

1.8.1   Corporate Accountability Ranking

Author(s): *CSR Network/AccountAbility*

Vodafone has topped the 2008 Accountability Rating, regaining the position it held in 2006. The Accountability Rating is a tool for measuring the extent to which companies have built responsible practices into the way they do business and their impact on the economies, societies and environments in which they operate. The Rating is applied annually to the Fortune Global 100 companies.

Key findings

Companies headquartered in Europe are the most accountable, with Asian companies retaining a slight lead over the 31 companies based in the United States.

- French companies are challenging the British leadership in corporate responsibility. There are now four British (average Rating score 59) and three French companies (average Rating score 55) in the top ten, together with one each from the US, Finland and Holland.
- Most companies within the G-100 (78%) are now disclosing targets for their environmental performance. However, a little less than half are actually saying when they plan to achieve these targets.

- 75% of companies are reporting on their carbon emissions, but despite major public awareness campaigns just 43% report emission reductions.
- Financial companies including HSBC and Barclays are showing continued improvement in the manner in which they discuss environmental, ethical and social responsibility aspects of their core business strategy. However, as the case of HBOS (5th) demonstrates, a strong performance on the Accountability Rating does not necessarily ensure companies have managed to protect themselves against the current challenging economic climate.
- The retail and fast moving consumer goods (FMCG) sector scores relatively poorly as companies struggle to manage social and environmental issues along their vast supply chains. Although there are significant improvements in performance from companies like Wal-Mart, only Tesco features in the top 25.
- The Rating website also features case studies of the top ten companies, highlighting examples of their best practice.

Rank	Company	Overall Score	SI	G&M	Eng.	OP
1	Vodafone	77.7	21.3	19.5	22.1	14.8
2	General Electric	70.2	20.6	19.6	17.6	12.3
3	HSBC	67.7	20.6	18.3	17.3	11.6
4	France Telecom	67.3	19.0	16.9	17.3	14.1
5	HBOS	66.2	18.5	17.8	15.8	14.1
6	Nokia	63.8	20.1	17.8	14.9	11.9
7	EDF	62.3	18.8	16.4	15.4	11.6
8	GDF Suez	61.8	14.7	16.2	13.2	17.7
9	BP	61.6	18.0	18.3	16.2	9.1
10	Royal Dutch/Shell	61.2	18.0	17.1	14.7	11.3

SI: Strategic Intent
G&M: Governance and Management
Eng.: Engagement
OP: Operational Performance

Source: CSR Research Digest, January 2009 (Vol. 1, No. 1)

1.8.2   100 Best Corporate Citizens

Author(s): *Corporate Responsibility Office*

The 2009 CRO 100 Best Corporate Citizens List has been released by Corporate Responsibility Officer. The list compares companies' performance in environment, climate change, human rights, employee relations, philanthropy, finance and governance.

Key findings

Rank	Company	Industry Subgroup
1	Bristol Myers-Squibb	Pharmaceuticals
2	General Mills, Inc.	Retail – Food
3	IBM Corp.	Computer Hardware
4	Merck & Co., Inc.	Pharmaceuticals
5	HP Co. LP	Computer Hardware
6	Cisco Systems, Inc.	Computer Hardware
7	Mattel, Inc.	Leisure Products
8	Abbott Laboratories	Pharmaceutical Manufacture
9	Kimberly-Clark Corp.	Personal Care Products
10	Entergy Corp.	Utilities - Electric

- In 2009, first-placed Bristol-Myers Squibb, No. 4 Merck, No. 5 HP, No. 7 Mattel, No. 11 Exxon Mobil and No. 29 Chevron, all came back from positions in CRO's 2008 Penalty Box for regulator-imposed sanctions.

Source: CSR Research Digest, April 2009 (Vol. 1, No. 4)

1.8.3   Corporate Responsibility Index

Author(s): *Business in the Community*

Business in the Community (BITC) has published its seventh annual Corporate Responsibility Index (CR Index) for 2008. Companies include those in the FTSE 250, sector leaders from the Dow Jones Sustainability Index, and BITC member companies that have a significant economic presence in the UK. This year, 141 companies participated in the CR Index.

Key findings

Platinum Scoring Companies (2007)		2009 Additions
Accenture	Lloyds TSB	Anglian Water Services
BAA	Pearson	British American Tobacco
Barclays	Pricewaterhouse-Coopers	BBC
BHP Billiton	Reckitt Beckiser	Carillion plc
Camelot Group	Reed Elsevier	Co-operative Group
Centrica	Rio Tinto	Deloitte LLP
Ernst & Young	Scottish Power	H M Revenue & Customs
J Sainsbury	Tesco	RSA Insurance Group
John Lewis Partnership	Unilever	RWE npower
Kelda Group	Veolia Water UK	
Kingfisher	WH Smith	
KPMG	Xstrata	

Source: CSR Research Digest, August 2009 (Vol. 1, No. 8)

1.8.4   10 Best Corporate Citizens

Author(s): Corporate Responsibility Magazine

Corporate Responsibility Magazine has for the first time released a ranking of industry-specific top ten in its ranking. The magazine releases an annual top 100 corporate citizens list.

Key findings

JP Morgan Chase & Co., Starbucks Corp. and Chevron Corp. are three of the winners.

- The winners in each category are:
  - Financials/Insurance/Real Estate – JPMorgan Chase & Co.
  - Information Technology – International Business Machines Corp.
  - Materials – E.I. DuPont De Nemours & Co.

- o Customer Items – Mattel, Inc.
- o Media & Entertainment – Starbucks Corp.
- o Business Services – Accenture Plc.
- o Consumer Staples – Campbell Soup Co.
- o Utilities – Pinnacle West Capital Corp.
- o Energy – Chevron Corp.
- o Healthcare – Bristol-Myers Squibb Co.

Source: Governance Research Digest, October 2011 (Vol. 2, No. 6)

1.8.5 Best Corporate Citizens in Government Contracting Corporate Responsibility

Author(s): CR Magazine

(CR) Magazine has released the 3rd annual Best Corporate Citizens in Government Contracting List. CR Magazine first introduced this list in 2010 to encourage government to take a broad set of factors – including transparency in reporting as well as key performance measures – into consideration when making buying decisions.

Key findings

Overall disclosure performance has improved by 5% over the prior year.

- Performance improvements are particularly strong among government contractors outside of the "best" of this year's list.
- While performance remains strong among the best, the "rest" showed 11% improvement in performance over 2011.
- At the same time, 3-year average returns to shareholders among the very best outpaced the rest by over 50%, demonstrating the financial benefits of transparency.
- IBM, Accenture and HP held on to their top positions in 2012, once again signifying their long-term commitment to openness in reporting.

Source: Governance Research Digest, July 2012 (Vol. 3, No. 7)

1.8.6 Top 10 Best Corporate Citizens

Author(s): CR Magazine

CR Magazine ranked the Top 10 Best Corporate Citizens by industry in 10 sectors — consumer items; consumer staples; energy; financial, insurance and real estate; healthcare; information technology; materials; media and entertainment; services; and utilities. It used publicly available data from Russell 1000 companies collected and analyzed by IW Financial, a Portland, Maine-based financial analysis firm.

Key findings

Nike, Campbell Soup and Chevron are among the best corporate citizens.

- The top three best corporate citizens in each industry are:
  - Consumer Items: Nike, Mattel, Gap
  - Consumer Staples: Campbell Soup, Sara Lee, Coca-Cola
  - Energy: Chevron, Occidental Petroleum, Hess Corporation
  - Financial/Insurance/Real Estate: JPMorgan Chase, Wells Fargo, State Street
  - Healthcare: Bristol-Myers Squibb, Abbott Laboratories, Johnson & Johnson
  - Information Technology: IBM, Microsoft, Texas Instruments
  - Materials: Freeport-McMoran Copper & Gold, International Paper, Mosaic Company
  - Media and Entertainment: McGraw-Hill, Starbucks, Walt Disney
  - Services: Accenture, ManpowerGroup, Waste Management
  - Utilities: Spectra Energy, Northeast Utilities, Duke Energy

Source: Governance Research Digest, October 2012 (Vol. 3, No. 10)

1.8.7   Thomson Reuters Corporate Responsibility Indices

Author(s): Thompson Reuters & S-Network

Thomson Reuters has launched a new family of environmental, social and corporate governance indices, developed jointly with Snetwork Global Indexes, a New York-based specialist index design firm. The new indices are powered by "dynamic" ratings based on the Thomson Reuters ASSET4 ESG database and they mirror the performance of major global benchmarks via companies that have substantially higher ESG ratings than the weighted average for such indices as the S&P 500 or MSCI EAFE.

Key findings

The ratings include a greater emphasis on quantitative outcomes than on qualitative corporate statements to ensure the indices are as objective and transparent as possible.

- The ratings include a greater emphasis on quantitative outcomes than on qualitative corporate statements to ensure the indices are as objective and transparent as possible.
- The first two sets of indices cover large capitalization stocks located in the US and the International Developed Ex- North America region (also known as EAFE).
- Composite ESG indices are available for these two regions, as well as indices for the two regions based on the individual economic, social and governance pillars.
- Real-time index values will be available on Thomson Reuters desktops and feed products starting May 30.
- The indices and ratings will also be available via an S-Network operated website, which will allow users an affordable way to benchmark against the index and rate ESG performance of a portfolio of stocks.
- The Thomson Reuters Corporate Responsibility Indices are:
  - The Thomson Reuters US Large Cap Environmental Index The Thomson Reuters US Large Cap Social Index
  - The Thomson Reuters US Large Cap Governance Index
  - The Thomson Reuters US Large Cap ESG Index
  - The Thomson Reuters Global Large Cap Environmental Index
  - The Thomson Reuters Global Large Cap Social Index
  - The Thomson Reuters Global Large Cap Governance Index
  - The Thomson Reuters Global Large Cap ESG Index

Source: Governance Research Digest, May 2013 (Vol. 4, No. 5)

1.8.8   CSR Ratings Study

Author(s): SustainAbility

SustainAbility has recently released its phase three of Rate the Raters study that tackles corporate sustainability ratings. The study covers in-depth evaluations of 21 ratings, in an attempt to shed light on how corporate sustainability ratings work in practice.

Key findings

With growing interest in ratings from a broader set of constituencies, it's becoming ever more important to ensure that the end results are accurate.

- In the race to build a better rating, ratings organizations have introduced considerable complexity in terms of their criteria, questions and scoring schemes.
- Yet it is found some of the best ratings in our review to be the simplest.
- As an increasing number of investors, consumers, employees and other stakeholders follow and make greater use of sustainability ratings, it is imperative that raters improve their efforts on quality assurance and control.
- Too many ratings focus on companies' past or current performance and not how they are positioned for the future.
- Lastly, raters won't be able to "Focus on the Future" unless they invest considerably more time directly engaging with the companies they rate.
- The majority of ratings today are based on arms-length assessments of performance.
- This is possible due to the nature (i.e. type of criteria) of today's ratings and often necessary given organizational limits and ratings' scope (i.e. small teams assessing large universes of companies).

Source: CSR Research Digest, March 2011 (Vol. 3, No. 3)

1.8.9   BITC Corporate Responsibility Index

Author(s): Business in the Community

Business in the Community published their 2014 Corporate Responsibility Index that provides insight into how leading companies are driving responsible business practice. This year the CR Index has identified six trends that are leading the responsible business agenda.

Key findings

Leading companies, such as those highlighted throughout this report, are linking their progress to remuneration, training and board development, but more progress is needed to ensure that sustainability is a priority at board and at a senior level.

- Many more companies need to move from passive integration to what we see as the next challenge, active and quality engagement, monitoring and empowerment of stakeholders.
- Currently, 80% of the CR Index companies' boards have agreed and monitored their policy on taxation, with half of CR Index participant companies publicly disclosing their policies.
- Sustainable production is an area of significant progress, with 63% taking steps to develop sustainable products and services, business processes or sourcing practices that have a longer return investment. But the vast majority of investments have focussed on responsible energy supply, rather than new products and services.

Source: CSR Research Digest, April 2014 (Vol. 6, No. 4)

1.8.10   100 Best Corporate Citizens

Author(s): Corporate Responsibility Magazine

Corporate Responsibility Magazine announced its 15th annual 100 Best Corporate Citizens List, recognizing the standout performance of public companies across the United States. The 100 Best List documents 298 data points of disclosure and performance measures—harvested from publicly available information in seven categories: environment, climate change, employee relations, human rights, governance, finance, and philanthropy.

Key findings

The top ten on the 2014 list include (in rank order): Bristol-Myers Squibb Co., Johnson & Johnson, Gap Inc., Microsoft Corporation, Mattel Inc., Weyerhaeuser Co., Ecolab, Inc., Intel Corp., Coca-Cola Co. and Walt Disney Co.

- 23 companies are on the 2014 list that were not on the 2013 list
- 17 companies have been on the list every year since 2008
- 33 companies rose an average of 20 ranks
- 42 companies fell an average of 17 ranks

Source: CSR Research Digest, May 2014 (Vol. 6, No. 5)

1.8.11   B Corp Best for the World 2014

Author(s): B Lab

B Lab announced its B Corp Best for the World List, with the 92 social enterprises creating the most positive overall social and environmental impact of the almost 1,000 certified B Corporations in operation. The winners earned a score in the top 10% of all certified B Corps on the B Impact Assessment, which is an evaluation of companies according to their impact on such factors as workers, suppliers, community, and the environment.

Key findings

This year there were 92 overall honorees: 56 micro-enterprises (companies with 0-9 employees), 26 small businesses (10-49 employees), and 10 midsize businesses (50 employees or more). The majority are service companies, but there's plenty of diversity: honorees come from 31 different industries. While financial and sustainability consulting firms have the most representation, other winners are in the business of everything from furniture to farmers' markets.

- This year's winners also came from all over the globe. About 25% of the B Corporation community is from outside the USA, so it's no surprise that 30% of Best for the World honorees were from our international community. In fact, 13% of winners were from emerging markets, including countries like Afghanistan, Nicaragua, Kenya, and Colombia. The Canadian community, as always, had a strong showing, with 12 different companies making the list.
- 15% of honorees are companies that made the Best for the World list for the first time in 2014, but have been certified for several years! These companies have not been content to merely make the 80-point bar; instead, they've worked to increase their score over the years, engaging in a "race to the top."

Among the top-scorers are:

- Echale a tu Casa (score: 168). Founded in 1997, the Mexico City-based company addresses the problem of inadequate housing in developing countries. Specifically, most families construct their own homes, but materials are expensive and financing is hard to get. Echale a Tu Casa, which calls itself a social housing production company, has a sustainable building model with innovations in construction, technology and finance. Some highlights: The lowest-paid workers receive 355% above the minimum wage, as well as free or subsidized housing. Eight-five percent of consumers using the company's services are from underserved populations.

- Re:Vision Architecture (score: 181). The Philadelphia company is an architecture, planning, and consulting firm specializing in sustainable design and development. To encourage collaboration among professionals from different fields and community members, the company holds multi-day design events during which participants work together to develop the most sustainable design or plan for a project. Some highlights: A bonus plan is paid to 100% of non-executive employees. Seventy-five percent of completed projects are LEED certified.

Source: CSR Research Digest, July 2014 (Vol. 6, No. 7)

II. TRANSPARENCY

2.1 CSR Communication and Social Media

2.1.1 CSR Information Disclosure on the Web: A Context-Based Approach Analysing the Influence of Country of Origin and Industry Sector

Author(s): L.S.O. Wandeley, R. Lucian, F. Farache, J.M. de Sousa Filho.

This study examines whether the CSR content on company websites is influenced by either country of origin or industry sector. The websites of 127 corporations from emerging economies including Brazil, Chile, China, India, Indonesia, Mexico, Thailand and South Africa, are examined. The companies represented are from the following industry sectors: Banking; Capital Goods; Conglomerates; Consumer Durables; Diversified Financials; Food, Drink and Tobacco; Insurance; Materials; Oil & Gas Operations; Retailing; Telecommunications Services and Transportation.

Key findings

Based on the data studied, country of origin has a more significant influence on online CSR disclosure than industry sector, although both are important.

- Although there are major problems related to social exclusion and poverty in the countries featured, and there is an expectation that companies should play a role as providers of social good for society, these two aspects alone do not give rise to like-minded corporate behaviour in different industry sectors and countries within the group of companies studied.
- The following factors are identified as inhibiting the development of CSR in developing countries: civil society is not well organised; the government does not strongly promote CSR; companies do not face strong, constant pressure; and the press has yet to assume the role of

watchdog.

- Information presented on the internet faces the challenge of a relative lack of credibility. Often, media coverage has greater credibility than communication the corporations themselves produce.

- The paper lists three factors that can facilitate success in CSR communications: source credibility of the communicator, honesty of the statements and the involvement of the audience with the topics that are being communicated.

- Further actions that can enhance source credibility are named as: ethics awards, evidence of contributions to NGOs, news coverage, avoiding spending more on advertising the action than on the CSR action itself and high involvement of the target group with a strong personal interest in the issue.

- CSR information disclosure on the web is strongly influenced by country of origin. All seven indicators (Code of Ethics; CSR Projects; CSR Project Results; CSR Partnerships; Social Reports; Corporate Values; the expression of CSR or Sustainable Development on the corporate homepage) used were confirmed as relevant.

- In the analysis of the relevance of industry sector, which was also proved to have a significant influence on online CSR disclosure, three of the seven indicators were confirmed as important (Social Reports, CSR expression on the corporate homepage, and CSR partnerships).

Source: CSR Research Digest, January 2009 (Vol. 1, No. 1)

2.1.2   CSR Communication of Corporate Enterprises in Hungary

Author(s): G. Ligeti, A. Oravecz

This study examines corporate communication of social responsibility actions. The study posits that most such actions are carried out primarily for purposes of marketing and corporate image. Interviews and observational studies were carried out with the top 20 companies in Hungary's TOP500 list. In addition, several small-scale investigations were carried out amongst a range of SMEs, and a consumer survey of 500 consumers was carried out by telephone.

Key findings

The main cause of difficulty in finding and integrating CSR solutions is that Hungarian companies tend to view CSR as a short term activity aimed at short term results.

- Economic interests are the decisive factor in Hungarian companies' approaches to CSR.
- Since the conditions for generating profits are provided by society, some companies are acknowledging the need to operate as a 'good citizen' as they 'have to return something' from their profit.
- The practice of relying only on customers' opinion when deciding upon potential social or environmental causes to support is widespread.
- However, decision makers' personal priorities and aversions are highly determining factors.
- Enterprises tend to think in terms of action, spectacular events that can be easily communicated than in terms of responsible functioning;
- Companies tend to choose among causes that 'can be undertaken' and 'can't be easily or properly communicated', instead of working for the indirect development of their own market environment standing against social exclusion.
- Respondent companies were asked what they consider to be 'socially responsible activities'.
- A large majority of respondents link these activities to complying with existing regulations.
- Approximately half of respondents believe addressing stakeholders' concerns and behaving ethically are socially responsible activities.
- Expectations shown by stakeholders also motivate many companies to activate themselves in the field of CSR. However, surveys of opinions and needs is usually absent from company CSR activity.
- Improving the well-being of employees in their workplace, making them more loyal and committed to their employer is also a motivating factor.
- This includes not only activities that directly influence employees, but also the 'good feeling' generated by corporate donations or voluntary action.

- The PR-aspect of CSR is particularly valued by companies which operate in markets where there are few other opportunities for differentiation.
- In companies where the CSR function is placed within a PR department, the communication focus tends to be on external communications.
- Where there is greater emphasis on employee commitment to social and environmental responsibility, and where CSR is generated by HR, internal communications tend to be stronger.
- For those companies that view CSR as a responsible way of operating business, corporate communication and responsibility are intrinsically connected.

Source: CSR Research Digest, March 2009 (Vol. 1, No. 3)

2.1.3   Making Sense of CSR Communication

Author(s): P. Ziek

This paper aims to provide an illustration of the behaviours that constitute CSR communication. Fifty US firms are examined for CSR actions within a variety of organizational contexts.

Key findings

Communicating CSR is limited to large organizations. Although there is variation in the actions utilized by these large firms, they do cluster regarding the actions chosen to depict the ethical and virtuous behaviors of the organization.

- Primarily, the organizations communicate CSR by conveying information about classically accepted CSR behaviours, such as philanthropy and codes of ethics.
- The overwhelming use of philanthropy (66% of firms in this study) and organizational codes (64%) infers that organizations rely on stakeholders' comprehension that the firm is indeed communicating CSR.
- With 56% of the companies publishing a dedicated CSR web page, use of the internet was the third, most-exercised move.
- 90% of the Top 5 in revenue and 60% of the Middle 5 in revenue and used the Web Page as a communications medium, compared to only

20% of the Bottom 5 in revenue.

- The remainder of the actions examined accounted for very little. The annual letter to shareholders and non-financial report was used by 24% of the companies.

- The debate concerning CSR is shifting from public relations, impression management and legitimacy to issues of competitive advantage and corporate governance.

- In an attempt to overcome criticisms, theorists, researchers and business professionals have demanded a transformation of organizational governance and decision-making that includes more representational voices; a move beyond organizationally controlled CSR to the acceptance and use of a stakeholder-managed model of environmental, social and governance issues.

- This partnership will require a shift in the logic that underlies the current model of communication and an acceptance of a logic that gives way to communication that allows an interaction of the support of information and statements as well as the opportunity for challenges of accounts.

Source: CSR Research Digest, August 2009 (Vol. 1, No. 8)

2.1.4 The Communication Patterns of Corporate Social Responsibility within and across Industries

Author(s): The Conference Board

This report examines how American corporations collectively describe their corporate social responsibility (CSR) activities based on an analysis of data collected from 103 Fortune 500 websites. The study examines CSR communication produced and disseminated by corporations across 11 industries to unpack the values presented in CSR communication.

Key findings

While there is commonality in CSR communication at the institutional level, differences exist across industries.

- The results present evidence of mimicry of CSR communication within industries, and they demonstrate that, at both the institutional and economic industry level of analysis, corporations give communication primacy to ethical and philanthropic responsibilities over legal and economic responsibilities.

- Such primacy suggests that corporations present CSR as a voluntary form of selfregulation.
- The results of analysis also identify welfare capitalism as a persistent institutionalized conceptualization of CSR.
- These findings suggest that, while CSR communication gives primacy to ethical and philanthropic responsibilities, CSR remains limited in its scope to those ethical and philanthropic responsibilities that benefit bottom line.

Source: CSR Research Digest, April 2012 (Vol. 4, No. 4)

2.1.5 CSR Communication Report

Author(s): Grayling

Grayling has released the latest results of Grayling PULSE, its quarterly global survey of inhouse communications professionals. Over 1,300 communications professionals worldwide participated in the third PULSE survey, the objective of which is to provide valuable data and insights upon which communications professionals can respond to, better plan and benchmark their organisation's approach to communications activities and their own internal PR resources.

Key findings

Most organisations (37 per cent) allocate just 10 per cent of their overall communications budget to CSR communications.

- Only half (52 per cent) of organisations believe their media is interested in covering CSR issues
- The sectors that believe they have the best performance in CSR & sustainability are Consumer & Retail (58%), Transportation, Automotive & Logistics (53%) and Energy, Environment & Industry (53%)
- The top three areas of focus for CSR / sustainability programmes are; Community and Corporate Social Responsibility (16%); Waste and Recycling (13%) and Philanthropy and Volunteering (11%)
- The most common ways for CSR / sustainability activity to be

communicated are; through Media Relations (25%) and Employee / Internal Communications (24.6%)

- Only 12 per cent of organisations are using social media to communicate their CSR / sustainability activity

Source: CSR Research Digest, April 2013 (Vol. 5, No. 4)

2.1.6   What Explains The Extent and Content of Social and Environmental Disclosures on Corporate Websites?

Author(s): *T. Tagesson, V. Blank, P. Broberg, S.O. Collin.*

This study examines the extent and content of companies' social and environmental disclosures via their websites. Annual financial statements are used as a source of data, alongside corporate websites. The financial statements and websites of 267 Swedish organisations (private companies and state–owned corporations) were analysed between April and May 2007.

Key findings

There is a positive relationship between both the firm's size and profitability, and the social and environmental information disclosed on its website.

- A relationship also exists between the industry sector a firm operates in and its online disclosures.
- State-owned enterprises tend to disclose more information than their privately-owned counterparts. It is suggested that this is due to pressure from both the State and national media.
- In Sweden there is a long tradition of transparency in the public sector, which is also legally regulated in the principle of public access to official records. This principle gives all Swedish citizens the right to inspect State documents and so may, in part, explain these high levels of disclosure.
- Corporations within the consumer goods industry disclose more about ethics than corporations in other industries.
- Corporations within the raw materials industry disclose more environmental information.
- The results for IT firms are not in line with theoretical assumptions.

Since IT corporations disclose less social information on the Internet than their counterparts in other industries, it could be assumed that they do not use their Internet expertise to disclose all kinds of information – not only social.

- One explanation for not disclosing much social information in particular could be that debate on social issues seems to be absent among these corporations.

Source: Environmental Research Digest, June 2009 (Vol. 1, No. 6)

2.1.7 Corporate Governance and Social Media: A Brave New World for Board Directors

Author(s): Global Corporate Governance Forum

The report provides insights on the power of new social technologies to shape boards' decisions and bolster stakeholders' influence. It showcases what board members should know about social media as it relates to a company's ability to do business and safeguard its image.

Key findings

Many companies are already leveraging social media as a powerful tool for connecting with stakeholders and building a trusted, reputable brand.

- Ethics, working conditions, and company culture take on new importance as employees become de facto examiners and raters of the company, putting the company in the public spotlight.
- Under these circumstances, it is key that boards guarantee the necessary resources for management to address social media opportunities and challenges.
- Boards also need to challenge management's assumptions, test the accuracy of the information the company is relying on, ask the right questions, and help establish the proper strategy.
- For boards, the first and most important social media question is one they need to ask themselves:
  - o Do they have the knowledge necessary to understand these changes and new technologies?
  - o Does the board need a change in composition to deal with the complexities of social media?

    o   Does the board need external support and training to do so?

Source: Governance Research Digest, July 2012 (Vol. 3, No. 7)

2.1.8 Who's Running the Company: A Guide to Reporting on Corporate Governance

Author(s): IFC Global Governance Forum and International Centre for Journalists

This media guide aims at helping business journalists report on corporate governance and raise public awareness of the impact it has on businesses, shareholders, and the broader community of stakeholders. Topics include the media's role reporting on corporate governance, how a board of directors functions, what financial reports reveal, and how to track down information that sheds light on a company's performance in an informed way.

<u>Key findings</u>

In an era of rapid globalization and volatility, entire economies can depend on how individual businesses are governed.

- There is a clear connection between well governed companies and better company performance, with benefits such as easier access to finance, improved efficiency, and enhanced market reputation.
- Corporate governance is at the heart of what goes right and wrong in business.
- Corporate governance describes the structures and procedures to direct and control companies, and the processes used by the board of directors to monitor and supervise management in discharging the board's accountability to shareholders for the running of the company and the performance of its operations.
- Corporate governance stories essentially are about people:
- Shareholders who want to change company policies; struggles between directors — who are charged with setting the company's strategy and policy — and managers, who might have different ideas.
- Transparency and accountability play a role in such stories, along with actions by regulators, stock exchanges, shareholders and stakeholders.

Source: Governance Research Digest, November 2012 (Vol. 3, No. 11)

2.1.9 State of Corporate Social Media 2013

Author(s): Nick Johnson (Founder, Useful Social Media)

Useful Social Media issued a free briefing on how large companies are using social media providing insight on organisational models for the best adoption of social media across the whole business. "The State of Corporate Social Media 2013" is based on responses from over 850 companies responsible for operations in the U.S., Europe, Asia, the Middle East, Africa and South and Central America.

Key findings

Social media's global relevance is a catalyst for change within large organizations.

- What was once seen as experimental is now an important part of how companies view, interact and learn about customers on a daily basis.
- Social media has encouraged (or force) companies to re-think how, when, where and why they communicate with their customers.
- Social technologies are enabling collaboration across previously siloed organizations.
- The development of multiple hub-and-spoke models requires new ways of thinking and forces teams to realize that social cannot be "owned" by a single team or business unit.
- Social media is becoming a CEO-level agenda. As social media practitioners become sought out in the boardroom, social goals, strategies, and tactics gain greater importance at the top, and this will further enable social media programs to scale as needed.
- b2c companies take the lead here. While 50% of b2c companies now use social media for customer service, the b2b community lags behind with only a 36% adoption.
- Corporations no longer have the power to dictate their own brand messaging: The company is now only one voice in the conversation, and the role of the communications department is only ever to influence, not dominate, discussion.

Source: Governance Research Digest, December 2013 (Vol. 4, No. 12)

2.1.10 CSR in the Blogosphere

Author(s): C. Fieseler, M. Fleck, M. Meckel.

This paper uses social network analysis to examine the interaction between corporate blogs devoted to sustainability issues and the blogosphere, a clustered online network of collaborative actors. The authors analyse the structural embeddedness of a prototypical blog in a virtual community, demonstrating the potential of online platforms to document corporate social responsibility (CSR) activities and to engage with an increasingly socially and ecologically aware stakeholder base. A case study of McDonald's corporate blog is used.

Key findings

Stakeholder involvement via sustainability blogs is a valuable new practice for CSR communications and stakeholder engagement.

- Sustainability blogs reach a very active and well-informed clientele, which is a customer demographic of great interest for marketers since they tend to be early adopters, influencers, and multipliers.
- However, even in the case of McDonald's, the influence of the company's blog on the overall network agenda remains marginal.
- The results from this research show that the discussions held on the McDonald's CSR blog do not necessarily permeate the blogosphere.
- Only those parts of the blogosphere bound tightly to the blog itself share issues and topics, whereas more distant parts tend to re ect the decentralized and heterogeneous character of the Internet.
- Blogs that are closely tied to the McDonald's blog discuss issues in a much more narrow sense and in a way that is more closely related to the initial character of a post, while more distant blogs discuss issues from a diverse set of perspectives.
- Nevertheless, both types of blogs enable McDonald's to diffuse into communities it would otherwise reach only with dif culty.
- The authors propose the concept of microdialogues to define the form of communication exemplified by blogs. Micro-dialogues are special in the sense that blogs and other participative media have almost no gatekeeping mechanism, enabling conversations without formal hierarchies.

- In the case of the McDonald's blog, stakeholders can freely and directly interact with a multinational company on critical issues such as working conditions or environmental stewardship.
- Instead of formal hierarchies; discussions in weblogs allow any and all interested parties to read and also comment, which results in a public review process that engenders authenticity, transparency, and credibility.
- The McDonald's CSR blog is strongly connected to various actors within the blogosphere, but the present study shows that only closely connected actors share topics with the focal blog.
- The influence of the focal blog shrank to marginal with another iteration, which leads to the conclusion that most micro-dialogues remain con ned within a certain community.
- There are several ways that companies can foster CSR engagement in the blogosphere.
- Every company can use publicly available data about weblogs as a starting point to analyze how embedded their own blog is within the larger blogosphere.
- One interesting variant of corporate blogging is for a company to blog about concrete challenges in its CSR strategy, or to let certain stakeholders write about their perspective on, or provide input about, CSR initiatives.
- Social media demand a certain amount of community self-management to ensure a successful platform with meaningful relationships. Companies that fear such openness may prefer to use media other than a blog.

Source: Social Research Digest, September 2009 (Vol. 1, No. 9)

2.1.11 CSR Communication Intensity in Chinese and Indian Multinational Companies

Author(s): C. Lattemann, M. Fetscherin, I. Alon, S. Li, A-M. Schneider.

This paper, which examines why companies in China, which have a higher level of economic development, communicate less CSR than their Indian counterparts. The authors use data from the 68 largest multinational companies in China and India. A review of CSR communications methods, such as company websites, annual reports and other publicly available documents, formed the basis of the empirical enquiry.

Key findings

China generally has lower CSR communications compared to India because India is a more rule-based culture, relative to China.

- The macro institutional environment in a country strongly affects companies' CSR behaviour.
- Industry also plays a significant role. Companies in the manufacturing sector are more likely to address CSR issues in their corporate communications than companies in service industries.
- Better internal corporate governance facilitates a higher level of CSR communications.
- Making improvements to the business environment, especially the governance environment, is a necessary condition to raising the CSR communications level in both countries
- Governments in more relation-based societies, such as China, should facilitate the transformation towards more rule-based governance, as in India.
- In particular, in its effort to improve the corporate image of Chinese rms, the Chinese government must consider improving its own institutions, rule of law, and governance environment, in addition to monitoring business rms more intensively.
- When a rule-based multinational corporation (MNC) sets up operations in a relation-based country, it may be dif cult for it to uphold its CSR standards in the host country due to the macro institutional environment that does not favour or facilitate a high level of CSR practices.
- Similarly, a rule-based MNC doing business in a relation-based country may nd that it is dif cult to require its local partner to adopt as high CSR standards as rule-based MNCs.
- On the other hand, a relation-based firm entering a rule-based market may find it difficult to meet the latter's CSR requirements.
- An understanding of the frictions between rule- based and relation-based countries in terms of CSR levels and expectations will help rms

navigate across countries and minimize unnecessary negative public images and unrealistic expectations in relation to CSR.

Source: Social Research Digest, October 2009 (Vol. 1, No. 10)

2.1.12 Sustainability 2.0: Current Trends at the Confluence of Social Media and CSR

Author(s): Sustainable Life Media

Sustainable Life Media (SLM) and research partner Zumer Interactive, Inc. announced the release of a new study entitled Sustainability 2.0: Current Trends at the Confluence of Social Media and CSR. The goal for Sustainability 2.0 was to understand how the intersection of social media and sustainability is being managed by successful brands.

Key findings

The intersection of social media and sustainability is a right-of-passage for companies seeking Authenticity, a momentum-changing force for companies in today's economy.

- Authenticity not only allows companies to more effectively manage their external reputations and brand perceptions, but it encourages greater employee engagement and improved recruitment opportunities.
- And the most authentic companies are able to open up new market opportunities because they avoid being defined by market perceptions.
- 70% of executives confirmed that social media and sustainability are at the forefront of their strategies to drive customer loyalty, retention and conversion.
- Reports are getting shorter and more interactive: the average sustainability report has reduced in length by more than 25% during the past four years while on average, 60% of companies are including videos in their sustainability reporting.
- 82% of companies will increase their investment in sustainability-focused activities on Facebook in 2011.
- Twitter is a magnifying glass for promoting corporate sustainability initiatives – corporate investment in the platform will double by 2015.

- While sustainability-themed blogging is still a minimal part of the overall blogosphere (1- 2%),there is untapped opportunity for companies that can effectively engage with bloggers to devise mutual solutions on sustainability issues.

Source: Social Research Digest, May 2011 (Vol. 2, No. 1)

2.1.13   The SMI-Wizness Social Media Sustainability Index

Author(s): SMI

The SMI-Wizness Social Media Sustainability Index is a special report offering indepth analysis of best practice social media sustainability communication. The report analyses leading social media programmes and campaigns, provides a guide to best practice in social media corporate reporting and highlights the creative ways companies are approaching social media storytelling.

Key findings

In this report SMI has selected 100 companies that have established dedicated social media channels for sustainability communications.

- The Index has been prepared specifically to provide key social media insight for Sustainability, CSR, internal comms, corporate communications and marketing professionals and the agencies that work with them.
- The report highlights:
  o how leading companies like GE, PepsiCo, BBVA and Timberland are using editorial techniques and effective storytelling to communicate sustainability initiatives;
  o how the Financial Services sector is pioneering social media thought leadership and new crowdfunding ventures;
  o how 10 companies are liberating their Sustainability Reports with social media innovation;
  o how companies are using more than 25 different types of social media platforms, apps and tools to connect with sustainability communities;
  o who is part of this year's Wizness Green Twitterati.

Source: Social Research Digest, January 2012 (Vol. 3, No. 1)

2.1.14 Social Media Sustainability Index

Author(s): The SMI-Wizness Social Media Sustainability Index 2012

This report demonstrates how 100 major companies are using social media to communicate sustainability and corporate social responsibility. The report was created by SMI and Custom Communication, and powered by Wizness Publisher, which is an online platform, which allows organizations of any shape and size to crate interactive sustainability report and exchange with their stakeholders.

<u>Key findings</u>

Levis Strauss, financial company BBVA, Danone and General Electric top the list. Telefonica, IMB, Marks & Spencer, FedEx and Microsoft rounded out the top 10 on the index.

- Out 100 companies 48 were from US, 45 Europe, 2 from each Brazil, Japan and Australia and 1 from India.
- 70 had dedicated sustainability blogs or magazines.
- 15 had Pinterest pages.
- Consumer goods was the best represented sector (23), followed by technology (17), industrial goods (14) and financial services (11).
- Oil and gas and real estate had one listing each.
- 40 had shareable sustainability reports and 4 shared those reports using Ipad apps.
- Facebook was the social media channel most favoured by corporate sustainability communicators, closely followed by twitter.

Source: Social Research Digest, March 2013 (Vol. 4, No. 3)

2.2   Country and/or Regional Reporting Trends

2.2.1   Best Practice in Sustainability Reporting

Author(s):   SustainAbility/UNEP/Fundacao   Brasileira   para   o Desenvolvimento Sustentavel (FBDS)

A new report, The Road to Credibility, assesses approaches to sustainability reporting in Brazil and highlights best practice in transparency and disclosure. 80 Brazilian companies issued sustainability reports in 2006-7. The Road to Credibility includes a rigorous analysis of the leading ten.

Key findings

Brazil is far ahead of many emerging economies in corporate disclosure of sustainability performance. In the same time period, only 8 such reports were produced by companies in China and 12 in India.

- The uptake of sustainability reporting in Brazil has been motivated by factors including: the country's increased exposure to international capital markets; the Sao Paulo Stock Exchange's (BOVESPA) introduction of the Novo Mercado listing for companies that voluntarily undertake to deliver corporate governance and transparency practices beyond compliance; and the 2005 launch of the socially responsible investment index, Indice de Sustentabilidade Empresarial (ISE).

Rank	Company	Industry	Report Year	GRI*	Score
1	Natura Cosmeticos	Personal Care Products	2007	A+	54%
2	Suzano Petroquimica	Chemicals	2006	C+	53%
3	Ampla Electric	Utilities	2007	A	52%
4	Coelce Electric	Utilities	2007	A	52%
5	Banco Real	Financial Services	2007	A+	51%
6	Energias do Brasil	Electric Utilities	2007	B+	47%
7	Sabesp Water	Utilities	2007	C	46%
8	Bunge Food	Processing	2007	A+	41%
9	Celulose Irani	Forestry and Paper	2007	B+	41%
10	Banco Itau	Financial Services	2007	A+	35%

- All of the Top Ten use the Global Reporting Initiative (GRI) third generation guidelines (G3).
- The Brazilian Top 10 were partly differentiated from others in the field by their focus on key material issues, although (with an average page

count of 161) there remains scope for far greater clarity, better prioritisation and more succinct analysis.

- In general, Brazilian reports lack strong stakeholder views on material issues and sustainability performance.
- Without external perspectives, many reports undermine their integrity and credibility by overemphasising good news, falling short on disclosure of hard indicators and targets, and also failing to communicate leadership vision and commitment.

Source: CSR Research Digest, January 2009 (Vol. 1, No. 1)

2.2.2 Factors Influencing Social Responsibility Disclosure by Portuguese Companies

Author(s): M. Castelo Branco, L. Lima Rodrigues

Companies disclose social responsibility information in order to present a socially responsible image, through which they aim to legitimise their behaviours to their stakeholder groups and influence the external perception of reputation. This study analyses the social responsibility disclosures of Portuguese companies via online corporate webpages and their annual reports. The data used was gathered in 2003 and 2004 and the companies selected were all listed on the Portuguese stock exchange.

Key findings

In the Environmental Disclosures category, the most frequently reported disclosure in both annual reports and online was a general environmental policy and company concern for the environment.

- 33% of annual reports and 35% of online statements made such a disclosure.
- The second most frequently reported environmental disclosures were, in terms of online reporting, general corporate sustainability, with 24% of participating firms covering this issue, and in annual reports, environmental management , systems and audit (29%).
- The least frequently reported environmental disclosures, both online and in annual reports, were: the energy efficiency of products; the prevention or repair of damage to the environment; and the discussion of specific environmental laws and regulations.

- Although product quality was mentioned by around 50% of annual reports and online statements, product safety was only mentioned by 12% and 14% respectively.
- Various forms of community involvement were more frequently reported online than in annual reports.
- Most reported were charitable donations and activities, and support for the arts and culture.
- The online prominence of community information is likely due to the wider audience of the general public.
- Overall, the results suggest that companies prefer the annual report as a means of providing social responsibility disclosures.
- Of the companies studied, 11 do not present CSR information online at all, whereas only 5 omit such information from their annual reports.
- Companies in the chemicals, construction and building materials, and forestry and paper sectors exhibit a tendency to disclose more environmental information than community involvement information.
- However, they do not necessarily disclose more environmental information than companies in less environmentally sensitive sectors.
- It seems there is no significant difference between the factors influencing CSR disclosure in Portuguese companies compared to companies operating in more developed capital markets.

Source: CSR Research Digest, February 2009 (Vol. 1, No. 2)

2.2.3 Corporate Social and Environmental Reporting and the Impact of Internal Environmental Policy in South Africa

Author(s): C. G. Mitchell, T. Hill

This paper investigates the development and use of corporate social and environmental reporting by businesses within a large municipality in South Africa. It finds a strong call for improved CSR and a greater degree of accountability and transparency by business. The survey was conducted following a structured questionnaire with the Global Reporting Initiative used as an appropriate framework.

<u>Key findings</u>

All companies assess environmental and social risks, most have an environmental management system in place, and the majority offer some form of CSR report.

- Many of the companies that took part are ISO14001 qualified and some a part of groups that report on the GRI.
- All the companies address human rights in policies, training, security and disciplinary proceedings, as the South African constitution requires this.
- However, few consider HR in their supply chains.
- Similarly, although all responding companies identify the sources of their inputs, very few have policies which address environmental issues upstream or downstream.
- The only sector that does address upstream/downstream affects is chemicals.
- All of the companies have policies against corruption. While not all of these were formalized, corruption was in all cases a disciplinary offence.
- Most companies measure their environmental impacts, although usually only annually.
- The sectors that provide least reporting are in the beverage, general retail, leisure, automotive and Engineering sectors.
- Although most companies are aware of the proportion of their product that is biodegradable and from renewable sources, few companies have a formal cradle to grave policy.
- Although those working in engineering functions in companies measure energy use and aim to improve efficiency, few know the energy footprint of their products.

Source: CSR Research Digest, February 2009 (Vol. 1, No. 2)

2.2.4   A Survey of Governance Disclosures in US Firms

Author(s): L. Holder-Webb, J. Cohen, L. Nath, D. Wood

This US study of governance disclosure practices and responses to regulation finds a high degree of variability in the presentation and reporting format choices for many elements of the governance structure.

The study examines a sample of 50 US firms and their public disclosure packages from 2004.

Key findings

The most commonly disclosed category of governance information is board structure and processes, followed by ethics matters. The least frequently disclosed major category is investor rights.

- Smaller firms offer fewer disclosures pertaining to independence, board selection procedures, and oversight of management (including whistleblowing procedures).
- Boards that are less independent offer fewer disclosures of independence and management oversight matters.
- Large firms provide more disclosures of independence standards, board selection procedures, audit committee matters, management control systems, other committee matters, and whistleblowing procedures.
- However, they do not appear to have a strictly superior information environment when compared to smaller firms.
- The most commonly released reporting format is a standalone governance document (e.g., committee charters ethics, whistleblowing policy, governance guidelines).
- Other common reporting formats for disclosing governance information are mandatory filings and websites, including IR websites.
- The most frequently reported elements of the voluntary disclosure package evaluated in this study are communications about committees other than the audit committee and change of control procedures, with 22.3% and 12.8% (respectively) of all governance disclosures including these types of information. (Change of control procedures include shareholder rights and other factors that would affect the ability of another entity to gain control of the company.)
- Board selection procedures were disclosed by only 39 firms (22% missing). Nine firms did not disclose independence standards, two did not disclose their ethics policy, and one did not disclose the executive compensation package (18%, 4%, and 2% of the sample, respectively).

Source: CSR Research Digest, March 2009 (Vol. 1, No. 3)

2.2.5 Is Corporate Responsibility Converging? A Comparison of Corporate Responsibility Reporting in the USA, UK, Australia and Germany

Author(s): S.Chen, P.Bouvain.

This study aims to move beyond the superficiality of previous analyses of CSR reports by using textual analysis software and a more robust statistical method to more objectively and reliably compare the CSR reports of firms in different industries and countries. The sample comprises leading companies (based on national stock market indices) from the US, UK, Australia and Germany. The analysis examines whether or not membership of the Global Compact makes a difference to CSR reporting and is overcoming industry and country specific factors that limit standardization.

Key findings

Businesses from different countries differ significantly in the extent to which they promote CSR and the CSR issues they choose to emphasise in their reports.

- In US company reports, a relatively high importance is placed on community and employee-related issues.
- In UK company reports employee and community-related issues remain significant, but are related to health and safety issues.
- The UK, which has a strong consumer awareness of ethical sourcing issues, displays much greater emphasis on customer and supplier-related issues in their CSR reports.
- In Australian company reports communities are discussed in connection with customers.
- German company reports are shown to be quite clearly distinct from US, UK, and Australian company reports. While employees remain central, there is a much clearer emphasis on social and environmental issues.
- In an examination of the relative importance (as measured by frequency of mention in the CSR reports) of each of the six areas of CSR (workers, customers, suppliers, community, environment, and society), countries showed significant differences in the mention of society, community, and customer issues.

- There was some overlap in the use of the terms 'social' and 'community' with German companies preferring the use of the word 'social' while US, UK, and Australian companies preferring the use of the word 'community' to describe similar activities.
- However, the differences appear to be more than semantic. For instance, one issue that was discussed at length by several German companies, but rarely by companies in the other countries was political dialogue and actively participating in the political process in their home country to bring about social change.
- Another significant difference between countries was in the use of third-party assurance of CSR reports. Here the UK stood out clearly as the country where third-party assurance was most frequently used and the US as the country where third-party assurance was least frequently used.
- There were few significant differences among industries. Industry made a significant difference only to frequency of mention of the environment.
- Multinationality of the company also had a significant effect on mention of the environment.
- Global Compact membership was shown to make a significant difference in mention of environmental and worker-related issues but not for mention of society, community, suppliers, and customer issues.
- Global Compact membership was also shown to have a significant effect on the inclusion of measured CSR performance statistics in the report.

Source: CSR Research Digest, May 2009 (Vol. 1, No. 5)

2.2.6 Revisiting the Practices of Corporate Social and Environmental Disclosure in Bangladesh

Author(s): F. Ahammad Sobhani, A. Amran, Y. Zainuddin.

This study attempts to revisit the state of CSR and environmental disclosures in Bangladesh, a review of which has not been conducted for a decade. The annual reports of 100 companies listed on both the Dhaka and Chittagong Stock Exchange form the basis of the analysis.

Key findings

While the overall level of disclosure has increased over the last ten years, in a global context, the level and extent of reporting remains meagre.

- All companies disclosed at least one issue related to HR.
- 47% made disclosures on community involvement, 23% on consumers, 19% on the environment, with 18% making disclosures in other areas.
- 76% of sample companies disclosed declarative types of information; 65% of companies disclosed non-monetary information; and 36% of companies disclosed monetary information.
- The analysis revealed that most of the companies (93%) disclose CSR and Environmental Disclosures (CSED) information in the form of 'good' news and only 2% sample companies disclose bad news.
- The banking sector most appreciates its staff, with 100% of sample banks disclosing information that suggests this level of care of its employees. In contrast, only 50% of garments and clothing manufacturers express appreciation of their staff.
- 60% of companies disclose information on their corporate directory, 32% on training and development, and 27% on health and safety.
- While information related to consumer and product issues remains relatively poor, there is a discernable upward trend.
- 30% of sample companies disclose information on community donations made, 14% refer to sponsorship and 6% to both poverty alleviation and women's development.
- Disclosure of information relating to pollution control and waste recycling for industrial concerns is very poor, 3% and 4%, respectively.
- 7% of the companies undertake tree plantation and other protective measures.
- Most of the CSED information is found to be disclosed in the 'message' of the Chairperson of the company or in the report of the Board of Directors. Quantitative information is very sparse, only located in the 'notes to accounts'.
- Earlier studies showed that CSED information under separate headings was very rare, but at present, 5% disclose CSED information under a separate title in their annual reports.
- 14% present CSED information under subtitles with any one of the themes categorized in this study; and 12% disclose HR information

under a separate heading or subheading namely HR Management or HR in their annual reports.

- Disclosure of social and environmental information under a separate heading like CSR is a distinct feature of the annual reports of many listed companies.

Source: CSR Research Digest, July 2009 (Vol. 1, No. 7)

2.2.7 A Longitudinal Study of Corporate Social Disclosures in a Developing Economy

Author(s): J. D. Mahadeo, V. Oogarah-Hanuman and T. Soobaroyen

The article examines corporate social disclosures (CSD) in an African developing economy (Mauritius). The findings draw from the annual reports of listed companies from 2004 to 2007.

Key findings

Informed by the country's context and legitimacy theory, the authors hypothesise that the extent and variety of CSD themes (social, ethics, environment and health and safety) will be enhanced post-2004, influenced by profitability, size, leverage and industry affiliation.

- Study finds a significant increase in the volume and variety of CSD, although information in relation to social activities remains the most prominent form of disclosure.
- Using a pooled regression analysis, authors also observe that size does explain variations in overall CSD and social disclosures, whilst leverage is positively related to changes in environmental and health and safety disclosures.
- There is no profitability relationship, and the effects of industry affiliation on CSD are nonsignificant or contrary to expectations.
- Overall, authors assert that legitimacy, as a strategic and managerially driven approach favouring symbolic actions, is the prevailing motivation underlying the progression of CSD in Mauritius.

Source: CSR Research Digest, January 2012 (Vol. 4, No. 1)

2.2.8 Sustainability Reporting – Practices and Trends in India 2012

Author(s): GRI, German Ministry of Economic Cooperation and Development (BMZ) and Thought Arbitrage Research Institute (TARI)

The new report explores sustainability reporting in India, and aims to establish factors that impede reporting. The report was commissioned by the German Ministry of Economic Cooperation and Development (BMZ) through a bilateral cooperation initiative supporting innovations in sustainability practices of Indian businesses.

<u>Key findings</u>

Awareness and use of sustainability reporting guidelines in India are restricted to large organizations.

- Companies say that they find it difficult to justify investments in sustainability initiatives, as the results and paybacks are not immediate.
- The authors of the report say smaller companies in India should start reporting their sustainability performance.
- The report also states that it is important to increase awareness and encourage the widespread adoption of sustainability reporting guidelines to support the transition to a sustainable economy.
- Indian companies have been reporting on sustainability parameters as a distinct section for about ten years now.
- However, the overall reporting initiatives have been sporadic and incomprehensive.
- It has been only over the past five years that a growing number of companies have been preparing separate sustainability reports.
- In view of the issues covered, this study is expected to establish a reference against which reporting efforts can be compared.
- Around 80 Indian companies from various sectors produce sustainability reports, and about 60 of these publicly declare that they use GRI's Sustainability Reporting Guidelines.

Source: CSR Research Digest, September 2012 (Vol. 4, No. 9)

2.2.9 Balanced Sustainability Reporting Study

Author(s): Ernst & Young

A new report from Ernst & Young, 'Keep The Balance Steady,' examines the quality of sustainability reporting by European companies. The study assessed reports from over 150 European companies included in the Financial Times top 500. The study focused on six aspects: stakeholder management, balance between positive and negative aspects, readibility, comparability, reliability, and corporate governance structures as regards sustainability.

<u>Key findings</u>

Sustainability reports place too much emphasis on completeness in the sense of covering many topics while lacking focus and a balanced discussion on the opportunities and challenges faced by the company

- Of the top 152 companies listed in the Financial Times top 500, 100 published a separate sustainability report in which they elaborate extensively on several aspects of sustainability.
- Some of the remaining 52 organisations have incorporated their sustainability report into their regular annual report. These reports were considered outside of the scope of this study.
- Sustainability reports no longer focus on environmental issues alone – as was the case a few years ago. 85% of organisations used their sustainability reports to define clear targets for people, planet and profit.
- Climate change was discussed in some form in 92% of surveyed reports.
- 44% of surveyed reports total 75 pages or more. In their ambition to gain legitimacy, a substantial number of organisations devote much of their sustainability report to a qualitative explanation of their sustainability performance.
- 76% of reports contain predominantly positive disclosures or include hardly any negative disclosures.
- Concerning stakeholder management, the sustainability reports do not explicitly indicate the approach they have taken or who are considered to be the organisation's stakeholders.

- 53% of reports do not indicate how stakeholder concerns are addressed.
- In many of the surveyed reports, the core message of how sustainability is embedded in the organisation is difficult to extrapolate.
- The increasing attention on disclosures related to management approaches may be attributable in part to the fact that the GRI focuses on this aspect.

Source: Governance Research Digest, March 2009 (Vol. 1, No. 3)

2.2.10 Lessons Learned: The Emerging Markets Disclosure Project 2008-2012

Author(s): Emerging Markets Disclosure Project (EMDP)

The Emerging Markets Disclosure Project released its final report, documenting a five year initiative championing greater transparency among emerging market companies on key environmental, social and governance (ESG) issues. The project attracted more than 50 participants, including asset owners, investment managers and service providers.

Key findings

A model for collaboration to improve sustainability reporting and practices in emerging and developing markets was established.

- It will be used by signatories to the United Nations (UN)-backed Principles for Responsible Investment (PRI) in the years ahead.
- It won the backing of 55 investors with more than $1 trillion in assets under management.
- A scorecard that enabled companies to benchmark their ESG performance and EMDP participants to assess companies' weaknesses in these areas was created.
- The Brazil country team contacted 102 companies and engaged 17 directly to encourage them to improve their sustainability reporting.
- All 17 either had plans to issue sustainability reports or were open to working towards this goal.
- The team in Indonesia convinced a listed polyester and petrochemicals company, Indorama Synthetics, to learn more about ESG best practices

and helped the firm identify and focus on several key sustainability issues: energy efficiency, waste treatment and corporate governance.

- The South Africa team won reforms from Aspen Pharmacare Holdings, Naspers, Sasol, Shoprite Holdings, Steinhoff International and Tiger Brands, including improvements in sustainability reporting and policies.
- In South Korea, the local EMDP team made steady progress on reporting with all 15 companies it engaged, including Hynix, LG Electronics, Samsung and Shinhan Financial Group.

Source: Governance Research Digest, October 2012 (Vol. 3, No. 10)

2.2.11 Internet-Based Corporate Disclosure and Market Value: Evidence from Latin America

Author(s): *U. Garay, M. Gonzalez, A. Gyzman and M. A. Trujillo*

Authors examine the relationship between an Internet-based corporate disclosure index and firm value, and evaluate the relatively understudied corporate use of the Internet by firms. These firms are listed in the seven largest stock markets of Latin America (Argentina, Brazil, Colombia, Chile, Mexico, and Peru).

Key findings

Authors find a positive and strong relation between the corporate governance disclosure index and the Tobin's Q for firms in Latin America.

- More specifically, authors find, after controlling for firms' characteristics, industry and country of origin, that an increase in 1% in the Internet-Based Corporate Disclosure Index causes an increase of 0.1592% in the Tobin's Q and an increase of 0.0119% in the firm's ROA.
- This result is statistically and economically significant for the sample of Latin American firms.
- These findings are robust after considering the potential endogeneity of the regression variables and after performing a battery of other robustness checks.
- The evidence shown here contributes to the mounting literature that suggest that firms can differentiate themselves by self-adopting better

corporate governance practices and, more specifically, better financial and corporate disclosure measures using the Internet.

- That is, even in a weak investor protection setting, firms can enhance their market value by self-adopting good corporate disclosure practices.

Source: Governance Research Digest, November 2012 (Vol. 3, No. 11)

2.2.12   ESG Reporting Trends

Author(s): Governance and Accountability Institute

Governance and Accountability Institute released its second yearly report examining corporate sustainability reporting trends by US-based companies. "2012 Corporate ESG/Sustainability/Responsibility Reporting: Does It Matter?", focused on S&P 500 and Fortune 500 companies.

Key findings

The number of S&P 500 and Fortune 500 companies managing and reporting performance on environmental, social and governance (ESG) issues more than doubled from 2010 to 2011.

- For the first time — non-reporters are in the minority.
- The research determined correlations between financial performance, equity indexes, Key Corporate Reputational Lists / Awards and Key Corporate Ratings & Rankings.
- Companies that measure and manage their sustainability issues perform better over the long-term in the capital markets.
- Companies that report on their sustainability strategies, initiatives, programs and performance appear to be more likely to be selected for key sustainability-reputation lists, ranked higher by sustainability reputation raters and rankers, and selected for inclusion on leading sustainability investment indexes.

Source: Governance Research Digest, December 2012 (Vol. 3, No. 12)

2.2.13   US Integrated Reporting Study

Author(s): Investor Responsibility Research Institute (IRRCI) and Sustainable Investments Institute (Si2)

Investor Responsibility Research Institute (IRRCI) and Sustainable Investments Institute (Si2) published a comprehensive empirical analysis of the sustainability disclosures of companies in the S&P 500 index, as reflected in 10-K filings, annual reports and proxy statements. The "Integrated Financial and Sustainability Reporting in the United States" report contains information on and analyzed 113 indicators for each of the 500 companies or 56,500 data points in all.

<u>Key findings</u>

1.4% of S&P companies have fully integrated reporting.

- American Electric Power, Clorox, Dow Chemical, Eaton, Ingersoll Rand, Pfizer and Southwest Airlines are the only companies in the S&P 500 — just 1.4% of the total — with fully integrated annual financial and sustainability reports.
- All seven companies, spread across different industry groups, used the Global Reporting Initiative guidelines as a reference or otherwise complied with one of GRI's most recent reporting frameworks.
- Zions Corporation was the only company not to include any sustainability disclosure across the various reports examined.
- Some 43.4% of the companies linked executive compensation to some type of sustainability criteria.
- Disclosure of capital expenditures on environmental controls were the most common, with 68% of companies sharing environmental management information. Many companies wrote about reducing overall operational risks, such as environmental spills and related cleanup and remediation costs and employee health and safety.
- Climate change, specifically in the context of potential regulation in the US and as a major concern among stakeholders, was mentioned by 66% of companies in the S&P 500.

Source: Governance Research Digest, April 2013 (Vol. 4, No. 4)

2.2.14 Transparency in corporate reporting: Assessing emerging market multinationals

Author(s): Transparency International

Transparency International issued an analysis of the public reporting practices of 100 emerging markets companies comprising a list of Global Challengers 2011. 'Transparency in corporate reporting: Assessing emerging market multinationals' is based on the methodology of previous Transparency International studies and presents data on three dimensions of transparency: Reporting on anti-corruption programmes (covering inter alia bribery, facilitation payments, whistleblower protection and political contributions), Organisational transparency (including information about corporate holdings), and Country-by-country reporting (including revenues, capital expenditure and tax payments).

Key findings

The disclosure practices of emerging market companies are inadequate.

- The observed levels of transparency fall short of the standards expected of large companies aspiring to become global players.
- Based on the data analysis, the average company score is 36 per cent (3.6 out of a maximum of 10 points in the overall index).
- Only one in four of the 100 companies achieved an overall score of at least 50 per cent.
- This result reflects a lack of recognition of the importance of transparency as a building block of good governance, including the management of corruption risks.
- The emerging market companies also lag behind in their acceptance of the responsibility that falls upon multinational companies to fulfil the transparency expectations of stakeholders.
- Results show that companies from China lag behind in every dimension with an overall score of 20 per cent (2 out of a maximum of 10).
- In contrast, Indian firms perform best in the BRICS with a result of 54 per cent (5.4 out of a maximum of 10) and several occupy the top positions in the overall Index.
- In the third (country-by-country reporting) dimension of the study, an area of disclosure that has proven to be a challenge for most companies, Indian firms stand out against the weaker performances of the other BRICS firms with a score of 29 per cent.

- Publicly listed companies, whose shares are traded on stock exchanges, perform considerably better than unlisted companies which include privately held and state-owned companies.

Source: Governance Research Digest, November 2013 (Vol. 4, No. 11)

2.2.15 2013 Review of the Implementation Status of Corporate Governance Disclosures: Brazil

Author(s): Dr. Marcelle Colares Oliveira, Professor at Federal University of Ceará, Brazil

The '2013 Review of the Implementation Status of Corporate Governance Disclosures: Brazil' employs the benchmark of good practices in corporate governance disclosure developed by UNCTAD's Intergovernmental Working Group of Experts on International Standards of Accounting and Reporting (ISAR).

Key findings

On the average, firms listed in the BM&Fbovespa index (IBOV) disclose more than three quarters of the items in the ISAR benchmark.

- 20 of the 52 items in the ISAR benchmark were disclosed by 90% or more of the firms, while 12 of the items were disclosed by all firms.
- The level of disclosure was low for certain items in the ISAR benchmark: four items were disclosed by less than 20% of the firms.
- The absolute number of items disclosed by each firm ranged from 26 to 50.
- The study concludes that the firms in our sample primarily disclosed items made mandatory by regulations issued by government agencies.
- On the other hand, several firms voluntarily disclosed nonmandatory items recommended by UNCTAD and by the Brazilian Institute of Corporate Governance (IBGC).

Source: Governance Research Digest, November 2013 (Vol. 4, No. 11)

2.2.16 US National Business Ethics Survey

Author(s): The Ethics Resource Center

The Ethics Resource Center generated the U.S. benchmark on ethical behavior in corporations which provides business leaders a snapshot of trends in workplace ethics and an identification of the drivers that improve ethical workforce behavior. ERC's 2013 report is the eighth in the series and it is an exacting longitudinal cross-sectional research effort in the field.

Key findings

Workplace misconduct is at an historic low, having steadily and significantly declined since 2007.

- 41% of over 6,400 workers surveyed said they have observed misconduct on the job, down from 55% in 2007.
- Over the last two years, observed misconduct fell in every one of the 26 specific categories ERC asked about.
- Pressure to compromise standards, often a leading indicator of future misconduct, also was down – falling from 13% in 2011 to nine percent in the latest survey.
- The dip in misconduct may reflect workers' tendency to take fewer risks when economic prospects seem weak or uncertain, given the relatively soft recovery since 2008. But it also is possible – and we believe probable – that businesses' continuing and growing commitment to strong ethics and compliance programs is bearing fruit and that ethical performance is becoming a new norm in many workplaces. That belief will be tested once economic growth becomes more robust and widespread.
- While misconduct is down overall, a relatively high percentage of misconduct is committed by managers – the very people who are supposed to set a good example of ethical conduct and make sure that employees honor company rules.
- Workers reported that 60% of misconduct involved someone with managerial authority from the supervisory level up to top management. Nearly a quarter (24%) of observed misdeeds involved senior managers.
- Workers said that 26% of misconduct is ongoing within their organization. About 12% of wrongdoing was reported to take place company-wide.

Source: Governance Research Digest, March 2014 (Vol. 5, No. 3)

2.3   Reporting (Best) Practices

2.3.1   Corporate Responsibility Reporting Awards

Author(s): Corporate Register

CorporateRegister.com has announced the winners of the second round of its corporate responsibility reporting awards. The awards identify the best corporate responsibility awards across nine categories.

Key findings

Category	Winner	First Runner-Up	Second Runner-Up
Best report	Vodafone Group PLC	Coca Cola Enterprises	Dell Inc.
Best first time report	Virgin Media	Deloitte	SolarWorld AG
Best SME report	Ecologic Designs Inc.	Australian Ethical Investment Ltd	RecycleBank LLC
Best integrated report	Novo Nordisk A/S	BASF SE	AXA SA
Best carbon disclosure	Royal Dutch Shell PLC	Bayer AG	Repsol YPF SA
Creativity in communications	Coca Cola Enterprises	LEGO Group	J Sainsbury PLC
Relevance and materiality	Vodafone Group PLC	Bayer AG	BP PLC
Openness and honesty	Co-operative Group Ltd	BP PLC	Royal Dutch Shell PLC
Credibility through Assurance	Vodafone Group PLC	Royal Dutch Shell PLC	BP PLC

Source: CSR Research Digest, May 2009 (Vol. 1, No. 5)

2.3.2   Sustainability Reporting Study

Author(s): PricewaterhouseCoopers

PricewaterhouseCoopers has recently released Creating Value from Corporate Responsibility report highlighting the need for investment-grade data along with growing interest in sustainability reports. The report goes on to note that half of the CEOs PwC recently surveyed plan to change their business strategies in the next three years because they expect their stakeholders to factor environmental and corporate responsibility into purchasing decisions.

Key findings

The quality of sustainability and corporate responsibility data that companies disclose will need to improve to keep pace with stakeholder expectations.

- The half of the CEOs PwC recently surveyed plan to change their business strategies in the next three years because they expect their stakeholders to factor environmental and corporate responsibility into purchasing decisions.
- Yet, today's corporate responsibility reports often don't have in place the rigorous processes that are ubiquitous in other areas of the business.
- Investors, regulators and NGOs are holding businesses to higher standards, and company reputations and valuations are hinging on their ability to report on their efforts in a quantitative way, said Kathy Nieland, PwC's US Sustainable Business Solutions leader.
- According to the report, some of the benefits of improved sustainability reporting include:
  - better assessment of risks and opportunities at all levels of the business;
  - ability to allocate resources and set appropriate performance goals
  - confidence that baseline measurements are accurate;
  - ability to enhance trust and promote value with key stakeholders;
  - improvements in delivering information in a timely and consistent way;
  - fewer errors and restatements;
  - less opportunity for manipulation.
- PwC's report notes that in the past year, activist shareholders targeted more than 80 US companies in various industries with resolutions for better disclosure on how they are managing potential business impacts

related to sustainability challenges and opportunities.

- Despite these higher expectations, a quarter of the companies that report to the Carbon Disclosure Project either do not disclose any information about how they evaluate uncertainty ranges of reported data or do not evaluate uncertainty at all.

Source: CSR Research Digest, February 2011 (Vol. 3, No. 2)

2.3.3 Multiple Messages: The Purpose and Future of Sustainable Development Reporting

Author(s): Acona / SABMiller

Acona and SABMiller have published new research to suggest how the best companies will report in ten years time. The report reviews the factors driving SD reporting, highlighting conflicting and competing pressures and asking some very basic unanswered questions over why companies do it.

Key findings

Discussions over the nature and practice of SD reporting are taking place in the shadow of a tidal wave of social and technological change that is fundamentally transforming the way we communicate.

- Social media, instant access, handheld devices, syndication, and all-powerful search engines have conditioned users to find the content that they want when they want it.
- At the same time the fast-rising BRICS economies are developing their own views on the role of companies in society and affecting the way global corporations think.
- The one-size-fits all, once-yearly SD Report is looking increasingly out of date.
- In the end, Multiple Messages concludes that the future of SD Reporting will be plural, bespoke and continuous:
- 'plural' in that the content will be spread through multiple documents and channels;
- 'bespoke' in that different audiences will require different content;
- and 'continuous' in that companies will be expected to communicate regularly – and the development of the story will become as important as the facts themselves.

- The set piece-multi-audience-once-a-year-third- party-assured-GRI-compliant report will be replaced by tailored multi-stranded communications to different audiences, using technology to allow regular update.
- This requires a more nuanced view of verification, breaking the task into pieces dependent on the nature of the content and the requirements of the audience.

Source: CSR Research Digest, July 2011 (Vol. 3, No. 7)

2.3.4 KPMG International Survey of Corporate Responsibility Reporting 2011

Author(s): KPMG

KPMG has analyzed the reports of more than 3,400 companies – the world's 250 largest, and the 100 largest in each of 34 countries. It then plotted each country in a quadrant based on quality of communications and level of process maturity.

<u>Key findings</u>

U.S. companies are "scratching the surface" of corporate responsibility, as a whole concentrating on communication more than performance.

- The U.S. falls into the "Scratching the Surface" quadrant.
- Companies in this quadrant have the highest risk of failing to deliver on their promises, and risk increasing investor pressure.
- The quadrant shows U.S. companies' level of process maturity ranking lower than every other country in the survey except Russia and Singapore.
- Most countries in the "Leading the Pack" quadrant are European nations, with the exception of Taiwan, Australia and India.
- These nations' companies have implemented information systems and processes to ensure reliable information, and have made few or no CR report restatements.
- They have asked for external assurance, apply GRI guidelines to their reports, and are taking steps towards integrated reporting.
- The report said that 71% of European companies are now reporting on CR, but the Americas are gaining ground with 69%, followed by the

Middle East and Africa, where 61% of companies now report on CR initiatives.

- Asia Pacific continues to trail, with 49% of its companies disclosing CR data to the markets.
- But the report found that Chinese and South Korean companies are doing a good job of implementing processes and systems to measure and govern corporate responsibility issues.
- Despite these varying levels of participation, CR reporting has become the "de facto law" for business.
- 95% of the 250 largest companies in the world (G250 companies) now report on their CR activities, a rise of more than 14% over KPMG's 2008 survey.
- Two-thirds of non-reporting G250 companies are based in the US and will therefore be likely to begin reporting on CR in the near future.
- Among the 100 largest companies in each of the 34 countries studied (N100 companies), the total number of reporting companies increased by 11%age points, to 64% in 2011.
- Sectors showing the greatest commitment to reporting include energy and natural resources.
- The pharmaceutical, construction and automotive industries deserve mention, with growth rates of 39, 33 and 29%age points, respectively.
- But the consultancy said it was surprised by the comparatively low ranking of other key industries.
- Transport, for example, has made great improvements incorporating low-emission policies into its business, but only 57% of these companies report on their CR activities.
- Trade and retail continue to rank last, though they picked up 26%age points since KPMG's 2008 survey.
- Among the N100, 69% of publicly traded firms conduct CR reporting, compared to just 36% of family-owned businesses, and about 45% for both cooperatives and companies owned by professional investors.
- Companies with revenues over $50 billion were twice as likely as those with revenues under $1 billion to report on their CR activities.
- Data quality appears to be a significant issue, with a third of G250 and over 20% of N100 companies issuing a restatement of their CR report.
- Over a third (35%) of G250 reporters with restatements admitted that

restatements were the result of an error or omission, which KPMG said is a far higher rate than is acceptable in financial statements.

- Other reasons for issuing restatements included updating the scope of reporting (42%), improving estimation or calculation methodology (44%) and updating CR definitions (28%).

Source: CSR Research Digest, December 2011 (Vol. 3, No. 12)

2.3.5 Building Trust in the Air: Is Airline Corporate Sustainability Reporting Taking Off?

Author(s): PwC

PwC has launched a report Building Trust in the Air, a survey of how well the world's airlines report on corporate sustainability. The report includes over 45 global airlines, from Cathay Pacific, Air France, Delta to British Airways and analyzed the 30 airlines that produced corporate sustainability reports.

Key findings

While there has been an increase in the number of airlines accounting their sustainability initiatives, there is still room for improvement.

- Airline industry urged to be clear and transparent in corporate sustainability reporting.
- No airline produced an 'excellent' report but more is being done.
- 10% gave data about lost baggage and around 25% reported on customer complaints.
- 70% are now stating total CO_2 emissions.
- 33% did not include any measures of fuel efficiency.
- 60% failed to report on waste production and water consumption.
- 77% are reporting on social activities such as education and volunteering schemes.
- No airline disclosed information around CS in relation to executives' take-home pay.
- Only a handful of airlines currently integrate their CS data into their overall annual report, and currently most CS reporting is voluntary.
- Companies that are concerned about the cost of producing such reports should start thinking now about the value-add it will give them in the

long run.

- Those that do take it seriously could get the edge in a very competitive market, the report says.
- Although 30 of the 46 sampled airlines produce a sustainability report, 62 of the top 100 airlines worldwide did not.
- Of the 30 PwC analysed, some of the best included Air France KLM, Iberia, Delta Air Lines, LAN Airlines, Lufthansa, Southwest Airlines and UPS.

Source: CSR Research Digest, December 2011 (Vol. 3, No. 12)

2.3.6   OS Knowledge Share 2011 Portfolio

Author(s): GRI

To showcase the experience and knowledge of the OS network, GRI launched the OS Knowledge Share Program in 2011. From January to December, various sustainability topics were discussed, in the form of chapter downloads and recorded webinars available exclusively to OS.

Key findings

The field of sustainability reporting, while still in its infancy compared to financial reporting, has evolved substantially over the past decade.

- The GRI Guidelines have become the world's most widely used sustainability reporting guidelines.
- Part of the reason for the Guidelines' popularity is their provision of a set of principles that organizations can use to define report content, a big challenge for most new reporters.
- IAG, Natura Cosméticos, ING and Shell each focused on one or more of the following principles for defining report content: materiality, stakeholder inclusiveness, sustainability context and completeness.
- From the resulting discussions, it was evident that most reporters felt that the principles are timeless - useful for new and seasoned reporters.
- The very process of applying the principles was seen by many as very useful to helping reporters manage their day-to-day operations through addressing material risks and opportunities and meeting stakeholder expectations.
- Change in the field of sustainability reporting is constant, as are critical

sustainability topics.

- Discussions by Ford, Norsk Hydro, Suncor and Westpac on mergers and acquisitions, human rights and environmental reporting, highlighted the importance of the materiality principle in helping reporters filter out topics to report on.

- Among other factors, organizational history and sector play a very important role in what topics reporters deem important to report on.

- Like many fields, sustainability reporting is not exempt from trends.

- Multi-tiered reporting, linking GRI reporting with AA1000 and integrated reporting were all trends followed by Telefónica, Vancity and Novo Nordisk respectively, and by many other reporting OS.

- Each trend comes with its own challenges in terms of application, but of particular note is the agreement among OS that while integrated reporting appears to be the way forward, the lack of an agreed-upon definition makes its application difficult.

- For many, the hope is that the outcome of the work of the International Integrated Reporting Council (IIRC), which GRI co-founded, will offer answers to this problem.

- Another major problem faced by many reporters is providing key stakeholders with access to their sustainability report.

- Codelco, whose key stakeholders are local communities, changed from traditional hardcopy reports to fully digital reports, only to shift back to hardcopies upon realizing that their report was not reaching key stakeholders.

- It was clear during the webinar on this topic that the starting point, before a decision is taken on report platforms, should be identifying key stakeholders and basing the choice of a report platform on which one would best meet their needs.

- Rabobank's feature in the project highlighted the less talked about aspect of reporting: what should be happening in between reports.

- Echoing the words of Peter Drucker (writer, professor and management consultant, 'What you can't measure, you cannot manage. What you can't manage, you cannot change'), general consensus among OS was that effective reporting should influence organizations' management of sustainability impacts.

Source: CSR Research Digest, May 2012 (Vol. 4, No. 5)

2.3.7 Adding Value through Sustainability Reporting

Author(s): Corporate Citizenship

Using an online questionnaire followed by individual interviews Corporate Citizenship took a snapshot of the current state of reporting as experienced by over 150 practitioners. Among other things consultancy asked them about their reporting audiences, formats used, preferred frameworks, attitudes to integrated reporting and the challenges they faced.

Key findings

The most popular reasons for companies to engage in sustainability reporting are stakeholder engagement and strategy formulation – not compliance or pushing the corporation's point of view.

- The results stand in contrast to popular opinion, which often holds that companies report because they have to, or as a way of greenwashing.
- The respondents ranked internal audiences as the most important readers for their sustainability reporting, at 40%, followed by analysts and financial stakeholders at 37%, and customers at 30%.
- Then came opinion formers at 20%, consumers at 15% and communities at 10%.
- These results show that reporting is becoming a more precise tool for stimulating change within the company.
- The survey found that while 64% of respondents use social media and video to communicate their sustainability programs, only 18% ranked these means as highly effective.
- A further 60% said social media is effective, and 65% said the same for video.
- In the survey, 16% of respondents said they are already using integrated reporting, which combines financial and sustainability reporting.
- Another 42% said they expect to produce their first integrated report within the next three years, but 20% said they do not expect to produce one for at least five years, or until such reporting is required.
- But overall the percentages above represent a significant shift to integrated reporting, which will benefit financial stakeholders.

Source: CSR Research Digest, August 2012 (Vol. 4, No. 8)

2.3.8   Strange   Bedfellows?   Voluntary   CSR   Disclosure   and   Politics

Author(s): P. A. Griffin and Y. Sun

Griffin and coauthor Yuan Sun analyzed extensive data on voluntary corporate social responsibility disclosures, campaign contributions and stock performance. To measure companies' social responsibility, the researchers studied more than 14,500 news releases posted between 2000 and 2011 by CSRwire.

Key findings

Companies that tout social responsibility and whose managers contribute to political action committees tend to provide higher returns to shareholders.

- The trend is especially prevalent in smaller, left-leaning companies.
- Companies were more likely to make social responsibility disclosures if they were headquartered in a so-called "blue state," or one that traditionally has voted Democratic in national elections.
- Companies that issue more press releases on CSRwire, an online news service that publishes reports issued by member organizations on issues related to sustainability and corporate social responsibility tend to have more
- management employees who contribute to political action committees.
- The correlation was strongest with individuals who donated to political action committees affiliated with the Democratic Party.
- Additionally, the stock market reacted favorably when corporations posted news releases on the CSRwire.
- This trend was most evident in organizations from the finance, green building and academia sectors.
- Those sectors recorded three-day excess market returns of 1.56%, 1.52% and 1.46% respectively in the three days after they released a corporate sustainability report.
- The worst performing sector post-CSR release was the green jobs and career news sector, which posted three-day excess returns of -1.33%
- The market effect intensified if company managers also made contributions to political action committees.

- While the correlations are strong, researchers need to look more closely at the underlying pathways whereby CSR disclosure and political contributions combine to produce shareholder gains.

Source: CSR Research Digest, November 2012 (Vol. 4, No. 11)

2.3.9   Reporting on Corporate Sustainability Performance

Author(s): Conference Board

The report analyses performance indicators disclosed in the sustainability reports of 94 for-profit Canadian corporations identifying 585 different indicators disclosed in the reports. The board focused on reports issued in 2008, drawn from 10 different sectors, including mining; oil and gas; retail and food; transportation, communication and services; insurance and other finance; banking; electricity; forestry and paper; engineering, construction and chemicals; and steel.

Key findings

Corporate sustainability reports have considerable variation in the types of performance indicators disclosed, a trend that could hinder benchmarking efforts and make it difficult to measure progress.

- Of the indicators disclosed, 22% were used by more than three corporations; 55% were used only once; 16% were used twice; and seven percent were used three times.
- If a small number of indicators are disclosed, there's a risk that key issues will not be addressed.
- On the other hand, if a report has a large number of indicators, it's possible readers will be overwhelmed and important issues could be lost.
- The incredible diversity in the indicators disclosed may have been caused by a number of factors including:
  o differing interpretations of sustainability;
  o a relative lack of mandatory standards for reporting;
  o the fact that different sectors have different reporting priorities;
  o and local circumstance.
- The analysis did find a balance between economic, environmental and social issues in the reports.

- In the reports, 42% of indicators were classified as economic, 33% were environmental and 25% were social.
- A number of voluntary guidelines for corporate sustainability reporting have emerged.
- The most prominent of these are the guidelines produced by the Global Reporting Initiative.
- Of the companies sampled for the study, 48% said they used the GRI guidelines.
- Only one-third of the reports had explicit summaries of their reporting on GRI indicators.
- And of the companies reporting on GRI indicators, only one reported on all 79 of the performance indicators suggested by the GRI; 10 reported between 50 and 78 indicators; seven reported between 30 and 49; and 13 reported between 10 and 29 indicators.

Source: CSR Research Digest, November 2012 (Vol. 4, No. 11)

2.3.10 How does it Stuck Up?

Author(s): Radley Yeldar

Communications agency Radley Yeldar has released a report revealing the top sustainability reporters. This year's study analyzes corporate sustainability reports from 35 of Europe's best sustainability reporters drawn from the FTSE Eurotop 100 index.

Key findings

Mining group Anglo American, energy company Centrica and finance group HSBC Holdings have been named the European companies with the year's best records of sustainability reporting.

- The top five European reporters are rounded out with drinks company Diageo and technology firm Siemens.
- The best sustainability reports show how sustainability is making a tangible difference to the business and detail "the good, the bad and the ugly" side of a company's sustainability efforts.
- Good reports also display information in a clear and concise manner and back narrative claims with evidence, letting sustainability data speak for itself.

- The best reporters are "saying more with less".
- Sustainability reporting has reached a crossroads, both as a piece of communication and a management tool.
- But in a year marked by high-profile ethical blunders and corporate scandals, the role of the sustainability report has been brought into question.
- While crucial narratives are being obscured by box ticking and standard disclosures, the wider use of Global Reporting Initiative guidelines and other external assurances is encouraging.

Source: CSR Research Digest, March 2013 (Vol. 5, No. 3)

2.3.11 The 2011 Black List

Author(s): Corporate Responsibility

The Corporate Responsibility magazine has unveiled its annual list of the least transparent companies in the Russell 1000. The list is an involuntary audit of presumptively public information of corporate America.

Key findings

As with last year's list, the members of this year's cohort have exactly zero points of relevant data that could be found to compare their transparency against the rest of the Russell 1000.

- The Financials industry was most represented, accounting for 32 of the list's members, or more than half.
- Next most common was the energy sector at 12% of the total, followed by consumer items and health care, at 10% each.

American Financial Group Inc.	Lincare Holdings Inc.
Assured Guaranty Ltd.	Leucadia National Corp.
Aspen Insurance Holdings	Markel Corp.
Ares Capital Corp.	Madison Square Garden Inc.
Axis Capital Holdings Ltd.	Nasdaq Omx Group Inc.
Bio-Rad Laboratories Inc.	National Fuel Gas Co.
Brown & Brown, Inc.	NII Holdings Inc.
Bancorpsouth Inc.	Annaly Capital Management Inc.
CareFusion Corp.	Realty Income Corp.

Chimera Investment Corp.	Omnicare Inc.
Core Laboratories N.V.	Partnerre Ltd.
Cooper Companies, Inc.	Patterson-UTI Energy Inc.
Dreamworks Animation Inc.	Everest Re Group Ltd.
Endurance Speciality Holdings	Regal Entertainment Group
Eaton Vance Corp.	RenaissanceRe Holdings Ltd.
Frontline Ltd.	SL Green Realty Corp.
Forest Oil Corp.	Solera Holdings Inc.
Frontier Oil Corp.	SXC Health Solutions Corp.
GenOn Energy, Inc.	Techne Corporation
Hansen Natural Corp.	TFS Financial Corporation
HCC Insurance Holdings, Inc.	Titanium Metals Corp.
Health Care Reit, Inc.	Torchmark Corp.
HCP Inc.	Trinity Industries, Inc.
Hospitality Properties Trust	Unitrin, Inc.
InterContinental Exchange Inc.	Ventas, Inc.
Lazard Ltd.	W.R. Berkley Corp.
Liberty Media Holding Corporation Capital	Wesco Financial Corp.
Liberty Media Holding Corporation Interactive	Alleghany Corp.
Liberty Starz Group	Zions Bancorporation

Source: Governance Research Digest, July 2011 (Vol. 2, No. 3)

2.3.12 Out with Transparency: In with Transparent Brands

Author(s): Cone

Cone has released highlights on the brand transparency. The paper examines elements of transparent brands.

Key findings

Transparent brands embrace transparency as an ethos.

- The ten elements of transparent brand:
    - lead with a clear purpose;
    - be laser-focused on issues that matter;

- o make operational commitments relevant to stakeholders;
- o use jargon-free and justified claims;
- o share operational challenges in a spin-free context to educate stakeholders;
- o create a personality, not just policies;
- o create and participate in a conversation, not a monologue;
- o embrace transparency as an ethos;
- o strive for honesty, not perfection;
- o provide accessible and deeper data for those who want it.

Source: Governance Research Digest, August 2011 (Vol. 2, No. 4)

2.3.13 CSR Reporting Study

Author(s): Leeds University / Euromed Management School

The Leeds study carried out jointly with Euromed Management School showcases "irrelevant data, unsubstantiated claims, gaps in data and inaccurate figures" in CSR reporting. Research covers analysis of more than 4,000 CSR reports, rankings and surveys published by companies over the past ten years.

Key findings

Incorrect and irrelevant data, unsubstantiated figures and major gaps abound in company CSR reports.

- Out of 443 European Union companies, fewer than one in six covered all corporate activities in their reporting of greenhouse gas emissions.
- Among the most colourful mistakes and omissions made by some of the world's biggest corporations were a company whose carbon footprint was four times that for the whole world, and a carmaker and power group which both, entirely legally, managed to excise a huge coal plant from their pollution record.
- More regular problems included companies ignoring data from individual countries or subsidiaries in their group – including many in China and Brazil – two of the world's biggest economies.
- Failing to collect or ignoring data from multiple sources was so endemic that BT, which has won awards for its CSR reporting, highlighted zero energy and water use, waste and transport for many of

its international operations in 2007; the following year the company did not claim they were zero but left more than half the table blank.

Source: Governance Research Digest, December 2011 (Vol. 2, No. 8)

2.3.14 On Materiality and Sustainability: The Value of Disclosure in the Capital Markets

Author(s): Harvard University

The Initiative for Responsible Investment at Harvard University has written a white paper on corporate disclosure entitled "On Materiality and Sustainability: The Value of Disclosure in the Capital Markets". The paper discusses the role of mandated corporate sustainability disclosure.

Key findings

The disclosure of corporate sustainability data should be mandated, as such information is critical for investors to make informed decisions.

- Sustainability data can help diminish financial risks and improve investment opportunities.
- It can also reduce distrust in capital markets, cut excess speculation and short-termism, and help prevent financial crises.
- There were $3.07 trillion of assets under responsible investment management in the US as of 2010, demonstrating the widespread interest in sustainability information.
- However, the growing interest in disclosure beyond financial data has led to numerous methods of sustainability reporting that vary greatly between corporations and industries in the US.
- While the need for such disclosure is crucial in today's market, inconsistency in reporting has raised more challenges than solutions.
- Much of the disparity is due to different interpretations of what is sufficiently "material" to report, as required by the Securities and Exchange Commission.

Source: Governance Research Digest, November 2012 (Vol. 3, No. 11)

2.3.15 Sustainability Reporting of World's Major Banks

Author(s): Claremont McKenna College's Roberts Environmental Center

Claremont McKenna College's Roberts Environmental Center released a detailed analysis of the social responsibility reporting efforts of the world's major banks. The report contains a compilation of Pacific Sustainability Index scores evaluating the environmental and social reporting of 27 banks, scoring them based on the reporting, intent, and performance of their environmental and social sustainability efforts.

<u>Key findings</u>

ANZ, National Australia Bank and Itaú Unibanco Holding are the top three sustainability reporting banks according to Pacific Sustainability Index.

- Major banks play a pivotal role in ensuring not only sustainable business in their own operations, but the operations of other industries as well.
- Providing finance for some projects results in environmentally harmful or socially unjust externalities, and by choosing not to support these projects, banks take a major step in setting precedence for other sectors.
- Focusing on more specific aspects of banks' operations is important in considering the sustainability of the banking sector. Of the direct environmental impacts from major banks' operation, perhaps the most obvious and notable is that of paper usage and recycling practices.
- For the Pacific Sustainability Index (PSI) scoring parameters, the importance of these practices is captured in both the "Green Purchasing," and "Supplier Screening"
- Sustainability Management points as well as Environmental Quantitative Data for "Waste Recycled: Office."
- Although many of the major banks have developed and implemented comprehensive policies addressing paper procurement, usage, and recycling practices, the overall waste management strategies for many of these banks seems to lack transparency.
- Aside from the sustainability of banks' own operations, project financing is perhaps the most important aspect of this sector's sustainability initiatives.
- Microfinance, community investment, and funding for environmentally sustainable projects are the most pertinent aspects of responsible financing.

- Aside from microfinance, another important means by which the banking industry can support communities and the economically disadvantaged is through community investment, which is intended to encourage depository institutions to help meet the credit needs of the communities in which they operate, including low and moderate income neighborhoods, consistent with safe and sound operations."

- Sustainable investments have an environmental dimension as well.

- Responsible finance practices in renewable energy sources have the potential to create a drastic impact on greenhouse gas emissions and global climate change ⬚ far beyond the reach of major banks' operations in reducing their own greenhouse gas emissions.

- Major banks play a pivotal role in ensuring not only sustainable business in their own operations, but the operations of other industries as well.

- Providing finance for some projects results in environmentally harmful or socially unjust externalities, and by choosing not to support these projects, banks take a major step in setting precedence for other sectors

Source: Governance Research Digest, September 2013 (Vol. 4, No. 9)

2.3.16   The Value of Sustainability Reporting

Author(s): Center for Corporate Citizenship and Ernst & Young LLP

The Center for Corporate Citizenship and Ernst & Young LLP conducted a survey on sustainability reporting, which was administered between February 26 and March 8, 2013. 'The Value of Sustainability Reporting' survey covered various aspects of an organization's ESG reporting and included the cost and benefits of reporting, as well as making connections to financial performance.

Key findings

A full 95% of the Global 250 issue sustainability reports.

- Sustainability disclosure can serve as a differentiator in competitive industries and foster investor confidence, trust and employee loyalty.

- Analysts often consider a company's sustainability disclosures in their assessment of management quality and efficiency, and reporting may provide firms better access to capital.

- The benefits of reporting include: better reputation, meeting the expectations of employees, improved access to capital, increased efficiency and waste reduction.
- Sustainability reporting requires companies to gather information about processes and impacts that they may not have measured before.
- This new data, in addition to creating greater transparency about firm performance, can provide firms with knowledge necessary to reduce their use of natural resources, increase efficiency and improve their operational performance.
- Moreover, sustainability reporting can prepare firms to avoid or mitigate environmental and social risks that might have material financial impacts on their business while delivering better business, social, environmental and financial value — creating a virtuous circle.

Source: Governance Research Digest, September 2013 (Vol. 4, No. 9)

2.3.17 Carrots and sticks: Sustainability reporting policies worldwide – today's best practice, tomorrow's trends

Author(s): KPMG, the United Nations Environment Programme (UNEP), Global Reporting Initiative (GRI) and the Centre for Corporate Governance in Africa at the University of Stellenbosch Business School

KPMG, the United Nations Environment Programme (UNEP), Global Reporting Initiative (GRI) and the Centre for Corporate Governance in Africa at the University of Stellenbosch Business School produced together an overview of global developments in policy and regulation for sustainability and Corporate Social Responsibility (CSR) reporting. KPMG, the United Nations Environment Programme (UNEP), Global Reporting Initiative (GRI) and the Centre for Corporate Governance in Africa at the University of Stellenbosch Business School produced together an overview of global developments in policy and regulation for sustainability and Corporate Social Responsibility (CSR) reporting.

Key findings

There is an increasing emphasis on a combination of complementary voluntary and mandatory approaches to organizational disclosure.

- The gradual integration of organizational performance data is on the rise, with attempts to combine corporate governance, financial and sustainability reporting.
- Going forward, it is likely that more governments will issue sustainability reporting policies.
- As reporting organizations voice their concerns about the various frameworks they may use or need to comply with, there will be increasing calls for the alignment and harmonization of frameworks.
- Report readerships will grow, and the discussion of sustainability data – including around its credibility – will continue to increase.
- This enhanced participation of report users will occur partly due to improvements in the userfriendliness of sustainability reports, utilizing XBRL and other reporting innovations.
- Reports will increasingly focus on sustainability issues that are material for stakeholders and investors, thereby providing the most accurate and relevant view of organizations' sustainability performance and impacts.

Source: Governance Research Digest, December 2013 (Vol. 4, No. 12)

2.3.18 Gender Diversity in Sustainability Reporting

Author(s): Global Reporting Initiative (GRI)/ International Finance Corporation (IFC)

A new report from the Global Reporting Initiative (GRI) and International Finance Corporation (IFC) states that, despite the presence of gender-related indicators in the sustainability reporting guidelines issued by the GRI, few companies report sufficiently on gender-related issues. The report highlights some of the existing and emerging business drivers for improving practices and reporting on material gender issues. It also offers practical steps on how to embed gender in sustainability reporting.

<u>Key findings</u>

Site of Gender Equality	Tips for Implementation
Organisational governance and	Clear and explicit commitment to gender diversity in missiont statement. Identify a board-level champion for

values	gender initiatives . Include gender as a performance indicator.
The workplace	Ensure fair and comparable wages, hours and benefits. Undertake recruitment and retention campaigns that target women and men. Encourage the employment of women and men in jobs that are not 'typical' for their gender.
The supply chain	Publish a clear policy statement to ensure wide awareness of company support for gender equality in the supply chain. Identify mechanisms to help suppliers meet gender-sensitive procurement policies.
The community	Ensure women have representation on decision-making bodies. Set up systems to consult with women in the community. Provide career information and training designed for both men and women in the local community.
With consumers	Establish ethical marketing policies that exclude any gender or sexual exploitation. Ensure products and services are accessible to both male and female consumers.
Investment	Establish processes to collect, analyzing and report gender-relevant information on potential investments. Avoid investing in organizations that do harm and/or violate human rights.

Source: Social Research Digest, December 2009 (Vol. 1, No. 12)

2.3.19 The KPMG Survey of Corporate Responsibility Reporting

Author(s): KPMG

KPMG launched their 2013 Survey of Corporate Responsibility Reporting marking 20 years since KPMG's first survey on CR reporting was published. The current survey is a deep-dive review into the quality of reporting among 4,100 companies in 41 countries.

Key findings

CR reporting sees exceptional growth in emerging economies.

- There has been a dramatic increase in CR reporting rates in Asia Pacific over the last two years. Almost three quarters (71%) of companies based in Asia Pacific now publish Cr reports – an increase of 22%age points since 2011 when less than half (49%) did so.
- The Americas has now overtaken Europe as the leading CR reporting region, largely due to an increase in CR reporting in Latin America. Seventy six percent of companies in the Americas now report on CR, 73% in Europe and 71% in Asia Pacific.
- The highest growth in CR reporting since 2011 has been seen in: India (+53%age points), Chile (+46), Singapore (+37), Australia (+25), Taiwan (+19) and China (+16).
- A narrowing gap between leading and lagging industry sectors. In all sectors more than half of companies report on Cr, meaning reporting can be considered standard global practice irrespective of industry.
- CR information in the annual report: now standard practice. Over half of reporting companies worldwide (51%) now include CR information in their annual financial reports. This is a striking rise since 2011 (when only 20% did so) and 2008 (only 9%).
- Use of Global Reporting Initiative (GRI) guidelines is almost universal
- 78% of reporting companies worldwide refer to the GRI reporting guidelines in their CR reports, a rise of 9%age points since the 2011 survey (over 90% do so in South Korea, South Africa, Portugal, Chile, Brazil and Sweden).
- Among the world's 250 largest companies the rate is even higher than the n100: 82% of G250 companies that report on CR refer to the GRI guidelines as opposed to 78% in 2011.
- Assurance among the largest companies has reached a tipping point
- Over half (59%) of the G250 companies that report CR data now invest in external assurance. This is up from 46% in 2011.
- Two thirds of those companies that invest in assurance choose to engage a major accountancy firm.

Source: Governance Research Digest, February 2014 (Vol. 5, No. 2)

2.3.20   Methodologie Review of Fortune 100 Corporate Reports

Author(s): Methodologie

Methodologie published its annual analysis of the reporting trends among the Fortune 100 companies. The fifth annual Review of Fortune 100 Corporate Reports tracks the evolution of trends, such as changing GRI standards for CSR reports, brand integration and technology.

Key findings

A majority of companies are continuing to leverage annual reports to communicate more than the standard financial requirements by going beyond 10-K reporting. There's still room for improvement in their overall storyline and transparency.

- Integrated reporting is not being heavily adopted. Integration seems like a logical concept: report and align on how you act on the values of your brand as a part of your financial picture. In reality, it's a much more complex practice and can have a fundamental change in the way you do business to report these together. Transition planning is critical.
- More CSR content is appearing in sections of the annual report, which indicates that companies are thinking about integration and its significance.
- The slight increase in CSR reporting overall may be attributable to the changing Global Reporting Initiative (GRI) standards and a desire to let the dust settle out between GRI3 and GRI4.
- The use of GRI reporting format and letters of assurance increased significantly. Both of these increases are great; however, the more systematic that reporting becomes, the more important it is that the strategic narrative should be told in the report so that the numbers provide a comprehensive and compelling storyline to support the brand

Source: Governance Research Digest, May 2014 (Vol. 5, No. 5)

2.3.21   The value creation journey: A survey of JSE Top-40 companies' integrated reports

Author(s): PriceWaterhouseCoopers South Africa

PriceWaterhouseCoopers South Africa conducted a survey on the Top 40 companies listed on the Johannesburg Stock Exchange based on the Content Elements for an integrated report presented in the IIRC's Consultation Draft of the International <IR> Framework. Findings in The value creation journey: A survey of JSE Top-40 companies' integrated reports are grouped by Content Element and then evaluated according to three broad categories: Clear opportunities to develop reporting; Potential to develop reporting; and Effective communication.

Key findings

The most effective communication was found in reporting on strategy and resource allocation, as well as reporting on business models.

- Reporting on governance activities showed the greatest room for improvement.
- Storytelling through images. Companies showed a definite willingness to tell their value creation stories in non-traditional ways. Use of information graphics and images that combined words and pictures were common throughout the reports.
- Governance in action. There was a definite tendency toward 'constrained' governance reporting. Companies seemed more comfortable reporting on board charters and terms of reference, rather than the actual activities undertaken by the board and committees during the year.
- Avoiding the 'crystal ball'. Historical reporting remains the focus, with companies shying away from broaching the topic of what the future may hold for them.
- 'Silo' reporting. It is evident that many companies are still taking their first steps on the integrated reporting journey. Stand-alone sections of reporting often provide excellent communication, but opportunities to connect this information to other areas in the report are often missed, especially in the segmental review.

Source: Governance Research Digest, May 2014 (Vol. 5, No. 5)

2.3.22 CR Perspectives 2013 — Global CR Reporting Trends and Stakeholder Views

Author(s): CorporateRegister.com

CorporateRegister.com released its annual free CR Perspectives report, combining data, insight and opinion to reveal how global CR reporting has developed and where it might be headed. CR Perspectives 2013 — Global CR Reporting Trends and Stakeholder Views looks at global CR reporting based on statistics derived from the world's largest CR reporting database (52,000 reports); and stakeholder views based on the inaugural CR Perspectives online survey, eliciting 300 participants' views on context, content, communication and credibility of CR reporting.

Key findings

Overall CR reporting quality has improved over the past ten years; and companies of all sizes, as well as other organizations, will eventually be expected to report on CR issues.

- It's best to follow a reporting framework, but not all frameworks are created equal; and respondents believe every CR report should include a materiality index.
- Employees are the single most important report audience, with the general public lowest priority; and while preferred reporting frequency is annual, ten percent of respondents would prefer continuous reporting.
- Including 'bad news' and data & targets is considered essential for a report to be credible; and the most credible report assurance statements declare their methodology — but if this methodology is desk research, this may detract from overall credibility

Source: Governance Research Digest, May 2014 (Vol. 5, No. 5)

2.3.23 See Change: How Transparency Drives Performance

Author(s): GlobeScan and SustainAbility

GlobeScan and SustainAbility released a survey that explores how transparency can be better leveraged to drive impact. The report, Towards Ethical Norms in International Business Transactions, aims to suggest, principally for boards of directors, one means of establishing the basis of trust for long term commercial relationships wherever they operate in the world.

Key findings

Sustainability reporting is stalled. That is, reporting is simply not driving as much impact as it could.

- Impact-wise, reporting has enabled efficiency gains, informed stakeholders about key issues, enhanced corporate reputations, and started to inform some investor decisions.
- However, at this stage in the global sustainability reporting journey, when we have access to a plethora of data, technology, and story-telling expertise, it is time for reporting to drive even more impact.
- Valuing and reporting on externalities, above many other possible transparency efforts, guides decision-making that leads to sustainable change within companies.
- This supports growing interest among many companies to better understand their material impacts, including relevant externalities, to mange their impacts on society and the environment.
- Sustainability experts believe transparency and sustainability reporting can bring more value to companies than it currently does: 79% of survey respondents indicate that corporate transparency positively impacts a company's sustainability performance.
- Respondents also suggest two top barriers to transparency driving more change—poor data accuracy and lack of focus on material issues. These experts pointed to mandatory non-financial reporting requirements and increased investor demand for integrated reporting as potential solutions to drive greater value from reporting

Source: Governance Research Digest, August 2014 (Vol. 5, No. 8)

2.3.24 EY's Excellence in Integrated Reporting Awards

Author(s): Ernst & Young

Ernst & Young released a survey of integrated reports from South Africa's top 100 JSE-listed companies and top 10 state-owned companies. The purpose of the survey "EY's Excellence in Integrated Reporting Awards" is to encourage excellence in the quality of integrated reporting to investors and other stakeholders by South Africa's top companies and state-owned companies (SOCs).

Key findings

Number of 'excellent', which includes top ten rankings of JSE listed companies increased to 35 (2014) from 28 in (2013).

- The top ten companies ranked in order
- Royal Bafokeng Platinum Ltd
- Standard Bank Group Ltd
- Sasol Ltd
- Truworths International Ltd
- Gold Fields Ltd
- Aspen Pharmacare Holdings Ltd
- Kumba Iron Ore Ltd
- Liberty Holdings Ltd
- Clicks Group Ltd
- Exxaro Resources Ltd
- Top three state-owned companies ranked Excellent*
- Eskom Holdings (SOC) Ltd
- Industrial Development Corporation of SA Ltd
- Transnet (SOC) Ltd
- 64 companies ranked as 'excellent' or 'good'
- Overall 22 companies moved up in rankings, whilst 16 moved down
- Average page length decreased to 159 pages (2013: 172 pages)
- 46 companies included summarised financials
- Average length of financial statements decreased to 45 pages (2013: 52 pages).

Source: Governance Research Digest, October 2014 (Vol. 5, No. 10)

2.3.25 Measuring Sustainability Disclosure: Ranking the World's Stock Exchanges

Author(s): Corporate Knights Capital

Corporate Knights Capital with the support of Aviva plc, Standard & Poor's Ratings Services and the Association of Chartered Certified Accountants (ACCA) issued their third annual study that researched how well global stock exchanges encourage listed companies to disclose basic corporate responsibility data and also ranks the world's stock exchanges on sustainability reporting performance. The report, "Measuring Sustainability Disclosure: Ranking the World's Stock Exchanges" analyses the extent to which the world's publicly traded companies are disclosing the seven basic 'first-generation' metrics; employee turnover, energy, greenhouse gas emissions, injury rate, payroll, water consumption and waste.

<u>Key findings</u>

Only three per cent of the world's largest listed companies* report on all basic sustainability metrics.

- Just over a third of large listed companies (39%) report on the amount of greenhouse gases they are emitting, but only a quarter disclose their water consumption (25%) and just 12 per cent report on their rate of employee turnover.
- Although the number of large companies disclosing basic sustainability indicators is increasing, the rate of uptake is flatlining. For example, the percentage of large listed companies who disclosed their energy use increased by 88 per cent from 2008 to 2012 but only by five per cent from 2011 to 2012. There is a similar slowdown in reporting occurring on the other sustainability indicators.
- The Helsinki Stock Exchange was the top-ranked exchange, moving up from second position in last year's assessment
- The Euronext Amsterdam took second spot, followed by the Johannesburg Stock Exchange, the only stock exchange in the top ten based in an emerging market
- This was followed by Euronext Paris and the Copenhagen Stock Exchange. The London Stock Exchange is ranked ninth the largest exchange inside the top ten, climbing from eleventh place over the past three years
- North American exchanges are noticeably absent.

Source: Governance Research Digest, November 2014 (Vol. 5, No. 11)

2.3.26 Transparency in Corporate Reporting: Assessing the World's Largest Companies (2014)

Author(s): Transparency International

Transparency International launched a report that evaluates the transparency of corporate reporting by the world's 124 largest publicly listed companies. The report, Transparency in Corporate Reporting: Assessing the World's Largest Companies, assesses the disclosure practices of companies with respect to their anti-corruption programmes, company holdings and the disclosure of key financial information on a country-by-country basis and follows on from a 2012 report which focused on the world's 105 largest publicly traded companies.

Key findings

Increasing numbers of global public companies are disclosing their anti-corruption programmes but they are still notably deficient in making public the full range of their corporate holdings and key financial information for each country where they operate.

- Country-by-country reporting is the dimension showing by far the weakest results.
- The vast majority (97 per cent) of assessed companies state publicly that they are committed to complying with all laws, including anti-corruption laws.
- Only 45 per cent of assessed companies prohibit facilitation payments. This is nevertheless an improvement over the results of our 2012 report showing that only 20 per cent banned the practice.
- Political contributions, especially those made abroad, are not transparent enough.
- The anti-corruption policies of UK companies are the most consistent with the criteria used to assess the anti-corruption programmes dimension in this report.
- With an average result of 58 per cent, the performance of financial sector companies is strikingly weak with respect to anti-corruption programmes.

Source: Governance Research Digest, December 2014 (Vol. 5, No. 12)

2.4   Environmental Disclosures

2.4.1   Environmental Disclosures of Palm Oil Plantation Companies in Malaysia: A Tool For Stakeholder Engagement

Author(s): R. Othman, R. Ameer

This paper examines annual environmental protection disclosures of palm oil companies in Malaysia that have significant implications for the preservation of earth, water and air quality. The empirical research used analysis of the annual reports of 60 listed companies in the plantation subsector of the palm oil industry on the Main Board of Bursa Malaysia.

Key findings

Some palm oil plantation companies provided only general statements on their awareness of environmental issues. Others offered no disclosure or acknowledgement at all.

- Some companies provide a lengthy section on the environment in the CSR section of their annual reports, with details including operational best practice, emissions reductions, carbon sequestration and conservation initiatives.
- Some companies' reports take a clearly defensive attitude in discussing their interactions with the environment.
- The most popular section of the annual report for environmental disclosures was the Chairman's Statement, as it is often used as a forum to make political or social comments about government, taxation, accounting standards or similar.
- The authors suggest that the limited information provided in palm oil plantation companies' annual reports have not satisfied stakeholders' appetites for more specific disclosures which accurately outline their environmental impacts.
- They suggest that accountants have a particularly important role in ensuring such non-financial information is embedded alongside financial details in annual reports.

Source: CSR Research Digest, March 2010 (Vol. 2, No. 3)

2.4.2   Corporate Reporting on Water Risk

Author(s): Ceres

A new report from Ceres, "Murky Waters? Corporate Reporting on Water Risk", aims to help investors and companies understand how companies in vulnerable sectors are evaluating, managing and disclosing water risks in their operations, supply chains and products. Companies from eight sectors (beverages, chemicals, electric power, food, homebuilding, mining, oil and gas, semiconductors) were reviewed and benchmarked against their peers. 100 companies were selected in total, based on their 2008 annual revenues and market capitalisation.

<u>Key findings</u>

Even for companies operating in sectors and regions of the world facing significant water risk, disclosure of risk and corporate water performance was weak. On a scoring scale that ranged from 0 to 100 points, no company surpassed 43 points.

- Diageo, the UK-based beverage company, received the highest score in the study.
- The mining sector performed best overall, followed by the beverage industry. Companies in the homebuilding sector received the lowest overall scores.
- The majority of participating organizations disclose exposure to water risks in annual reports or similar documents, but the language employed is vague.
- Companies are failing to reference specific at risk operations or supply chains, and do not attempt to quantify or monetize risk. Only six companies report any water accounting data within their financial findings.
- 73% of the companies surveyed report some exposure to water-related physical risks such as drought.
- Only nine companies report reputational risks related to water. These include companies in the beverage, mining and oil and gas sectors.
- 67% of companies disclose some level of water-related regulatory risk, with the highest exposure in the mining, electric power, and oil and gas sectors.

- Nearly half (48%) report some level of litigation risk.
- Although the majority of companies disclosed key water risk factors in their financial filings or annual reports, some restricted this discussion to their sustainability reports, reflecting an ongoing lack of integration between voluntary reports and regulated financial filings.
- Few companies provide performance data at the local level. Nearly two-thirds of the reviewed companies report total water use data, but only 17% report this data down to the site or regional level.
- Only a handful of companies put their water use in context by noting the number or percent of facilities operating in water-stressed regions. These included BP, Diageo, Heineken, Nestle and SABMiller.
- 24% of companies detail specific policies, standards or management systems to reduce water-related risks and costs.
- Only 21% disclose quantified targets to reduce water use. Three of these companies – Diageo, DuPont, and Xstrata – had reduction targets that were differentiated by the level of water stress facing specific facilities. Only 15 companies had goals to reduce wastewater discharge.
- No companies provided comprehensive data on their suppliers' water performance. A few – including Danone, SABMiller, and Unilever – provide estimates of the water use embedded in their supply chains.
- Twelve companies disclose working with their suppliers to help them reduce water use or wastewater discharge.
- Companies in sectors with a significant proportion of their water footprint embedded in the supply chain – food, beverage, electric power, and oil and gas – largely did not report engaging their suppliers on water management.
- Just under one-third of companies report collaborating in some way with local stakeholders on efforts to protect or restore watersheds and ecosystems near their operations.
- Despite reputational risks linked to siting water-intensive projects or facilities, only five companies – all in the mining or oil and gas sector – disclose engaging or consulting with stakeholders on the water impacts of siting or expanding operations.

Source: CSR Research Digest, March 2010 (Vol. 2, No. 3)

2.4.3 Environmental, Social and Governance (ESG) Disclosure Report

Author(s): Emerging Market Disclosure Project (EIRIS/Korean CSR Research Services/Responsible Research Singapore)

The Emerging Market Disclosure Project has released a report detailing the ESG disclosure practices of ten major South Korean companies. The companies featured are: Hynix, Hyundai Motor, KEPCO, KT, LG Chemical, LG Electronics, POSCO, Samsung Electronics, Shinhan Financial Group and SKT.

Key findings

The report finds strong reporting on environmental issues but a relatively poor understanding of social issues, particularly human rights.

- Many Korean companies, even large listed, do not publish CSR reports, and it is hard to find any reporting within financial services and amongst holding companies
- However, for those that do report, environmental disclosure is strong. All of the companies analyzed cover environmental issues in some depth and some display excellent reporting on the following: environmental policies, management systems, global coverage, board-level responsibility for environmental issues, quantitative emission data and quantitative reduction targets
- Reporting on human rights is mostly ignored, with disclosure on the issue being non-existent or superficial. Many commentators also find a worrying imbalance between the treatment of workers in South Korea and the treatment of the company's employees in overseas subsidiaries
- Most companies disclosed on at least three indicators relevant to corporate governance. However, on the issue of separation of chairman and CEO, only five companies met this challenge, a pattern similar to other large Korean companies
- Korean companies exhibit poor reporting of policies on political donations, which is a corruption issue very specific to Korea, where 'facilitation payments' to bureaucrats have emerged as a new form of bribery.
- Based on the report's findings, the groups recommend that Korean

companies begin to incorporate more systematic stakeholder involvement into their ESG strategies, monitor, audit and report social performance, and disclose political contributions.

- Each of the 10 companies analyzed disclosed some information on their anti-bribery activities, but few disclosed political donations.

Source: CSR Research Digest, May 2010 (Vol. 2, No. 5)

2.4.4   Water Disclosure Report

Author(s): Carbon Disclosure Project

Carbon Disclosure Project (CDP) launches first water disclosure report on world's largest companies. CDP Water Disclosure sent its first annual questionnaire to the world's largest companies asking for information on their water use and other water-related business issues.

Key findings

The report findings show that water is already impacting business operations with 96% of responding companies able to identify whether or not they are exposed to water risk and more than half of those reporting risks classifying them as current or near-term (1-5 years).

- 39% of companies are already experiencing detrimental impacts relating to water including disruption to operations from drought or flooding, declining water quality necessitating costly on-site pre-treatment, and increases in water prices, as well as fines and litigation relating to pollution incidents.
- Water security is already high on the corporate agenda with 67% reporting responsibility for water-related issues at the board or executive committee level.
- The majority of companies (89%) have already developed specific water policies, strategies and plans, and 60% have set water-related performance targets.
- Business engagement on water issues differs widely across different industry sectors: 100% of companies in the chemicals sector responded compared with just 29% in the oil & gas, and construction, infrastructure & real estate sectors.
- Responses were received from companies in a total of 25 countries,

with the most responses coming from the USA (59, 57% responding), the UK (14, 64% responding) and Japan (13, 45% responding). The highest response rates were from South Africa (100%), Germany (83%) and Switzerland (71%).

- A high number of corporations (62%) are identifying a wide range of water related business opportunities in areas such as water management, water efficiency and reduction, and wastewater treatment.

- Just 53% of companies are able to identify whether they are exposed to water risks in their supply chains, as opposed to the high levels of awareness (96%) of water risks in their own operations.

- Sectors reporting the greatest exposure to water risks include food, beverage & tobacco and metals & mining, with chemicals and technology & communications the least exposed.

- Physical risks to direct operations from drought and flooding were most frequently cited, but companies also recognize risks from changing regulations and reputational damage.

- Companies exhibiting best practice in water management include Anglo American, Colgate- Palmolive, Ford, GE, PG&E and Taiwan Semiconductor Manufacturing.

Source: CSR Research Digest, December 2010 (Vol. 2, No. 12)

2.4.5   Corporate Water Reporting Report

Author(s): Pacific Institute

A new report from the Pacific Institute suggests that companies have improved their practices in reporting water use and its effects, but efforts must still be made to provide greater disclosure and enable understanding of the risks and impacts of corporate water needs. The report, commissioned by the UN Global Compact, looked at corporate reporting on water sustainability by 110 companies across 11 waterintensive sectors.

Key findings

62% of companies analysed adhered to at least one of the factors used to evaluate reporting methods and approaches.

- While more frequent and broader engagement of stakeholders may strengthen the depth, breadth, and legitimacy of corporate responsibility reports, currently, less than half of the companies assessed mention utilizing stakeholder input to inform their reporting.

- The criterion met by the highest number of companies (89%) was that for quantified water quantity data. This was followed by specified targets for water performance (66%), trend water performance data (66%) and quantified water quality data (64%).
- There is a clear need to further expand corporate reporting to include common approaches to describing actions and impacts outside of direct operations.
- Water reporting would be advanced by the development of harmonized sector-specific indicators on water.
- There is a need for practical guidance on how companies can carry out water-focused materiality assessments to assist in determining reporting content.
- More work needs to be done to ensure more responsible conformity to and harmonization with existing corporate reporting guidelines.
- There is significant potential for cross-sectoral learning with regard to water reporting.
- Companies can provide greater detail in reporting on individual corporate actions. This would include more substantive descriptions of the objectives, scope, and impacts of corporate actions, particularly for supplier engagement, partnerships, community engagement, and public policy work.
- Company reporting should also elaborate on the specific role they played in each project and the corporate resources dedicated.

Source: Environmental Research Digest, May 2009 (Vol. 1, No. 5)

2.4.6   Electric Utilities Carbon Disclosures Report

Author(s): Carbon Disclosure Project

The Carbon Disclosure Project has released its 2009 Electric Utilities Report. The report examines the carbon reporting of the world's 249 largest publicly traded electric utilities. As carbon emissions constraints get ever tighter, electric utilities must work hard to reduce fossil fuel use.

Key findings

The majority of the world's largest electricity utilities have no emission reduction targets in place and many are not even providing investors with information on which fuels they are using to generate power.

- Just 16% have set and disclosed absolute emission reduction targets.
- Moreover, of the 110 companies that responded to requests for information on their climate change strategy, 41% had no emission reduction plans in place, while under half disclosed information on their current electricity generation capacity and fuel mix.
- The highest scoring electric utilities for CDP6 (2008) are Endesa, Iberdrola, and AGL Energy with 85, 82 and 81 points respectively, out of 100 total possible points.
- These utilities are providing comprehensive descriptions of company-specific climate change risks and opportunities as well as their strategies to integrate climate change into core business strategies.
- Out of the 110 electric utility responses analyzed for this report, 93 companies (or 85%) provided quantitative GHG emissions data (either direct Scope 1 or indirect Scope 2 emissions) in their CDP6 responses.
- Fewer companies reported on standard metrics of emissions intensity (emissions released per unit of output). 90% of European companies reported emissions intensity figures, whereas only 52% of North American and 31% of Asian companies did so.
- For those companies that reported emissions intensity figures in metric tonnes of carbon dioxide equivalent per Megawatt-hour (CO_2-e/MWh), American Electric Power and TransAlta Corp. are among those with the most carbon emissions-intensive generation, while Entergy Corp. and FPL Group have some of the least intensive electricity production, due to their use of nuclear power and renewables.
- Out of the 110 unique responses analyzed for this report, 61% of respondents say they are forecasting future GHG emissions and 59% say they have an emissions reduction plan in place.
- Forty-eight companies also provided specificvdetails on the baseline years and target strength of their emissions reduction targets.
- Numerous companies included disclosure on a range of investment opportunities from renewable energy installations and demand side management (DSM) programs to facility upgrades, fuel switching and

research and development of carbon sequestration and storage (CCS).

Source: Environmental Research Digest, June 2009 (Vol. 1, No. 6)

2.4.7   Energy Companies' Climate Risk Disclosures Report

Author(s): Ceres/Environmental Defense Fund

A new report from Ceres and the US Environmental Defense Fund, "Climate Risk Disclosure in SEC Filings," analyzes recent 10-K filings from global industries. Companies were evaluated on their absolute levels of disclosure on climate risk relative to the Global Framework for Climate Risk Disclosure. Companies were selected for this study based on their involvement in the coal, electric utilities, oil and gas, insurance, and transportation industries. The 100 largest companies by market capitalization and annual revenue were selected as the sample.

Key findings

While the energy industries are disclosing climate change risks to a greater extent than other sectors, the detail and depth of those disclosures are far from sufficient to help investors make wise choices.

- For electric utilities, disclosure was widespread but minimal. None of the 26 companies studied achieved a "Fair" rating on disclosure of emissions and climate change position.
- Only 3 out of 26 electrical utilities companies (12%) ranked "Fair" on climate risk assessment, and only 2 out of 26 companies (8%) provided "Fair" disclosure of actions to address climate change.
- Seven of the electrical utilities companies studied provided no information on actions to address climate change.
- Nevertheless, the electric power sector ranked higher than the other sectors and had three of the highest disclosing companies in the study— AES, Xcel, and PG&E.
- All six coal companies surveyed included some disclosure of climate change issues in their 10-K filings, though only one achieved a "Fair" score in any of the three categories analyzed.
- Coal companies' strongest disclosure was in the area of risk assessment; five of the companies provided disclosure in this category that was rated "Limited" or "Fair."
- Rio Tinto provided the best disclosure, including valuable information

on emissions, while Yanzhou Coal Mining Co. performed the worst overall.

- The majority of the 23 oil and gas companies studied provided some disclosure on climate risk assessment, but disclosure was weak with none ranking "Fair" and 22 out of 23 (96%) scored as "Limited" or "Poor."

- Disclosure in the other two categories was even more limited. Twelve out of 23 oil and gas companies (52%) provided no disclosure on actions to address climate change, while 17 out of 23 companies (74%) disclosed no information on their emissions or climate change position.

- Apache, Exxon Mobil and Anadarko were noted for particularly weak overall disclosure, while Shell scored best across the board.

- Companies in the transportation sector provided minimal disclosure in SEC filings. Only 5 of 19 (26%) disclosed their emissions or their climate change position, and none were ranked as "Fair" for this disclosure.

- General Motors was the only company to provide information on past emissions from its operations, while not a single company disclosed emissions associated with vehicle use.

- Transportation companies provided somewhat more informative disclosure on climate risk and actions to address climate change, with 68% providing some disclosure in each of these categories. The disclosure was weak, however, and did not meet investors' needs.

- Only three transportation companies scored "Fair" on climate risk assessment and two scored "Fair" on their actions to address climate risks.

- Honda, Daimler and General Motors scored the highest overall.

- Although prudent risk assessment is the basis for a viable insurance industry, the 27 insurance companies studied in this sector provided the least disclosure across the board compared to other sectors.

- Eighteen out of 27 companies (67%) had no mention of climate change or related risks anywhere in their SEC filings.

- Twenty-three out of 27 insurance companies (85%) failed to disclose their emissions or a statement on climate change, while 24 out of 27 companies (89%) omitted disclosure on actions to address climate change, despite the wide range of opportunities for new, climate-related insurance products.

- The handful of companies that did provide more informative disclosure—Swiss Re, Munich Re and Zurich Financial—were all non-U.S. companies.

Source: Environmental Research Digest, July 2009 (Vol. 1, No. 7)

2.4.8   Carbon Disclosures Report

Author(s): Carbon Disclosure Project

The Carbon Disclosure Project has released its annual report into the climate change-related performance and disclosures of UK companies. The companies featured in the report comprise the UK FTSE 350.

<u>Key findings</u>

Topping the league table for both disclosure and efforts to reduce carbon emissions are Centrica and consumer goods company Reckitt Benckiser.

- The following companies were also highlighted for being near the top of the table: Interserve, National Grid, Royal Dutch Shell, Scottish & Southern Energy, Tesco, Unilever, and United Utilities.
- Rate credits in property policies (i.e. for those who institute loss control measures);
- In total, only 35% of the FTSE 350 have disclosed emissions reductions targets.
- The best-performing companies in the survey all showed that they had incorporated upcoming regulation into their thinking and had shown carbon reduction activities that delivered results.
- The report found that the utilities sector was most aware of upcoming regulation and was the strongest-performing sector in terms of disclosure, with more than two thirds having already achieved positive results in emissions reduction.
- Transportation and utility firms demonstrated both the largest financial commitment to curbing emission and the most aggressive reduction targets, with Bayer, BASF, HSBC, Rio Tinto and Carnival topping the Carbon Disclosure Leadership Index.
- 55% of respondents view the introduction of the Carbon Reduction Commitment in April 2010 as a risk, with 24% seeing it as an

opportunity.

- This round of the CDP maintained an overall response rate of 67% and an increase in responses from the FTSE 100 of 4%, suggesting that, despite the economic downturn, climate change remains high on the agenda.

Source: Environmental Research Digest, October 2009 (Vol. 1, No. 10)

2.4.9   Corporate Environmental Disclosure Report

Author(s): Greenpeace

A new report from Greenpeace China analyses the progress made towards environmental disclosure by some of the largest Chinese companies and multinationals operating within the country. The scope of the study encompasses enterprises belonging to either the 2008 Fortune Global 500 or the 2008 Fortune China 200, and that were discovered to be exceeding discharge standards by environmental protection departments. A total of 25 factories belonging to 18 companies feature in the research.

Key findings

Serious shortcomings were discovered in the extent to which companies complied with environmental information disclosure measures enacted by the Chinese Ministry of Environmental Protection (MEP). None of the 25 factories disclosed the information required within the stipulated 30 days time limit.

- Two of the companies failed to disclose environmental information even though local environmental authorities reported them as either using or discharging hazardous chemicals.
- These companies were the Aluminum Corporation of China and the Hunan Nonferrous Metal Corporation.
- The four factories belonging to three companies (Samsung Electronics, China Coal Energy, Weichai Power) that did eventually disclose environmental information only disclosed extremely limited data.
- Two of the four factories gave details of only two pollutants. The third and fourth factories – both belonging to Samsung Electronics – gave information on six and four pollutants each.
- The authors believe that this information is unlikely to be complete.

- In many of their operations in developed countries, the eight multinationals regularly disclose comprehensive data on factory emissions. In China, only Samsung Electronics out of the eight multinational companies disclosed data of their factories 'blacklisted' by local environmental protection bureaus.

- The results demonstrate widespread noncompliance and disregard for Chinese environmental regulations. This corporate disobedience is, in part, encouraged by local governments' weak enforcement of the Ministry of Environmental Protection's measures.

- Ambiguities existing within the MEP's measures may also be a significant contributing factor to weak corporate environmental information disclosure.

- The authors outline a list of demands to both industry and government. These include corporates' obligation to comply with MEP measures in China; as well as release and transfer information on all pollutants listed in the standards that apply to their specific activities.

Source: Environmental Research Digest, December 2009 (Vol. 1, No. 12)

2.4.10   CDP Water Disclosure Global Report 2011

Author(s): Carbon Disclosure Project

CDP Water Disclosure's goal is to aid the transformation by encouraging meaningful and systematic reporting on water globally so that investors and other stakeholders can understand how companies are building water into their core business strategies, and so that leading practices can be shared. The survey being sent to 315 companies on the Global 500 index, all identified as operating in the most water-stressed locations or sectors, this year had a 60% response rate.

Key findings

Only 57% of organizations report board-level oversight of water policies, strategies or plans, compared with 94% for climate change.

- The different approaches to carbon and water are surprising, given that most reported waterrelated risks are near-term: companies in the water survey identified 64% of direct operational risks and 66% of supply chain risks as occurring between now and 2016.

- More than one third of respondents (38%) have already experienced waterrelated business impacts, such as operational disruptions from severe weather or water shortages.
- One company reported that it had already experienced a water-related impact at a cost of $200 million.
- Meanwhile, 59% of companies reported exposure to water-related risks.
- Companies said the biggest water risk for direct operations is water stress or scarcity (41%), followed by flooding (24%), reputational damage (23%), and higher compliance costs (21%).
- Energy companies report a high level of risk at 72%, yet CDP said they reported the lowest levels of board oversight, at 36%.
- 63% of respondents said water presents commercial opportunities, with 79% of those opportunities being near-term.
- The most commonly cited opportunities were cost reductions from water efficiency, revenue from new water-related products or services, and strengthened brand value.
- For example, Colgate Palmolive said an improved cleaning process at site in South Africa has saved the company 388,000 liters of water a year, and increased product output by two tons daily because of reduced downtime.
- In a collaboration with three printed circuit board assembly partners, Cisco Systems instituted a new soldering practice that eliminated the need for a water-intensive wash stage, saving over $1 million a year.
- The report found that respondents' ability to provide water-related usage data has improved.
- The proportion of companies able to report water withdrawals (95%) has increased since 2010 (86%), as has the ability to report water recycling/reuse data (58% compared to 42% in 2010).
- A new paradigm is emerging for water management, with initiatives including improved data and analytics, improved efficiency, energy-efficient water treatment technologies, and efforts to extract energy and nutrients from wastewater.
- In the report, companies indicated that they mostly understood the relationship between water and energy use, with 72% reporting linkages or trade-offs between water and carbon emissions.

- But 38% of companies were unaware of whether they are exposed to water risk in their supply chains, compared to only 7% for direct operations.
- CDP said that the consumer discretionary sector is particularly exposed to supply chain risk, but 41% of respondents in this sector cannot state whether their supply chain is exposed to water-related risk.

Source: Environmental Research Digest, December 2011 (Vol. 2, No. 8)

2.4.11 Clearing the Waters: A Review of Corporate Water Risk Disclosure in SEC Filings

Author(s): Ceres

The report analyzes changes in water risk disclosure by more than 80 companies between 2009 and 2011. The report covers water use in eight water intensive sectors: beverage, chemicals, electric power, food, homebuilding, mining, oil & gas and semiconductors.

Key findings

Overall corporate disclosures of water-related risks have increased since 2009, but most reporting remains weak and inconsistent.

- Significantly more companies are disclosing exposure to water risk, with a focus on physical risk.
- 87% of companies now report physical risk exposure versus 76% in 2009, with the biggest increases coming from the oil and gas sector.
- More companies are making the connection to climate change.
- In 2009, only eight of the 82 companies assessed (10%) disclosed that climate change posed growing physical risks in the form of water scarcity, flooding or quality issues to their operations and supply chains. In 2011, that number jumped to 22 (27%).
- There is a continued lack of quantitative data and performance targets.
- Despite improvements in overall disclosure, data on company water use and the financial impacts of water-related risks remain infrequent in financial filings.
- There is growing, but still limited, disclosure on water management systems and performance.
- In light of these risks, the report recommends that companies:

- undertake ongoing and more robust analysis of potential water-related risks;
- augment qualitative disclosure with more quantitative data in SEC filings;
- ensure compliance with the SEC's guidance on climate change disclosure;
- provide investors with information on how they are mitigating water risks.

Source: Environmental Research Digest, July 2012 (Vol. 3, No. 7)

2.4.12   Environmental Tracking Carbon Rankings

Author(s): Environmental Investment Organisation

Environmental Investment Organisation published the Environmental Tracking Carbon Rankings, which examine the GHG emissions and transparency of the 800 largest companies globally. This latest set of Carbon Rankings build on the methodology established previously for the ET 2011 Carbon Rankings, where companies were placed into one of four Disclosure and Verification categories and then ranked by carbon intensity (tonnes of CO2 equivalent per million US dollars of turnover) based on Scope 1, 2 & 3 emissions.

Key findings

Only 37% of the world's largest companies report their greenhouse gas emissions fully and correctly.

- BASF, (Complete & Verified), comes top, disclosing all 15 Scope 3 Categories, according to the GHG Protocol Scope 3 Reporting Standard, with a combined Scope 1, 2 & 3 emissions intensity of 932.74 tCO2e/$M turnover.
- US based First Energy comes last, with no public data and an inferred combined Scope 1, 2 & 3 emissions intensity of 10,342.03 tCO2e/$M turnover.
- RWE, (Complete & Verified), has the highest publicly disclosed Scope 1 & 2 figure of 166,200,000 tCO2e, with a combined Scope 1, 2 & 3 intensity of 3,870.19 tCO2e/$M turnover.

- Europe leads the world on all disclosure metrics: 35% of companies report complete and independently verified data. This compares to 11% for the BRICS, the lowest of any region.
- 8 of the top 10 companies in the ET Global 800 are Europe based.
- 267, or 33%, of companies within the ET Global 800, report one or more Scope 3 categories. However, only 15, or 2%, report 5 or more Scope 3 categories.

Source: Governance Research Digest, May 2013 (Vol. 4, No. 5)

2.4.13 Sustainability goals and reporting

Author(s): Grant Thornton

Grant Thornton published a report that gives insight on the current state of sustainability reporting among SEC registrants and highlights unregulated proposals and frameworks. The data for the report "Sustainability goals and reporting" comes from in-depth interviews conducted by Financial Executives Research Foundation Inc. (FERF) and Grant Thornton LLP, as well as a review of more than 25 Fortune 500 companies' publicly available sustainability reports.

Key findings

Financial executives are not as involved in corporate social responsibility matters and reporting as perhaps they should be.

- The finance function's involvement in sustainability reporting (internal and external) adds credibility and confidence in the measurement, data collection and analysis processes.
- Stand-alone sustainability reporting will become accepted practice, but it is likely to be an interim step.
- Reporting that integrates sustainability and social responsibility with financial goals and results to describe for all stakeholders the company's past and future creation of value is likely to be the ultimate objective.
- Financial executives need to play a greater, if not leading, role in these developments.

Source: Governance Research Digest, April 2014 (Vol. 5, No. 4)

2.4.14 Cool Response: The SEC & Corporate Climate Change Reporting

Author(s): Ceres

Ceres released a report that examines the state of corporate reporting and associated SEC comment letters on climate change, based on a survey of more than 40,000 SEC comment letters sent to companies in the last four years and an analysis of the state of S&P 500 company reporting on climate disclosure through the end of 2013. The report, Cool Response: The SEC & Corporate Climate Change Reporting also provides recommendations for the SEC and companies on improving the quality of reporting and calls on the SEC to prioritize the disclosure of material climate risks, focusing on companies in the most at-risk sectors and on recent regulatory developments.

Key findings

The majority of financial reporting on climate change is too brief and largely superficial, and that most companies are failing to meet SEC requirements.

- The SEC is not prioritizing the financial risks and opportunities of climate change as an important disclosure issue. Based on the low number and content of SEC comment letters in the last four years; the small number of letters to high carbon emitters and insurance companies; the SEC's decision not to convene a planned 2010 roundtable on climate disclosure; and the lack of SEC public statements, trainings, or supplemental guidance for registrants, it is clear that the SEC has not prioritized improving climate disclosure in financial filings.
- The SEC issued 49 comment letters that addressed the adequacy of climate change disclosure in 2010 and 2011, but only 3 comment letters in 2012 and none in 2013.
- Most comment letters—38—were issued in 2010 following the release of the interpretive guidance. Since then, there has been a significant fall-off in SEC attention to this area.
- Most S&P 500 climate disclosures in 10-Ks are very brief, provide little discussion of material issues, and do not quantify impacts or risks. Based on this report's 0-100 scoring scale, electric power companies

received an average score of 16.7 for the quality of their SEC reporting—by far the highest industry average. Even within this group there was high variability in the quality of reporting.

- Most S&P 500 companies that disclose via the CDP provide significantly more detailed information in voluntary climate reporting compared to mandatory 10-K filings. Seventy percent of the 332 S&P 500 companies that responded to the 2013 Carbon Disclosure Project questionnaire scored 70 or above on a CDP 0-100 scale designed to evaluate the quality of reporting in response to the questionnaire. Only 14% of the 488 S&P 500 companies that filed 10-Ks in 2013 scored above 5 on this report's 0-100 scoring scale for their SEC climate reporting. A score of 5 amounts to about one short paragraph or a couple of lines focused on climate-related risks or opportunities.

- A large number of companies fail to say anything about climate change in their annual filings with the SEC. Forty one percent of S&P 500 companies did not include any climate related disclosure at all in their 10-K filings in 2013.

- Over the last four years the state of corporate climate reporting in response to the SEC's Guidance has improved—at best—marginally. Still, the vast majority of financial reporting on climate change does not meet SEC requirements.

- Most companies are not discussing company specific material information and are not quantifying risks or past impacts. Most are briefly discussing climate change using boilerplate language of minimal utility to investors, providing few materials details about climate risks and opportunities facing them.

Source: Governance Research Digest, July 2014 (Vol. 5, No. 7)

2.4.15 Corporate Water Disclosure Guidelines: Towards a Common Approach to Report Water Issues

Author(s): The CEO Water Mandate in collaboration with CDP, Global Reporting Initiative, PricewaterhouseCoopers, and World Resources Institute

The CEO Water Mandate in collaboration with CDP, Global Reporting Initiative, PricewaterhouseCoopers, and World Resources Institute developed a set of guidelines aimed to harmonize reporting approaches, minimizing reporting burdens so companies spend less time on different reports and more time actively managing water. The Corporate Water Disclosure Guidelines: Towards a Common Approach to Report Water Issues is the product of a multi-year, highly-collaborative effort, informed not only by project partners with expertise in water resources and corporate reporting, but also by business representatives, civil society organizations, and UN agencies.

Key findings

Disclosure supports a more sustainable and equitable management of water resources by improving the ability of stakeholder audiences to evaluate a company's water practices and make comparisons across companies. It thus fosters greater corporate accountability.

- Disclosure can support business viability in many ways, including:
- Improving a company's understanding of its water risks, opportunities, and impacts and the effectiveness of its responses
- Providing an opportunity to demonstrate progress and good practices to external stakeholders, thereby improving the company's reputation and building investor confidence
- Establishing a dialogue and building credibility with key stakeholders, paving the way for future partnerships that advance shared water-related goals
- Water disclosure can serve a number of functions. It can:
- Act as the foundation of a standalone report on the company's water management activities
- Serve as a component of broader sustainability reports
- Inform the company's financial filings
- Augment information on company websites
- Be a starting point for dialogue with company stakeholders.

Source: Governance Research Digest, December 2014 (Vol. 5, No. 12)

2.5 External Monitoring and Assurance

2.5.1 The Impact of External Monitoring and Public Reporting on Business Performance in a Global Manufacturing Industry

Author(s): J.P. Katz, E. Higgins, M. Dickson, M. Eckman.

This study examines the importance of external monitoring and public reporting on the performance of firms in the global apparel industry. The authors focus on the impact of details released by a third party monitor for company's financial performance and stock market reaction.

Key findings

The external monitoring of business activities reduces the level of unknown information (which can threaten an organization's reputation) allowing society to more accurately assess business reputation and determine risks associated with valuing the firm.

- External monitors also act as a check on managerial control in firms with a dispersed ownership structure.
- The authors note that, in some instances, some firms experienced negative rates of return in response to monitoring announcements. They account for this in terms of media coverage that included claims from experts and activists who did not feel that the monitoring went far enough.
- Stakeholders may pull their investments from markets when they see brands at risk from association with poor performance, such as poor working conditions in apparel factories.
- The authors suggest that reports of standards violations worry investors in the short term, but company credibility and value increase with continued involvement in compliance related activities and a history of transparent reporting.
- Also, investors may recognize that external monitoring may have some initial cost but will improve performance in the long term.

Source: CSR Research Digest, June 2010 (Vol. 2, No. 6)

2.5.2 Beyond Transparency: Information Overload and a Model for Intelligibility

Author(s): R.L. Laud, D.H. Schepers

This paper presents a new model that contributes to improving the quality of corporate information by providing not more but better information through increasing its intelligibility. Using examples from a number of forward-thinking firms that have found alternative means to provide better information and strengthen their companies, the authors offer a stakeholder-centric model (SCM) for improving information intelligibility.

Key findings

The implementation and incorporation of external stakeholders in company operations and reporting, as featured in the proposed model, provides the added benefit of reputational enhancement.

- By already using intelligible external input from social responsibility groups, firms such as Dow Chemical, Xerox, and McDonald's have accrued benefits beyond those of their competitors who have had a more internal singular focus.
- Social movements, activists and NGOs are invited to provide inputs to the model.
- Although it may seen counterintuitive to invite watchdog groups to comment on internal documents, these groups can provide valuable insights and assist in the distribution of more reliable and useful information.
- For example, toy company Mattel regularly invites the International Center for Corporate Accountability (ICCA) to audit its overseas subcontractors to provide third-party assurance that subcontractors have safe plants and employees are treated according to Mattel's guidelines.
- Many organisations could optimise coordination among the internal reporting functions and external stakeholder-oriented groups much like consumer goods companies link internal marketing functions with external research.
- The SCM model also provides benefits by leveraging reputational assets and potentially reducing liability "tax", and lowering the cost of capital.

- Increased intelligibility increases other stakeholder benefits as well – among them increased reliability of information, comprehensive firm data and the potential for greater financial returns.
- Through the SCM model, stakeholders receive a more comprehensive view of the firm, which, in turn, would prompt organisations to set higher standards.
- By gaining the additional insights offered by the proposed model, the authors suggest that company information processors, including directors, firm management and auditors, will have a better and broader sense of the firm's real financial position and overall risk exposure.
- External input groups can provide an important check and balance on both how the information is processed and what it is intended to demonstrate in an unintelligible format.
- The model also offers scope for improving corporate governance, ethics and transparency. Adding intelligibility to reported information should increase the drive to better governance and more ethical behaviour.

Source: Governance Research Digest, December 2009 (Vol. 1, No. 12)

2.5.3 Multinationals' Accountability on Sustainability: The Evolution of Third-party Assurance of Sustainability Reports

Author(s): P. Perego and A. Kolk

This article explores how multinational corporations (MNCs) adopt assurance practices to develop and sustain organizational accountability for sustainability. Using a panel of Fortune Global 250 firms over a period of 10 years, authors document the diffusion patterns of third-party assurance of sustainability reports.

Key findings

The results illustrate great variability in the adoption of assurance practices in the formative stages of this novel market.

- The descriptive analysis indicates the relevance of external institutional pressures as well as internal resources and capabilities as underlying factors driving the adoption of assurance.

- The evidence also suggests that several MNCs project a decoupled or symbolic image of accountability through assurance, thereby undermining the credibility of these verification practices.
- The paper contributes to the emerging literature on international accountability standards and emphasizes the need to enhance theory-based, cross-disciplinary knowledge related to auditing and accountability processes for sustainability.

Source: Governance Research Digest, September 2012 (Vol. 3, No. 9)

2.5.4 Trends in External Assurance of Sustainability Reports – Spotlight on the USA

Author(s): GRI in collaboration with Bloomberg LP and G&A Institute

GRI in collaboration with Bloomberg LP and G&A Institute launched a special US study showcasing trends on assurance of sustainability information. GRI did this by means of a webinar with over a 100 attendees. The 'Trends in External Assurance of Sustainability Reports – Spotlight on the USA' study was undertaken in order to shed light on which companies utilize assurance providers for their sustainability reporting and their reasons for doing so.

<u>Key findings</u>

In the USA, only 10% (26 out of 269) of GRI-based sustainability reports obtained external assurance in 2011.

- The international percentage is much higher at 38%.
- GRI's Sustainability Reporting Guidelines, introduced the Application Level system with A, B and C indicating the level of transparency of the report.
- Most assured reports (in this report, those designated with a "+" symbol) in the USA in 2011 are Application Level B GRI-based sustainability reports.
- Globally, these were more likely to be on the highest level of transparency, namely Application Level A reports.
- Some of the 26 assured reports contained more than one assurance statement; 30 assurance statements were identified.

- The 30 assurance statements identified (from reports designated with a "+" symbol) were performed by different assurance providers: accountancy, engineering or professional service firms.

Source: Governance Research Digest, January 2014 (Vol. 5, No. 1)

2.5.5   Green Quadrant: Sustainability Assurance (Global)

Author(s): Verdantix

Verdantix issued their third benchmark of sustainability assurance providers. The report, Green Quadrant: Sustainability Assurance (Global), identifies 29 notable providers of sustainability assurance and compares them against 63 assessment criteria.

Key findings

Bureau Veritas, Deloitte, DNV, EY, KPMG and PricewaterhouseCoopers (PwC) are the six leading suppliers of sustainability assurance.

- Increased scrutiny of environmental, social and governance disclosures in financial and sustainability reports will require Fortune 500 firms to seek much more comprehensive assurance of their sustainability data and controls in 2014.
- The six market leaders have established market positions ahead of other firms due to their:
- Long client lists across all sectors and geographies. Leading firms provide an assurance statement for at least 100 sustainability reports annually. For example, Bureau Veritas has assured the reporting of AstraZeneca, Lukoil, Nestlé and Network Rail.
- Broad service offerings that integrate many expertise areas. Financial audit firms staff assurance teams with experts from their audit practices, sustainability consulting teams and industry practice groups — meeting the buying criteria of complex, global corporations.
- Commitment to shaping market standards. The leaders shape the market through the technical committees and working groups of organizations such as the CDP, the Global Reporting Initiative, the International Accounting Standards Board, and the International Integrated Reporting Council.

- Long-running marketing programs to drive awareness. The Big Four financial audit firms in particular have published numerous thought leadership reports on sustainability reporting and assurance to help corporations understand the value of assurance.
- Innovation for product and supply chain sustainability. DNV earned the top score for product sustainability assurance. It has invested in product water footprints as well as creating its own standard, ProSustain, against which clients can have their management system or products certified.

Source: Governance Research Digest, February 2014 (Vol. 5, No. 2)

2.5.6   The 2013 Ratings Survey: Polling the Experts

Author(s): GlobeScan and SustainAbility

GlobeScan and SustainAbility conducted a survey that took the pulse of experts from around the world on topics including rating credibility, drivers of such credibility and the importance of ratings in driving improved corporate performance. The aim of the 2013 Ratings Survey: Polling the Experts was to provide perspectives from experts that can help companies, investors and other stakeholders make sense of and get more value from ratings.

Key findings

NGOs are most trusted by experts to judge corporate sustainability performance, but ratings are catching up. Governments and journalists remain least trusted.

- The five most credible ratings remained the same as in 2012, although the order shuffled. The top five in 2013 are CDP, the Dow Jones Sustainability Index, Access to Medicines Index, the FTSE4Good Index Series and oekom Corporate Ratings.
- A number of ratings including Bloomberg, Climate Counts and MSCI ESG Research experienced notable increases in credibility in 2013.
- The most mentioned drivers of credibility are 1) having a positive impact on corporate sustainability performance and 2) focusing on the right issues.

- To improve corporate performance, experts suggest that raters make results fully available to stakeholders and ask more sector-specific questions – two points that were prominent in the third and fourth phases of Rate the Raters.
- Experts are optimistic about the future of ratings: 63% believe they will be more important three years from now in driving improved corporate sustainability performance.

Source: Governance Research Digest, February 2014 (Vol. 5, No. 2)

2.6 Reporting Systems

2.6.1 Rate the Raters: The Necessary Future of Ratings

Author(s): SustainAbility

Rate the Raters is a fourphase research program in which SustainAbility is working to better understand the universe of corporate sustainability ratings in order to influence and improve their quality and transparency. In this phase four paper it was elected, in part based on the counsel of the advisory panel and sponsors, to succinctly present a vision for the future of ratings along with concrete recommendations for change.

Key findings

There will be greater demand for fewer, higher quality ratings in the future.

- We will likely see further growth and diversification in ratings over the next few years, particularly in relatively new markets (e.g. India), as organizations continue to experiment with new approaches and business models.
- Ultimately the market will settle on a few "winners" in different ratings types.
- For example there will be a small number of consumer-facing, broad sustainability rankings, a few water ratings, etc.
- Quality will be the key driver in determining which ratings survive, and those which do will have greater resources to invest in people, training, quality management and other areas that will result in better ratings (thus creating a virtuous circle).

- In the future, we envision a more clearly segmented ratings value chain, with a small handful of players specializing in data compilation, others using this data to compete on research and analysis, and others still competing on packaging this research and analysis into rankings and products or services.
- This specialization will bring greater efficiency (for raters and companies) and will allow the different players to hone expertise in distinct arenas.
- It will also foster competition in research and analysis, which from our perspective is the most important link in the value chain.
- Future ratings will need to find the right balance between being consistent and adaptive.
- On the former, companies and users benefit from the certainty that comes with constancy in ratings' methodologies over time — they want the goalposts to remain the same.
- Yet, the sustainability agenda is evolving as our understanding of issues improves, and ratings of corporate sustainability performance should adjust to reflect this.

Source: CSR Research Digest, August 2011 (Vol. 3, No. 8)

2.6.2   Towards Integrated Reporting – Communicating Value in 21st Century

Author(s): International Integrated Reporting Committee

A discussion paper Towards Integrated Reporting – Communicating Value in the 21st Century was released by the International Integrated Reporting Committee. The paper lays out a proposed integrating reporting framework, which focuses on a company's business model.

Key findings

Integrated reporting holds the prospect of removing "clutter" that obscures important information in company reports.

- Corporate reports are long and in many cases getting longer, raising the likelihood that excessive detail will obscure critical information.
- An Integrated Report provides a clear reference point for other communications, including any specific compliance information, such

as investor presentations, detailed financial information, operational data and sustainability information.

- Much of this information might move to an online environment, reducing clutter in the primary report, which will focus only on the matters that the organization considers most material to long-term success.
- Integrated reporting aims to combine the most material elements of information currently reported in separate reporting strands (financial, management commentary, governance and remuneration, and sustainability) in a coherent whole.
- Most importantly integrated reporting shows the connectivity between these elements, and explains how they affect the ability of an organization to create and sustain value in the short, medium and long term.
- The main output of Integrated Reporting is an Integrated Report: a single report that the IIRC anticipates will become an organization's primary report, replacing rather than adding to existing requirements.
- Such a report enables evolving reporting requirements, both market-driven and regulatory, to be organized into a coherent narrative.
- Integrated reporting should provide insights about significant external factors that affect an organization, the resources and relationships used and affected by the organization, and how the business model interacts with both of these to create and sustain value over time.
- The committee argues that five guiding principles underpin the preparation of an integrated report: strategic focus, connectivity of information, future orientation, responsiveness and stakeholder inclusiveness, and conciseness, reliability and materiality.
- The content of an integrated report should include six key elements, the IIRC says: organizational overview and business model; operating context, including risks and opportunities; strategic objectives and strategies to achieve these objectives; governance and remuneration; performance; and future outlook.
- These content elements are fundamentally linked to each other and should be presented in a way that makes the interconnection between them apparent, rather than as isolated, stand-alone sections.
- Many organizations are taking innovative approaches to "aspects of reporting that are often consistent with the concept of Integrated

Reporting.

- These include the 2010 annual report by AkzoNobel, Annual Review and Summarized Financial Information by Sasol, 2010 Annual Report by BHP Billiton and 2010 annual report by Anglo American.
- But few organizations, if any, however, could claim to have achieved the ideal of Integrated Reporting.

Source: CSR Research Digest, October 2011 (Vol. 3, No. 10)

2.6.3   GRI: Inside [and] out

Author(s):: GRI

Following its own guidelines GRI has launched its annual Sustainability Report 2010/11. This year, the report is based on the G3.1 Guidelines and the NGO Sector Supplement – tailored guidance suitable for nonprofit organizations like GRI.

Key findings

Transparency of organizations worldwide is boosted by the work of GRI.

- GRI's biggest impacts are indirect, through the use of its Sustainability Reporting Framework, improving the sustainability and transparency of thousands of organizations worldwide.
- Recent research shows that sustainability reporting is becoming more standard practice, with 95% of the world's 250 biggest companies producing reports on their sustainability performance.
- GRI's Sustainability Report 2010/11 aims to show how GRI's work with its network influences transparency worldwide, focusing on its programs, policy and partnerships.

Source: CSR Research Digest, March 2012 (Vol. 4, No. 3)

2.6.4   GRI Application Levels: Why Strive for an A?

Author(s): BrownFlynn

In the report BrownFlynn defines and examines the underlying structure of the GRI Framework and the differences between the Application Levels. The study demonstrates why companies with a higher Application Level are better able to manage their sustainability impacts and provides evidence of a correlation between a company's GRI Application Level and its reputation for sustainability performance.

Key findings

Companies with a higher Global Reporting Initiative application level are better able to manage their sustainability impacts than those with a lower application level.

- Companies with a GRI application level of A receive an average sustainability rating of 57.4 out of 100 from sustainability ranking aggregator CSRHub.
- Those with an application level of C receive an average sustainability rating of 54.9.
- As GRI application levels relate to transparency rather than sustainability, the consultancy says that at first glance application levels can appear insignificant as a measure of sustainability performance.
- But when looking at the specifics of the required disclosures, implicit quality controls built into GRI application levels facilitate a company's greater commitment to sustainability.
- This in turn encourages high quality disclosures.
- In addition, companies seeking an application level of A or B have to have in place "established policies, procedures, training, goals and internal controls" to manage their sustainability programs.
- A or B companies also enjoy a better reputation for sustainability performance.

Source: CSR Research Digest, May 2012 (Vol. 4, No. 5)

2.6.5   Integrated Reporting Draft Framework Outline

Author(s): IIRC

The International Integrated Reporting Council (IIRC) has released the Draft Outline of its Integrated Reporting Framework. The Outline establishes for the first time the basic structure of the Framework and is intended to keep stakeholders informed as the Framework is developed.

Key findings

The successful company of tomorrow will have an integrated strategy to achieve financial results and create lasting value for itself, its stakeholders and society.

- Clear links must be made between a company's 'single bottom line' and the sustainability impacts caused - or the value created -in generating its financial results.
- The Framework should help those companies producing an integrated report to also integrate sustainability into their strategy.
- The process to establish an internationally accepted Integrated Reporting Framework is in its early days at the IIRC, and has already attracted important players in the corporate reporting field, such as reporting standard
- setters, large auditing companies, accountancy boards, large companies, financial market institutions, and NGOs.
- The new Draft Outline aims to keep stakeholders informed of the likely structure and general content of the Framework as work on its development progresses, taking into account:
- Feedback received on the Discussion Paper;
- Engagement with the Pilot Programme participants, the Investor Network and others;
- Additional research and work being conducted by the IIRC Secretariat.
- Other details on the technical content are expected to be released in late 2012, followed by a draft Framework for public consultation in early to mid-2013.
- 'Version 1.0' of the Framework will be released in late 2013.

Source: CSR Research Digest, August 2012 (Vol. 4, No. 8)

2.6.6   Integrated Reporting: Driving Value

Author(s): Ernst & Young

Ernst & Young's recent report outlines four initial steps that companies should take to implement integrated reporting. In addition, it discusses the benefits and challenges of integrated reporting.

<u>Key findings</u>

Companies aiming to combine financial and nonfinancial material into a single, integrated report should begin by framing their business goals and environmental and social objectives with capital opportunities and risks.

- Once goals have been defined, companies should complete a thorough materiality analysis to determine what integrated reporting risks and opportunities are important to their leadership, investors and stakeholders.
- Their responses should be prioritized to determine material issues and related business strategies.
- The third step is to evaluate integrated reporting best practices and select the methods that best fit that company's particular needs.
- Executives should mirror the quality, processes and controls of these leading companies and organizations.
- Finally, companies should create a road map.
- Begin by prioritizing reporting on the environmental, social and fiscal activities and projects that further the company's ability to create and preserve value.
- The road map should include processes and controls that support credible, high-quality reporting.
- Executives building the road map should engage leadership, investors and stakeholders to prioritize projects that best ensure return on investment and communicate those successes to an outside audience.

Source: CSR Research Digest, December 2012 (Vol. 4, No. 12)

2.6.7 Understanding Transformation: Building the Business Case for Integrated Reporting

Author(s): Black Sun and International Integrated Reporting Council (IIRC)

The report tracks the behavioral changes during the first year of the IIRC's pilot program initiative which aims to help develop an International Integrated Reporting Framework. The pilot program involves more than 80 private and public companies such as Volvo Group, Danone and Microsoft, and 25 institutional investors.

Key findings

Almost 93% of businesses say integrated reporting breaks down barriers between teams and leads to better connected departments.

- 98% agreed that the shift towards integrated reporting leads to a better understanding of how the organization will create value over time.
- 74% agreed that it will lead to more consistency in external communications.
- 93% agreed that it leads to better quality data collection.
- 64% say analysts will benefit significantly from integrated reporting in future.
- 95% say employees will benefit from it in the future.
- 28% report they are already seeing significant benefit to the board from integrated reporting and 56% expect to see significant benefit to the board in future.
- 97% expect a positive benefit overall to the board in the future.

Source: CSR Research Digest, January 2013 (Vol. 5, No. 1)

2.6.8   Event Organizers Sector Supplement

Author(s): GRI

Event organizers can now report on sustainability issues like impacts on communities, natural environments, and local and global economies, thanks to new guidance just published by the GRI. The sustainability reporting guidance, tailored for the events sector, aims to make reporting more relevant for event organizers by defining how to provide qualitative and quantitative information on sustainability issues.

Key findings

The events sector is diverse: its activities range from business meetings, conferences, and exhibitions to sports and cultural festivals -- all of which have impacts on the economy, environment and society.

- These impacts need to be considered, measured and shared in order to improve the sustainability performance of the events industry.
- The Event Organizers Supplement provides organizations in the sector with a tailored version of GRI's Reporting Guidelines.

- It includes the original Guidelines, which set out the Reporting Principles, Disclosures on Management Approach and Performance Indicators for economic, environmental and social issues.
- The Event Organizers Supplement's additional commentaries and Performance Indicators, developed especially for the sector, capture the issues that matter most for event organizers:
  - site selection;
  - transport of attendees;
  - recruiting and training of the event workforce, participants and volunteers;
  - sourcing of materials, supplies and services;
  - managing impacts on communities, natural environments, and local and global economies;
  - planning and managing potential legacies;
  - accessibility of an event.

Source: Governance Research Digest, January 2012 (Vol. 3, No. 1)

2.6.9 The Oil and Gas Sector Supplement

Author(s): GRI

GRI provides sector guidance for the oil and gas industry, enabling oil and gas companies to measure and report their sustainability performance. The Supplement was developed according to a multi-stakeholder process, with experts from oil and gas companies and stakeholder institutions brought together in a Working Group to develop the guidance.

Key findings

Today's new guidance will help companies in the oil and gas sector to report their sustainability performance – including around issues such as environmental management, health and safety and emergency preparedness.

- The Supplement covers the following key issues for the sector, expanded from the Reporting Guidelines:
  - market presence, including local content;
  - volume and characteristics of estimated proved reserves and production;

- o research towards, and amount of renewable energy generated;
- o assessment and monitoring of risks for ecosystem services;
- o policies, programs and processes to involve indigenous communities;
- o existence of emergency preparedness programs;
- o decommissioning of sites due to company's operations.

Source: Governance Research Digest, March 2012 (Vol. 3, No. 3)

2.6.10 Stock Exchange Benchmark on Non-Financial Reporting Rules

Author(s): Verdantix

The Verdantix report "Stock Exchange Benchmark On Non-Financial Reporting Rules" assesses the sustainability disclosure requirements for ten stock exchanges around the world with combined market capitalization of $15 trillion representing more than 15,600 listed firms. The focus is on rules, policies, scope, current status, enforcement, penalties, format and frequency of non-financial reporting.

Key findings

Despite widespread praise for the introduction of new environmental and social reporting requirements none of the stock exchanges operates demanding green reporting rules.

- Rules on social responsibility disclosures are prominent in emerging economies like India where investment in extractive industries can have significant impacts on local communities
- Integrated reporting of financial and sustainability performance has been spearheaded in South Africa by the King Code of Governance Principles
- Broader reporting of material environmental and social risks has been driven up the agenda by the Australian Corporate Governance Principles and Recommendations
- National legislation requiring environmental disclosures in the French market requires firms listed on NYSE Euronext to report against 42 Environment, Social and Governance indicators

- From April 2013, 1,800 firms listed on the London Stock Exchange must disclose GHG emissions data due to a new UK government regulation implemented by the LSE.

Source: Governance Research Digest, December 2012 (Vol. 3, No. 12)

2.6.11 Sustainability Reporting Platform

Author(s): PE International

PE International released the next generation of its SoFi software platform, SoFi 5 '13 Release, to help sustainability novices and mid-sized companies advance from spread sheet use to a faster and more reliable process for sustainability data aggregation, validation, analysis and reporting. For organizations with mature sustainability programs in place that are looking to further improve, the SoFi 5 '13 Release also offers configurable features including new modules for sustainability performance management, EHS reporting, and fully automated data capture from enterprise systems.

Key findings

The new SoFi 5 '13 Release was designed to deliver faster, more accurate data aggregation through efficient workflows and a wide range of options for automated data input, direct system integration with ERP and Building Management Systems, Smart Meters and more.

The new modules in the SoFi 5 '13 Release include:
- SoFi Environmental Health & Safety Management
  - It adds incident reporting, compliance and audit management capabilities to the platform.
  - Developed in collaboration with SoFi clients from the pharmaceuticals, technology and utility sectors, the new module enables EH&S managers to streamline reporting and automatically calculate common KPIs such as accident frequency/severity rates.
  - It also helps to identify potential risks and cases of non-compliance that need immediate attention as well as plan and manage audits of ISO 14001 environmental management systems or suppliers.
- SoFi Sustainability Performance Management
  - It fulfills the advanced data mining, modeling and forecasting needs of power users.

- The SoFi performance visualization is now integrated with new scenario and trend analysis capabilities and an extended best practice project library to further assist sustainability planning and risk assessment.
- These upgrades make it easier for users to identify trends and relationships in sustainability data to better forecast future performance.
- SoFi Connection Center
  - It meets complex requirements for data exchange between the SoFi platform and an organization's existing IT infrastructure.

Source: Governance Research Digest, June 2013 (Vol. 4, No. 6)

2.6.12 US Health Care Sustainability Accounting Standards

Author(s): US Sustainable Accounting Standards Board (SASB)

The US Sustainable Accounting Standards Board (SASB) has developed sustainability accounting standards to help publicly listed corporations report sustainability issues to investors and the public. The new sector-specific SASB provisional standards are aimed at industries in the health care sector, including biotechnology, pharmaceuticals, medical equipment and supplies, health care delivery, health care distributors and managed care.

Key findings

For the biotech and pharmaceuticals industries, companies must disclose ways they offer medicines to high-priority countries, recalls, unused product takebacks and safety issues, such as adverse side effects.

- Companies must discuss clinical trial safety protocols and any legal or regulatory fines or settlements therein.
- They must divulge how product prices compare to the Consumer Price Index.
- Fines or settlements for false advertising, corruption and poor manufacturing practices also must be revealed, while employee recruitment, retention and training programs must be elucidated.
- Product traceability, manufacturing energy and water use, and waste procedures also are measured.

- Other sustainability topics for the biotech and pharmaceutical standards address supply chain management, consumer access, safety, employee relations, marketing, pricing, corruption, counterfeiting and natural resource and energy conservation.
- These companies also must share their strategies for facilitating access for low-income patients, including alternative pricing mechanisms, billing and pricing frameworks.
- Patient privacy procedures must meet a high standard.
- Employee turnover and talent recruitment and retention strategies also are assessed, as are incidents of fines and settlements for Medicare and Medicaid fraud.
- In the environmental arena, energy use and waste generation are evaluated, while companies must reveal strategies for how climate change risks may affect business operations.
- Both the health care delivery and managed care subsectors must discuss access, privacy, transparency, fraud, employee relations, improved outcomes, plan literacy and performance, energy and waste efficiency, and climate change impacts on human health.

Source: Governance Research Digest, September 2013 (Vol. 4, No. 9)

2.6.13 Beverage Industry Environmental Roundtable (BIER) Sector Guidance for GHG reporting

Author(s): Beverage Industry Environmental Roundtable (BIER)

Beverage Industry Environmental Roundtable (BIER) has released a sector guidance for greenhouse gas emissions reporting whose goal is to achieve alignment on the different value chain elements, per beverage category. The document is aligned with the protocols developed by World Business Council for Sustainable Development (WBCSD) and World Resources Institute (WRI): the GHG Protocol (most widely used international accounting tool for enterprise-level reporting), the Corporate Value Chain (Scope 3) Accounting and Reporting Standard (allows to assess the entire value chain emissions impact and identify the most effective ways to reduce emissions) and the Product Life Cycle Accounting and Reporting Standard (used to understand the full life cycle emissions of a product and focus efforts on the greatest GHG reduction opportunities).

Key findings

- The beverage industry can be proactive by inventorying and reporting GHG emissions in a way that will help to meet growing demands from key organizations and stakeholders, such as:
- Governments that seek to regulate and provide incentives for businesses to reduce their GHG footprints;
- Influential beverage customers that have begun to engage their suppliers for GHG emissions accounting;
- Individual consumers who are increasingly aware of the environmental impacts of the products they purchase and of the businesses that provide them.
- Consumers can choose, and are choosing, to buy environmentally-friendly products and to avoid companies that are less sensitive to reducing their environmental footprint;
- Trade organizations that represent a broader base of companies active in the beverage industry.
- While the Beverage Industry Sector Guidance for Greenhouse Gas Emissions Reporting allows for a consistent approach to identifying life cycle impacts, this guidance is not designed to be used to directly compare products.
- Its purpose is to clarify the perspective of the industry as to what is included in GHG emission reporting and how boundaries are set.
- The Beverage Industry Sector Guidance for Greenhouse Gas Emissions Reporting is organized as follows:
- Section 1, Alignment with Recognized Protocols. Reviews the major protocols and evaluates their application to the beverage industry.
- Section 2, Approaches to Emissions Estimation and Reporting. Includes the Enterprise Inventory Approach, which defines specifics and calculation methods relating to the calculation of an enterprise inventory of GHG emissions; also includes Product Carbon Footprint Approach, which defines specifics and calculation methods relating to the calculation of a product carbon footprint.
- Section 3, Beverage Sector Value Chain Overview.
- Section 4, Data Reporting. Provides data reporting guidelines with emphasis on the calibration of reports to ensure industry consistency.
- Section 5, Individual Beverage Category Alignment.

- Section 6, Glossary.
- Section 7, Appendices.

Source: Governance Research Digest, February 2014 (Vol. 5, No. 2)

2.6.14 G4 Guidelines and ISO 26000 in conjunction

Author(s): GRI

Global Reporting Initiative published a linkage document that relates the social responsibility guidance given in ISO 26000 to the reporting guidance provided by GRI. The publication, GRI G4 Guidelines and ISO 26000: 2010 How to use the GRI G4 Guidelines and ISO 26000 in conjunction provides cross-references between the two documents – enabling organizations to take advantage of the synergies and complementarities that the two initiatives share.

Key findings

- Both GRI G4 and ISO 26000 guidelines cover the most common economic, environmental and social topics and impacts that ought to be addressed by organizations. However, while ISO 26000 is intended to give guidance on the actions and expectations for organisations to address each of these topics, the GRI Guidelines provide guidance on what to report for each of these topics specifically.
- Both GRI and ISO 26000 define two steps for identifying what are the relevant topics and prioritizing the most important ones. In the first step, both standards use the term 'relevance', but in the second step, GRI uses the term 'materiality' while ISO 26000 uses the term 'significance'.
- GRI uses the terms 'relevance' and 'materiality' in the context of reporting and communication to identify the issues that are important enough to be reported on.
- ISO 26000 uses the terms 'relevance' and 'significance' for identifying issues to be managed, improved and communicated.
- ISO 26000 calls for communication on the performance of social responsibility of organisations and GRI's Guidelines provide a comprehensive set of Standard Disclosures for organizations to report on their performance against implementing ISO 26000 and against its core subjects.

- However, it is important to note that the GRI Standard Disclosures related to the clauses of ISO 26000 should not be understood as the only nor the complete set of disclosures required satisfying the scope of each particular ISO clause.

Source: Governance Research Digest, May 2014 (Vol. 5, No. 5)

2.6.15 Ready to Report? Introducing Sustainability Reporting for SMEs

Author(s): GRI

GRI launched a new booklet aimed at SMEs who are considering whether sustainability reporting is relevant for them, and how they can start the reporting process in a realistic way that relates to their own context and circumstances. The publication, Ready to Report? Introducing Sustainability Reporting for SMEs provides a simple introduction to sustainability reporting (using the GRI G4 Guidelines) in order to help SMEs take the first small steps in their sustainability journey and it focuses on the relevance and value of reporting for SMEs and GRI Reporting Process for SMEs.

Key findings

- Section A looks at the internal and external benefits of sustainability reporting based on the experiences and testimonies of SMEs that GRI has engaged with in a number of projects since 2008. This section is intended to make the case for sustainability reporting for SMEs.
- Section B details the steps for creating a GRI sustainability report using the five phase GRI model for a sustainability reporting. It introduces five steps to preparing a sustainability report process and also includes proposals for actions that a company can undertake to address its sustainability impacts and the plans needed to support these actions.

Source: Governance Research Digest, May 2014 (Vol. 5, No. 5)

2.6.16 Realizing the Benefits: The Impact of Integrated Reporting

Author(s): The Black Sun, in partnership with the International Integrated Reporting Council (IIRC)

The Black Sun, in partnership with the International Integrated Reporting Council (IIRC), conducted research that highlights the significant positive impact of Integrated Reporting on those businesses who have taken a lead on making their corporate reporting and thinking fit for purpose. The study, Realizing the Benefits: The Impact of Integrated Reporting was conducted with participants of the three year IIRC Pilot Programme – a network of 140 influential businesses such as HSBC and Marks & Spencers, and investors from 26 countries that have helped the IIRC develop and test the International Integrated Reporting Framework, building on earlier research from 2012.

Key findings

As organisations work together differently and use new information to assess their performance there have been important breakthroughs in organisations' understanding and articulation of how they create and destroy value – 92% say it has improved understanding.

- As the understanding of value creation changes, decision making changes - 79% report improvements. These are largely attributed to changes in management information, particularly information provided to boards, with many noting that the most important benefit they experienced was a change in conversations between the board and management – 78% see more collaborative thinking about goals and targets by the board, executives and strategy departments
- 84% see a current benefit regarding data quality
- 65% see a current benefit of better long term decision making
- 68% see a better understanding of the business risks and opportunities

Source: Governance Research Digest, December 2014 (Vol. 5, No. 12)

III.   ETHICAL BEHAVIOUR

3.1   General Rankings, Awards and Benchmarks

3.1.1   Corporate Ethics Ranking

Author(s): Covalence

Covalence has released a corporate ethics ranking which reviews the actions of companies from 2002 up to 31 December 2009. 581 multinational companies across 18 industry sectors are featured in the ranking.

<u>Key findings</u>

IBM and Intel Corp (from the technology sector) and HSBC Holdings (banking) top the ranking for the whole of 2009.

- These three leaders are followed by: Marks and Spencer; Unilever; Xerox; General Electric; Cisco Systems; Dell Inc.; Procter & Gamble.
- Environmental initiatives, eco-innovative products and social sponsorships have enabled companies to generate positive coverage in 2009.
- Issues related to downsizing, CO_2 emissions and working conditions caused the most criticisms.
- The most active criteria in 2009 were, among positive news: Environmental Impact of Production (15% of all positive news), Eco Innovative Product (12%), Social Sponsorship (12%), and Information to Consumers (4%).
- On the negative side, the most active criteria were: Downsizing (23%), Environmental
- Impact of Production (10%), Labour Standards (10%), and Wages (8%).
- Of the most recently included companies, the best ranked are: Sodexo (Travel & Leisure), Mitsubishi Electric Corporation (Industrial Goods & Services), and Visa Inc. (Financial Services).

- New companies appearing at the bottom of the ranking are: Philip Morris International Inc. (Personal & Household Goods), Hess Corporation (Oil & Gas), and Mega Financial Holding Co. Ltd (Financial Services).

Source: CSR Research Digest, March 2010 (Vol. 2, No. 3)

3.1.2 Ethical Reputation Ranking

Author(s): Covalence

Ethical reputation organization, Covalence, has released its report for the first quarter of 2010. Covalence analyses data from 581 companies across 18 sectors in its quarterly reports, and the data informing this report spans the five years from 2005-2010 (March).

Key findings

The top ten leaders across all sectors are: (1) IBM Corp., (2) Intel Corp., (3) Cisco Systems, Inc., (4) HSBC Holdings plc, (5) Unilever, (6) Marks and Spencer Group plc, (7) General Electric Co., (8) Pepsico Inc., (9) Xerox Corp., (10) Dell, Inc.

- Sector Leaders
  - Automobiles and Parts: BMW Group
  - Banks: HSBC Holdings
  - Basic Resources: Alcoa Inc.
  - Chemicals: DuPont
  - Construction and Materials: Holcim
  - Financial Services: American Express
  - Food & Beverages: Unilever
  - Health Care: GlaxoSmithKline
  - Industrial Goods & Services: General Electric
  - Insurance: Swiss Re
  - Media: Walt Disney Co.
  - Oil & Gas: Suncor Energy Inc.
  - Personal & Household Goods: Procter & Gamble
  - Retail: Marks & Spencer
  - Technology: IBM
  - Telecommunications: AT&T Inc.
  - Travel and Leisure: Starbucks

o   Utilities: PG&E Corp.

Source: CSR Research Digest, May 2010 (Vol. 2, No. 5)

3.1.3   Annual Ethical Companies Ranking

Author(s): Covalence

Covalence has published its annual ethical ranking. The findings cover an enlarged group of 541 multinationals over 18 sectors. The data used to build the ranking covers the period 2002-2008.

Key findings

The overall leaders this year are HSBC, Intel and Unilever. Also in the top ten are Marks & Spencer, Xerox, Alcoa Inc., Rio Tinto, General Electric, Dell Computer and DuPont.

- New entrants to the top ten are Xerox in fifth place, General Electric in eighth and DuPont in tenth.
- They replace IBM which slips to 14th, Hewlett Packard that falls to 30th, and Toyota that falls to 34th.

Leaders Across Sectors	
Automobiles & Parts	Nissan Motor
Banks	HSBC Holdings
Basic Resources	Alcoa, Inc.
Chemicals	DuPont
Construction & Materials	Holcim
Financial Services	Goldman Sachs
Food & Beverages	Unilever
Health Care	GlaxoSmithKline
Industrial Goods & Services	General Electric
Insurance	Swiss Re
Media	Pearson PLC
Oil & Gas	Petrobras
Personal & Household Goods	Sony
Retail	Marks & Spencer
Technology	Intel Corp.
Telecommunication	Vodafone

Travel & Leisure	Starbucks
Utilities	PG&E Corp

- The most active criteria in 2008 have been: Environmental impact of production, Social sponsorship, Waste management, Information to consumer, Eco-innovative product, International presence, Downsizing, Product environmental risk, Labour standards, and Anti-corruption policy.

Source: Governance Research Digest, February 2009 (Vol. 1, No. 2)

3.1.4   Global Companies Ethical Ranking

Author(s): Covalence

Covalence has published the results of its ethical ranking for the first quarter of 2009. The ranking covers a total of 541 multinationals over 18 industry sectors.

<u>Key findings</u>

New entrants to the top ten are IBM (3rd) and Cisco Systems (9th), replacing DuPont (which fell to 11th) and Rio Tinto (13th).

- During Q1 of 2009, the following criteria have gained importance, relative to Q4 of 2008: international presence, wages, eco innovative product, downsizing, anti-corruption policy.

Leaders Across Sectors			
1	Intel Corp.	6	Alcoa Inc.
2	HSBC Holdings	7	Dell Inc.
3	IBM	8	Xerox
4	Unilever	9	Cisco Systems
5	Marks & Spencer	10	General Electric

Sector Leaders			
Automobiles & Parts	Honda Motor	*Insurance*	Swiss Re
Banks	HSBC Holdings	*Media*	Walt Disney Co.
Basic Resources	Alcoa, Inc.	*Oil & Gas*	Statoil Hydro

Chemicals	DuPont	Retail	Marks & Spencer
Construction & Materials	Holcim	Personal & Household Goods	Proctor & Gamble
Financial Services	Goldman Sachs	Technology	Intel Group
Food & Beverages	Unilever	Telecommunications	Vodafone
Healthcare	Bristol Myers Squibb	Travel & Leisure	Starbucks
Industrial Goods & Services	General Electric	Utilities	PG&E Corp.

Source: Governance Research Digest, April 2009 (Vol. 1, No. 4)

3.1.5 World's Most Ethical Companies

Author(s): Ethisphere

Ethisphere has released its 2009 list of the world's most ethical companies. This year 99 companies make the list. Twenty companies have been removed and 25 appear for the first time. 44 companies are "threepeats" making the list every year for the last three years.

Key findings

Sector	Company (Country)
Aerospace/ Defence	Honeywell International (US); Aerospace Corporation (US); Harris Corporation (US).
Apparel	Nike (US); Patagonia (US).
Automotive	BMW (Germany); Cummins (US); Johnson Controls (US); Toyota Motor (Japan).
Banking	HSBC (UK); Rabobank (Netherlands); Standard Chartered Bank (UK); Westpac Banking Corporation (Australia)
Business Services	Accenture (Bermuda); Pitney Bowes (US); Dun & Bradstreet (US).
Chemicals	Ecolab (US).
Computer Hardware	Dell (US); Hewlett-Packard (US); Ricoh Company

	(Japan); Xerox (US);Oracle (US); Salesforce.com (US); Symantec (US).
Consumer Products	Henkel (Germany); Kao (Japan); Mattel (US); SC Johnson & Son (US); Unilever (UK/Netherlands).
Diversified Industries	General Electric (US).
Electronics and Semiconductors	Freescale Semiconductor(US); Intel (US); Texas Instruments (US).
Energy and Utilities	Duke Energy (US); FPL Group (US); Sempra Energy (US); Statkraft (Norway); Wisconsin Energy (US).
Engineering and Construction	CRH (Ireland); Fluor (US); CH2M Hill (US); Holcim (Switzerland).
Environmental Services and Equipment	Waste Management (US).
Financial Services	American Express (US); Hartford Financial Services (US); The Principal Financial Group (US).
Food and Beverage	Danone (France); General Mills (US); Kellogg Company (US); PepsiCo (US); Stonyfield Farm (US).
Food Service	Sodexo (France).
Food Stores	Safeway (US); Trader Joe's (US).
Forestry, Paper, Packaging	International Paper (US); Stora Enso (Finland); Svenska Cellulosa (SCA)(Sweden); Weyerhaeuser (US).
General Retail	Target (US).
Healthcare	Cleveland Clinic (US); Johns Hopkins Hospital (US); Premier (US).
Hotels, Travel, Hospitality	Accor (France); Marriot International (US).
Industrial Manufacturing	Caterpillar (US); Eaton Corporation (US); John Deere (US); Milliken (US); Rockwell Automation (US).
Insurance	Aflac (US); Sompo (Japan); Swiss Re

	(Switzerland).
Internet	Google (US); Zappos.com (US).
Media, Publishing, Entertainment	Thomson Reuters (Canada); Time Warner (US).
Medical Devices	Baxter International (US); Becton Dickinson (US); Royal Philips (Netherlands).
Oil and Gas	Flint Hills Resources (US); Petro-Canada (Canada).
Pharma and Biotech	AstraZeneca (UK/Sweden); Novartis (Switzerland); Novo Nordisk (Denmark); Novozymes (Denmark).
Real Estate	Jones Lang LaSalle (US).
Restaurants and Cafes	McDonald's (US);Starbucks (US).
Speciality Retail	Best Buy (US); Gap (US); IKEA (Sweden); Marks & Spencer (UK); Ten Thousand Villages (US).
Telecom Hardware	Avaya (US); Cisco Systems (US).
Telecom Services	T-Mobile (US); Vodafone (UK).
Transportation and Logistics	Nippon Yusen Kaisha (Japan); UPS (US).

Source: Governance Research Digest, June 2009 (Vol. 1, No. 6)

3.1.6   2011 World's Most Ethical Companies

Author(s): Ethisphere

The Ethisphere Institute announced its fifth annual selection of the World's Most Ethical Companies. Ethisphere highlights 110 organizations that lead the way in promoting ethical business standards – companies that go beyond legal minimums, introduce innovative ideas benefiting the public and force their competitors to follow suit.

<u>Key findings</u>

The World's Most Ethical ("WME") Companies prove a clear correlation between ethical business practices and improved financial performance.

- WME companies, if indexed together, have routinely and significantly outpaced the S&P 500 every year since the recognition was developed in 2007.
- On average, the WME companies outperformed the S&P 500 by 7.3% each year.
- The 2011 World's Most Ethical Companies have already surpassed the S&P 500 year to date.
- A record number of nominations and applications from companies this year is evidence of both the award's growing prominence and companies' desire to be acknowledged for their high ethical standards.
- The 2011 list is the largest since the award's inception in 2007.
- Of the 110 companies honored this year, 74 are returners from the 2010 list.
- An increasing number of global companies are also placing added emphasis on their ethical standards, with 42 winners coming from outside of the United States, including six from Japan.
- The list also features 36 first time winners, including eBay, Hitachi Data Systems, Adidas, Stonyfield Farm and Singapore Telecom.
- eBay Inc. is honored to be included in this year's impressive list of Ethisphere's World's Most Ethical Companies.
- eBay was founded on the belief that strangers could trust and connect with one another through global commerce.

Source: Governance Research Digest, May 2011 (Vol. 2, No. 1)

3.1.7   American Business Ethics Award

Author(s): Foundation for Financial Service Professionals

The Foundation for Financial Service Professionals recently announced company recipients of the 2011 American Business Ethics Award (ABEA). ABEA recognizes companies that exemplify high standards of ethical behavior in their everyday business conduct and in response to specific crises or challenges.

Key findings

Kimberly-Clark Corporation was announced as the large company recipient of the 2011 American Business Ethics Award.

- Kimberly-Clark's ethical way of life is rooted in core values that require authenticity, accountability, innovation and caring as the driving influence in all its business decisions, transactions and initiatives.
- Conducting business in accordance with these core values starts at the top and carries through to each of the 57,000 Kimberly-Clark employees, whether those employees are based in the United States, China, Australia, South Africa, Brazil or any other of the 36 corporate locations the company maintains worldwide.
- Kimberly-Clark's code of conduct, which is available in 27 languages, focuses on the higher standard of doing the right thing, not just that which is legally required.
- To stress the importance of living by this code, Kimberly-Clark requires formal training, team leader coaching and publishes "Ethical Moments," a series of articles that focus solely on the ethical dilemmas the company's employees may encounter in the workplace.
- Other recipients of the 2011 American Business Ethics Award were Corgan Associates (midsized company) and the Eye & Laser Center (small company).

Source: Governance Research Digest, November 2011 (Vol. 2, No. 7)

3.1.8   2013 Ethics & Compliance Leadership Survey Report

Author(s): LRN Knowledge Service Provider

LRN Knowledge Service Provider released their sixth annual report that uncovers the key drivers of effectiveness in E&C programs with the Program Effectiveness Index (PEI), a benchmark for evaluating which program factors are most highly correlated with ethical employee behaviors and reduced employee misconduct. The findings of '2013 Ethics & Compliance Leadership Survey Report' are based on an in-depth survey of more than 180 ethics and compliance leaders from across industries and geographies.

Key findings

More than 80% of respondents see business performance and value creation as the greatest benefits of an ethical culture, surpassing compliance for the first time.

- Goals matter when building an effective Ethics and Compliance program.
- The E&C Leadership Survey Report finds that programs with the primary mandate of "ensuring ethical behavior and alignment of decision-making and conduct with core values" score higher on the Program Effectiveness Index than those focused solely on "ensuring compliance with rules and regulations."
- The majority of executives surveyed feel that data privacy (74%), conflicts of interest (70%), electronic data protection (68%), and bribery and corruption (62%) are 2013's top ethics and compliance risks.
- Social media is also now considered a top risk by 41% of E&C leaders.

Source: Governance Research Digest, August 2013 (Vol. 4, No. 8)

3.1.9 The 2013 Ethics and Compliance Hotline Benchmark Report

Author(s): NAVEX Global

NAVEX Global issued a report that shares the latest 2012 trends and benchmarking data from the NAVEX Global reporting database—the largest database of its kind in the world. 'The 2013 Ethics and Compliance Hotline Benchmark Report' is a resource that can be used to benchmark your compliance program against industry standards and provide actionable insights into policy management, training, awareness, and more.

Key findings

The last few years have seen a rise in the reporting rate.

- This rise in reporting may be due to:
  1. Increasing sophistication of ethics and compliance programs' communications and training strategies
  2. Involvement and accountability of the board and executive leadership
  3. Media coverage of whistle blower lawsuits and awards
  4. Encouragement from government officials to report observed misconduct

- Despite the potential bias against anonymous allegations among some leaders and even some investigators, the gap in average overall substantiation rate between allegations made by reporters has remained at 7% or less over the last four years, indicating that such reports are valuable and credible.
- Helpline/hotline data that is carefully tracked, reviewed, benchmarked, and presented with sufficient context often provides the early warning signs needed to detect, prevent, and resolve problems.

Source: Governance Research Digest, December 2013 (Vol. 4, No. 12)

3.1.10 World's Most Ethical Companies

Author(s): The Ethisphere Institute

The Ethisphere Institute, an independent center of research promoting best practices in corporate ethics and compliance, announced today the selection of the 2014 World's Most Ethical Companies. The World's Most Ethical Company designation recognizes companies that truly go beyond making statements about doing business ethically and translate those words into action.

<u>Key findings</u>

This year's 144 honorees represent 41 industries and include 21 first-time honorees. In this eighth year of recognizing companies, Ethisphere is honoring the largest group of organizations based outside the U.S. – 38 organizations from 21 countries and 5 continents.

- The World's Most Ethical Company assessment is based upon the Ethisphere Institute's Ethics Quotient™ framework. The Ethics Quotient framework has been developed over years of effort to provide a means to assess an organization's performance in an objective, consistent and standardized way.
- Scores are generated in five key categories: ethics and compliance program (25%), reputation, leadership and innovation (20%), governance (10%), corporate citizenship and responsibility (25%), and culture of ethics (20%).

Source: Governance Research Digest, April 2014 (Vol. 5, No. 4)

3.2   Sectoral Reviews

3.2.1   Banking Sector Report

Author(s): Covalence

Covalence Banking Sector 2010 report covers the progress in ethical reputation of the banking sector. The report analyses and compares the ethical reputation of 29 international banks, internally as well as against the 18 sectors benchmark covering 581 large companies.

Key findings

The ethical reputation of banks shows a smaller progress than other sectors mainly due to a low volume of positive news regarding products, as well as criticisms related to remunerations and gender discriminations.

- The Impact of Product criteria group only represents 16% of positive news registered on banks, against 37% for the 18 sectors benchmark.
- Banks are shy in demonstrating the social utility of their products and in presenting their innovations in this field.
- Many banking activities can be described in terms of contribution to sustainable development but banks don't use these terms much.
- The low level of criticisms targeting banks' products can be interpreted as a lack of incentives.
- Secondly, bankers seem to consider that highlighting their sustainable products may be counterproductive to the serious, conservative, cautious, and money-oriented corporate culture and image they show to their clients.
- Next to the usual suspects (tax issues), wages was the most active criteria.
- CEO compensation, traders' bonuses, and the differential between the highest and the lowest salaries within banks have been abundantly criticized.
- This report also highlights an increasing amount of negative comments about the status of women at work (discrimination on wages and promotions, a work atmosphere described as unfriendly to women).
- On the positive side, banks registered the most points on social sponsorship (philanthropic donations, community investments) and on

climate change mitigation.

- Some banks are less shy than others in their offering of sustainable products, which allows them to score well in Covalence EthicalQuote Ranking.
- For example, they communicate on their involvement in microfinance and renewable energy projects, on interest rates favorable to green buildings, or on their signing of the UN Principles for Responsible Investment.

Source: CSR Research Digest, September 2010 (Vol. 2, No. 9)

3.2.2   Retail Industry Ethical Ranking

Author(s): Covalence

Wal-Mart jumps from last place (2007) to third place (2008) in Covalence's ethical ranking of the retail sector. Geneva-based ethical research firm, Covalence, has released its 2008 Retail Industry Report, which tracks the ethical reputation of multinationals in the media.

Key findings

Marks and Spencer claims first place, followed by Home Depot and Wal-Mart.

- The lowest ranked companies in 2008 were PPR; Bed, Bath and Beyond; and TJX.
- The industry as a whole has made major advances in tackling poor working conditions in its supply chains, an issue which has in the past led to a number of ethical controversies.
- Retailers have taken most action on environmental criteria in 2008, with the environmental impact of production and waste management being reported as the two most frequently addressed areas.
- Despite being placed in the top three, Wal-Mart remains the most criticized retailer, with 48% of the negative news naming retailers.
- In the last year, the provision of information to consumers, external working conditions, products' environmental risks and the launch of eco-innovative products have all attracted fewer positive news stories.

- The areas in which there were most significant increases in the number of positive news stories were waste management and social sponsorship.

Rank	Company	Positive Stories	Negative Stories	Ethical Rate
1	Marks & Spencer	643	83	77%
2	Home Depot	447	145	51%
3	Wal-Mart Stores	1517	1285	8%
4	Tesco plc	542	326	25%
5	Gap Inc	327	161	34%
6	Best Buy Co.	206	44	65%
7	Carrefour SA	257	104	42%
8	Hennes & Mauritz	188	46	61%
9	Lowes Cos	124	29	62%
10	eBay Inc	132	53	43%
23	Westfarmers	20	6	54%
24	Sears	83	79	2%
25	TJX Companies	26	27	-2%
26	Bed Bath & Beyond	24	27	-6%
27	PPR	41	63	-21%

Source: Governance Research Digest, January 2009 (Vol. 1, No. 1)

3.2.3 Ethical Review of Food and Beverages Sector

Author(s): Covalence

Covalence has released its Food and Beverages Sector Report based on findings from 2008. Following its reference index Dow Jones Sector Titans, Covalence now categorizes Monsanto in the Food & Beverage sector. This sector covers a large spectrum in Covalence's Ethical Ranking. The sector averages 7th place out of 18 sectors in Covalence's EthicalQuote score for the period 2002-2008.

Key findings

Generally speaking, the food and beverage sector has increased its ethical reputation, despite the inclusion of Monsanto, a major producer of GMOs.

- The top producers of positive news in January to December 2008 have been Coca Cola Company, Nestlé, PepsiCo and Unilever, while Monsanto, Nestlé, Coca Cola Company, and Unilever come first for negative news.
- Compared to the 18-sector benchmark, Food & Beverages are the subject of significantly more negative news in the area of Impact of Product.
- The human risks of product were seen in relation to GMOs and other nutrition-related issues such as children's health, melamine, fat, and marketing practices; major environmental risks of products were seen in relation to Monsanto's production of GMOs and pesticides.
- The critical situations of Archer Daniels Midland and Monsanto reflect the challenges along the supply chain and the potential risks that lie in the sector for big consumer brands.
- Criteria gaining weight within positive news in 2008 have been: Waste Management, Joint Venture, Labour Standards, International Presence and Social Impact.
- Findings also show that the Food & Beverage sector seems to face fewer ethical consequences from the current economic crisis compared to the benchmark (fewer criticisms related to job-cuts).
- The Food and Beverages sector shows competitive advantages on criteria such as social Sponsorship, United Nations Policy, and Social Stability (community initiatives).
- There is also evidence from this sector that companies understand the importance of partnerships with renowned social and environmental organizations as a powerful means to increase trust in global brands.

Source: Governance Research Digest, March 2009 (Vol. 1, No. 3)

3.2.4 Garment Industry Ethical Report

Author(s): Oxfam

A new Oxfam report has released its findings on the transparency of labour and ethical standards in the supply chains of 26 Hong Kong garment companies. The report was undertaken between May and October 2008. The companies investigated produce garments for over 1,000 brands, make over HK$170 billion in annual turnover, and operate in more than 40 countries. Oxfam rated the companies on the transparency of their ethical and labour practices, not on whether they actually engaged in unethical practices.

Key findings

The Esquel Group of Companies (clients include Tommy Hilfiger, Hugo Boss, and Abercrombie and Fitch) were the most transparent. The company achieved a rating of 70% (equivalent to average ratings in Canada and therefore a good score).

- The success of the Esquel Group is considered particularly impressive since it is a private company and has made such progress on its own initiative.
- In contrast, the next company, Li & Fung Limited (Liz Claiborne), only scored 33%.
- 19 out of the 26 companies scored zero.
- In addition to Esquel and those companies taking part in the garment roundtable, Glorious Sun, Chickeeduck and Hembly have engaged with Oxfam Hong Kong and CSR Asia during the research period.
- These three companies have some good practices in place, which are not fully reflected in their public reporting at this time.
- Overall, the report found that despite the increase in awareness of the need for transparent reporting along the supply chain, the implementation of measures to report supply chain management procedures was still below standards.
- Currently, Hong Kong apparel companies are facing limited or no market and consumer pressures for increased transparency of their supply chain practices.
- However, several companies are beginning to feel increased pressure from investors and clients about their supply chain labour practices.
- As a result of this research, more companies showed concern about the research and engaged with Oxfam and CSR Asia to better understand the research criteria and how to cooperate with the research.

- Based on the heightened level of interest, it looks likely that reporting will become a trend among the more socially responsible companies in Hong Kong in the near future.
- Many of the companies that did receive a score this year are not yet providing sufficient, credible and verifiable information to consumers or shareholders to allow informed ethical choices.
- Compared with other stakeholders of Hong Kong apparel brands, the Hong Kong Exchanges and Clearing Limited (HKEx) is the most influential.
- During interviews, companies implied that if improved transparency was required by HKEx, they would certainly respond.
- A few of the larger companies are beginning to feel pressure from investors about their social compliance.
- They find that they are fielding more and more requests about supply chain practices from institutional investors, socially responsible investors and NGOs.
- There is consensus that a major obstacle to ethical supply chain practices is the price squeeze being felt by suppliers from large multinational apparel clients in parallel to increasingly stringent supplier codes of conduct requirements.

Source: Governance Research Digest, May 2009 (Vol. 1, No. 5)

3.2.5 Consumption of Personal and Household Goods Ranking

Author(s): Covalence

Covalence has released its 2009 ethical ranking of companies in the personal and household goods sector. 32 companies appear in the ranking, which has been compiled using data spanning 2002-2009.

Key findings

Sector Ranking	Ranking Across All Sectors	Company
1	14	Procter & Gamble
2	16	Sony Corp
3	37	Philips Electronics
4	60	Nike

5	61	Henkel
6	79	L'Oreal
7	99	Panasonic
8	100	LG Electronics
9	104	Sharp
10	106	Clorox
11	118	Eastman Kodak
12	175	Sanyo Electric
13	224	Avon Products
14	255	LVMH
15	263	Colgate-Palmolive
16	280	Reckitt Benckiser
17	291	Richemont
18	322	Adidas
19	348	Kimberly Clark International
20	362	Svenska Cellulosa
21	375	Kao Corp
22	390	Imperial Tobacco
23	419	Electronic Arts Inc
24	457	Coach Inc
25	468	Pioneer Corp
26	502	Reynolds American
27	504	Nintendo
28	507	British American Tobacco
29	510	Altria
30	511	Mattel
31	513	D.R. Horton
32	522	Japan Tobacco

Source: Governance Research Digest, May 2009 (Vol. 1, No. 5)

3.2.6 Automobile Manufacturers Ethical Ranking

Author(s): Covalence

Ethical quotation company, Covalence, has released its second-quarter ranking of automobile and parts manufacturers. The ranking, published quarterly, uses integrated data covering the period 2002-present.

Key findings

Ranking (Previous Ranking)	Company	Ranking (Previous Ranking)	Company
1 (6)	Johnson Controls	**16 (16)**	General Motors Corp.
2 (4)	Ford Motor Co.	**17 (12)**	Daimler
3 (3)	Toyota Motor	**18 (17)**	Aisin Seiki
4 (5)	BMW	**19 (19)**	Yamaha Motor Co.
5 (1)	Honda Motor	**20 (23)**	Suzuki Motor
6 (2)	Nissan Motor	**21 (25)**	Bridgestone
7 (7)	Mazda Motor	**22 (13)**	Michelin
8 (10)	Peugeot SA	**23 (24)**	Fuji Heavy Industries
9 (9)	Denso Corp.	**24 (20)**	Harley-Davidson
10 (8)	Fiat	**25 (28)**	Porsche
11 (14)	Renault	**26 (22)**	Valeo
12 (15)	Mitsubishi Motors	**27 (26)**	Magna International
13 (11)	Kia Motors	**28 (29)**	Genuine Parts Co.
14 (21)	Volkswagen	**29 (27)**	GKN plc
15 (18)	Hyundai Motor	**30 (30)**	Continental AG

Source: Governance Research Digest, July 2009 (Vol. 1, No. 7)

3.2.7   Ethical Reputation of Banks Report

Author(s): Covalence

Ethical quotation company Covalence has recently released its 2009 Banking Sector Report. Banks rated 18th out of 18 industry sectors in Covalence's EthicalQuote which covered the period June 2008 – May 2009.

Key findings

HSBC by far leads the field in the top four companies in Covalence's all-time ethical ranking. It is followed by Barclays Bank, Bank of America and Royal Bank of Canada.

- Royal Bank of Scotland and UBS are the laggards of the sector.
- Five banks appear to have registered important ethical reputation gains during the last 12 months. These are: HSBC, BNP Paribas, BBVA, Scotiabank, and Royal Bank of Canada.
- These banks benefited from innovative products (SRI, microfinance, social entrepreneurship), employee-related initiatives (diversity) and social sponsorship.
- The banking sector once led in setting goals to reduce carbon emissions; now, other sectors are following suit.
- In addition, more sceptical observers are monitoring project financing and the real achievements of banks in climate change mitigation.
- Companies the most exposed to the sub-prime crisis contributed greatly to the downturn (UBS, Citigroup, Royal Bank of Scotland, Bank of America). The Economic Impact and Downsizing criteria were the most active.
- For the first time, Europe and North America generated a majority of negative news.
- Compared to the 18 sectors, Banks receive relatively more positive news on Social Sponsorship and Social Stability criteria, and more negative news with the criteria Fiscal
- Contributions and Downsizing: banks are strong on philanthropy and community support, but weak on tax issues.
- Tax issues dampened the ethical reputation of UBS last year. It is likely that banks favoring individual and corporate tax avoidance will also generate unfavorable media coverage in the future.
- The philanthropic legitimacy of tax avoidance is becoming increasingly difficult to justify, as modern governments are increasingly democratic.

Source: Governance Research Digest, August 2009 (Vol. 1, No. 8)

3.2.8   Mining and Metals Sector Ethical Report

Source: Governance Research Digest, September 2009 (Vol. 1, No. 9)

Author(s): Covalence

Covalence has released its latest EthicalQuote annual ranking for the mining and metals sector. 32 companies comprise the sector analysis. The data that informs the report is drawn from the period January 2002 to June 2009.

Key findings

The mining and mineral sector ranks 17th out of 18 sectors. In the last 24 months, the sector has lost nearly half of its past gains, while the overall benchmark doubled.

- Alcoa is the leading company in the sector (#9 out of 541 companies), followed by Rio Tinto (#14), UPM-Kymmene Ojy (#151).
- The lowest placed companies are Freeport- McMoRan (#537), Grupo Mexico (#535) and Harmony Gold (#529).
- Alcoa received the most positive news stories (16% of the total positive news stories identified), closely followed by Arcelor Mittal (15%). However, Arcelor Mittal also received by far the most negative press (20%).
- In the last twelve months the most significant progress has been accomplished by International Paper and Peabody Energy, while Arcelor Mittal, Impala Platinum, Freeport- McMoRan and Barrick Gold suffered the most.
- Criticisms have strongly increased in 2008 and 2009. The recent economic down-turn is certainly an important explanation, as downsizing and jobs cuts have weighted heavily on the sector's ethical performance.
- In the last year the major positive issues in the mining and metals sector have been: Climate Change (emissions, energy); Commitment (policies, programs and initiatives); Community issues (health, family).
- The major negative issues have included: union action and strikes; job cuts; legal issues relating to water usage; community issues and SRI governance.
- The current inflation of negative news naming basic resources companies can also be interpreted in terms of CSR dialectics, since this socially and environmentally exposed sector has always had to face various ethical challenges.

- Non Governmental Organizations (NGOs) and alliances, local groups and communities watch companies in this sector closely. It has therefore been strongly stimulated to develop CSR strategies.

3.2.9 Healthcare Sector Ethical Ranking

Author(s): Covalence

Ethical company Covalence has released its latest ranking of companies in the healthcare sector. Across the full universe of eighteen industry sectors, healthcare is currently placed eighth.

Key findings

Pharmaceutical companies involved in consumer health activities achieve the best ethical reputation.

- Among the seven leaders in the healthcare sector ranking, five companies are following a diversified business strategy and operate in consumer health (such as over-the-counter drugs, eye and dental care).
- These companies are: GlaxoSmithKline; Bristol Myers Squibb; Novartis; Abbott; and Johnson & Johnson.
- These companies have also communicated with the public on subjects such as social sponsorship, climate change and community.
- Future success for diversified healthcare companies will be driven by their ability to create brand loyalty through strong ethical behaviour.

Rank	Company	Rank	Company
1	GlaxoSmithKline	17	Merck & Co.
2	Bristol Myers Squibb	18	Takeda
3	Novartis	19	Deiichi Sankyo
4	Roche	20	WellPoint
5	Abbott	21	Medco Health Solutions
6	Boehringer Ingelheim	22	CIGNA Corp
7	Johnson & Johnson	23	Genentech
8	Astra Zeneca	24	Boston Scientific
9	Novo Nordisk	25	Amgen
10	United Health	26	Medtronic
11	Baxter International	27	Zimmer Holding

12	Aetna	28	Astellas Pharma
13	Eli Lilly	29	Wyeth
14	Sanofi Aventis	30	Schering Plough
15	Pfizer	31	Gilead Sciences
16	Becton-Dickinson		

Source: Governance Research Digest, October 2009 (Vol. 1, No. 10)

3.2.10 Uplifting the Earth: The Ethical Performance of Luxury Jewellery Brands

Author(s): Fair Jewelry Action / Lifeworth Consulting

Published by Fair Jewelry Action, a non-profit organisation promoting fairly traded jewellery, and strategy advisers Lifeworth Consulting, the report benchmarks ten prestigious jewellery brands on their social and environmental performance. The report provides guidance on how brands can move beyond a negative risk management approach to their ethical considerations, and instead use social and environmental issues as a creative inspiration and collaborate to make jewellery a positive force for all involved.

Key findings

Top jewellery brands are failing to meet the growing expectations of customers for ethical sourcing of metals and gemstones, thereby providing opportunities for new brands to emerge.

- The comparison of brands performance with innovations in the ethical sourcing of precious metal and gemstones finds them significantly lagging behind, with the sole exceptions of Cartier and Boucheron, which are recognised for taking useful steps.
- The research also found that six of the ten brands still offered to sell Burmese rubies from the shop floor in London or Geneva boutiques last year, despite an EU embargo.
- One reason for the lack of comprehensive action from prestigious brands is identified as the absence of a positive vision for the ethical role of the jewellery industry.

- Although a decade of effort to reduce conflict and environmental damage from jewellery supply chains has curbed some of the worst practices, it has failed to identify an aspirational role for jewellery.
- Today, the efforts of responsible jewellery pioneers are outlining a vision of ethical excellence.
- By comparing the actions of ten luxury brands with this new vision, the report finds luxury jewellery firms risk being left behind in an increasingly aspirational marketplace.
- More people recognise something is beautiful if it has been made beautifully, which involves all aspects of its creation.
- Some in the industry understand that, and need help to get buy-in from their colleagues.
- Interviews with international experts identified new brands that embody a new approach to jewellery, including CRED Jewellery, Fifi Bijoux, JEL and Brilliant Earth.
- The big brands must get their act together if they are not going to lose customers to the companies that really care.
- They can't hide behind vague statements or the Kimberley Process any more, because others are showing what's possible.

Source: Governance Research Digest, July 2011 (Vol. 2, No. 3)

3.3   Moral Reasoning and Perceptions

3.3.1   A Survey of Manager's Perceptions of Corporate Ethics and Social Responsibility and Actions that may Affect Companies' Success

Author(s): R. Cacioppe, N. Forster, M. Fox

This exploratory study examines how managers and professionals regard the ethical and social responsibility reputations of 60 well-known Australian and International companies. The study also considers how this in turn influences managers and professionals attitudes and behaviours towards these organizations. More than 350 MBA students, other postgraduate business students and participants in Australian Institute of Management management education programmes took part in the survey.

Key findings

Top ten ethically Responsible organisations		Top ten socially Responsible organisations	
Rank	Company	Rank	Company
1	The Body Shop	1	The Body Shop
2	Royal Automobile Club	2	Royal Automobile Club
3	Australian Institute of Management	3	Lotteries Commission of Australia
4	University of Western Australia	4	Australia Post
5	Wesfarmers	5	University of Western Australia
6	Australia Post	6	Ben and Jerry's
7	Lotteries Commission of Australia	7	Australian Institute of Management
8	Ben and Jerry's	8	Water Corporation
9	Alinta	9	Wesfarmers
10	Curtin University	10	Alinta

- In the bottom five places, the least ethically responsible organizations were viewed to be: Reebok; News Corporation; International Olympic Committee; Nike; British American Tobacco.
- The least socially responsible organizations were viewed to be: News Corporation; Reebok, Exxon Mobil; Nike; British American Tobacco.
- Respondents cited a number of characteristics as indicative of a companies' ethical and social behaviour, including: whether the company or its employees break the law; how they deal with their employees in Australia and in developing countries; the extent to which they put their employees and customers before profits; and how they treat the environment.
- In a purchasing situation, most respondents reported that, if the price and quality of the goods were the same, they would buy from the company with the stronger ethical and social reputation.
- Further actions that respondents stated that they might take in response to ethically or socially irresponsible companies were: not applying for jobs at that company; not buying that company's products;

and not buying stock in that company, even if the respondent stood to make money from the transaction.

Source: Governance Research Digest, January 2009 (Vol. 1, No. 1)

3.3.2 The Impact of Perceived Organisational Ethical Climate on Work Satisfaction

Author(s): M. Elçi, L. Alpkan

This empirical study investigates the effects of nine ethical climate types on employee work satisfaction. These types are: self-interest, company profit, efficiency, friendship, team interest, social responsibility, personal morality, company rules and procedures, and lastly laws and professional codes. Staff and managers from 62 different telecommunication firms in Turkey took part in the research, and produced 1174 usable questionnaires.

Key findings

Creating, announcing, and encouraging a convenient ethical climate appears to be a must to increase work satisfaction in organizations and obtain both managerial and economic benefits.

- Firms can exhibit various types of ethical climates at different levels of intensity.
- A climate of self-interest affects work satisfaction negatively. In contrast, climates of team interest and social responsibility affect work satisfaction positively.
- Climates relating to law and professional standards were also found to affect work satisfaction positively.
- Recognizing the significant impact of principled cosmopolitan climate on employees' work satisfaction, managers need to communicate universal principles and professional codes to all of the members of the organization.
- A code of ethics and company policies that ensure that employees comply with professional standards may guarantee such a principled climate.
- Social responsibility climate had the highest level and personal morality climate was the lowest one among other ethical climate types in the telecommunication firms.

- Those who believe that their organization had team interest (caring) and social responsibility (caring) type ethical climates are also satisfied.
- Training programs that emphasize utilitarian (benevolent) reasoning may ensure such a caring environment.
- This study confirms that a self-interest ethical climate has a significant negative influence on work satisfaction.
- Strategies that organizations may use to diminish such self-centered concerns include ethics audits and the use of personal moral development level as selection and promotion criteria.
- Finally, the study also indicates that climates based on company profit, efficiency, friendship, personal morality, company rules, and procedures have no impact on work satisfaction.

Source: Governance Research Digest, March 2009 (Vol. 1, No. 3)

3.3.3 Does A 'Care Orientation' Explain Gender Differences In Ethical Decision-Making?

Author(s): R.Bampton, P. Maclagan

This paper explores the notion that women are more inclined than men to subscribe to an 'ethic of care' in the context of ethical decision making in organizations, and that once this perspective is adopted a pattern is discernable. The empirical study was conducted in the UK with 98 students of accounting. Two thirds of participants were male, and two thirds were under 21 years of age.

Key findings

Where a 'care' orientation is invited, women judge situations differently from men.

- More specifically, without saying that women are 'more ethical' than men, the female subjects in this study demonstrated more of a concern for human welfare, and also for the protection of the environment.
- Men do not consider personal gain to be acceptable when in conflict with proper practice.
- Men are more likely to support the impersonal values of profit or 'business', and perhaps proper procedures, or law and order.

- For these male students 'acceptable business practice' could mean 'profitable' in a narrow commercial sense, rather than 'ethical' in the sense that a wider range of stakeholders are 'cared' for,
- In the context of this study, women tend to view actions which offend the ethic of care (broadly defined) as unacceptable, while men may allow regard for profit and proper procedures to override such 'human' (or 'green') concerns.

Source: Governance Research Digest, May 2009 (Vol. 1, No. 5)

3.3.4 What would Confucius Do? – Confucian Ethics and Self-Regulation in Management

Author(s): P. R. Woods and D. A. Lamond

The study examined Confucian moral philosophy, primarily the Analects, to determine how Confucian ethics could help managers regulate their own behavior (selfregulation) to maintain an ethical standard of practice. In addition, it was examined some of the unique Confucian practices to achieve self-regulation including ritual and music.

Key findings

Some Confucian virtues relevant to self-regulation are common to Western ethics such as benevolence, righteousness, wisdom, and trustworthiness.

- Some are relatively unique, such as ritual propriety and filial piety.
- Seven Confucian principles we identified and discussed how they apply to achieving ethical self-regulation in management.
- Authors balanced the framework by exploring the potential problems in applying Confucian principles to develop ethical self-regulation including whistle blowing.
- Confucian moral philosophy offers an indigenous Chinese theoretical framework for developing ethical self-regulation in managers.
- This is relevant for managers in Confucian-oriented societies, such as China, Korea, Japan, and Singapore.
- Authors recommend further research to examine if the application of the Confucian practices outlined here actually work in regulating the ethical behavior of managers in modern organizations.

Source: Governance Research Digest, August 2011 (Vol. 2, No. 4)

3.3.5 The Credit Crisis and the Moral Responsibility of Professionals in Finance

Author(s): J. J. Graafland and B. W. van de Ven

Starting from MacIntyre's virtue ethics, authors investigate several codes of conduct of banks to identify the type of virtues that are needed to realize their mission. Article compares and contrast the codes of conduct with the actual behavior of banks that led to the credit crisis.

<u>Key findings</u>

Based on this analysis, authors define three core virtues: honesty, due care, and accuracy.

- It was found that in some cases banks did not behave according to the moral standards they set themselves.
- However, although banks and the professionals working in them can be blamed for what they did, one should also acknowledge that the institutional context of the free market economy in which they operated made it difficult to live up to the core values lying at the basis of the codes of conduct.
- Given the neo-liberal free market system, innovative and risky strategies to enhance profits are considered desirable for the sake of shareholder's interests.
- A return to the core virtues in the financial sector will therefore only succeed if a renewed sense of responsibility in the sector is supported by institutional changes that allow banks to put their mission into practice.

Source: Governance Research Digest, November 2011 (Vol. 2, No. 7)

3.3.6 Moral Intensity, Issue Importance and Ethical Reasoning in Operations Situations

Author(s): S. Valentine and D. Hollingworth

The study investigates the relationships among moral intensity, perceived ethical issue importance, and three stages of the ethical reasoning process: recognition of an ethical issue, ethical judgment, and ethical intention. Using an internet-based, selfreport survey containing two operations management scenarios and various ethics measures, information was collected from business professionals working for a Midwestern financial services organization.

Key findings

The hierarchical regression results indicated that some dimensions of moral intensity were positively related to perceived importance of an ethical issue, ethical issue recognition, and ethical judgment.

- Perceived importance of an ethical issue was associated with increased ethical issue recognition and ethical judgment.
- The steps of ethical reasoning were also positively interrelated.

Source: Governance Research Digest, July 2012 (Vol. 3, No. 7)

3.3.7   The Ethics of Gifts and Hospitality

Author(s): IBE

A new briefing from the IBE considers some of the ethical issues around the giving and accepting of corporate gifts and hospitality and outlines good practice. The report outlines what organisations and their employees need to bear in mind when giving or accepting gifts and hospitality.

Key findings

The acceptance of gifts, services and hospitality can leave an organisation vulnerable to accusations of unfairness, partiality or deceit, or even unlawful conduct.

- Commercial relationships may be subject to bias and an organisation's reputation for 'doing business ethically' will be put at risk.
- Companies which operate outside their home market need to be particularly aware of crosscultural differences in what is considered appropriate in gift giving and accepting.
- Although in some markets gifts and hospitality are a prevalent and fundamental part of business transactions, the extraterritorial reach of the UK Bribery Act (2010) has made the giving and accepting of gifts and hospitality a real concern for businesses and their employees around the world.

- Companies help prevent their employees giving or accepting inappropriate gifts/hospitality by providing guidance, usually in the company code of ethics (or equivalent document).
- The code will outline the company's position on gifts and hospitality and set out good practice for employees. Codes of ethics will often reference a gifts and hospitality policy which expands on the guidance in the code.
- Corporate gifts and hospitality policies typically set out:
  - clear definitions of what constitutes 'gift giving' or 'hospitality';;
  - what type of gift/hospitality can and cannot be given or accepted;
  - the financial value of gifts/hospitality that can be given or accepted without disclosure;
  - how and where gifts/hospitality should be recorded when given or accepted i.e. on a gifts and hospitality register;
  - how employees can refuse gifts or hospitality without causing offence;
  - how staff can seek further guidance;
  - standards for the giving and accepting of gifts and hospitality in the markets the company operates in and how the company responds to cultural differences in these markets.

Source: Governance Research Digest, November 2012 (Vol. 3, No. 11)

3.3.8 Corporate Value Clusters Study

Author(s): K. G. Jin, R. Drozdenko and S. DeLoughy

Scientists for the Ancell School of Business and Western Connecticut State University have created a conceptual framework for the empirical, ethical, and corporate social responsibility study of financial professionals. Their findings were published in an article highlighting the relationships among four constructs—financial professionals' perceived organizational value clusters, ethics, corporate social responsibility, and corporate performance.

Key findings

Organizational core values significantly affect corporate ethics, social responsibility, and financial performance.

- Organizations in the financial industry can move toward being more ethical and socially responsible by adopting organic core values (e.g., democratic, open, trusting, enterprising, creative, stimulating) and moving away from mechanistic values (e.g., structured, regulated, procedural, authoritarian, closed, callous).
- The adaptation of organic core values does not require the organization to suffer a loss in financial performance.

Source: Governance Research Digest, January 2013 (Vol. 4, No. 1)

3.3.9 Reframing the Business Case for Diversity: A Values and Virtues Perspective

Author(s): H. van Dijk, M. van Engen and J. Paauwe

The paper provides an ethical evaluation of the debate on managing diversity within teams and organizations between equality and business case scholars. Authors' core assertion is that equality and business case perspectives on diversity from an ethical reading appear stuck as they are based on two different moral perspectives that are difficult to reconcile with each other.

Key findings

It is pointed out how the arguments of equality scholars correspond with moral reasoning grounded in deontology, whereas the foundations of the business case perspective are crafted by utilitarian arguments.

- The problems associated with each diversity perspective correspond with the traditional concerns with the two moral perspectives.
- To resolve this stalemate position, it is argued that the equality versus business case debate needs to be approached from a third, less wellknown moral perspective (i.e. virtue ethics).
- Authors posit that a focus on virtues can enhance equality by reducing prejudice and illustrate this by applying it to the HRM domains of recruitment and selection and of performance management.
- Subsequently, it is argued that values are key to aligning virtues with each other and with corporate strategy, delineate our values and virtues perspective on diversity, and argued why and how it can enhance organizational performance.

Source: Social Research Digest, December 2012 (Vol. 3, No. 12)

3.3.10 Managers' Moral Decision-Making Patterns over Time: A Multidimensional Approach

Author(s): J. Kujala, A. Lämsä and K. Penttilä

Taking multidimensional ethics scale approach, the article describes an empirical survey of top managers' moral decision-making patterns and their change from 1994 to 2004 during morally problematic situations in the Finnish context. The survey questionnaire consisted of four moral dilemmas and a multidimensional scale with six ethical dimensions: justice, deontology, relativism, utilitarianism, egoism and female ethics.

Key findings

This study proves that managers' moral decision making patterns change.

- According to the results of this research, managers' moral decision-making became more multidimensional during the study period.
- The change is explained by:
  1. the inclusion of female ethics items in the scale which allows managers to show more diversity in their decision-making;
  2. the change in the Finnish economic context from depression to economic prosperity and growth during the study period, which is conducive to the spread of post materialist values, such as the importance of social relations and;
  3. the increasing public discussion of the importance business ethics.

Source: Governance Research Digest, May 2011 (Vol. 2, No. 1)

3.3.11 A Model for Ethical Decision Making in Business: Reasoning, Intuition, and Rational Moral Principles

Author(s): J. Woiceshyn

The article proposes a model for ethical decision making in business in which reasoning (conscious processing) and intuition (subconscious processing) interact through forming, recalling, and applying moral principles necessary for long-term success in business. The study is based on data from a study on strategic decision making by 16 effective chief executive officers (and three not-so-effective ones as contrast).

Key findings

Following the CEOs in the study, author employs a relatively new theory, rational egoism, as the substantive content of the model and argues it to be consistent with the requirements of long-term business success.

- Besides explaining the processes of forming and applying principles (integration by essentials and spiraling), author briefly describes rational egoism and illustrates the model with a contemporary moral dilemma of downsizing.
- Study concludes with implications for further research and ethical decision making in business.

Source: Governance Research Digest, December 2011 (Vol. 2, No. 8)

3.3.12 Personalist Business Ethics and Humanistic Management: Insights from Jacques Maritain

Author(s): A. Acevedo

The article examines the conceptual relationship between personalism and humanism. This article furthers that research by arguing that a true humanistic management is personalistic.

Key findings

Article claims that personalism is promising as a sound philosophical foundation for business ethics.

- Insights from Jacques Maritain's work are discussed in support of these conclusions.
- Of particular interest is his distinction between human person and individual based on a realistic metaphysics that, in turn, grounds human dignity and the natural law as the philosophical basis for human rights, personal virtues, and a common good defined in terms of properly human ends.
- Although Maritain is widely regarded as one of the foremost twentieth century personalist philosophers, his contribution has not been

sufficiently considered in the business ethics and humanistic management literature.

- Important implications of Maritainian personalism for business ethics as philosophical study and as practical professional pursuit are discussed.

Source: Governance Research Digest, January 2012 (Vol. 3, No. 1)

3.3.13 The Impact of Ethical Ideologies, Moral Intensity, and Social Context on Sales-Based Ethical Reasoning

Author(s): S. R. Valentine and C. R. Bateman

The study explores the influence of idealism and relativism, perceived moral intensity in a decision-making situation, and social context on the recognition of an ethical issue and ethical intention. Utilizing a sales-based scenario and multiple ethics measures included on a self-report questionnaire, data were collected from a regional sample of business students, most of whom had modest work experience.

Key findings

The results indicated that perceived moral intensity was associated with increased ethical issue recognition and ethical intention.

- Idealism was also associated with increased ethical issue recognition, and relativism was associated with decreased ethical intention.
- Social consensus was positively related to ethical issue recognition and intention, while competitive context was inversely related to ethical intention.
- Finally, ethical issue recognition was associated with increased ethical intention.
- Idealism, moral intensity, social consensus, and work experience worked together as predictors of ethical issue recognition, whereas recognition of an ethical issue, relativism, moral intensity, social consensus, and competitive context worked together to predict ethical intention.

Source: Governance Research Digest, September 2011 (Vol. 2, No. 5)

3.3.14 Data Brokers: A Call for Transparency and Accountability

Author(s): Federal Trade Commission

The Federal Trade Commission undertook a study of nine data brokers to shed light on the data broker industry. The report, "Data Brokers: A Call for Transparency and Accountability" finds that data brokers operate with a fundamental lack of transparency.

<u>Key findings</u>

Data brokers obtain and share vast amounts of consumer information, typically behind the scenes, without consumer knowledge.

- Data brokers sell this information for marketing campaigns and fraud prevention, among other purposes. Although consumers benefit from data broker practices which, for example, help enable consumers to find and enjoy the products and services they prefer, data broker practices also raise privacy concerns.
- Data brokers collect and store billions of data elements covering nearly every U.S. consumer. Just one of the data brokers studied holds information on more than 1.4 billion consumer transactions and 700 billion data elements and another adds more than 3 billion new data points to its database each month.
- Data brokers collect consumer data from extensive online and offline sources, largely without consumers' knowledge, ranging from consumer purchase data, social media activity, warranty registrations, magazine subscriptions, religious and political affiliations, and other details of consumers' everyday lives.
- Consumer data often passes through multiple layers of data brokers sharing data with each other. In fact, seven of the nine data brokers in the Commission study had shared information with another data broker in the study.
- Data brokers combine online and offline data to market to consumers online.
- Data brokers combine and analyze data about consumers to make inferences about them, including potentially sensitive inferences such as those related to ethnicity, income, religion, political leanings, age, and health conditions. Potentially sensitive categories from the study

are "Urban Scramble" and "Mobile Mixers," both of which include a high concentration of Latinos and African-Americans with low incomes.

- The category "Rural Everlasting" includes single men and women over age 66 with "low educational attainment and low net worths." Other potentially sensitive categories include health-related topics or conditions, such as pregnancy, diabetes, and high cholesterol.
- Many of the purposes for which data brokers collect and use data pose risks to consumers, such as unanticipated uses of the data. For example, a category like "Biker Enthusiasts" could be used to offer discounts on motorcycles to a consumer, but could also be used by an insurance provider as a sign of risky behavior.
- Some data brokers unnecessarily store data about consumers indefinitely, which may create security risks.
- To the extent data brokers currently offer consumers choices about their data, the choices are largely invisible and incomplete.

Source: Governance Research Digest, May 2014 (Vol. 5, No. 5)

3.3.15 A crisis of culture: Valuing ethics and knowledge in financial services

Author(s): Economist Intelligence Unit (EIU)

Economist Intelligence Unit (EIU), sponsored by CFA Institute, released a report that examines the role of integrity and knowledge in restoring culture in the financial services industry and in building a more resilient industry. The report, A crisis of culture: Valuing ethics and knowledge in financial services draws on three main sources for its research and findings: a global survey of 382 financial services executives conducted in September 2013, a global survey of 50 executives from firms supporting the financial services industry across a number of areas, including technology, marketing and business processes and a series of in-depth interviews with senior financial industry executives and experts.

Key findings

Most firms have attempted to improve adherence to ethical standards. Global institutions, from Barclays to Goldman Sachs, have launched high-profile programmes that emphasise client care and ethical behaviour.

- Over two-thirds (67%) of firms represented in the survey have raised awareness of the importance of ethical conduct over the last three years, and 63% have strengthened their formal code of conduct and the system for evaluating employee behaviour (61%). Over two-fifths (43%) of respondents say their firms have introduced career or financial incentives to encourage adherence to ethical standards.

- Despite a spate of post-crisis scandals that suggest continued profit-chasing behaviour, large majorities agree that ethical conduct is just as important as financial success at their firm. Respondents would also prefer to work for a firm that has a good reputation for ethical conduct than for a bigger or more profitable firm with questionable ethical standards. Nearly three-fifths (59%) personally view the industry's reputation on ethical conduct positively; and 71% think their firm's reputation outperforms the industry's.

- Executives struggle to see the benefits of greater adherence to ethical standards. While respondents admit that an improvement in employees' ethical conduct would improve their firm's resilience to unexpected and dramatic risk, 53% think that career progression at their firm would be difficult without being flexible on ethical standards. The same proportion thinks their firm would be less competitive as a consequence of being too rigid in this area. Less than two-fifths (37%) think their firm's financials would improve as a result of an improvement in the ethical conduct of employees at their firm.

- To become more resilient, financial services firms need to address knowledge gaps. The increasingly complex risk environment has made advancing and updating knowledge of the industry crucial for those working in or serving the financial services industry. Nearly three fifths (59%) of respondents identify better knowledge of the industry as the top priority for making their firm more resilient to risk. Three fifths think gaps in employees' knowledge pose a significant risk to their firm.

- Nonetheless, a lack of understanding and communication between departments continues to be the norm. Many argue that ignorance was a key contributor to the global financial crisis: managers signed off complex products they did not understand, while HR departments agreed to incentives they did not realise encouraged risk-taking.

Source: Governance Research Digest, June 2014 (Vol. 5, No. 6)

3.4 Cross-Cultural Differences

3.4.1 Codes, Ethics and Cross-Cultural Differences: Stories from the Implementation of Corporate Code of Ethics in a MNC Subsidiary

Author(s): S. Helin, J. Sandström

This research focuses on the cross-cultural aspects of the implementation of an American company's code of ethics into its Swedish subsidiary. 19 members of staff in the Swedish subsidiary (500 employees), from product assemblers to the CEO, were interviewed in early 2005 and mid-2006. A total of 48 interviews were conducted, including a number with the Head of Communications.

Key findings

The majority of respondents expressed that they were not comfortable with the code set by the US owners. A number of the negative reactions to the code were based in cross-cultural differences between Americans and Swedes.

- The following issues were identified as particularly problematic:
- Incompatibility between legal systems: The parent company insisted that US legislation be followed, whereas the subsidiary operated under Swedish regulations and as such was bound by the Swedish legal system.
- Inconvenient content: A "clash of cultures" meant that Swedish staff found some of the US codes unsuitable and inappropriate within their own culture.
- Inconvenient style: It was felt that some of the language used was unnecessarily patronizing.
- "The American Way": Swedish employees found that the parent company insisted on more documentation and process than they had previously used. Swedes felt that their existing processes were more ethical.
- Risk of being sued: Swedes were uncomfortable with the Americans' litigious culture.

- Trust and mistrust: Corporate scandals in US companies led the parent company to instinctively mistrust the Swedish employees.
- Differences in norms and values: Respondents felt that the code being implemented was based on US values and did not consider the importance of Swedish values in this new context.
- The need for an adapted translation: Building on a number of the points above, it was felt that the code was a clumsy, direct translation from the American version, not a translation adjusted to Swedish culture and conditions.
- Importantly, it is noted that, in spite of the above challenges, none of the staff took issue with the spirit of the code and all were willing to sign up to it. In doing so, they did not initiate a conversation about company ethics in relation to the code.
- An exercise that was meant to create a stronger commitment to shared core values and behaviours throughout the group inadvertently had the opposite effect.
- The code strengthened the divide between 'us' and 'them', shifting self and others' identities into the single category of 'nationality'.

Source: Governance Research Digest, January 2009 (Vol. 1, No. 1)

3.4.2. Collective Versus Individualist National Cultures: Comparing Taiwan and US Employee Attitudes Towards Unethical Business Practices

Author(s): R.L. Sims

This study considers the national cultural dimension of collectivism versus individualism in the context of unethical business practices. Survey data were gathered from 252 full-time employees working in the collective country of Taiwan and the individualist country of the United States of America.

Key findings

Organizations working across national borders should understand that employees from collective cultures may be more willing to withhold the truth from out-group members to benefit in-group members than might be expected from employees from individualist cultures.

- Employees within a collective culture (Taiwan) are more likely to indicate they would make an unethical decision that benefits the organization.
- It was expected that because employees from collective cultures may be more loyal to their organizations, they would extend this loyalty if faced with an ethical dilemma that indicated that the organization and coworkers were in need of help that could be provided with the withholding of truth from someone outside the group.
- Employees within individualist cultures (US) are not more likely to indicate they would make an unethical business decision for personal benefit.
- Employees within individualist cultures are more likely to report a tendency to openly question an unethical practice by their organization.
- This is due to significant cultural differences: collective cultures are still to a large extent characterized by differentiated rights amongst different social groups. (This would be understood as discrimination in many individualized cultures.)
- There are no differences in reported likelihood of making an unethical business decision between collective and individualist cultures when there is no apparent benefit.
- Employees who have bonded with their organization are more likely to follow the ethical rules set.
- Even in individualist cultures, the whole truth is not always seen as the most ethical option.
- Given that the entire organization may suffer the consequences of a poor reputation, honesty to out-group members may become the expected standard even within a collective culture.
- The authors suggest that training programs or codes of ethics could be developed specifically addressing this type of situation.

Source: Governance Research Digest, April 2009 (Vol. 1, No. 4)

3.4.3 A Cross-Cultural Construct of the Ethos of Corporate Codes of Ethics: Australia, Canada, Sweden

Author(s): G. Svensson, G. Wood, J. Singh, and M. Callaghan.

This paper aims to develop and describe a construct of the ethos of the corporate codes of ethics across three countries: Australia, Canada and Sweden. Questionnaires were sent to the top 500 companies operating in the private sectors within each country. Targeted companies were also asked to supply a copy of their corporate code of ethics.

Key findings

77% of the companies which took part indicated possession of a code of ethics. Australian and Canadian companies were more likely to have a code of ethics (89% and 96% respectively) than Swedish companies (61%).

- Five factors are identified in the findings that correspond with the pre-specified dimensions of the construct. These are:
- Surveillance and training
    - o More specifically, ethics audits alongside the establishment of an ethics training committee and staff training in ethics.
    - o Furthermore, the authors contend that the appointment of an individual to the role of 'ethical ombudsman' can help to enhance the ethical health of an organisation.
- Guidance
    - o This consists of a number of subareas and may be seen as a complement to surveillance and training.
    - o If companies accept that it is good corporate practice to align their codes with their strategic planning processes, then they should not only use the ethos of the code as a guide in their strategic planning process but they must also make that final comparison of the strategic plan against the code.
    - o Congruence between the strategic plan, which drives the organisation's actions, and the ethical views of the company should also make it easier for employees to act.
    - o Previous studies have shown that the most common areas in which these companies had utilized the code in the marketplace were for customers, suppliers and the environment.
    - o Previous research also found that a large proportion of companies were convinced that their corporate codes of ethics had an impact on the bottom line.
- Internal and external communication

- o It has been suggested that codes should be public documents that have an external as well as an internal focus and that organisations should be cognizant of the relationship of the organisation with all stakeholders.
- o An organisation's customers and suppliers should be informed of the existence of the company's code.
- Sustainability
  - o Within a corporate code of ethics, provision should be made for enforcement.
  - o If organisations are to evolve into ethical entities, both individual and collective action must be taken by individuals to change practices that they view as being contrary to the ethical health of the organisation.
  - o Formal guidelines to support whistleblowers should be considered, since if standards are to be set it will be necessary to ensure that either violations or breaches will be reported, reviewed and corrected.

Source: Governance Research Digest, August 2009 (Vol. 1, No. 8)

3.4.4 Implementation, Communication and Benefits of Corporate Codes of Ethics

Author(s): G. Svensson, G. Wood, J. Singh, M. Callaghan.

This paper examines the implementation, communication and benefits of corporate codes of ethics by the top companies operating in Australia, Canada and Sweden. The authors present an international comparison based on data from a longitudinal study comprised of national surveys conducted in 2001-2 and 2005-6.

Key findings

In all three countries, large organisations indicate a substantial interest in corporate codes of ethics. There are, however, differences in the ways that the companies in each country implement and communicate their corporate codes of ethics and the benefits they perceive as being derived from them.

- Data from the 2005-6 survey shows that 89.4% of Australian companies have a code of ethics, compared with 96.2% of Canadian companies, and 61.1% of Swedish companies.
- The involvement of corporate officials goes across the middle and higher levels of managers and boards, with senior managers and CEOs most closely involved for all three countries.
- The most widely-cited reason for developing codes of conduct is to support the corporate culture. Following this, staff integrity is cited by Australian and Canadian respondents, and core competence by Swedish respondents.
- Ethics codes are primarily communicated through booklets. Inductions and electronic communications.
- Companies inform new staff of the code by issued copies, training and discussion, and during induction programmes.
- More companies inform customers of their corporate code of ethics than do not.
- Communication is usually via the company website.
- Suppliers are more informed of their codes and communication with them is more formal that with customers.
- Focusing on communication with suppliers may be the result of a company drive to encourage supplier commitment to the ethos of the company ethics programme.
- Perceived benefits of codes of ethics include dealing responsibly with customers and the environment.
- Less than half the companies in Australia and Canada claim to use their ethics codes to resolve ethical problems in the marketplace.

Source: Governance Research Digest, December 2009 (Vol. 1, No. 12)

3.4.5   Corporate Ethics Policies & Programmes

Author(s): IBE

The IBE surveys UK companies every three years on the use of their codes of ethics. For the first time, the survey also included companies listed on the stock exchanges of Spain, Italy, France and Germany.

Key findings

In 2010, six out of ten UK companies provide training in business ethics for all their staff.

- This is a drop in 10% from 2007, when training was provided by seven out of ten UK companies.
- Although we are living in a time of austerity, cutting back on ethics training is a short-sighted thing for companies to do.
- Author(s)s to the corporate code of ethics in the recruitment process are more likely to be made by continental European-based companies - (Spain (60%); Italy (60%); France (57%); Germany (50%) - than those in the UK (38%).
- The Boards of larger UK companies are increasingly involved in reviewing the effectiveness of their organisation's ethics policies and programme.
- Bribery, corruption and facilitation payments along with discrimination issues and speak up policies lead the list of 'significant issues' for UK companies. In 2007 it was 'safety and security' and 'environmental impact'.
- Nearly all UK and continental European companies surveyed said they provided a mechanism for raising ethical concerns.
- 83% of responding UK companies screen suppliers and other business partners for ethical standards.
- Continental European companies are more likely to have a stand-alone ethics/compliance function with responsibility for the code and ethics programme than UK companies.

Source: Governance Research Digest, May 2011 (Vol. 2, No. 1)

3.4.6 What Ethical Leadership Means to Me: Asian, American and European Perspectives

Author(s): C. J. Resick, G. S. Martin, M. A. Keating, M. W. Dickson, H. K. Kwan and C. Peng

This study examines the meaning of ethical and unethical leadership held by managers in six societies with the goal of identifying areas of convergence and divergence across cultures. More specifically, qualitative research methods were used to identify the attributes and behaviors that managers from the People's Republic of China (the PRC), Hong Kong, the Republic of China (Taiwan), the United States (the U.S.), Ireland, and Germany attribute to ethical and unethical leaders.

Key findings

Despite the increasingly multinational nature of the workplace, there have been few studies of the convergence and divergence in beliefs about ethics-based leadership across cultures.

- Across societies, 6 ethical leadership themes and 6 unethical leadership themes emerged from a thematic analysis of the open-ended responses.
- Dominant themes for ethical and unethical leadership for each society are identified and examined within the context of the core cultural values and practices of that society.

Source: Governance Research Digest, August 2011 (Vol. 2, No. 4)

3.4.7 Doing Business in South Africa: An Overview of the Ethical Aspects

Author(s): Institute of Business Ethics

The Institute of Business Ethics offers a synopsis of the current trends and challenges in business ethics and corporate responsibility in South Africa. The new occasional paper explores the particular cultural factors influencing business ethics in South Africa, the salient business ethics challenges that companies face.

Key findings

There are high expectations for companies to contribute significantly to social development.

- Under the Government's B-BBEE Act (2003), companies doing business with public bodies are required to show how they are sharing their wealth with South Africa's poorest.
- Every company listed on the Johannesburg Stock Exchange (JSE) has a code of ethics and has some form of ethics management programme in place as a result of the requirement to adhere to King III.
- Priority areas for businesses operating in South Africa are:

- o speaking up: an effective means of reducing bribery, corruption and fraud is to encourage and support employees to report their concerns;
- o conflicts of interest management: South Africa became quite an insular economy as a consequence of apartheid and one of the responses of the population was to start small businesses;
- o diversity and B-BBEE: given the diversity of the population, the legacy of apartheid, and the economic empowerment strategy in place (B-BBEE), promoting and supporting diversity in the workforce is a fundamental aspect of any corporate ethics programme in South Africa;
- o HIV/AIDS: the duty of care for employees with HIV/AIDS and their families is a material aspect of CR programmes.

Source: Governance Research Digest, September 2011 (Vol. 2, No. 5)

3.4.8 Ethical Cultures in Large Business Organizations in Brazil, Russia, India and China

Author(s): A. Ardichvili, D. Jondle, B. Kowske, E. Cornachione, J. Li and T. Thakadipuram

The study focuses on comparison of perceptions of ethical business cultures in large business organizations from four largest emerging economies, commonly referred to as the BRICs (Brazil, Russia, India, and China), and from the US. The data were collected from more than 13,000 managers and employees of business organizations in five countries.

Key findings

The study found significant differences among BRIC countries, with respondents from India and Brazil providing more favorable assessments of ethical cultures of their organizations than respondents from China and Russia.

- Overall, highest mean scores were provided by respondents from India, the US, and Brazil.
- There were significant similarities in ratings between the US and Brazil.

Source: Governance Research Digest, January 2012 (Vol. 3, No. 1)

3.4.9 The State of Business Ethics in Israel: A Light Unto the Nations?

Author(s): M. S. Schwartz

To examine the current state of business ethics in Israel, the study examines the following: (1) the extent of business ethics education in Israel; (2) the existence of formal corporate ethics program elements based on an annual survey of over 50 large Israeli corporations conducted over 5 years (2006–2010). In addition it examines perceptions of the state of business ethics based on interviews conducted with 22 senior Israeli corporate executives.

Key findings

In general, Israel might be considered to have made great improvements in the state of business ethics over the years.

- In terms of business ethics education, the vast majority of universities and colleges offer at least an elective course in business ethics.
- In terms of formal business ethics program elements, many large companies now have a code of ethics, and over time continue to add additional elements.
- Most respondents believed they worked in ethical firms.
- Despite these developments, however, there appears to be significant room for improvement, particularly in terms of issues like: nepotism/favoritism; discrimination; confidentiality; treatment of customers; advertising; competitive intelligence; whistleblowing; worker health and safety; and the protection of the environment.
- When compared with the U.S. or Europe, most believed that Israeli firms and their agents were not as ethical in business.
- A number of reasons were suggested that might be affecting the state of business ethics in Israel.
- A series of recommendations were also provided on how firms can better encourage an ethical corporate culture.

Source: Governance Research Digest, January 2012 (Vol. 3, No. 1)

3.4.10 The Effects of Corporate Ethical Values and Personal Moral Philosophies on Ethical Intentions in Selling Situation: Evidence from Turkish, Thai, and American Businesspeople

Author(s): J. Marta, A. Singhapakdi, D.-J. Lee, S. Burnaz, Y. I. Topcu, M. G. S. Atakan and T. Ozkaracalar

The goals of this study are to test a pattern of ethical decision making that predicts ethical intentions of individuals within corporations based primarily on the ethical values embedded in corporate culture, and to see whether that model is generally stable across countries. The survey instrument used scales to measure the effects of corporate ethical values, idealism, and relativism on ethical intentions of Turkish, Thai, and American businesspeople.

Key findings

The study is positioned within a fairly new stream that assesses patterns across countries, rather than differences between them, in a way that might be called "culture free."

- The results show a generally positive influence between cultural ethical values and ethical intentions.
- The results also indicate that the positive effect of corporate ethical values on ethical intentions is greater for managers with low idealism and high relativism.
- Authors also discuss the implications of the results for managers of international businesses.

Source: Governance Research Digest, March 2012 (Vol. 3, No. 3)

3.4.11 Globalising a Business Ethics Programme

Author(s): IBE

The IBE Good Practice Guides offer practical assistance and guidance for making ethics policies and programmes effective. It helps organisations achieve consistent standards of business practice by recognising the cultural attitudes and practical issues they will face when communicating their ethical values to a global workforce.

Key findings

Corporate ethics programmes can be ineffective on a global scale if they are perceived locally as irrelevant or inappropriate.

- Different approaches to conflicts of interest: In Africa, where family bonds are highly valued nepotism is common and often seen as in the best interest of the business.

- Different gift giving practices: In parts of Asia, token cash gifts are routine in business relationships at special occasions like the birth of a child or New Year. Not being able to give a "red envelope" could result in the loss of face. In some African countries, businesses might ask suppliers to sponsor a son or daughter's wedding. Not doing so could be considered insulting.

- Perceptions of reporting channels: Negative historical events (such as the Cultural Revolution in China or the Stasi in East Germany) which have fostered cultural fears of retaliation may mean that reporting or speak up lines are better referred to as opportunities to raise concerns.

- Types of ethics training: In many parts of Africa where story-telling and group discussion is part of the culture, games, case studies and role play are effective, but lecture-style training is not. In contrast, in Asia, where the education system relies on lecture, employees will not be so comfortable discussing ethics matters in an open manner. Training audiences in Europe may not be as open to games which they may see as trivialising the topic.

- Translation of idioms: One code of ethics suggested that employees should "take a step back", meaning to reflect, but the code was translated literally as "we need to move backwards"! Translators of fiction rather than technical experts may have a better grasp of idiom and so be more appropriate as translators of ethics materials.

- Many companies launch their ethics programmes from the head office without proper adaptation to international locations where the company does business.

- This Guide will help them review their programme so that it has relevance wherever they operate and actually makes a difference to business practice.

Source: Governance Research Digest, May 2012 (Vol. 3, No. 5)

3.4.12 Doing Business in China: An Overview of Ethical Aspects

Author(s): IBE

The paper reviews the business ethics climate within China and explores the operating environment for business and considers the cultural characteristics which underpin this. It also looks at current business ethics and corporate responsibility trends and identifies the key ethical challenges facing businesses seeking to operate with high ethical standards in the Chinese market might encounter.

<u>Key findings</u>

Whilst China is still developing a robust corporate governance framework and universal rule of law, the pace of change in China is fast and the scale of their ambition in areas such as corporate governance, sustainability and anti-corruption is growing.

- With the advent of the UK Bribery Act and its extra-territorial reach, it is imperative for companies entering the Chinese market to be mindful of particular cultural traits (such as gift giving traditions and personal networks) when rolling out training and guidance designed to establish and ensure high ethical standards of business practice among employees.
- Business ethics and CSR in China are maturing fields.
- Heavily influenced by the state and traditional Confucian values, there are high expectations on business to play a part in addressing social inequalities and issues such as bribery and corruption, discrimination, human rights and environmental degradation.
- The Chinese government expects ethics and CSR programmes to be in line with the country's long term strategy for social improvement as outlined in its Five Year Plan.
- It is important that Western companies acknowledge the roles that personal connections (guanxi) and respect or 'avoiding loss of face' (mianzi) play when guiding employees on how to manage business relationships appropriately.
- Other Confucian influences on employees' behaviour include:

- o a reluctance by staff to speak up against colleagues (particularly their superiors) or use a reporting hotline as they are taught unquestioning respect for authority and loyalty to their group;
- o the need when training staff for small group sizes of the same rank, as the presence of superiors may inhibit employees to be frank and open in their discussion.

Source: Governance Research Digest, July 2012 (Vol. 3, No. 7)

3.4.13 Socio-Cultural Change and Business Ethics in Post-Soviet Countries: The Case of Belarus and Estonia

Author(s): C.J. Rees, G. Miazhevich

This study explores the influence of socio-cultural factors on business ethics in post-soviet countries with dissimilar cultural contexts. Belarus and Estonia were identified as being among the most noteworthy examples of culturally different post-soviet countries in transition.

Key findings

There are significant socio-cultural differences between the business norms of Belarus and Estonia, and these should not be overlooked in generalized views of the business ethics of 'former soviet states.'

- There are contradictory manifestations of mixtures of business norms in the two countries, which are conditioned by the merger of an autocratic bureaucratic soviet system with more participative and empowering forms of western management.
- The most persistent changes in business culture are moves from patriarchal and paternalistic types of relationship.
- Additionally, Belarusian business culture is characterised by the pervasiveness of double ethics while dealing with the state, the importance of informal networks and low work motivation.
- Overall, residual soviet ideology appears to be more persistent in Belarus than in Estonia.
- In Belarus, factors such as the discontinuity with its pre-revolutionary past and values, the strong influence of the communist regime, the slow transition to a market economy, and moral relativism, are relatively important when considering business ethics in this context.

- In contrast, soviet work values and double morality are reported as generally despised in Estonia while cherished pre-revolutionary values including values of work, farming, diligence and individualism appear to have survived the soviet occupation and are relevant to current business ethics in this context.

Source: Social Research Digest, June 2009 (Vol. 1, No. 6)

3.4.14 Cultural Dimensions, Ethical Sensitivity and Corporate Governance

Author(s): A. W. H. Chan and H. Y. Cheung

This study examines the differences in Corporate Governance practices in firms across different countries using the concept of ethical sensitivity. It is based on the regression analysis of 271 firms in 12 countries and regions.

<u>Key findings</u>

It is found that Hofstede's cultural dimensions can explain the differences in Corporate Governance practices.

- Furthermore, the results demonstrate the influence of culture on ethical sensitivity, which eventually determines the Corporate Governance practices in different regions.

Source: Governance Research Digest, September 2012 (Vol. 3, No. 9)

3.4.15 Ethical Ideology and Ethical Judgements in the Portuguese Accounting Profession

Author(s): P.A. Marquez, J. Azevedo-Pereira

This study examines the attitudes of Portuguese chartered accountants to the ethical questions that arise in their professional activity. 276 accountants completed a questionnaire that was circulated during two conferences.

<u>Key findings</u>

Respondents' ethical judgments did not differ significantly based on their ethical ideology, supporting the idea that ethical ideology is not an important determinant of ethical judgments.

- Gender seems to be the most important determinant of ethical judgments.
- Age, however, was shown to have little influence on ethical judgments.
- Against expectations, men evidenced significantly stricter judgments than women in two of the five ethical scenarios presented in the questionnaires.
- Neither gender nor education had an effect on accountants' sense of relativism.
- Age, however, was demonstrated to be significant, suggesting that, as experience is gained, chartered accountants are less willing to follow rules.
- Older accountants also generally expressed greater leniency in the ethical scenarios.
- Relativism may have a stronger effect on ethical judgments than idealism, but the results from this study were not conclusive.

Source: Governance Research Digest, June 2009 (Vol. 1, No. 6)

3.4.16 Ethical Leadership Across Cultures: A Comparative Analysis of German and US Perspectives

Author(s): G.S. Martin, C.J. Resick, M.A. Keating, M.W. Dickson.

This paper examines beliefs about four aspects of ethical leadership – Character/ Integrity, Altruism, Collective Motivation and Encouragement – in Germany and the United States. The study uses data from Project GLOBE (Global Leadership and Organizational Behaviour Effectiveness) and a supplemental analysis.

Key findings

The mean level of endorsement for each of the four dimensions of ethical leadership by American and German middle managers was 5.9 or higher for three of the four dimensions, namely Character/Integrity, Encouragement and Collective Motivation.

- This suggests that middle managers from each society viewed these dimensions as important components of effective leadership.
- For 10 of the 15 attributes, 57% or more of the German respondents viewed the attribute as indicative of ethical leadership.

- For the Character/Integrity and Encouragement dimension, German respondents generally indicated that the attributes composing these two dimensions were reflective of ethical leadership. The Encouragement dimension was also strongly endorsed by US managers.
- However, for Character/Integrity, a lower percentage of German respondents (57%) selected three of the four attributes – honest, just and sincere – than their US counterparts.
- A somewhat different pattern emerged for the Altruism and Collective Motivation dimensions. Regarding Altruism, less than half of the German respondents found two of the four attributes – modest (42.9%) and fraternal (42.9%) – to be indicative of ethical leadership.
- For Collective Motivation, less than one-third of the German respondents rated three of the five attributes composing this dimension as representing ethical leadership. These attributes include communicative (14.3%), group-oriented (28.6%) and team-builder (28.6%).
- Equally, the results provide an indication that Altruism and Collective Motivation are less central aspects of ethical leadership in Germany than in the United States.
- The results also suggest that middle managers from these societies had a more neutral view of the importance of Altruism for providing effective leadership.
- While middle managers from the United States endorsed each dimension to a significantly different degree than German middle managers, the level of endorsement among middle managers from the former West and East Germany did not differ significantly.
- Among the four ethical leadership dimensions in the current study, the greatest differences between German and US respondents existed for the Collective Motivation dimension.
- While German middle managers endorsed this dimension to a strong, but somewhat lower extent than US middle managers, a smaller percentage of the German respondents indicated that three of the four attributes characterizing this dimension – communicative, group orientation and team builder – represented ethical leadership.
- Collective Motivation may, therefore, be less central to an understanding of ethical leadership in Germany than in the United States.

- In Germany, relationships between managers and workers are more trusting and confident, perhaps explaining why 100% of the German respondents identified confidence builder as an attribute of ethical leadership.

Source: Governance Research Digest, July 2009 (Vol. 1, No. 7)

3.4.17 Ethical Standards and Behaviour in Workplace

Author(s): IBE

This survey report published by the Institute of Business Ethics aims to uncover the views of employees on ethical standards and behavior in their workplace. The survey report specifically looked at employees in Great Britain and Continential Europe (France, Germany, Italy an Spain).

Key findings

Majority of British (84%) than Continental European (77%) claim that honesty is practiced "Always/Frequently" in their organization.

- Of the 20% of British employees and 28% of Continental European employees aware of misconduct in their workplace actually reported it.
- Attitudes of indifference ('it's none of my business') and belief that no punitive action will be taken, deters employees who are aware of misconduct from raising their concern.
- Aspects of a formal ethics programme is more established in Britain evidenced by increases in the number of British workers claiming that their organization provides four aspects:
  - o Written standards on ethical business behavior: up from 66% in 2008 to 73% in 2012
  - o Anonymous mechanism for reporting misconduct: up from 54% to 69%
  - o Training on ethical standards: up from 55% to 62%
  - o Information helpline on ethical issues: up from 49% to 59%
- In comparison, Continental Europe is less positive; less than half of employees say their organizations provides each of the aforementioned four aspects.

Source: Social Research Digest, January 2013 (Vol. 4, No. 1)

3.5 Role Models and Leadership

3.5.1 Most Influential People in Business Ethics

Author(s): Ethisphere

Ethisphere, a New York-based international think-tank dedicated to best practices in business ethics, has published its annual list of the 100 Most Influential People in Business Ethics. In a year when many headlines pertaining to issues of legal compliance, business ethics, sustainability or social responsibility were for negative actions, Ethisphere found individuals who stood out for their positive achievements in the business ethics world.

Key findings

Rank	Name	Role	Category	Action
1	Liu Qi	Chairman, 2008 Olympic Organizing Committee	Government & Regulatory	New stringent levels of anti-corruption
2	Neelie Kroes	European Commissioner for Competition	Government & Regulatory	Cartel-busting
3	Heinrich Kieber	Former IT technician, LGT Bank	Media & Whistleblowers	Blowing whistle on tax evasion
4	Kim Yong-chul	Former inhouse lawyer for Samsung	Media & Whistleblowers	Blowing whistle on bribery
5	Mark F. Mendelsohn	Deputy Chief, Department of Justice Fraud Section	Government & Regulatory	Enforcement of Foreign Corrupt Practices Act
6	Lee Scott	CEO, Wal-Mart	Business Leadership	Investment in clean energy
7	Shan Rambu-ruth	Head, South African Competition Commission	Government & Regulatory	Probing of SA food industry

8	Bobby Jindal	Governor of Louisiana	Government & Regulatory	Championed tough ethical laws
9	Myron Steele	Chief Justice, Delaware Supreme Court	Government & Regulatory	Action on corporate governance law
10	Philip Collins	Chairman, UK Office of Fair Trading	Government & Regulatory	Offering of rewards

Source: Governance Research Digest, February 2009 (Vol. 1, No. 2)

3.5.2 An Empirical Study of Leader Ethical Values, Transformational and Transactional Leadership, and Follower Attitudes Toward Corporate Social Responsibility

Author(s):: K. S. Grover and M. A. LaRocca

The study investigates transformational and transactional leadership styles and their impact on follower CSR attitudes. Data from 122 organizational leaders and 458 of their followers was collected to examine the relationships.

Key findings

Leader deontological ethical values (altruism, universal rights, Kantian principles, etc.) were strongly associated with follower ratings of transformational leadership.

- While leader teleological ethical values (utilitarianism) were related to follower ratings of transactional leadership.
- As predicted, only transformational leadership was associated with follower beliefs in the stakeholder view of CSR.
- Implications for the study and practice of ethical leadership, future research directions, and management education are discussed.

Source: Governance Research Digest, November 2011 (Vol. 2, No. 7)

3.5.3 CEO Ethical Leadership, Ethical Climate, Climate Strength, and Collective Organizational Citizenship Behavior

Author(s): Y. Shin

The present study conducted firm-level analyses regarding the relationship between chief executive officer (CEO) ethical leadership and ethical climate, and the moderating effect of climate strength (i.e., agreement in climate perceptions) on the relationship between ethical climate and collective organizational citizenship behavior (OCB). Self-report data were collected from 223 CEOs and 6,021 employees in South Korea.

Key findings

In spite of an increasing number of studies on ethical climate, little is known about the antecedents of ethical climate and the moderators of the relationship between ethical climate and work outcomes.

- As predicted, CEOs' self-rated ethical leadership was positively associated with employees' aggregated perceptions of the ethical climate of the firm.
- The relationship between ethical climate and firm-level collective OCB was moderated by climate strength.
- More specifically, the relationships between ethical climate and interpersonally directed collective OCB and between ethical climate and organizationally directed collective OCB were more pronounced when climate strength was high than when it was low.

Source: Governance Research Digest, May 2012 (Vol. 3, No. 5)

3.5.4 Leadership and Change: The Case for Greater Ethical Clarity

Author(s): B. Burnes and R. T. By

This article addresses the relationship between the ethics underpinning leadership and change. It examines the developments in leadership and change over the last three decades and their ethical implications.

Key findings

The study adopts a consequentialist perspective on ethics and uses this to explore different approaches to leadership and change.

- In particular, the article focuses on individual (egoistic) consequentialism and utilitarian consequentialism.
- The article argues that all leadership styles and all approaches to change are rooted in a set of values, some more likely to lead to ethical outcomes than others.
- It concludes that, to achieve sustainable and beneficial change, those who promote and adopt approaches to leadership and change must provide greater ethical clarity about what they are championing.

Source: Governance Research Digest, June 2012 (Vol. 3, No. 6)

3.5.5   The Ethics of the Management Profession

Author(s): R. Khurana & N. Nohria

The authors of this Harvard Business Review paper argue that, in order for managers to regain the legitimacy that has been lost through the widespread institutional breakdown of trust, business leaders must view their role as one that incorporates a civic and personal commitment to their duty as institutional custodians. Such a reconceptualisation of the role of managers should, it is argued, include a code of conduct. Managers should also be accountable to a governing body which oversees members' compliance.

Key findings

The article suggests wording for a Hippocratic oath for managers:

- As a manager I serve as society's fiduciary for one of its most important institutions: enterprises that bring people and resources together to create valued products and services that no single individual could produce alone.
- My purpose is to serve the public's interest by enhancing the value my enterprise creates for society. Sustainable value is created when the enterprise produces an economic, social, and environmental output that is measurably greater than the opportunity cost of all the inputs it consumes.

- In fulfilling my role:
    - I recognize that any enterprise is at the nexus of many different constituencies, whose interests can sometimes diverge. While balancing and reconciling these interests, I will seek a course that enhances the value my enterprise can create for society over the long term. This may not always mean growing or preserving the enterprise and may include such painful actions as its restructuring, discontinuation, or sale, if these actions preserve or increase value.
    - I pledge that considerations of personal benefit will never supersede the interests of the enterprise I am entrusted to manage.
    - The pursuit of self-interest is the vital engine of a capitalist economy, but unbridled greed can be just as harmful. Therefore, I will guard against decisions and behavior that advance my own narrow ambitions but harm the enterprise I manage and the societies it serves.
    - I promise to understand and uphold, both in letter and in spirit, the laws and contracts governing my own conduct, that of my enterprise, and that of the societies in which it operates.
    - My personal behavior will be an example of integrity, consistent with the values I publicly espouse.
    - I will be equally vigilant in ensuring the integrity of others around me and bring to attention the actions of others that represent violations of this shared professional code.
    - I vow to represent my enterprise's performance accurately and transparently to all relevant parties, ensuring that investors, consumers, and the public at large can make well-informed decisions.
    - I will aim to help people understand how decisions that affect them are made, so that choices do not appear arbitrary or biased.
    - I will not permit considerations of race, gender, sexual orientation, religion, nationality, party politics, or social status to influence my choices.
    - I will endeavor to protect the interests of those who may not have power, but whose well-being is contingent on my decisions.
    - I will manager my enterprise by diligently, mindfully, and conscientiously applying judgment based on the best knowledge available.

- o I will consult colleagues and others who can help inform my judgment and will continually invest in staying abreast of the evolving knowledge in the field, always remaining open to innovation.
- o I will do my utmost to develop myself and the next generation of managers so that the profession continues to grow and contribute to the wellbeing of society.
- o I recognise that my stature and privileges as a professional stem from the honour and trust that the profession as a whole enjoys, and I accept my responsibility for embodying, protecting, and developing the standards of the management profession, so as to enhance that respect and honour.

Source: Governance Research Digest, February 2009 (Vol. 1, No. 2)

3.5.6 Critical Role of Leadership on Ethical Climate and Salesperson Behaviours

Author(s): J.P. Mulki, J.F. Jaramillo, W.B Locander

This study identifies a type of leadership style that can help firms develop an ethical climate. Responses from 333 salespeople working for a North American subsidiary of an international pharmaceutical company were used to analyze the impact of instrumental leadership on ethical climate. The effect of ethical climate on effort, satisfaction with the supervisor, and job satisfaction were also examined.

Key findings

There is a positive and significant relationship between instrumental leadership style and ethical climate and between considerate leadership and satisfaction with the supervisor.

- Ethical climate positively influences satisfaction with supervisor, job satisfaction, and employee effort.
- Supervisory satisfaction has a positive link with job satisfaction.
- Job satisfaction influences job performance directly and indirectly though effort.

- Establishing ethical guidelines, demonstrating adherence to formal guidelines, and having zero tolerance of unethical activities are all effective ways of influencing salesperson's ethical behaviors.
- The study also shows that establishment of ethical guidelines may not necessarily be the result of a 'consensus' team effort where everyone's views are considered and accommodated.
- Instrumental leadership is crucial for implementing an ethical climate as it defines clear boundaries of ethical behavior.
- By spelling out the "dos & donts" of ethical behavior, a directive leader prescribes the "empowered space" which still leaves enough latitude for decision making. This reduces uncertainty, increases effort, and ultimately improves job performance.
- In terms of unethical behaviors, salespeople prefer to know that certain activities are completely off limits.
- When principled behavior enjoys a top priority, salespeople can come to enjoy their job without the temptation to "just slightly" cross the line in order to save the business.

Source: Governance Research Digest, June 2009 (Vol. 1, No. 6)

3.5.7 Ethical Duties of Organizational Citizens: Obligations Owed by Highly Committed Employees

Author(s): C. Caldwell, L. A. Floyd, R. Atkins and R. Holzgrefe

Individuals who demonstrate organizational citizenship behavior (OCB) contribute to their organization's ability to create wealth, but they also owe their organizations a complex set of ethical duties. Although, the academic literature has begun to address the ethical duties owed by organizational leaders to organizational citizens, very little has been written about the duties owed by those who practice OCB to their organizations.

Key findings

In this article, authors identify an array of ethical duties owed by those who engage in extra-role behavior and describe those duties in context with personality theory.

- Employees who understand the complex nature of OCB and the associated duties they owe to others are more likely to reach their potential and make greater contributions within their organizations.

Source: Governance Research Digest, October 2012 (Vol. 3, No. 10)

3.5.8 Evolving Responsibilities & Liabilities of Ethics Representatives: a practical guide

Author(s): European Business Ethics Forum & IBE

A report published by the European Business Ethics Forum prompts corporate Ethics Representatives (ERs), and their employers, to consider the extent to which their evolving responsibilities are likely to pose any increase in personal and legal liability. "Evolving Responsibilities & Liabilities of Ethics Representatives: a practical guide" explains what can be done to support employees and mitigate concerns.

Key findings

ERs are unlikely to have specific legal risk attached to them as long as they are diligent in fulfilling their responsibilities, ask the right questions and inform the right people of concerns that arise.

- As a result of the evolving nature of their responsibilities as well as developments in the legal and regulatory context within which they operate, the report explores the extent to which ERs may find themselves exposed to legal, personal and professional risks in the line of promoting and upholding ethical standards.
- While there is as yet very little case history around legal liabilities occurring due a to a failure to act, concerns are likely around the consequences of fulfilling their responsibilities, for example, being ostracized or dismissed for reporting misconduct, or stepping into sensitive areas, finding something suspicious, but being unable to act without fear of getting fired.
- To ensure that the often voluntary role remains attractive to employees, the report calls for organisations to fulfill their duty of care to their ethics representatives by helping them to perform their roles effectively and reinforcing the opportunities the role brings.

- They need to reassure themselves and staff that any personal and legal risks are understood.

Source: Governance Research Digest, January 2013 (Vol. 4, No. 1)

3.5.9 Authentic Leadership and Behavioral Integrity as Drivers of Follower Commitment and Performance

Author(s): H. Leroy, M. E. Palanski and T. Simons

The literatures on both authentic leadership and behavioral integrity have argued that leader integrity drives follower performance. Yet, despite overlap in conceptualization and mechanisms, no research has investigated how authentic leadership and behavioral integrity relate to one another in driving follower performance.

<u>Key findings</u>

In this study, authors propose and test the notion that authentic leadership behavior is an antecedent to perceptions of leader behavioral integrity, which in turn affects follower affective organizational commitment and follower work role performance.

- Analysis of a survey of 49 teams in the service industry supports the proposition that authentic leadership is related to follower affective organizational commitment, fully mediated through leader behavioral integrity.
- Next, authors found that authentic leadership and leader behavioral integrity are related to follower work role performance, fully mediated through follower affective organizational commitment.
- These relationships hold when controlling for ethical organizational culture.

Source: Governance Research Digest, April 2012 (Vol. 3, No. 4)

3.6   Organisational Integrity

3.6.1. The Codes of Ethics of S&P/MIB Italian Companies: An Investigation of Their Contents and Factors That Influence Adoption

Author(s): E. Lugli, U. Kocollari, C. Nigrisoli.

This article discusses the results of a survey into the contents, role and effectiveness of company codes of ethics in Italian companies. The companies surveyed are all listed on the Italian stock exchange (S&P/MIB). 40 companies representing the industrial, financial and service sectors took part.

Key findings

71% of companies in the financial sector have a company code of ethics. The figure is 92% for the service sector and 100% for industry.

- The various functions stated in different codes of ethics can be subdivided into three further categories: the function of preserving the firm's good image and reputation; the function of preventing illegal behaviour and the function of making the firm's values explicit.
- Across the three sectors, the most widespread code function was "making the firm's values explicit" (52% on average), in comparison with the function of "preserving the firm's image and reputation" (34% on average) and the least mentioned aim of "preventing illegal behaviour" (17% on average).
- The percentage for the function of "preserving the firm's image and reputation" was higher in the financial (40%) and service (45%) sectors than in the industrial sector (12%).
- The generally low percentage scored by "preventing illegal behaviour" may mean that codes of ethics are generally considered more as tools of external communication than as regulatory tools.
- Five categories of general principles were found in codes' contents: compliance with the law and regulations; honesty; transparency; integrity; and impartiality and independence in decision-making.

- In the financial sector an objective principle such as compliance with the law and regulations (30%) is less widespread than subjective principles such as honesty (80%) and integrity (90%).
- It appears that the financial sector pays more attention to honesty and integrity because these principles are considered the cornerstones of businesses like banking and insurance.
- While transparency is a principle equally present in all sectors, we notice a predominance of subjective over objective principles even in the service and industrial sectors, although the difference appears less significant than in the financial sector.
- Customer focus is a social value given a particularly high degree of consideration in the service (55%) and financial sectors (40%) while in the industrial sector its score is considerably lower (25%).
- Another major difference regards the particular attention paid by the financial sector (60%) to a trust-based relationship between the firm and its stakeholders. In contrast, this social value is completely absent in the industrial sector (0%).
- The observance of social responsibility turns out to be particularly significant in the financial sector (80%). Firms operating in the service (73%) and industrial (75%) sectors are more involved in environmental protection.
- The importance of the human factor in the running of the firm receives most consideration in sectors like service (82%) and finance (70%).

Source: Governance Research Digest, April 2009 (Vol. 1, No. 4)

3.6.2   Corporate Communication, Ethics and Operational Identity: A Case Study of Benetton

Author(s): J.L.Borgerson, J.E. Schroeder, M. Escudero Magnusson, and F. Magnusson.

This article investigates conceptual and strategic relationships between corporate identity, organizational identity and ethics, utilizing the Benetton Corporation as an illustrative case study. A multi-method case study, including interviews at retail outlets and trade events, sheds light on several important yet under-studied components of corporate identity, including stakeholders such as retail managers and contract employees.

Key findings

Benetton failed to use its socially responsible visual identity to inform and inspire its organisational identity via retail managers, contract employees and trade events.

- While Benetton had built a viable ethical and socially responsible identity via both communication and action, it failed to operationalise that identity throughout the organisation.
- In acting like a 'mere clothing retailer', Benetton may lose opportunities to connect consumers with its powerful ethical identity, built up via an enormously successful campaign that created a leading global brand.
- By overlooking their operational identity, companies may fail to connect their ethical values to this aspect of organisational identity by missing out on the added value to be gained from building ethical values and socially responsible attributes into their business identity.
- Consistency in communicating ethical values and socially responsible attributes, and coherence in connecting these values throughout business identity, do influence the relationships between organizational identity, corporate identity and ethical values.

Source: Governance Research Digest, August 2009 (Vol. 1, No. 8)

3.6.3 Ethics in Decision-making

Author(s): IBE

The new report from the Institute of Business Ethics draws on the experience of UK and international companies, as well as psychological and behavioural research, to provide practical assistance on how to encourage and embed ethical values and commitments across all decision-making. The Good Practice Guide will be useful for organisations looking for ways to instil ethical awareness and reasoning across all their decision-making.

Key findings

Faced with the pressures of business – demands to succeed, to 'make the numbers', to deliver on time, to follow the boss's orders – it is often too easy to make decisions without considering the ethical implications.

- High profile business scandals have shown that organisations' failure to instil the habit of ethical awareness and reasoning across all decision-making can lead to significant reputational and financial hits.
- Ethics in decision making is about maximising the conditions that best support any decision in an organisation, so that it has the desired outcome with respect to its ethical commitments.
- The Guide provides a framework for understanding the key conditions for and barriers to bringing ethics into business decisionmaking.
- It includes real examples of how companies facilitate, promote and embed ethics in decision-making.
- It includes chapters that focus on assistance for employees, managers and senior leaders.

Source: Governance Research Digest, June 2011 (Vol. 2, No. 2)

3.6.4 The Ethical Challenges of Social Media

Author(s): IBE

This briefing aims to raise awareness of the ethical challenges social media presents for companies. It also considers good practice in providing guidance for employees on its use whether for business or personal use.

<u>Key findings</u>

The unique characteristics of social media pose ethical challenges for business, through employees" use of social media on behalf of the company, as well as their personal use.

- In an IBE survey of large companies(2), 6 of 7 respondents identified integrity risk as the main ethical challenge with regard to social media.
- To address the ethical challenges that social media presents, companies need to fully assess the risks and be aware of the challenges presented by social media before using it.
- Through a social media policy companies can provide guidance to employees on how to address the ethical challenges.
- The policy needs to be consistent with the company's ethics policy and overlap with other existing policies around communication.
- The policy would provide guidance on two main areas; employees" use of social media on behalf of the company, and employees" personal use

of social media, including issues such as bullying and harassment, speaking up and employees" right to privacy.

Source: Governance Research Digest, December 2011 (Vol. 2, No. 8)

3.6.5 Surveys on Business Ethics 2011

Author(s): IBE

The Institute of Business Ethics' annual summary of the findings of selected surveys on business ethics issues carried out in the previous year. Publication includes the IBE/Ipsos MORI survey on Attitudes of the British Public to Business Ethics, the Edelman Trust Barometer, the ILM Index of Leadership and Trust and surveys on whistleblowing, fraud and antibribery and corruption.

Key findings

Nearly two thirds of people believe business behaves ethically; a third do not.

- Trust in NGOs, business and government declines globally.
- Employees trust their CEOs more now than in 2009.
- 55% of organisations provide whistleblowing facilities to external stakeholders and 35% to the general public.
- Only 56% are aware that their company has an anti-bribery policy.
- 29% of UK companies have „just a little" knowledge about the Bribery Act.
- 92% of FTSE 100 companies provide no metrics on ethics in their annual report.

Source: Governance Research Digest, February 2012 (Vol. 3, No. 2)

3.6.6 Concerns & Ethical Lapses, 2010 & 2011

Author(s): IBE

This new IBE Briefing provides an overview of major ethical concerns and lapses, as recorded in the IBE's weekly media monitoring in 2010 and 2011. The news stories involve UK companies or multinationals with a UK presence.

Key findings

The IBE media monitoring reported 928 cases of ethical lapses in 2010 and 2011.

- Finance (includes insurance companies) received by far the most news coverage (295 news stories).
- This is consistent with previous years.
- Retail was the next most reported on sector in the media, closely followed by the technology (includes IT companies) and extractive (oil, gas, metal and mining) sectors.
- The tobacco, chemicals, construction and property sectors were least mentioned in the news.
- The most commonly reported on ethical issue was bribery, corruption and fraud, followed by executive remuneration, corporate governance and fair competition.
- News items reporting on whistleblowing/speaking up, lobbying/donations, discrimination, and human rights were less common.
- There were some notable differences in reporting on concerns and ethical lapses in 2011 compared with 2010.
- The number of news stories involving the extractive sector almost doubled.
- Conversely coverage on utilities companies decreased by two thirds, and in the food and drink sector, by more than half.
- In terms of ethical issues, the number of cases involving corporate governance issues more than trebled from 2010 to 2011.
- Similarly, reporting on incidents of bribery, corruption and fraud almost doubled over this period.
- It is worth noting that in 2010 there were 87 cases relating to executive remuneration but this dropped to 33 in 2011.
- Only 3 of the 27 new stories on lapses in product safety and only 1 of 12 reports on lobbying/donations occurred in 2011. The number of news stories on marketing/advertising and on supply chain/procurement issues fell by more than half from 2010 to 2011.

Source: Governance Research Digest, March 2012 (Vol. 3, No. 3)

3.6.7 Sustainability with Integrity: Organisational Change to Collective Action

Author(s): UN Global Compact

A new report by the UN Global Compact was developed to highlight the importance of ethics and compliance in delivering corporate sustainability's full potential. The publication illustrates a range of corporate actions to implement the Global Compact's tenth principle on anti-corruption around the world.

Key findings

Over the last ten years, the field of anti-corruption, ethics and compliance has developed significantly as corporate awareness of these issues increases with changing legal and social environments.

- However the 10th Principle Against Corruption remains one of the most difficult areas to implement.
- Anti-corruption is also a least-reported issue area among UN Global Compact participants' annual Communications on Progress.
- Exciting promises of a low-carbon economy and sustainable future are often constrained by weak governance and rampant corruption.
- Transparency and strong anti-corruption measures will contribute significantly to realising sustainability priorities.
- Since the introduction of the 10th Principle in 2003, the UN Global Compact has led efforts to integrate the anti-corruption agenda into the corporate sustainability movement by building the business case, developing tools and resources, and convening collective action at the country level.
- Highlighting the potential of collective action as an effective mechanism to address corruption risks, the publication features five organisations from Brazil, China, Kenya, Serbia and the United Kingdom, and their approach to anti-corruption collective action.

Source: Governance Research Digest, June 2012 (Vol. 3, No. 6)

3.6.8 Business Ethics & Human Rights

Author(s): Institute of Business Ethics

An IBE Briefing explores the link between business ethics and human rights with a brief overview of the current business and human rights landscape. It also looks at how businesses seek to respect human rights and avoid human rights violations in their business operations and relationships.

Key findings

Attention to human rights has been shown to have a positive impact on business performance through improved stakeholder relations, positive corporate reputation and brand image, and employee motivation and retention.

- 'Doing business ethically' necessarily involves respecting human rights in the course of business operations.
- A company that is wishing to be considered as ethical will need to be mindful of human rights within the responsibilities of business and consistent with local law.
- Although respecting human rights can be considered integral to a business ethics agenda, IBE research (2012) found that only half of FTSE100 companies (52%) explicitly consider human rights in their code of ethics in some way.
- The positive and negative duties to protect human rights are still firmly with national governments.
- However, trends such as globalisation and the increasing presence of multinational corporations, pressures from NGOs, and reputation risk management, has meant there are increasing expectations of business in respecting human rights.
- The Briefing explores how companies are responding to this and the mechanisms they are using to express commitment and avoid human rights violations.

Source: Governance Research Digest, September 2012 (Vol. 3, No. 9)

3.6.9 Promoting Cultures of Integrity: Six Ethical Issues for Business Education

Author(s): Institute of Business Ethics

The report presents key thoughts from an ongoing consultation exercise on embedding business ethics into business education. IBE surveyed the Human Resource professionals across 40 large UK companies.

Key findings

80% felt business ethics should be taught as a compulsory module.

- The majority of business studies courses have ethics as an elective module, if it is taught at all.
- All respondents believed that ethical sensitivity was an important criterion in selecting employees, assessed through behavioural/competency-based interviews with dilemma cameos or reference made to the company's values.
- Furthermore, when asked whether MBA candidates were deemed to be adequately knowledgeable about business ethics, only 20% said 'yes' with the remainder saying 'somewhat'.

Source: Governance Research Digest, November 2011 (Vol. 2, No. 7)

3.6.10 2013 Corporate Governance and Compliance Hotline Benchmarking Report

Author(s): The Network, Inc., and BDO Consulting

The Network, Inc., a provider of integrated governance, risk and compliance (GRC) solutions, and BDO Consulting, a division of BDO USA, LLP, released its eighth annual statistical study of compliance hotline-related activity for the past five years. The goal of the 2013 Corporate Governance and Compliance Hotline Benchmarking Report is to identify emerging best practices for hotlines and other mechanisms for reporting misconduct and to provide a framework by which companies can assess their own ethics and compliance programs.

Key findings

The cross-industry incident-reporting rate increased to 9.27 reports per 1,000 employees, an eight percent increase from the previous year.

- In addition, the Corporate Fraud Index for 2012, which measures the percentage of fraud-related incidents across all reports, rose to 23.6%, an all-time high since the Index was first reported in 2005.

- Retaliation: Retaliation, an ongoing issue for organizations as they work to promote ethical workplaces, was cited as a factor in approximately two percent of cross-industry reports covering a broad variety of ethics and governance-related issues. Retaliation was highest in the Transportation, Communications & Utilities industry, followed closely by Construction.

- Actionability (Case Outcome): The actionability rate, which measures the percentage of reports warranting further investigation, rose to 72% in 2012. Actionability for reports involving retaliation was significantly higher, at 79%.

- Web Reporting: In 2012, 14% of reports were submitted via the web, a slight increase.

- Anonymity: The rate at which reports were made anonymously remains relatively stable, at 49%; however, only 21% of employees submitting an anonymous report had previously notified management.

- Industry Trends: The Construction industry showed a dramatic 197% increase in the reporting rate to 18.03 reports per 1,000 employees; the next largest increase came in the Wholesale Trade industry, at 19%. Both the Retail Trade and Services Industries saw a reporting rate decrease.

- Incident Categories: In 2012, three categories saw slight increases to reporting rate: Employment Law Violation; Corruption & Fraud; and Environment, Health & Safety. Despite a slight decrease in reporting, the Personnel Management category continues to lead all industries by a wide margin.

- Prior Management Notification: The majority of employees submitting a report – 72% – did not previously express their concerns to management prior to the employee utilizing the hotline.

Source: Governance Research Digest, January 2014 (Vol. 5, No. 1)

3.6.11 2013 Corporate Ethics Policies and Programmes: UK and Continental Europe Survey

Author(s): Institute of Business Ethics

The Institute of Business Ethics published its seventh survey exploring the mechanisms used by large companies to embed ethical values within business practice and provide guidance to staff. The 2013 Corporate Ethics Policies and Programmes: UK and Continental Europe Survey is unique in its ability to track changes that have occurred in the UK FTSE350 since 1995 in the way business organisations develop and implement their ethics policy and programmes.

<u>Key findings</u>

There is evidence of increased investment into ethics programmes over the last 3 years by corporate management. Seven out of ten respondents said this compared to five out ten in 2010 (68% of UK and 82% of Continental European respondents).

- What is more, 87% of UK respondents state that a member of the board of directors takes ultimate responsibility for the ethics programme. This suggests that the embedding of ethical values is being given a higher priority at this level. However, ethics is only a regular board agenda item for 65% of UK respondents and 70% of other European companies.
- Despite the increased investment in ethics programmes, a fifth of companies seem to offer training only once to general employees and managers, and only a third routinely train staff and managers once a year and (24%) of FTSE 350 respondents offer ethics training to the board only once.
- Bribery, corruption and facilitation payments continues (as in 2010) to be viewed as the most significant ethical issue for respondent companies – nearly 80% selected it.

Source: Governance Research Digest, January 2014 (Vol. 5, No. 1)

3.6.12   2013 Compliance and Ethics Benchmarking Survey

Author(s): SAI Global and Baker & McKenzie

SAI Global and Baker & McKenzie released the results of their 2013 Compliance and Ethics Benchmarking survey. The survey report also includes demographic breakdowns of the respondents' organization, size, industry, and global reach.

Key findings

- When asked about their title, 38% of respondents of respondents indicated they were employed as Vice President, Chief Compliance Officer, or general counsel at their organizations.
- When asked about their full-time, dedicated compliance and ethics staff, 38% of respondents said the overall compliance and ethics staffing levels at their organization have increased over the past year.
- However, 43% of respondents indicated they did not have sufficient staff, control, authority, and budget to effectively measure, manage, and mitigate compliance risks at their organization.
- When asked about their hotline and case management systems, a majority (56%) of those who completed the survey said their organizations use an outside vendor to manage their whistleblower hotline.
- Nearly half of respondents (45%) indicated they conduct risk assessments to address C&E risks on an annual basis.
- Almost 80% of respondents brief their boards on at least an annual basis, with 62% of them briefing their boards on a quarterly basis.

Source: Governance Research Digest, January 2014 (Vol. 5, No. 1)

3.6.13   2014 Ethics Communications Best Practices Report

Author(s): Ethisphere Institute

The Ethisphere Institute released a report that highlights strategies and tactics for leveraging ethics and integrity as differentiating brand attributes, citing key takeaways from the second-annual Best Practices in Ethics Communications Workshop, which was held at the New York Stock Exchange on October 24 2013. The 2014 Ethics Communications Best Practices Report features insights and perspectives from several recognized leaders in communications, academia, and legal and compliance and includes best practices that enabled companies to attain WME recognition.

Key findings

Transparency remains a priority issue, and the report suggests that an emphasis on ethics communications can drive greater profitability and mitigate risks.

- Communicating across cultures. Leaders need to be sure they are communicating effectively across different countries and cultures, which can define ethics very differently. Multinational corporations need to understand these differences and communicate accordingly.
- We all own ethics. No one person in an enterprise owns ethics, just as no one person owns trust. While compliance officers can help lead the dialogue, it is everyone's responsibility to spark conversations around ethics, regardless of his or her role in the enterprise.
- Reputations are not managed, they are earned. Companies need to understand that today's marketplace is drastically different from even five years ago, when enterprises relied purely on operational data to measure success. To thrive today, companies need to be strong from a communications, trust and ethical standpoint.
- Communications must be bold, deliberate. You can't take 'no' for an answer if what you propose is the right thing to do. Communication requires courage, especially in today's transparent environment.

Source: Governance Research Digest, July 2014 (Vol. 5, No. 7)

3.6.14 Towards Ethical Norms in International Business Transactions

Author(s): Institute of Business Ethics

The Institute of Business Ethics released a report that describes the macro economic development of recent decades and the international commercial values that now exist and explores the challenges of developing a generally agreed set of values for international business transactions. The report, Towards Ethical Norms in International Business Transactions, aims to suggest, principally for boards of directors, one means of establishing the basis of trust for long term commercial relationships wherever they operate in the world.

Key findings

Eliminating the causes of the erosion of trust between buyer and seller is seen as fundamental to sustainable economic activity.

- To underpin trust, the challenge then is to find a way to harmonise the ethical values which underlie all economic transactions wherever they take place.
- The Golden Rule implies openness in negotiations rather than what appears afterwards to be deception. It also has the merit of overriding some cultural differences that can create misunderstanding between contracting parties.
- A further challenge is for international companies themselves to be more resolute about applying their core ethical values throughout their worldwide operations.
- A zero tolerance policy to all forms of bribery, corruption and other forms of misconduct should be a basic commitment.
- A way forward would be for multinational companies, wherever headquartered, to include in all contracts a section on the standards they expect of theiremployees and their business partners in conducting business anywhere in the world.
- If agreement can be reached on a universal set of core ethical values or norms for international business, based on common and long held moral principles, then economic activity in all its different aspects will have an important new facilitator of economic output. This in turn would enhance the prospect that more of the world's population would be enabled to escape from poverty and benefit from expanded wealth creation

Source: Governance Research Digest, July 2014 (Vol. 5, No. 7)

3.6.15 Embedding ethical values in the corporate culture: Zambia

Author(s): The Chartered Institute of Management Accountants (CIMA)

CIMA published a paper that discusses ethical challenges that can be faced in corporate life as well as giving recommendations on how best to safeguard against risk and how to strengthen a culture of integrity. The paper, 'Embedding ethical values in the corporate culture: ZAMBIA' summarises 1. Who is responsible for ethical conduct and how is it communicated and supported?, 2. What can be done to combat corrupt business practices and how can the external environment be influenced? and 3. What ethical information is useful and what is the role of finance?

Key findings

Although the majority of organisations recognised that the board and senior management have overall responsibility, a number of companies do put an emphasis on raising awareness among all staff. It was more likely to be the largest organisations, or those with international presence, that put shared responsibility into practice. This was most apparent in regard to staff training, awareness raising and engagement.

- Although all organsations had a code of ethics, or relevant policies related to ethical conduct, not all of them were sure that staff would be aware of such guidelines or their responsibilities. Best practice examples included having an ethical champion, mandated by the leadership, who was able to promote ethical behaviour and formally raise ethical issues and concerns on behalf of the staff. Ethical champions included a nominated member of staff, or a member of a management committee.
- An ethics programme of training and communication which continues to remind staff of their duties and obligations is important in order to establish an ethical culture. The example was cited of a professional services company where it was mandatory for all staff to complete e-tests on ethics which have to be passed and which are repeated throughout the year. Penalties for incomplete tests ensure that they are not seen as 'optional'. This was backed by wider awareness raising activities, such as ethical messages appearing on computer screens. Another regional financial services organisation routinely tested their employees to assess their level of understanding and awareness of their code.
- It is important to document the activities that are taking place in an organisation to embed ethical behaviour and to emphasise the organisation's values. Therefore it is advised to track staff that have undergone training and assess their understanding of their commitments.

- Due diligence should be exercised with employees, suppliers, customers and partners who will be associated with the organisation, and the outcomes tracked. Risk and compliance departments can assist in collecting and acting upon such information but will need the support of other business units such as HR, procurement and sales.
- Contracts should be revisited to ensure that they align with a company's values and operating standards. If a hotline or similar reporting mechanism is in place, any issues arising should be discussed at leadership level and a response to concerns should be documented to show how issues are resolved and dealt with. Whistleblowing legislation has recently been introduced in Zambia and companies should seek advice and support from the relevant authorities and advisors in this regard.

Source: Governance Research Digest, August 2014 (Vol. 5, No. 8)

IV. RESPONSIBLE INVESTMENT

4.1 Investor Portfolio Management

4.1.1 Integrated ESG Analysis

Author(s): United Nations Principles for Responsible Investment (UNPRI)

UN Principles of Responsible Investment prepared a study showcasing how investors and analysts are integrating ESG factors into fundamental equity valuation. Integrated Analysis: How investors are addressing environmental, social and governance factors in fundamental equity valuation includes economic analysis, industry analysis, company strategy, financial reports and valuation tools.

Key findings

ESG analysis is used in all aspects of fundamental equity valuation, particularly in industry analysis, forecasting earnings and adjusting discount rates.

- ESG issues are assessed through standard models of business performance and valuation.
- We believe that any investor could make use of the research we reviewed.
- The reliance on traditional valuation tools can create a tension between their relatively short timeframes and the longer timeframes needed for many ESG issues to impact companies.
- Much of the analysis focused on situations where ESG issues were becoming more urgent or where investors are beginning to look to the longer term.
- ESG information remains more resource intensive to acquire and assess than audited financial information.
- The difficulty of acquiring consistent, comparable, audited information remains a significant hurdle to integrated analysis.

- Whilst for some ESG factors there is broad consensus that the issue could have a significant impact on a firm's performance, the materiality of other aspects depends on individual investors' processes, investment horizons, risk budgets and performance targets.

Source: Governance Research Digest, February 2013 (Vol. 4, No. 2)

4.1.2   Guide to Ethical Funds

Author(s): Blue and Green Tomorrow

Blue and Green Tomorrow released a guide that builds the case for ethical and sustainable investment in the UK. 'The Guide to Ethical Funds' aims to encourage potential investors to make a more informed investment choice in the future, relying on ethical, sustainable and responsible options.

Key findings

Sustainability megatrends continue to make the case for long-term, sustainable investment.

- There is a growing need to 'do more with less' in the context of population growth, climate change and resource availability, particularly with regards to pollution, and the consumption of energy and water resources.
- Companies that use more resources than they need (energy, water, minerals) are inefficient and are unnecessarily reducing their profitability.
- Companies that neglect the communities, in which they are based or operate, erode or antagonise their customer base.
- Those investors that reduce risk and maximise investment opportunities by seeking out companies which have the best performance on environmental, social and governance (ESG) issues, or by engaging with companies to improve performance, will be best placed to manage the global challenges that are coming our way.
- Mainstreaming green and ethical investment is about ensuring a good range of green and ethical financial products are available to all consumers across all aspects of ethical finance

Source: Governance Research Digest, August 2013 (Vol. 4, No. 8)

4.1.3 What Investees Think

Author(s): Keystone Accountability

Keystone Accountability conducted a survey of 330 investees providing anonymous feedback on seven leading impact investors. The 'What Investees Think' report identifies a significant opportunity to redress the gap in existing measurement, reporting and rating tools with systematic investee feedback and highlights areas of strength and areas in need of improvement.

Key findings

Investees don't really know what their social and environmental results may be.

- They have no idea what investors do with the reports that they prepare for them.
- They note that investors do not provide sufficient resources or expertise to enable investees to meet their reporting requirements.
- There is a significant opportunity for impact investors to encourage and support investee efforts to get client feedback. When they do they will find that end client feedback is not only useful to investees, it is also useful for investment decisions.
- The weakest areas have to do with value adding through non-financial support and transparency while the strongest areas are their technical competence, efficiency and credibility.
- Weaknesses are mainly in the nature of omissions – things they don't do, but should – and strengths flow from the exemplary comportment of their staff.
- While investees indicate inadequacies in current non-financial support, they express a strong demand for it.
- Across the board, impact investors would benefit from being more proactive in soliciting advice and guidance from their investees.

Source: Governance Research Digest, October 2013 (Vol. 4, No. 10)

4.1.4   What do investors expect from non-financial reporting?

Author(s): European Sustainable Investment Forum (EUROSIF) and the Association of Chartered Certified Accountants (ACCA)

The European Sustainable Investment Forum (EUROSIF) and the Association of Chartered Certified Accountants (ACCA) conducted a survey of 94 analysts and investors from large mainstream to small specialist funds located across 18 countries in order to gather the views and opinions of the investment community on their use of ESG information and the proposed reporting regime. The 'What do investors expect from non-financial reporting?' survey follows a European Commission proposal in April to establish new requirements for disclosure of non-financial information for all large companies in the EU.

Key findings

The most important sources of non-financial information for investors are sustainability/CSR reports and annual reports.

- A majority of respondents agree that current non-financial information published by companies is linked to the CSR policy.
- However, they disagree that current reporting is linked to business strategy and risk, and disagree that sufficient information is provided to assess financial materiality.
- In order for non-financial information to be useful to investors it must be comparable across companies.
- Respondents state that current non-financial reporting is not sufficiently comparable and agree that nonfinancial information should be better integrated with financial information.
- Qualitative policy statements are important to assess financial materiality, but quantitative key performance indicators (KPIs) are viewed as essential.
- Accountability mechanisms should be part of non-financial reporting, either through new board oversight mechanisms, third-party assurance and/or shareholder approval at AGMs.

Source: Governance Research Digest, November 2013 (Vol. 4, No. 11)

4.1.5 Investment With A Conscience: Examining The Impact of Pro- Social Attitudes and Perceived Financial Performance on Socially Responsible Investment Behaviour

Author(s): J. Nilsson

This study aims to examine the impact of a number of prosocial, financial performance, and socio-demographic variables on socially responsible investment (SRI) behavior in order to explain why investors choose to invest different proportions of their investment portfolio in SRI profiled funds. The study was conducted in Sweden and used data generated from 528 returned questionnaires. Responses were gathered from investors with differing investment behaviour – from those with no SRI investments to those whose portfolios are predominantly comrpised of SRI funds.

Key findings

Positive views on pro-social attitudes related to the issues addressed in SRI indicated that such issues are important to most investors. However, the investors who invested more of their portfolio in SRI generally displayed stronger pro-social attitudes than the investors who invested less.

- The levels of both trust and perceived consumer effectiveness (PCE – the notion that consumers are more likely to act on a social issue if they believe that their behaviour helps to solve the issue in question) for the most part increase with the amount invested in SRI.
- Almost 27% of the sample perceived that SRI profiled mutual funds perform worse than regular mutual funds.
- 20.5% thought that SRI will outperform regular funds in the long run while the bulk of the respondents (52%) held the perception that financial return will not be lower or higher than in regular mutual funds.
- Similar results can be observed in perceptions of investment risk, where 63% of the sample perceives similar risk levels for regular and SRI mutual funds.
- 13% of the sample thought that SRI is riskier while 24% perceived that risk is reduced in SRI funds.

- Men have a tendency to invest a smaller proportion of their investments in SRI.
- Education also proved a significant predictor of SRI behaviour as consumers without a university degree invested less in SRI.
- Three further socio-demographic variables (income, place of residence, and age) did not significantly impact SRI behaviour.

Source: Social Research Digest, February 2009 (Vol. 1, No. 2)

4.1.6 Fostering Labour Rights in Developing Countries: An Investor's Approach to Managing Labour Issues

Author(s): R.H. Montgomery and G.F. Maggio.

This paper presents a methodology to assist investors in large scale private infrastructure and other industry sector projects to utilize internationally recognized core labour rights and related standards for fostering sound labour management. The methodology involves due diligence or analysis of labor conditions and subsequent supervision and monitoring of performance and promotes the use of best practices to complement existing minimum requirements. Case study examples are presented and challenges in applying the approach are discussed.

Key findings

Unlike many other initiatives, which focus compliance primarily in relation to the core labour rights, the methodology addresses additional labour standards, such as the special circumstances of indigenous workers, personnel management, and workplace accommodations for projects undertaken in remote areas.

- The methodology offers a framework for assessing compliance with host country laws and recognized international labour rights norms, and for promoting best practices that go beyond compliance.
- The questions and indicators provide identifiable bases for measuring improvements to realize compliance and best practices objectives.
- The approach is designed to provide flexibility to address unique labour management circumstances in a variety of contexts.
- The methodology is not intended to replace or circumvent host country labour laws or other procedures for redressing violations. It was

designed to complement other existing avenues for achieving compliance with national law and international standards.

- Where ILO standards exceed national law on a particular issue, companies should strive to go beyond minimum national law requirements and conform to applicable international norms and best practices.

- Depending on the composition of the workforce as well as local political and economic circumstances, there can be substantial opportunities and risks in managing labour issues in large private sector resource extraction, infrastructure, or other projects.

- Assessing compliance with labour rights requirements involves a number of challenges.

- In some situations it will not be easy to fully conform to a particular labour rights standard, such as implementing an equal opportunity employment program that does not inadvertently discriminate against the labour rights of other workers.

- A further challenge is agreeing on the breadth of the labour management system's coverage for contractors, subcontractors, and other persons or units providing services to the project.

- An important question is determining who will actually perform the due diligence and supervision. In making this decision, key factors to consider include how best to ensure objectivity, integrity, and efficiency in the process.

- Depending on the situation, appropriate reviewers could be members of company staff, the investor's staff (if applicable), or independent third parties.

- Reviewers should have sufficient combined expertise in labour rights law and policy, auditing projects for labour rights compliance, and a knowledge of engineering and sociopolitical issues connected with large private sector development projects. In some complicated cases, a team may be needed.

- Due to their nature, large-scale private sector infrastructure projects may be more likely than smaller-scale enterprises to comply in practice with certain core labour standards, such as the prohibition of child labour in hazardous activities, and the use of forced labour.

- The issue of whether to make public the results of a compliance review of the labour management system is an open issue for many companies.

Factors relating to confidentiality and avoidance of legal liability need to be addressed.

Source: Social Research Digest, August 2009 (Vol. 1, No. 8)

4.1.7   ESG Indices for Bond Market

Author(s): Barclays and MSCI

Barclays and MSCI launched a new family of fixed income indices based on environmental, social and governance (ESG) factors, which they say could stimulate sustainable investment through the bond market. The Barclays MSCI ESG Fixed Income Indices comprise more than 500 bespoke and standard indices and are thought to be the first of their kind for the bond market, although a range of similar indices exist for equity investors, including the FTSE4Good and the Dow Jones Sustainability Indices.

Key findings

- The new portfolio provides asset owners and managers with a comprehensive series of performance benchmarks.
- Three sets of indices have been issued.
- The Sustainability Indices will only include companies performing well in terms of ESG factors compared to their competitors.
- The Social Responsibility Indices excludes companies engaged in activities such as tobacco production or nuclear power that might deter values-based investors.
- A third weighted set does not exclude any companies, but will over-weight or underweight firms within a bond index based on ESG ratings.
- Institutional investors should be able to leverage these indices to create index-linked investment products, such as Exchange Traded Funds (ETFs), separately managed accounts, and structured products, based on ESG investment themes.

Source: Governance Research Digest, June 2013 (Vol. 4, No. 6)

4.1.8   Proxy Voting for Sustainability

Author(s): Ceres

Ceres released a resource guide to help global investors respond to environmental, social and governance, or "ESG," issues that are increasingly the subject of shareholder resolutions filed with U.S. publicly held corporations. It includes more than 75 specific best practice examples of proxy guidelines compiled from leading public pension funds, asset managers, socially responsible investment funds, labor unions and foundations.

Key findings

Although there has been much progress in support for both governance and sustainability resolutions put forward by shareholders since 2004, the largest asset managers often fail to take advantage of this opportunity to promote key governance and sustainability reforms at large public companies, including the types of reforms that may have averted the recent financial crisis.

- Ceres reviewed the proxy voting guidelines of large asset managers in the U.S. and found that many institutions' guidelines are not detailed or comprehensive enough to guide voting on specific governance and sustainability issues.
- However, some institutional investors like the Florida and Connecticut state retirement systems, CalSTRS, PaxWorld Management, Calvert, Northern Trust and the AFL-CIO, have developed partial proxy voting guidelines on sustainability-focused resolutions.
- Among the specific best practice guidelines highlighted in the report's appendix:
  o water availability: Florida's state retirement system will support resolutions seeking disclosure about a company's water supply dependency or preparation of reports pertaining to sustainable water supplies for a company's operations;
  o greenhouse gas emissions: Connecticut's state retirement system will vote for resolutions requesting company disclosure on greenhouse gas emissions from their operations and products;
  o policy lobbying: Calvert will support resolutions asking companies to disclose budgets dedicated to public policy lobbying activities;
  o board independence: the AFL-CIO, Florida retirement system and other investors support resolutions seeking stronger composition of independent board members on corporate boards.

Source: Governance Research Digest, September 2011 (Vol. 2, No. 5)

4.1.9   Eurosif Media Sector Report

Author(s): Eurosif

A report by Eurosif, based on research by Ethix SRI Advisors, describes the key environmental, social and governance issues facing the sector and their importance in investment decisions. These include trust and freedom of expression issues as well as privacy and intellectual property, environmental and content diversity issues.

Key findings

Investors are aware that the media sector faces specific risks particularly relating to trust and ethics which can have very significant financial impacts, as seen in the UK's phone hacking case.

- Authors recommend that publishers are more transparent about the reliability of their sources, adhere to accepted ethical standards and distinguish more clearly, fact and opinion.
- By enhancing trust, publications grow their audience and advertising revenue, which appeals to investors.
- Alma Media, a new case-study in the report, is experimenting with several imaginative techniques to build trust with its readers.
- The media sector is going through huge changes driven by new technologies, the convergence of the media sector with the technology and communications sectors, and the need for companies to radically transform their business models as growing number of consumers expect to access content anywhere anytime, without charge.
- What this means is that companies need to be acutely aware that their business risk profile may be changing dramatically: software companies may be sued for breaches of copyright law, telecommunications companies may find that their overall footprint increases as they partner with traditional print media companies, all companies will be under pressure to properly manage personal data and information.
- From an investment perspective, it is very difficult to assess the investment implications of ESG issues at a sectoral level.
- Instead analysts will need to analyse these issues at the individual company level and frequently at the level of individual business lines.

- Moreover, this analysis is not static; the rate of change in the sector means that, now more than ever, investors need to look forward and try and understand how the company and the sector as a whole are changing.

Source: Governance Research Digest, May 2012 (Vol. 3, No. 5)

4.1.10 A New Foundation for Portfolio Management

Author(s): Portfolio 21 Investments

Portfolio 21 Investments, a Portland-based investment management firm, has published a report highlighting significant factors and trends impacting investors in the 21st Century. The publication offers a new framework for managing ecological risks and emerging opportunities, and meeting the multi-faceted needs of today's investors.

<u>Key findings</u>

The paper proposes three new investment decisionmaking principles related to risk, growth, and utility: Integrated Risk, Selective Growth, and Multidimensional Utility Functions.

- The three principles are founded on observed facts and market behavior in contrast to simplified assumptions and generalizations.
- These New Foundational Principles should form the basis for investment decision-making in place of a theory that can only be substantiated by making unwarranted and unrealistic assumptions about risk, growth and utility.
- Integrated Risk includes the externalities that are not priced in the market but which threaten to inhibit or shift returns.
- Integrated Risk considers the potential impact of ecological limits as they manifest in business disruptions, shortages, and social/political upheaval.
- The end of growth does not mean the end of the economy, but, because the economy must curtail throughput, there will be clear winners and losers.
- Rather than a "rising tide lifting all boats", the new economy will resemble a zero sum game with respect to throughput-driven growth.

- The term Selective Growth refers to the fact that growth can occur even if average economic growth is zero or negative, but it will be unique to particular sectors and companies rather than a function of rising per capita material consumption.
- The existence of Multidimensional Utility Functions means that clarity with respect to the unique purpose and goals of each asset owner should be central to the investment process.
- But, unless this is specifically called out, there is a tendency for investors, advisors, and consultants to default to the language and practices of Modern Portfolio Theory, despite the shortcomings identified here and elsewhere.

Source: Governance Research Digest, January 2012 (Vol. 3, No. 1)

4.1.11 Finding Common Ground on the Metrics that Matter

Author(s): IRRC Institute

This report explores and documents the extent to which corporate ESG information tracked and managed internally by companies is consistent with analogous information sought by external parties, and in particular, by ESG investors and the research companies that serve them. To conduct analysis, authors obtained corporate data from the results of a recent "Green Metrics that Matter", and developed ESG researcher/investor data by collecting and compiling publicly available information from company web sites and other sources.

Key findings

There is general agreement about the key corporate sustainability issues, but not necessarily on the specific form and number of metrics used to measure them.

- There is also a fundamental difference in the purpose(s) to be served by examining corporate ESG information between corporate executives and ESG researchers/investors.
- Increasingly, corporate managers and ESG researchers/investors believe that the same ESG issues are important, but may track them at very different levels of detail.

- Corporate ESG metrics and approaches to managing to them are based on business fundamentals (e.g., benefits/costs, importance to customers, possibility of impact).
- Disclosure of the ESG metrics of common interest is very uneven, with some being disclosed by a great many companies and others disclosed by very few.
- ESG researchers are concerned both with corporate accountability and with predicting the future, and their information requests and collection methods reflect the need to both receive appropriate assurances and to inform a judgment about the management quality of companies.
- Both ESG researchers/ investors and corporate EHS managers and executives approach ESG issues from a risk mitigation perspective, not a value creation perspective.
- Most specific indicators used by corporate EHS managers and executives and investors focus on identifying negative attributes or downside risk.
- While the members of both groups are interested in the potential for ESG-related financial value creation, their interactions are generally devoid of information speaking directly to this crucial issue.
- Future improvements in corporate disclosure quality and in efficient and adroit collection and use of these data in investment analysis will require improved clarity and more effective and consistent communication between companies, researchers, and the consumers of information.
- Substantial, non-incremental progress depends on clear articulation, from both companies and ESG researchers/investors, of corporate financial value creation through advancements in managing ESG issues and their results.
- Typical ESG metrics reporting practices and guidelines have advanced, but also have had some unintended and unfortunate consequences, including too few companies reporting, and some researchers requesting a substantial number of additional (non-GRI) metrics.
- These adverse outcomes often reinforce one another.
- More widespread and consistent disclosure on fewer indicators might create more utility for both corporations and investors.

- Greater dialogue and sharing of information and perspectives is essential for both sides to understand the other's needs and constraints, and to forge communication mechanisms that are more effective and less burdensome than current practices.

Source: Governance Research Digest, June 2012 (Vol. 3, No. 6)

4.1.12   Toniic E-Guide to Early-Stage Global Impact Investing

Author(s): The Toniic Institute—in collaboration with Duke University

The Toniic Institute—in collaboration with Duke University's CASE i3— released a first-of-its-kind online primer, a 7-step framework to global early-stage impact investing. The "Toniic E-Guide to Early-Stage Global Impact Investing" is a fundamental reference for anyone seeking to understand how to successfully invest at the early stage for both a financial return and social or environmental impact.

Key findings

Impact investing in early-stage enterprises, although challenging, can be extremely rewarding and potentially provide both financial and social or environmental returns. It allows investors to improve the lives of the poor or vulnerable—locally and globally—while providing a return on capital. Yet few comprehensive guides exist for investors.

- In early-stage impact investing, the investees are social enterprises that are either pre-revenue or just earning revenue. Early-stage enterprises are an important investment focus for impact investors because the groundwork is laid during this phase for the company's customers, revenue model, impact thesis (its theory of change about how it will create social value), and overall sustainability.

Source: Governance Research Digest, April 2014 (Vol. 5, No. 4)

4.1.13 Understanding   investors: the   changing   corporate   perspective

Author(s): ACCA (the Association of Chartered Certified Accountants)

ACCA (the Association of Chartered Certified Accountants) issued its last report in a four-part series examining what investors want from corporate reporting and how organisations are responding to their needs. The report, Understanding investors: the changing corporate perspective, examines current trends in reporting and the audit relationship from the perspective of the CFO, with a particular emphasis on real-time and integrated reporting.

Key findings

The speed with which companies release their annual accounts is seen as an important indicator of efficient management and good governance.

- Almost two-thirds of CFOs say that external stakeholders see a speedy close as a sign of good management.
- A majority of CFOs have already made efforts to close their accounts more quickly, and most intend to reduce closing times further over the next three years.
- A broad majority of respondents believe that faster closing has not only improved their reporting culture, but it has also led to better decision making in the corporate reporting cycle.
- Moreover, the reduction in closing time has allowed companies to re-allocate important resources in their finance departments to make them more efficient.
- There is cautious support for a move to real-time reporting. Two-thirds of CFOs surveyed would welcome a move towards greater adoption of real-time reporting, but they also worry that this could compromise competition-sensitive information and lead to misstatements. In addition, 45% of respondents said that the difficulty of instituting effective controls to ensure accuracy is a major obstacle to more widespread use of real-time financial reporting.
- Many companies have already taken steps to secure 'real-time' information within the business, but others still have considerable work to do. Up-to-the-minute information about key performance metrics is a vital source of competitive advantage, because it helps companies to become more agile, meaning they can respond more quickly to market changes.
- Real-time information within a business only has value if executives can have confidence in the underlying data.

- Accessing accurate, complete data is a major challenge, particularly in companies where data is distributed widely across multiple applications and silos. Making data more consistent, standardised and accurate remains a key goal for many companies.

- Investors value more frequent, rapid reporting and CFOs are, for the most part, supportive of this trend. Nonetheless, care must be taken to strike a balance between speed and the need for assurance. Releasing information quickly has no benefit if that information is subsequently found to be subject to misstatements or reporting errors.

- The research has found strong support for integrated reporting among investors. Most of the CFO respondents also indicate that they will ultimately move towards this model. There is, however, some reluctance among companies to be a first mover. Although policymakers need to do more to educate and engage corporates in the benefits of integrated reporting, CFOs should develop a better understanding so they can determine the right time to transition.

Source: Governance Research Digest, June 2014 (Vol. 5, No. 6)

4.1.14 COPING, SHIFTING, CHANGING: Strategies for Managing the Impacts of Investor Short-Termism on Corporate Sustainability

Author(s): Global Compact LEAD and the Principles for Responsible Investment (PRI)

Global Compact LEAD and the Principles for Responsible Investment (PRI) launched a joint report that examines what companies can do to reduce the negative impacts of short-termism on their long-term strategies and investments. The report, COPING, SHIFTING, CHANGING: Strategies for Managing the Impacts of Investor Short-Termism on Corporate Sustainability outlines three broad corporate strategies: 1) Cope with prevailing short-termism in their existing investor base (in the near-term), 2) Shift to a more long-term oriented investor base (in the medium-term) and 3) Support wider systemic change in the capital markets (over the medium to long-term).

Key findings

Eliminating the causes of the erosion of trust between buyer and seller is seen as fundamental to sustainable economic activity.

- Recommendation 1: Companies need to understand the diverse needs and interests of their current investor base and of potential (or target) future investors.
- Recommendation 2: Companies should analyse how investor short-termism has affected their business strategy, their capital investment and their financing of the business.
- Recommendation 3: Companies need to define the outcomes – coping, shifting, changing – they wish to achieve from their efforts to alleviate the impacts of investor short-termism on their businesses.
- Recommendation 4: Companies need to develop performance measures that they can use to track progress against these outcomes.
- Recommendation 5: Companies should monitor the results of their efforts to cope with short-termism, to shift their investor base and to change the capital markets. They should share their knowledge and experiences with other companies.
- Recommendation 6: Companies should develop and implement sustainability strategies that, as far as possible, provide clear financial benefits (e.g. cost reduction, improved efficiency) over the short-term.
- Recommendation 7: Companies should communicate the short- and the long-term financial benefits of their sustainability-related strategies and activities. They should highlight metrics that are of relevance to short-term investors and clearly articulate how the company's longer-term investments positively affect its net present value.
- Recommendation 8: Companies should confidently communicate and demonstrate how their business strategy, including their approach to sustainability, will create long-term value for their investors.
- Recommendation 9: Senior management remuneration should depend on the long-term performance of the business, across a range of financial and non-financial metrics, of the business.
- Recommendation 10: Companies should consider whether they should stop producing quarterly earnings guidance and instead report on issues and metrics that are of relevance to the longer-term success of the business.

- Recommendation 11: Boards of directors should produce formal statements that set out their duties as stewards of the company and that commit them to long-term decision-making. Within these statements, they should explain how they define long-term, and explain how this relates to their business and investment cycles.
- Recommendation 12: Companies should proactively meet with current and potential investors to discuss the company's approach to creating and protecting value. These meetings should cover issues such as sustainability, long-term strategy, performance, governance, culture, risk and reputation, and should occur outside of the results season.
- Recommendation 13: Companies should provide policymakers with evidence (case-studies and data) of how investor short-termism has affected their business strategy, their capital investment decisions, their approach to sustainability and their ability to create long-term business value.
- Recommendation 14: Companies should encourage policymakers to take action to address the negative consequences of short-termism and to adopt measures that enable companies to take a longer-term approach to sustainability-related activities and investments.
- Recommendation 15: Companies should take a long-term approach in their own investment practices and in the investment practices of their pension funds.

Source: Governance Research Digest, September 2014 (Vol. 5, No. 9)

4.2   Country Investment Trends

4.2.1   European SRI Study 2012

Author(s): Eurosif

Marking their 10th anniversary, Eurosif has recently released the 5th European Sustainable and Responsible Investment Study. It is the the organization's fifth report of the SRI industry in European markets.

<u>Key findings</u>

All responsible investment strategies have gained market share, with four of the seven having grown more than 35% per year since 2009.

- Although the growth is not uniform across the various European markets, the fastest growing strategy is Norms-based screening, with Exclusions and Best-in-Class also ranking highly.
- With the rapid growth of "Impact Investing" as an investment philosophy, European and national politicians have begun to strongly pursue initiatives aimed at strengthening the segment.
- Eurosif estimates the current European market of Impact Investing at €8.75 billion.
- This comes at a time when financial regulations seek to reconcile financial markets and create infrastructure for sustainable, long-term economic growth.
- The majority of respondents to the 2012 study saw regulatory drivers as one of the leading growth catalysts for SRI in Europe, in conjunction with institutional investors.

Source: Governance Research Digest, October 2012 (Vol. 3, No. 10)

4.2.2 Responsible Investment and the Chinese Stock Market

Author(s): M. Barnett and J. Chen

The study's authors studied the effect of environmental, social, and governance (ESG) risks on securities' performance in terms of alpha for Chinese firms. This study was the first of its kind to research the link between ESG risk assessment and financial performance in the Chinese stock market.

Key findings
The study conclusively determined a continuing opportunity for greater than expected return on investment for ESG risk, referred to as "ESG alpha" in the study.

- There are three necessary considerations to be made when assessing the Chinese stock market with ESG criteria:
  o in-depth ESG risk data for Chinese firms;
  o distinction between Chinese firms listed predominantly for Chinese and western institutional investors;
  o discrepancies between western and Chinese definitions of ESG criteria.

- While the report shows significant investment opportunities using Chinese ESG criteria within the Chinese markets, the alpha is generally lower when using Western ESG criteria for Chinese listings.
- Additionally, research has not yet shown a potential for ESG on Chinese stocks that are listed internationally.

Source: Governance Research Digest, October 2012 (Vol. 3, No. 10)

4.2.3   2012 Report on Sustainable and Responsible Investment Trends in the United States

Author(s): Forum for Sustainable and Responsible Investment

A new report was released tracking growth and reflecting trends within the sustainable, responsible, impact (SRI) investment industry in the U.S. It measures ESG integration (environmental, social, governance) in investment analysis and portfolio selection, the filing of shareholder resolutions on ESG issues, and community impact investing.

Key findings

As of year-end 2011, the overall total of professionally managed SRI assets in the U.S. was $3.74 trillion, up by 22% from 2009.

- The total is 486% greater than in 1995, the first year that US SIF began measuring the size and scope of the SRI industry—in sharp contrast to the 376% growth of professionally managed conventional assets over the same time period.
- The gain in market share is attributed to increasing client demand for ESG investing strategies and growth of community development bank assets, as consumers switch from large banks, are credited with much of the impetus for growth.
- The report highlights progresses made on a variety of fronts in recent years, including the fact that now over 50% of S&P 500 companies have agreed to disclosure and board oversight of corporate political spending.
- It's also noted that environmental and social proxy ballot issues are garnering more shareowner votes and more money managers are filing shareowner resolutions.

- Alternative investment vehicles, such as private equity and venture capital funds, responsible property funds, and hedge funds have experienced as much as 250% asset growth just since 2010.
- Sudan topped the list of avoidance policies, with nearly $1 trillion invested in U.S.- domiciled accounts that eschew investments in companies doing business there.

Source: Governance Research Digest, November 2012 (Vol. 3, No. 11)

4.2.4   Emerging Markets Custom Index

Author(s): Northern Trust (Nasdaq: NTRS), in collaboration with MSCI ESG Research's and Institutional Shareholder Services' (ISS) ESG screens

Northern Trust (Nasdaq: NTRS), in collaboration with MSCI ESG Research's and Institutional Shareholder Services' (ISS) ESG screens, announced the first emerging markets custom index which integrates Environmental, Social and, uniquely, Governance (ESG) screens. The MSCI Emerging Markets Custom ESG Index and Northern Trust's corresponding fund are designed to enable institutional investors across the globe to gain exposure to the potential growth and diversification benefits of emerging markets investment, while incorporating traditional environmental and social screening, as well as a unique governance screen.

Key findings

The index is a passive investment vehicle that filters out companies with less satisfactory governance criteria, using three screens applied to the MSCI EM Index universe, followed by a sequence of checks on governance and executive independence.

- The first three screens were determined based on common factors for norms based and industry screening criteria identified in consultation with Northern Trust's existing European investor clients.
- The first eliminates constituent companies of the MSCI EM Index that have been found to be in breach of the UN Global Compact's ten principles.
- The second screen removes manufacturers of controversial weapons such as cluster bombs and landmines and finally tobacco manufacturers are excluded.

- Following these exclusions, any constituents lacking sufficient independence across ownership, board representation, key corporate committees and audit and remuneration committees are filtered out.

Source: Governance Research Digest, June 2013 (Vol. 4, No. 6)

4.2.5   Global Sustainable Investment Review

Author(s): Global Sustainable Investment Alliance

Global Sustainable Investment Alliance produced the first report to collate the results from the market studies of regional sustainable investment forums from Europe, the US, Canada, Asia, Japan, Australia and Africa. The "Global Sustainable Investment Review 2012"report is based on the work of seven sustainable investment forums which, using detailed surveys, localized knowledge, and secondary sources, have evaluated and compared the sustainable investment practices of asset owners, asset managers and individual investors around the world and it includes all major asset classes, from public equities and fixed income to hedge funds and microfinance.

<u>Key findings</u>

Globally, at least US$ 13.6 trillion worth of professionally managed assets incorporate environmental, social and governance (ESG) concerns into their investment selection and management, representing 21.8% of the total assets managed professionally in the regions covered by the report.

- Europe is the largest region with about 65% of the known global sustainable investing assets under management.
- The three biggest regions—Europe, the United States, and Canada— together account for 96% of such assets.
- The most common sustainable investing strategy used globally is negative/exclusionary screening, with US$ 8.3 trillion in assets.
- This is followed by integration (US$ 6.2 trillion) and corporate engagement/shareholder action (US$ 4.7 trillion).
- Norms-based screening is also significant at US$ 3.0 trillion, but this approach is currently only found on a large scale in Europe.

- Positive/best-in-class screening stands at just over US$ 1.0 trillion, while impact investing and sustainability themed investments are comparatively small at US$ 89 billion and US$ 83 billion respectively.
- There are large differences in the popularity of specific strategies employed across regions.
- For instance, the US market contributes most of the global assets invested in positive screening and impact investing, while most thematic investments originate from Europe and Africa.
- All the regions expect the proportion of assets managed with reference to ESG considerations to rise, as more and more investors realize the importance of sustainable investment to risk management and long-term performance and as the salience of ESG issues grow.

Source: Governance Research Digest, June 2013 (Vol. 4, No. 6)

4.2.6   SME Funding Study

Author(s): Heart and Mind Strategies, commissioned by Shell Foundation and Citi Foundation

Heart and Mind Strategies published research meant to capture the current SME finance environment and "market offerings" for the Missing Middle in the Middle East with a view to understanding the opportunities for promoting growth finance into the region. This research looked beyond what is already "known" to assess what current financing strategies SMEs are using, the size of the funding gap, the potential for growth and the kind of service offering that would suit their needs.

<u>Key findings</u>

Although there is a number of existing SME support programs in the region, they need to go beyond the provision of limited subsidized loans and preinvestment training to adequately support the Missing Middle SMEs throughout their business lifecycle.

- Missing Middle SMEs have four critical interrelated needs for sustainable success: 1) flexible patient capital structured to fit the needs of each SME; 2) sustainable and customized business development assistance targeted to each SME's needs;; 3) market linkages to supply chains to ensure SMEs have an adequate access to market opportunities; and 4) an enabling business environment that addresses the barriers to their development and growth.

- There is near unanimous agreement among SMEs and intermediaries interviewed in this study that addressing these needs in a focused and sustained manner would increase the survival rates and sustainability of SME businesses.

- An integrated system that offers a one-stopshop facility where SMEs can access a range of services from information about starting a business to support on how to effectively manage and sustain a growing business is much needed.

- To make SME support programs more effective, a more coordinated, customized and sustained model of support that is sustained throughout the various stages of business development and growth, and is capable of addressing not only barriers to starting up a business, but also barriers to operating a business and achieving growth, should be adopted.

Source: Governance Research Digest, February 2013 (Vol. 4, No. 2)

4.2.7   UK Impact Investment Report

Author(s): UKSIF

UKSIF released a report that brings together insights from leading UK impact investment specialists drawn from UKSIF's membership. Their dialogue in 'The Future of Investment: Impact Investing' demonstrates the different motivations which drive activity: from costcutting by Government, to belief driven by personal experience, expectations that market-level returns are possible from certain impact investments, the wide range of opportunities which are already apparent, the extent to which the UK is a global leader in the field and how investors of all sizes will be offered the chance to impact invest.

Key findings

In the UK, there has been a growing awareness of the need to broaden the funding available to social purpose organisations and build a social investment market.

- Impact investments are made with the intention to generate measurable social and environmental impact alongside a financial return.
- The criteria to evaluate the positive social and/or environmental outcomes of investments are an integrated component of the investment process.
- In contrast, practitioners of socially responsible investing also include negative or avoidance criteria as part of their investment decisions.
- The social investment market offers a choice of risk, reward and impact from each investment across the spectrum.
- Some investments seek to achieve market-rate risk-adjusted financial returns whilst others offer below-market risk-adjusted financial returns in return for the impact created – socalled 'blended value' investments.
- The regulatory barriers that constrain impact investing in the UK are, firstly, tax disadvantages related to the fact that the investments tend to be long-term and illiquid.
- Taking into account the tax regime in the UK (applied to say pension contributions, ISAs etc) all of the benefits are di rected towards liquid investments on capital markets.
- Even in more flexible vehicles (such as SIPPs) unlisted investments are hard to make and can come with prohibitively expensive fees.
- Other support mechanisms, such as EIS and VCT regimes may apply in some circumstances for equity investments but the fit between EIS/VCT rules and impact investments is quite patchy with some areas heavily covered (such as solar VCTs up u ntil 2011) and others sparsely covered.
- Community Interest Tax Relief can be used in certain circumstances (e.g. Bristol Together CIC) but is fairly inflexible as a scheme

Source: Governance Research Digest, August 2013 (Vol. 4, No. 8)

4.2.8   Impact Investing in Canada: State of the Nation

Author(s): Purpose Capital and the MaRS Centre for Impact Investing

Purpose Capital and the MaRS Centre for Impact Investing jointly authored a report that provides updated information and analysis that can inform both new and existing actors in the impact investment sector. The State of the Nation report on impact investing in Canada responds to a need to better understand the nature of impact investing activity in Canada, the ways in which it is evolving and maturing, and the areas in which it could grow or falter.

Key findings

Impact investing in Canada is characterized by a diversity of approaches and organizations.

- Unsurprisingly, given the size of the country, impact investing in Canada spans a wide range of motivations, forms and uses.
- Challenges remain in several important areas: Looking beyond established sectors and regions, there is still much work to be done to create supportive infrastructure for impact investing.
- At a basic level, there is a misalignment between capital and opportunity; more often than not, entrepreneurs continue to identify finance as a key barrier to growth, and investors continue to rank deal-flow and investment readiness as a fundamental issue.
- The search and transaction costs of deals remain relatively high, even without accounting for issues such as impact measurement and a restrictive regulatory system. These and other issues require concerted and sustained effort in order to stimulate more activity.
- Industry building will require coordinated action and leadership: Even if the practice of impact investing is not new—and there are certainly good examples of successful organizations—there is much work to be done to nurture and celebrate Canadian exemplars. Creating the conditions for all market actors to harness the potential of impact investing will require coordinated action within and across sectors and regions.

Source: Governance Research Digest, September 2014 (Vol. 5, No. 9)

4.3 Green Investment

4.3.1 Do Corporations Invest Enough in Environmental Responsibility?

Author(s): Y. Kim and M. Statman

The article addresses the conflict of environmental investments and shareholder interest. Authors examine the appropriate approach for investment in the environment to align with the interest of shareholders.

Key findings

Corporations increase their investment in environmental responsibility when an increase improves financial performance and reduce when a decrease improves financial performance.

- Proponents of corporate environmental responsibility argue that corporations shortchange shareholders by investing too little in environmental responsibility.
- They claim that corporations can improve their financial performance by increasing their investment in environmental responsibility.
- Opponents of corporate social responsibility argue that corporations shortchange shareholders by investing too much in environmental responsibility.
- They claim that corporations can improve their financial performance by reducing their investment in environmental responsibility.
- Yet, others claim that corporations serve their shareholders well by investing just enough in social responsibility, not too little and not too much.
- If so, corporations increase their investment in environmental responsibility when an increase improves financial performance and reduce their investment in environmental responsibility when a decrease improves financial performance.
- Authors find that the behavior of corporations is consistent with the claim that they act in the interest of shareholders, increasing or decreasing their investment in environmental responsibility as necessary to improve their financial performance.

Source: Environmental Research Digest, January 2012 (Vol. 3, No. 1)

4.3.2 The Challenge of Institutional Investment in Renewable Energy

Author(s): Climate Policy Initiative

Climate Policy Initiative issued a report that mapped the potential of institutional investors to bridge the financing gap more cost effectively and identified the barriers to achieving it. The report, "The Challenge of Institutional Investment in Renewable Energy" analyzed the investment portfolios of more than 25 pension funds and insurance companies across North America, Europe, and Australia, along with global and national data on institutional investors.

Key findings

If all policy barriers were removed and investors optimized their renewable energy related investment practices, institutional investors could supply one quarter to one half of the investment needed to fund renewable energy projects through 2035.

- The long-term, reliable returns offered by green energy should align with institutional investors' objectives, rather than those seeking short term gains.
- By making green energy investments, institutions could enhance the performance of their portfolios and lower the cost of capital for renewable energy while removing some of the financial burden of supporting clean energy infrastructure from cash-strapped governments.
- However, direct investment in renewable energy projects remains challenging for institutional investors, while backing for companies with some clean energy in their portfolios may not necessarily spark further investment in the clean energy sector.
- Tapping into this finance may require pooled investment vehicles that create liquidity, increase diversification, and reduce transaction costs, or the development of direct investment teams specialising in clean energy.
- Policy barriers discouraging institutional investors from contributing to renewable energy projects should also be removed

- These include perceived policy uncertainty, such as retrospective cuts to subsidies, and inconsistent legislation.

Source: Governance Research Digest, March 2013 (Vol. 4, No. 3)

4.3.3   Green Investment Report

Author(s): Green Growth Action Alliance Initiative & Accenture

In collaboration with the World Economic Forum's Green Growth Action Alliance Initiative, Accenture released a report that informs policy-makers and public and private finance providers how to close the gap in delivering inclusive, sustainable growth. The Green Investment Report: The Ways and Means to Unlock Private Finance for Green Growth highlights that governments need to strategically target their public finance to attract private capital into green investment through measures such as guarantees, insurance products and incentives, combined with the right policy support.

Key findings

Approximately US$ 34 billion in additional public funding is needed to stabilize global temperatures at an acceptable level.

- By increasing climate-related public funding from its current level of US$ 96 billion to around US$ 130 billion, it could mobilize private capital in the range of US$ 570 billion.
- This would address the US$ 700 billion in investment that the Report finds is required to put the world on a climate-resilient path towards green growth.
- Greening investment at scale is a precondition for achieving sustainable growth.
- The investment required for the water, agriculture, telecoms, power, transport, buildings, industrial and forestry sectors, according to current growth projections, stands at about US$ 5 trillion per year to 2020.

Source: Governance Research Digest, March 2013 (Vol. 4, No. 3)

4.3.4   UNEP Carbon Accounting Briefing

Author(s): UNEP FI

The United Nations Environment Programme Finance Initiative (UNEP FI) and a group of investors including Allianz, HSBC, Pax World Investments and Trillium Asset Management published a briefing on how investors should use to understand, assess and mitigate portfolio carbon risk. The briefing also lays the foundations for the development of a new market standard to measure, disclose and reduce greenhouse gas emissions associated with their investments and portfolios so as to reduce policy, regulatory and financial risks associated with these emissions.

Key findings

Carbon footprinting is one of several key tools that investors should use to understand, assess and mitigate portfolio carbon risk.

- There are three key quantitative approaches that investors can take to reduce carbon risk exposure:
  - Invest in assets belonging to less carbon-intensive sectors relative to benchmark (asset allocation).
  - Select assets with a lower carbon footprint within each sector relative to benchmark (stock selection) or select companies with particularly sound decarbonisation strategies and ambitious targets even if, momentarily, they may seem relatively carbon-inefficient.
  - Engage with carbon-intensive investee companies to encourage carbon efficiency gains over time (shareholder engagement).

Source: Governance Research Digest, July 2013 (Vol. 4, No. 7)

4.3.5   Global Investor Survey on Climate Change

Author(s): Global Investor Coalition, Mercer

The networks in the Global Investor Coalition commissioned Mercer to conduct a survey on climate-related investment practice by members of the GIC networks, focusing on the integration of climate change considerations into investment processes and actions taken during 2012. The 'Global Investor Survey on Climate Change' provides an overview of emerging best practices of 84 participating investors with assets in excess of USD14 trillion, based in ten countries.

Key findings

Despite the ongoing economic challenges and continuing policy uncertainty, members of the GIC networks have retained and, in many cases, advanced their practices to address climate change in their investment activities.

- There is a clear trend in the results showing that climate risk analysis is performed within asset classes and for specific investments rather than at the portfolio level.
- Climate risk analysis in equity portfolios for example is performed by almost 100% of respondents and real estate and infrastructure portfolios are receiving increasing levels of attention with respect to physical climate and policy or regulatory impacts.
- Around half of asset owners undertook a climate risk assessment at the portfolio level, and around half of these made changes to their investment activities as a result.
- This year's report highlights allocations to 'low carbon investments' and the way investors think about risk analysis, particularly in relation to 'emissions intensive investments'.
- A number of respondents are either divestingor electing not to invest, based on climate change concerns, although the extent to whichthese practices apply across portfolios will require further examination in future years.
- Seeking better information on low carbon and emissions intensive investments within portfolios appears to be one of the major areas of opportunity arising from this year's survey.
- Engagement by Asset Owners and Asset Managers with policy makers and companies remain core tools for addressing climate change risks with high levels of activity in these areas.
- Institutional investors in large diverse markets continue to face challenges to diversifying away from emissions exposures when policy signals do not sufficiently support changes.

Source: Governance Research Digest, September 2013 (Vol. 4, No. 9)

4.3.6   Ceres Blueprint for Sustainable Investing

Author(s): Ceres

Ceres published a report intended to guide investors along a path to becoming "sustainable" —investors who understand that the 21st century economy will be shaped by powerful forces such as climate change, population growth, rising demand for energy, declining supplies of fresh water and other natural resources, and protection of human rights and worker health and safety. 'The 21st Century Investor: Ceres Blueprint for Sustainable Investing' is designed to help investors act on their growing concern about sustainability by providing a set of 10 concrete action steps that will move them along a path towards becoming sustainable investors.

Key findings

To protect current and future beneficiaries, and maximize risk-adjusted returns, sustainable investors will need to mitigate the risks and seize the opportunities arising from these sustainability challenges.

- The Blueprint recommends 10 action steps for institutional investors seeking to become sustainable investors.
- Step 1: Establish a Commitment to Sustainable Investment Through a Statement of Investment Beliefs
- Step 2: Establish Board Level Oversight of Sustainability Policies and Practices.
- Step 3: Identify Sustainability Issues Material to the Fund.
- Step 4: Evaluate Asset Allocation for Material Sustainability Risks
- Step 5: Select an Investment Strategy and Integrate Sustainability Criteria.
- Step 6: Require Sustainable Investment Expertise in Manager and Consultant Procurement.
- Step 7: Evaluate Manager Performance Against Sustainable Investment Expectations.
- Step 8: Establish Engagement Strategies and Proxy Voting Guidelines Consistent with Sustainable Investment Goals
- Step 9: Support Policies and Market Initiatives that Promote a Sustainable Global Economy.
- Step 10: Integrate Sustainable Investment Criteria Across All Asset Classes and Strategies.

Source: Governance Research Digest, October 2013 (Vol. 4, No. 10)

4.3.7   Investing in Conservation: A Landscape Assessment of an Emerging Market

Author(s): EKO Asset Management Partners, JPMorgan Chase, The Nature Conservancy, the David and Lucile Packard Foundation, and the Gordon and Betty Moore Foundation

EKO Asset Management Partners, JPMorgan Chase, The Nature Conservancy, the David and Lucile Packard Foundation, and the Gordon and Betty Moore Foundation produced the first-ever study of the market for conservation-related impact investments. The report, Investing in Conservation: A Landscape Assessment of an Emerging Market presents findings from a survey of 56 investors, including five for-profit and nonprofit development finance institutions (DFIs) and 51 private investment organizations.

Key findings

Private investments in this space are expected to more than triple over the next five years (2014-2018). A substantial amount of potential private capital has not been deployed, demonstrating the need for a significant increase in the number of risk adjusted investment opportunities.

- Conservation investments, also referred to as conservation impact investments, are intended to return principal or generate profit while driving a positive impact on natural resources and ecosystems.
- A fast-growing market totaling approximately $23 billion in the five-year period from 2009-2013.
- The approximately $23 billion committed to conservation impact investments from 2009-2013 was invested in three main categories:
- Water quantity and quality conservation, including investments in watershed protection, water conservation and storm water management, and trading in credits related to watershed management
- Sustainable food and fiber production, including investments in sustainable agriculture, timber production, aquaculture, and wild-caught fisheries
- Habitat conservation, including investments in the protection of shorelines to reduce coastal erosion, projects to Reduce Emissions from

Deforestation and Degradation (REDD+), land easements, and mitigation banking

- Private investoConservation investments, also referred to as conservation impact investments, are intended to return principal or generate profit while driving a positive impact on natural resources and ecosystems.
- A fast-growing market totaling approximately $23 billion in the five-year period from 2009-2013. rs expect to deploy $1.5 billion of already-raised capital over the next five years, and to raise and invest an additional $4.1 billion
- Of the nearly $2 billion already invested by private investors, 80% came from only 10 sources
- The total market for conservation investment is expected to increase to $37.1 billion over the next five years
- Of the three categories of conservation investment studied, DFIs invested largely in water quality and quantity projects ($15 billion), while private investors invested largely in sustainable food and fiber production (about $1.2 billion)
- Survey respondents noted a shortage of investable projects and opportunities, indicating that they need more deals with adequate risk-return ratios and more seasoned management teams.

Source: Governance Research Digest, December 2014 (Vol. 5, No. 12)

4.3.8   Peak: Investing at the Edge of Ecological Limits

Author(s): Portfolio 21 Investments

Portfolio 21 Investments, a Portland-based investment management firm, has published a report highlighting significant factors and trends impacting investors in the 21st Century. The publication offers a new framework for managing ecological risks and emerging opportunities, and meeting the multi-faceted needs of today's investors.

Key findings

Unlimited growth has been the expectation for as long as there's been a stock market. It is the foundation of all traditional investment strategies, which is to manage volatility within an ever- expanding market.

- The simple story of endless growth is giving way to something far more complex – a landscape of entirely different risks and opportunities.
- Portfolio 21 Investments' strategy favors companies that:
  o adapt business models to seek competitive advantages in the face of declining natural systems and resources (e.g., fresh water, oil, and other raw materials);
  o take advantage of efficiencies offered by emerging local and regional economies;
  o do more with less by re-using resources and creating closed-loop systems;
  o avoid legal, financial, and reputation risks associated with greenhouse gases, superfund sites, spills, and toxic releases;
  o build competitive advantage through ecologically-focused R&D and capital investments;
  o reduce environmental impacts and liabilities with outcome-driven initiatives accompanied by environmental accounting and thorough, relevant reporting.

Source: Environmental Research Digest, February 2012 (Vol. 3, No. 2)

4.3.9   Climate Change and Investment Research

Author(s): Carbon Disclosure Project

New research from the Carbon Disclosure Project has shown that investment decisions are increasingly impacted by climate change information. The Investor Research Project set out to capture information on how climate change and CDP data is being used by investors. The report summarises the responses from 87 signatory investors who took part in an online questionnaire in late 2008.

Key findings

More than three-quarters of respondents (77%) said they factor climate change information into their investment decisions and asset allocations.

- CDP is the leading source of climate change information among respondents.
- More than 80% of respondents said they consider climate change to be important relative to other issues impacting their portfolio.

- Four-fifths of respondents said they found CDP data useful and valuable. Institutional investors cited carbon risk and potential legislation as the primary motivators for utilizing CDP data.
- Corporate engagement emerged as the principal area in which investors are currently using CDP data, both as a stand alone resource and to back up information from other sources.
- A number of investors commented that systematically incorporating CDP data into financial analysis is in progress and a key goal.
- The majority of respondents are willing to ask companies to do more than just disclose information on climate change. For example, many are willing to ask for emissions reductions.
- The vast majority of investors cited "carbon risk" and "potential regulation" as motivation for using CDP data.
- Investors' determination of carbon risk is challenged by the unpredictability of future carbon prices and the absence of a clear regulatory framework in many jurisdictions.
- Investors overwhelmingly indicated in their written responses that the materiality of climate change depends on the nature of the investment being considered (i.e. sector, company, and geography) and other important factors such as oil and other energy prices, current and potential regulations, scientific findings and consumer sentiment.
- The responses provided indicate that investors expect CDP data to increase in significance and applicability. As climate change regulation matures and expands around the globe, members of the investment community will be increasingly compelled to analyse climate risks and opportunities in detail.

Source: Environmental Research Digest, March 2009 (Vol. 1, No. 3)

4.4   State of the Market

4.4.1   Impact Investment Market Report

Author(s): J.P. Morgan and the Global Impact Investing Network

J.P. Morgan and the Global Impact Investing Network (GIIN) released a "Perspectives on progress", a report that reveals the experiences, expectations, and perceptions of 99 impact investors in 2012, as well as their plans for 2013. Investors surveyed for the report include fund managers, development finance institutions, foundations, diversified financial institutions, and other investors with at least USD 10 million committed to impact investment.

Key findings

Americans believe businesses are better suited than the government to cope with climate change.

- Though the impact investing market is relatively new, a majority of respondents report that some or many investments passed their initial screens in nearly all regions of the world, with U.S. & Canada, South Asia, and Latin America & the Caribbean providing the most robust pipelines to surveyed investors.
- However, respondents believe the market is still challenged by a lack of appropriate capital across the risk/return spectrum and a shortage of high-quality investment opportunities.
- Encouragingly, surveyed investors indicate that progress was made in these areas and across other indicators of market growth in 2012.
- Respondents also highlight the importance of impact measurement for both raising capital and general industry development.
- Notably, 96% of respondents measure their social and/or environmental impact, with most utilizing third-party standards, including the Impact Reporting and Investment Standards (IRIS) metrics

Source: Governance Research Digest, January 2013 (Vol. 4, No. 1)

4.4.2   The Impact of Sustainable and Responsible Investment

Author(s): US SIF Foundation

The US SIF Foundation published a paper that highlights the positive impact that sustainable and responsible investing has had on investors and the investment industry, on companies, on individuals and communities, and on public policy. 'The Impact of Sustainable and Responsible Invesment' report examines how sustainable and responsible investors have engaged the investment industry, companies, individuals, communities and governments–either individually or collectively–to address environmental, social and governance (ESG) challenges and to reform the way business is conducted.

Key findings

Sustainable and responsible investors have been, and continue to be, a force for positive change in the US.

- The growth of the sustainable investing field and the mainstreaming of ESG integration have led to diverse SRI initiatives, such as program- and mission-related investing campaigns by foundations and impact investments by institutions and individuals.
- Individual investors have benefited by gaining access to retirement plans with SRI options and having the ability to work with specialized SRI financial advisors.
- Individual investors also benefit from their ability to invest in communities directly through banks,credit unions, and other community development.
- Investors—often in concert with civil society organizations and multi-stakeholder groups—have persuaded numerous publicly held companies to:
  1. Improve climate risk disclosure
  2. Adopt sustainable forestry practices
  3. Address poor labor and human rights conditions in their global supply chains
  4. Pledge not to discriminate against employees on the basis of their sexual orientation
  5. Disclose health, safety and environmental risks associated with hydraulic fracturing
  6. Improve accountability of executive pay practices
  7. Promote gender and racial diversity on their boards of directors, and
  8. Issue detailed reports on sustainability

Source: Governance Research Digest, November 2013 (Vol. 4, No. 11)

4.4.3   ESG Atlas and Risk Calculator

Author(s): Maplecroft

Maplecroft has released its 2012 findings of the ESG Atlas and Risk Calculator. The ESG Atlas and Risk Calculator includes 49 ESG risk indices, evaluating 197 countries, which investors can choose from to create country scorecards and a bespoke global ESG dashboard.

Key findings

Complicity in the violation of human rights constitute the most significant environmental, social and governance (ESG) risk faced by investors in the fast growing BRIC economies of Brazil, Russia, India and China.

- The 10 countries with the highest levels of ESG risk are Somalia, North Korea and Myanmar, which are classified as 'extreme risk,' while South Sudan, Haiti, DR Congo, Sudan, Zimbabwe, Afghanistan and Pakistan sit within the 'high risk' category.
- However, global investment is centred in the new financial powerhouses of the BRICs, along with other emerging growth markets, such as Indonesia, Mexico, Nigeria, the Philippines and Viet Nam, and it is in these countries where responsible investors will be particularly exposed to ESG risks.
- All of the BRICs are classified as posing high ESG risks in Maplecroft's overall results, with the exception of Brazil, which is categorised as 'medium risk.'
- It is within the area of human rights though that investors face the biggest challenges.
- Within the 14 human rights categories assessed by the ESG Atlas and Risk Calculator, Brazil performs the best of the BRICs, but is still classified as 'extreme risk' in five categories: child labour, working conditions, minority rights, indigenous peoples' rights and security forces.
- Brazil also exhibits high levels of environmental risk and it is among the world's worst performers for threats to biodiversity, deforestation and GHG emissions.
- Russia is classified as 'extreme risk' in nine of the 14 human rights categories, but it is China and India which pose the most risk to investors in this regard.
- Both feature in the 'extreme risk' category of 12 of the human rights indices, including six of the seven labour rights risks.

- China is also among the lowest performers for democratic governance and, along with Russia, has one of the least independent legal systems, while India is the 12th poorest performing economy for environmental risk.
- Of the total of 22 countries in the 'low risk' category of the ESG Atlas and Risk Calculator results, 19 are located in Europe signalling that the region remains an ethical safe haven for responsible investors due to established legal and regulatory systems and good governance.
- The best performing countries include: Norway, Sweden, Denmark, Finland, Switzerland, Germany and Austria.
- New Zealand, Australia and Canada are the only countries located outside of Europe classified as 'low risk'.

Source: Social Research Digest, January 2012 (Vol. 3, No. 1)

4.4.4 Environmental, Social and Governance (ESG) Investment Trends Study

Author(s): IFC/Mercer

A new report from the IFC and Mercer finds growth in sustainable investing in emerging markets, but also notes the need for improvement in such areas as active ownership. The report's authors focused their inquiry into four major emerging markets: China, India, South Korea, and Brazil.

Key findings

Investment in sustainable investment funds in emerging markets has grown more than fivefold between 2003 and 2008, to more than $300 billion.

- $50 billion of this amount reflects funds which are specifically branded as socially responsible or sustainable, while the remaining amount represent mainstream managers who take environmental, social, and governance (ESG) issues into account.
- In response to environmental concerns, China has developed a Green Security Index that requires heavy polluting companies to undergo an environmental assessment before they seek listing on Chinese stock exchanges.
- The report found that ESG improvements at a business level are

challenged by China's position as a world factory whose pursuit of profits too often excludes consideration of ESG factors. Corporate regulatory compliance is more often driven by fear of sanction than by a belief in ESG practices.

- India was found to have the lowest standards of ESG implementation of the countries surveyed in the report.

- While some investment managers displayed awareness of local social issues, especially on poverty reduction, access to clean water, and sanitation, active ownership of Indian companies was absent.

- However, the Stock Exchange in Mumbai does have a sustainability index. The S&P ESG India Index, which was initiated and sponsored by the IFC, comprises 50 Indian companies that meet ESG criteria.

- South Korea has seen the largest increase of sustainable investment (SI) labeled funds, which grew from two in 2005 to 45 in 2008.

- The South Korea Exchange is developing an eco index listing, and plans to establish a socially responsible investment (SRI) index in the future.

- However, in general there was a lack of good reporting on ESG standards, and little willingness to engage companies was in evidence.

- In Brazil, where the concept of sustainability led to the creation of an SRI labeled fund in 2001, engagement with companies on the issue of corporate governance has become fairly common, and the practice of proxy voting has begun to take root as well.

- Investment managers in Brazil tend to offer specialty products, rather than integrating ESG into mainstream products.

- However, the UN Principles for Responsible Investment (PRI), a major driver for global sustainable investment, has 28 signatories in Brazil, including 18 pension funds, 8 asset managers and 2 professional service providers.

Source: CSR Research Digest, May 2009 (Vol. 1, No. 5)

4.4.5 Sustainable Investing: Establishing Long-Term Value and Performance

Author(s): DB Climate Change Advisors

A report published by Deutsche Bank outlines a history of Sustainable Investing (SI), from Ethical negative screens, to Socially Responsible

Investing (SRI) to Responsible Investing (RI). It is a review of 100 academic studies of sustainable investing, as well as 56 research papers, two literature reviews and four meta-studies.

Key findings

Companies with a higher CSR ranking typically have a lower cost of capital and represent a lower risk to investors.

- Socially responsible investors have traditionally found it difficult to demonstrate outperformance in the broad SRI category.
- However, Deutsche Bank has been able to identify the source of value created by SRI by defining three specific categories:
  - SRI,
  - CSR, and
  - ESG (Environmental, Social Governance).
- Of the 100 studies examined 89% show that companies with a high rating for ESG factors also exhibit market-based outperformance.
- Approximately 85% of the studies indicate these companies report accounting-based outperformance.
- Deutsche Bank believes that incorporating ESG factors into investment methodologies is emerging as best practices.
- ESG is also promoted by the UN Principles for Responsible Investing (UN PRI), backed by over 1,000 signatories.

Source: CSR Research Digest, July 2012 (Vol. 4, No. 7)

4.4.6   Responsible Investment Report

Author(s): EIRIS

Environmental, social, and governance (ESG) disclosure by companies in emerging markets is becoming an increasingly important issue of concern to sustainability investors in the developed world. A new report by EIRIS analyzes the results of an investor survey to gain a better understanding of investment activities in emerging markets. The report features responses of 67 sustainability investors, mostly from North America and Europe, who manage over $130 billion of emerging market assets.

Key findings

70% of respondents say that lack of ESG disclosure by companies in emerging markets hampers their efforts to increase investments.

- Responsible investors, especially those located in Europe, already have extensive experience in investing in emerging markets, some for longer than six years.
- Brazil is making the most progress toward ESG disclosure.
- Investors cite two important developments in Brazil that allow the government there to pressure companies to improve transparency. First, the Bovespa Sustainability Index integrates sustainability into lending and investment in emerging markets. And second, the presence of local ESG investment research activity in Brazil provides vital information to potential investors from the developed world.
- Investors reported that South Africa, China, South Korea, and India were also making progress toward improved ESG disclosure.
- Improved ESG disclosure in Asian countries was influenced by the onset of globalisation and the resulting need to operate to global standards along with changes in government legislation.
- These findings mirrored an earlier report, coauthored by EIRIS in March 2009, entitled A Review of ESG Practices in Large Emerging Market Companies, which found "that the large South African and Brazilian companies had adopted higher levels of corporate responsibility than their peers in other emerging market countries."
- Among the companies cited by respondents as being their top holdings were Petrobras of Brazil, Samsung Electronics of South Korea, and China Mobile.
- North American respondents rated the lack of company ESG disclosure most often as a key challenge to investing in emerging markets, whereas the European group most often cited corporate culture as a key challenge.
- The European group cited language difficulties approximately twice as often as their North American counterparts, while the North American group cited a lack of investment research far more often than the European group.
- Investors have particular leverage in raising awareness and building demand for improved ESG disclosure.

- There is significant scope for improvements by companies in the levels of disclosure and the quality and consistency of information provided.
- The report recommends that companies seek help in their ESG reporting from such established initiatives as the Carbon Disclosure Project (CDP) and the Global Reporting Initiative (GRI).

Source: CSR Research Digest, August 2009 (Vol. 1, No. 8)

4.4.7 Socially Responsible Investing and Sustainability Study

Author(s): Thomson Reuters/UKSIF

Thomson Reuters and UKSIF, the sustainable investment and finance association, announced the results of the eighth annual Thomson Reuters Extel/UKSIF Socially Responsible Investing & Sustainability Survey. The 2010 Survey represents the views of over 450 investment professionals from 16 countries, making it the most extensive assessment of socially responsible investing (SRI) in the European investment community.

Key findings

Buyside firms are placing more emphasis on sustainability issues in the research & advisory services they receive from brokers.

- Nearly 90% of buyside firms are planning to increase SRI & sustainability asset allocation in the coming year.
- Key rankings from the Thomson Reuters Extel/UKSIF Survey include (2009 ranking in brackets):
  - Leading Brokerage Firm for SRI Research
    - Société Générale (1)
    - CA Cheuvreux (2)
    - UBS (4)
  - Leading Brokerage Individual for SRI Research
    - Sarj Nahal, Société Générale (1)
    - Valery Lucas-Leclin, Société Générale (3)
    - Julie Hudson, UBS (2)
    - Leading Brokerage Firm for Corporate Governance Research
    - Oddo Securities (1)
    - UBS (4)
    - CA Cheuvreux (3)

- ○ Leading Quoted Company for Sustainability Communications
  - ▪ Royal Dutch Shell plc (8)
  - ▪ Tesco plc (3)
  - ▪ Novo Nordisk (-)
  - ▪ Leading Fund Management Firm for SRI
  - ▪ Threadneedle Asset Management (3)
  - ▪ Aviva Global Investors (2)
  - ▪ BlackRock Investment Management (4)

Source: CSR Research Digest, October 2010 (Vol. 2, No. 10)

4.4.8 Measuring Investors' Socially Responsible Performance in Mutual Funds

Author(s): I. Barreda-Tarrazona, J. C. Matallín-Sáez and M. R. Balaguer-Franch.

The aim of the study is to analyze investor behavior towards socially responsible mutual funds. The analysis is based on an experimental study where a sample of individuals takes investment decisions under different parameters of information about the investment alternatives and expected returns.

Key findings

The results obtained suggest that although individuals' criteria for investment are essentially guided by returns and diversification, participants invest significantly more in a fund when they are explicitly informed about its SR nature.

- In particular, participants who declare being concerned about SR actually invest significantly more in the SR alternative.
- Furthermore, the level of SR faithfulness among a small group of investors is such that they invest the main share of their budget in the SR fund, even when the return differential is highly unfavorable.
- Providing clear information about the SR characteristics of an investment is crucial to help investors express their preferences.

Source: Governance Research Digest, October 2011 (Vol. 2, No. 6)

4.4.9 Responsible Investment: Creating Value from Environmental, Social and Governance Issues

Author(s): PwC

PwC survey seeks to explore the private equity industry's response whether managing ESG issues really help to create value. The report also examines what drives PE houses to focus on responsible investment, and how they are tackling the challenge of valuing and measuring their efforts.

Key findings

Some 94% of private equity houses expect environmental, social and governance issues to become more important to their business in the next five years.

- Investor pressure on such firms is the main, or in some cases the only, driver for this change of tack.
- But 94% of private equity firms also believe that ESG activities can create investment value, with many identifying cost savings, incremental revenue generation through new products, or enhanced reputation.
- Despite this increasing pressure from investors and a the wide acceptance of profit in ESG activities, only 20% of the private equity houses surveyed have put systems in place to measure value created from ESG activities.

Source: Governance Research Digest, April 2012 (Vol. 3, No. 4)

4.4.10 WEF Impact Investment Report

Author(s): World Economic Forum, in collaboration with Deloitte Touche Tohmatsu

The World Economic Forum, in collaboration with Deloitte Touche Tohmatsu, launched a report that provides a market assessment and recommendations for how mainstream investors can more actively engage in impact investing. The report, 'From the Margins to the Mainstream: Assessment of the Impact Investment Sector and Opportunities to Engage Mainstream Investors', highlights the impact investing to generate market returns while addressing key social and environmental challenges.

<u>Key findings</u>

To reach a 2020 market projection of more than US$ 500 billion, the impact investment sector needs to grow significantly.

- 79% of impact investors are already targeting market rates of return.
- Currently, capital of less than US$ 40 billion is committed to impact investments out of the trillions in global capital.
- According to World Economic Forum estimates, the impact investment sector would need to grow aggressively to reach an optimistic 2020 market projection of more than US$ 500 billion.
- While 80% of US-based pension fund managers are familiar with impact investing, only 9% felt that it is a viable investment approach.
- To move impact investing from the "margin to the mainstream" will require efforts among stakeholders and innovative strategies.
- Several key recommendations for how the impact investment sector can reach scale: calling on impact investment funds to be transparent about the financial returns that are generated; for impact enterprises to proactively measure and report on social and environmental impact; for governments to provide tax relief for early-stage investments in which public benefit is created; and for philanthropic endowments to commit to impact investments and not just to programmatic allocations.

Source: Governance Research Digest, September 2013 (Vol. 4, No. 9)

4.4.11 Impact Investment: The Invisible Heart Of Markets

Author(s): The Taskforce on Social Impact Investment

The Taskforce on Social Impact Investment, established by UK Prime Minister David Cameron under the UK's presidency of the G8, and chaired by Sir Ronald Cohen, launched a report that highlights the potential that impact investment has to help solve some of society's most pressing issues, and lays out several clear recommendations, devised by government and private sector experts from across the G7, EU, and Australia. The report entitled Impact Investment: The Invisible Heart of Markets – Harnessing the power of entrepreneurship, innovation and capital for public good calls on governments and the financial sector to take action to unleash $1 trillion of private sector impact investment to tackle social problems.

Key findings

The Age of Impact Entrepreneurship focuses on removing constraints on the growth of organisations established or now led by impact entrepreneurs.

- Those who seek to deliver impact need better recognition and better tools and support to get things done at scale. This includes mechanisms to protect social mission in businesses, such as the new benefit corporation structure that is catching on among impact entrepreneurs in the US and many other countries.
- High-level recommendations
  o Set measurable impact objectives and track their achievement
  o Investors to consider three dimensions: risk, return and impact
  o Clarify fiduciary responsibilities of trustees: to allow trustees to consider social as well as financial return on their investments
  o Pay-for-success commissioning: governments should consider streamlining pay-for-success arrangements such as social impact bonds and adapting national ecosystems to support impact investment
  o Consider setting up an impact investment wholesaler funded with unclaimed assets to drive development of the impact investment sector
  o Boost social sector organizational capacity: governments and foundations to consider establishing capacity-building grants programs
  o Give Profit-with- Purpose businesses the ability to lock-in mission: governments to provide appropriate legal forms or provisions for entrepreneurs and investors who wish to secure social mission into the future
  o Support impact investment's role in international development: governments to consider providing their development finance institutions with flexibility to increase impact investment efforts. Explore creation of an Impact Finance Facility to help attract early-stage capital, and a DIB Social Outcomes Fund to pay for successful development impact bonds.

Source: Governance Research Digest, October 2014 (Vol. 5, No. 10)

4.4.12 Environmental, Social and Governance Performance Report

Author(s): EABIS

The European Academy of Business in Society (EABIS) has released a report detailing how the ESG (environmental, social and governance) performance of companies might impact on the drivers of business success. The report draws heavily on material generated by laboratory meetings, focus groups, interviews, and working papers which formed part of the two-year research project.

Key findings

There are a number of obstacles to mainstreaming ESG factors in investment decisions.

- These tend to fall in one of two categories: obstacles with investors, and obstacles inside companies.
- Obstacles with investors
  - Investors' mindsets tend to be skewed towards quantitative analysis and short-termism. This is often accompanied by a slightly inflexible analytical framing of issues.
  - While ESG data is more geared towards qualitative analysis and long-term investment decisions, sometimes quantification and shorttermism negatively rubs off on to ESG issues.
  - Where data are collected on ESG issues, they are often undermined by inconsistencies and insufficiencies arising mainly from the differences of ESG data in terms of actors, industries, regions and countries.
  - Most investors tend to think that ESG issues are complex, expansionary, and, therefore, contestable. They see ESG issues as presenting a high degree of complexity which makes them difficult to articulate, assess and integrate into investment decisions.
- Obstacles inside companies
  - Companies are at different stages of corporate responsibility (CR) maturity and so only some companies will have significant ESG performance improvements to report.

o Even many of the more mature companies when it comes to embedding CR and sustainability have only recently made the explicit link between this commitment and their overall strategy; others have still to do so.

o Many have struggled with how to explain this linkage satisfactorily, in terms of how the failure to link creates corporate risks, and how making this link creates opportunities.

o Senior managers may not, therefore, yet appreciate the significance of ESG performance data presented to them in terms of potential or actual impact on business performance.

Source: Governance Research Digest, November 2009 (Vol. 1, No. 11)

4.4.13 Green Transition Inflection Point: Green Transition Scoreboard® 2013 Report

Author(s): Ethical Markets

Ethical Markets published "Green Transition Inflection Point: Green Transition Scoreboard® 2013 Report" tracking private investments in the green economy worldwide since 2007. GTS data sources include the highly respected Cleantech, Bloomberg, Yahoo Finance, Reuters and many UN and other international studies, NASA and individual company reports.

Key findings

The year 2012 was an inflection point for the green transition worldwide, with $4.1 trillion invested or committed in the green economy as of Q4 2012.

- Renewable Energy - Important to this rapidly expanding sector is the growth of renewable energy in developing countries.
- Green Construction - This is the most conservatively under-reported sector of this report, counting only green construction materials, not including labor.
- Energy Efficiency - Investments include conservation efforts and initiatives and products focused on lowering energy needs or using less energy than a comparable product, as companies now recognize efficiency investments' rapid payback periods.

- Green R&D - Significant company investments show sustainability is integrated into its core strategy, serving as a strong indicator for investors. This data helps identify innovative companies ahead of the curve in responding to heightening environmental risks and regulations.
- Cleantech - As Cleantech grows, energy storage increases in importance, at the level of power plants and grid electricity and at retail and local levels with improvements in batteries, fuel cells, flywheels, ultra capacitors, flow batteries, compressed air as well as metering of use at all levels.
- The GTS omits nuclear, clean coal, carbon capture & sequestration, and biofuels from feedstocks other than sea-grown algae.

Source: Environmental Research Digest, March 2013 (Vol. 4, No. 3)

4.4.14 Green Transition Scoreboard 2012: From Expanding Cleantech Sectors to Emerging Trends in Biomimicry

Author(s): Ethical Markets Media

The Green Transition Scoreboard® (GTS) is a timebased, global tracking of the private financial system for all sectors investing in green markets. The GTS tracks five sectors: Renewable Energy, Green Construction and Efficiency, Cleantech, Smart Grid and Corporate R&D.

Key findings

Asia, Europe and Latin America catching up with the USA in total non-government investments and commitments for all facets of green markets.

- 2011 ended with a GTS total of $3,306,051,439,680, starting from 2007.
- Given the many studies indicating that investing $1 trillion annually until 2020 will accelerate the Green Transition worldwide and the over 100 research reports and articles referenced in this years' update, the report definitively shows green investments are becoming the norm.
- Institutional investors are shifting away from more speculative sectors such as hedge funds, private equity, oil and commodity ETFs.
- Ethical Markets hopes global investors are redeploying at least 10% of their portfolios directly in companies driving the Green Transition, putting green markets on track to reach the $10 trillion goal by 2020.

- The GTS data provides investment advisors the foundation to update their asset allocations to include green sectors, which Mercer, LLC, advises should represent 40% of portfolios – half to offset climate risk and half to capitalize on these opportunities.

Source: Environmental Research Digest, March 2012 (Vol. 3, No. 3)

V.   RESPECT FOR STAKEHOLDERS' INTERESTS

5.1   Corporate Responsiveness

5.1.1   Investigating Stakeholder Theory and Social Capital: CSR in Large Firms and SMEs

Author(s): A. Russo, F. Perrini

This paper argues that the idiosyncrasies of large firms and SMEs explain their different approaches to CSR. The authors suggest that the notion of social capital is a more useful way of understanding the CSR approach of SMEs, whereas stakeholder theory more closely addresses the CSR approach of large firms.

<u>Key findings</u>

In general, large firms with a consolidated strategic orientation to CSR represent the idealised scenario, in which the stakeholder view of the firm predicts extensive and responsible behaviours.

- SMEs follow the principles of social capital, operating within a less structured context made up of trust, informality, and networking.
- SMEs exploit their strong relationship built out of trust, reputation, and legitimacy with specific stakeholders (e.g. the suppliers, customers, competitors, and local community) sufficiently to improve their license to operate.
- Nevertheless, SMEs remain unable to formalize such relational capital through specific managerial tools (e.g. ethical codes, non financial reports, and in general organizational and managerial procedures), which might be helpful to the long-term process of value creation.
- Social capital can also be relevant to the large firms, which can be considered as social capital developers, even though they do that intentionally by managing CSR according to a stakeholder approach.
- Large firms comprehend the relevance of identifying their relationships with stakeholders, but still lack the ability to integrate the management

of these specific relationships into their corporate strategy.

- Therefore, relationships, trust, legitimacy, openness, and in general the key drivers of sustainability that researchers are promoting as the basis of social capital should be prioritized by large firms.
- The cultivation of close relationships with workers and the social or business environment makes it possible to establish expectations in social relationships and ensures collective action through increased confidence.

Source: CSR Research Digest, March 2010 (Vol. 2, No. 3)

5.1.2 Configuration of External Influence: The Combined Effects of Institutions and Stakeholders on Corporate Social Responsibility Strategies

Author(s): M-D. P. Lee

The article introduces a theoretical framework that combines institutional and stakeholder theories to explain how firms choose their corporate social responsibility strategy. Organizational researchers have identified several distinct CSR strategies (e.g., obstructionist, defensive, accommodative, and proactive), but did not explain the sources of divergence.

Key findings

This article argues that the divergence comes from the variability in the configuration of external influences that consists of institutional and stakeholder pressures.

- While institutions affect firms' social behavior by shaping the macro-level incentive structure and sources of legitimacy (distal mechanisms), firms' stakeholders can amplify or buffer the institutional forces by acting as mediators (proximate mechanisms).
- The two dimensions are interdependent in that stakeholders draw legitimacy and power from institutions, and institutions are often actualized through stakeholder mechanisms.
- Together, they form a particular configuration of external influences that shapes how focal firms construct their CSR strategy.

Source: CSR Research Digest, September 2011 (Vol. 3, No. 9)

5.1.3 Drivers of Long-term Business Value: Stakeholders, Stats and Strategy

Author(s): Deloitte

This paper seeks to shed light on stakeholders, taken as a whole, and when they might have a material economic impact on the company and thereby impact valuations. While demonstrating that ESG performance does matter for financial valuation in the near term, the statistical evidence also points a way to long-term business value creation.

<u>Key findings</u>

A growing number of stakeholder groups are raising the bar on corporate performance. To create value for diverse stakeholders companies must understand the value of environmental, social and governance (ESG) issues to each group.

- Stakeholder perceptions of a company as well as its impact on society and the environment represent an important driver for a firm's longterm success.
- NGOs, trade unions, social activists and business associations influence a firm's sustainability strategy and policy.
- Similarly, shareholders are increasingly taking ESG measures into account to determine a company's valuation.
- Finding the value in ESG management is becoming central to how many companies craft their sustainability strategy.
- Finally, the report describes strategic considerations for engaging with stakeholders in ways that create mutual value.

Source: CSR Research Digest, July 2012 (Vol. 4, No. 7)

5.1.4 The ABC of CSR for Small and Medium Enterprises

Author(s): BRASS / ACCA

Cardiff University's Centre for Business Relationships, Accountability, Sustainability and Society (BRASS) has developed a guide on CSR for SMEs, in partnership with Association of Chartered Certified Accountants in Wales. The guide concentrates on how the business can voluntarily engage with key stakeholders to determine how to 'do good while doing good business'.

Key findings

The guide focuses on four key CSR issues that are likely to be important to the business.

- These four key issues are:
  - o Employees - practical guidance on steps you can take to provide an excellent place to work in, and to balance the needs of your company with the needs of individual employees, to the benefit of both;
  - o Environment - practical solutions to minimize negative environmental impacts that will arise from the operation of your business, your use of resources and generation of waste;
  - o The community - practical suggestions on how to engage with your local community for mutually beneficial outcomes;
  - o The supply chain - advice on how to work with your customers and suppliers to maximize quality, environmental protection and health and safety standards while maintaining labour and human rights standards throughout your supply chain.
- The 'how to' section of the guide provides practical ideas on developing and implementing a CSR strategy.
- These three steps are:
  - o Getting Started - initial practical ideas for how to get started with CSR;
  - o More Ideas - more advanced ideas and initiatives for those who have already started to adopt some CSR measures;
  - o Taking Things a Step Further - for those companies ready to formalize their CSR programmes.

Source: CSR Research Digest, December 2011 (Vol. 3, No. 12)

5.1.5 Corporate Responsibility Analysis

Author(s): Ethical Corporation

Ethical Corporation published a report that analyzes how CSR initiatives are influenced by finance, laws, religion and culture. The Corporate

Responsibility Analysis features insight into the relationships between companies and stakeholders and provides 15 sustainability communication tips.

Key findings

Teaming up with a charity offers corporations a reputational boost.

- For those bent on pursuing the partnership approach under a charitable banner, the establishment of clear rules of the game is critical.
- While the tactical mix of NGO campaigning hasn't changed much – press releases, protests and rallies, legislative lobbying, consumer and corporate pressure – that mix is now deployed more strategically, thoughtfully and internationally than ever before.
- Advances in communications have played a fundamental role in the way western NGO campaign groups mobilise their supporters and members.
- Labels force more transparency on corporations and are often a blunt way to evaluate ethical corporations and products.
- In UAE cultural and religious traditions are the key factors that drive corporations to engage in corporate responsibility and most of them lack a strategic business element.
- Honesty makes the difference and authentic stories from a sustainability report are what will improve corporate reputation.

Source: Governance Research Digest, May 2013 (Vol. 4, No. 5)

5.1.6 Corporate Responsiveness to Community Stakeholders: Effects of Contextual and Organisational Characteristics

Author(s): N. Kobeissi, F. Damanpour

Corporate community responsiveness relates to business activities that are integral parts of a firm's operations and are designed to benefit the firm through benefiting communities. Using data from US commercial banks gathered between 1997 and 2000, this study measures banks' corporate community responsiveness and examines the influence on this responsiveness of a number of factors including company profitability, ownership and risk.

Key findings

The negative relationship between community income and community loans suggest that banks are complying with Community Reinvestment Act (CRA) recommendations to boost their lending in low- and moderate-income neighbourhoods.

- However, the negative relationships between minority populations and both community loans and CRA rating provide strong support to those who contend that financial institutions continue to discriminate against minority populations.
- This may be because banks pursue a defensive-reactive strategy towards their social obligations, focusing on a narrow interpretation of social responsibility based on economic and legal criteria only.
- Also, some borrowers, owing to mistrust, feelings of intimidation and negative past experiences, may perceive that banks are not for them and therefore create self-exclusion barriers.
- In more competitive markets, banks provide more CRA loans to their local communities as a differentiation strategy to distinguish them-selves from rivals and improve their image among customers.
- The data revealed that younger banks tended to be more involved in small business and community development loans.
- This may be because newly established banks tend to abandon small business lending once the banks attains a particular size.
- Younger banks also focus on their immediate geographic location, have a particular competitive advantage in serving small business customers, and are likely to pursue new customers in order to grow.
- The data from this study supports previous research findings in suggesting that superior financial performance leads to additional resources that can then be invested in social issues.
- The findings suggest that lower-risk firms have a greater ability to implement stakeholder- related activities. This is particularly true for undercapitalized banks where excessive risk might result in forgoing community activities for safety reasons.
- Institutional ownership was not found to have a significant impact on an organisation's stakeholder engagement.

- Mergers and acquisitions showed a weak positive effect on community loans, which contradicts other studies that propose that mergers and acquisitions have an impending effect on stakeholder activities.

Source: Social Research Digest, November 2009 (Vol. 1, No. 11)

5.1.7 Do Firms Practice What They Preach? The Relationship Between Mission Statements and Stakeholder Management

Author(s): Barbara R. Bartkus, Myron Glassman.

This study explores the relationship between mission statement content and stakeholder management actions. The sample for this study comprised the top 100 firms listed in the Fortune 500 published in 2001.

<u>Key findings</u>

The most commonly included elements in company mission statements are the least likely to have an impact on company actions.

- Although social issues such as the environment and diversity are less frequently included, their mention in mission statements is associated with positive company behaviours related to these issues.
- Organisations' actions are not always aligned with the commitments outlined in their mission statements. False or misleading statements can damage a firm's reputation.
- If, as has been posited, credibility and reputation are important issues in stakeholder management, then the accuracy of mission statements may be critical to effective stakeholder management and subsequent organizational success.
- The inclusion of primary stakeholders and social issues in mission statements suggests that some stakeholder groups are more salient to managers than others.
- These stakeholders have their own goals that may impact upon the organisation's long-term survival.
- Companies may use mission statements to pay lip service to key social issues in order to access resources controlled by primary stakeholders.

- No relationship was found between firms with a mission statement that mentions specific stakeholder groups (employees, customers or the community) and behaviours regarding these stakeholders.
- This suggests that the inclusion of specific stakeholder groups in mission statements is likely due to institutional pressure, while specifying social issues is related to policy decisions.
- It was hyphesised that firms with mission statements that include stakeholder issues would be more likely to successfully address these issues in practice than firms with missions that omit them.
- Although a strong relationship was not found in general, the study did find that companies that include diversity in mission statements experience significantly fewer diversity concerns.
- While companies that do mention the environment in their mission also demonstrate more environmental strengths, no relationship was found between environmental concerns and mission content.
- This suggests that the finding is not industry-related.
- It is suggested that the reason why companies are inclined to "walk the talk" when it comes to environmental and diversity issues is due to the fact that inclusion of these issues is not prescribed.

Source: Social Research Digest, January 2009 (Vol. 1, No. 1)

5.2 Stakeholder Pressure

5.2.1 Bringing About Changes To Corporate Social Policy Through Shareholder Activism

Author(s): M. Rojas, B. M'Zali, M-F. Turcotte, P. Merrigan

This study examines shareholder initiated social policy proposals' capacity to exert pressure on management to force it to adopt suggested changes in policy. Throughout the period examined (1997–2004), firms in the United States received nearly 300 social policy shareholder resolutions per year. These proposals were transferred into a coded database for analysis.

Key findings

The analysis suggests that the capacity to influence management is higher for some types of issues presented in the resolution, such as those related to board diversity, energy and environment, and international labour and human rights.

- The capacity to exert pressure on firms can be substantially higher for some types of filers, notably pension funds and mutual funds.
- Firms, for instance, are requested to advance actions as diverse as protecting animal rights, encouraging diversity in the board room, or respecting local or indigenous rights.
- In spite of this diversity, the demands concentrate on a few big items.
- Roughly one in four proxies (Energy & Environment) seeks to improve the environmental performance of firms, requesting the companies to better report on the environmental impact of their operations, or to abandon projects that are deemed extremely dangerous for ecosystems, or to reduce carbon emissions.
- One proxy in five (18%) demands corporate action to ensure respect for labour and human rights in corporations' overseas operations.
- One proxy in 10 requests corporations to advance actions able to assure that firms offer a discrimination-free environment for their employees (equal employment).
- Similarly, slightly lower proportions were observed for requests intended to favour corporate contribution to the achievement of fairer societies (such as voluntarily shortening the lifespan of the drugs that companies produce, promoting the use of certified fair coffee in commercial operations, or promoting access of economically disadvantaged populations to bank credit).
- This group of requests, labeled "Fairness in society," accounted for roughly 9% of all proposals received.
- Resolutions requesting tobacco companies to adopt self-restraining policies in marketing and production decision making, or termination of involvement with the tobacco industry in the case of suppliers of goods and services to this industry, accounted for nearly 7% of proxies filed during the period.
- The 10% of successful withdrawn resolutions represents a modest, although not negligible, capacity to change corporate social policy.

- Success in the social policy filing scene is, however, much lower than the level attained in its corporate governance counterpart by large institutional investors.
- Championing new causes can imply higher levels of failure because it may take time to be able to create a critical mass of support among the shareholder base over an issue.
- The group of the 19 most targeted companies received a lower percentage of proposals dealing with board diversity, equal employment, and international labour and human rights, which were the most successful issues, and a higher percentage of some of the least successful groups of issues, such as tobacco issues.
- Likewise, the most targeted firms seem to disproportionately attract the least skilled types of filers in terms of capacity to influence management (individuals and advocacy groups) vis-à-vis the larger sample.
- Given the low chances of success, it could reasonably be asked why shareholders pursue this tactic. The authors offer some suggestions:
  - It is less costly than other forms of corporate campaign.
  - Advancement of careers of people involved in filing decision could lead to oversupply of the activity.
  - Large firms tend to be repeatedly targeted by socially concerned investors. The decisions adopted by very large firms, arguably the leaders in their industry, may be adopted by other competitors, by mimesis or out of fear of losing reputation and, consequently, considerable segments of their client base.
  - In many cases, corporate governance resolutions going above the threshold 20% or more (which is modest by the standards of corporate governance activism) made management uncomfortable enough to satisfy shareholder demands.
  - Social policy filing may be reinforced by other forms of activism, such as demonstrations, criticism of targeted firms in the media, and letter campaigns.

Source: CSR Research Digest, August 2009 (Vol. 1, No. 8)

5.2.2 Why Do Patterns of Environmental Response Differ? A Stakeholders' Pressure Approach

Author(s): J.L. Murillo-Luna, C. Garcés-Ayerbe, P. Rivera-Torres

This study analyses the strategies or patterns of adaptation of firms in responding to environmental requirements or expectations. Specifically, the focus of the analysis is on the influence of various stakeholders on the degree of proactivity of these patterns. The findings are based on the questionnaire responses of environmental managers (or equivalent) at 240 small, family-owned firms based in Aragón, north-eastern Spain. The study was conducted in 2003.

Key findings

Nearly 50% of respondents stated that their environmental responses are driven primarily by legislation.

- 22% of respondents paid most attention to the actions of stakeholders, while 20% described their response as "passive". Only 9% reported a focus on "total environmental quality".
- The greater the stakeholder pressure perceived by managers, the more proactive the company's response. This trend is similar for all types of stakeholders.
- The greater the environmental demand perceived by managers, the more solutions the firm tends to adopt beyond the mandatory environmental requirements established by the authorities, and even beyond market or society expectations.
- While the analysis was able to identify five distinct stakeholder groups (corporate government; internal economic; external economic; regulatory; external social), the results also showed that managers perceive only one dimension of stakeholders' demand for environmental protection. Thus, when a company perceives pressure from one stakeholder group they also perceive pressure from the rest.
- It is suggested that an explanation for this may be the fact that values, characteristics and attitudes of managers influence how they interpret environmental issues. This may bias the intensity of their perception of environmental pressure.
- Managers attach the greatest importance to regulatory stakeholders

(e.g. legislation) and corporate government stakeholders (e.g. the company Board).

- The study recommends a more in-depth analysis be conducted of the relationship between different pressure groups and the forms of environmental response they solicit from companies.

Source: Environmental Research Digest, January 2009 (Vol. 1, No. 1)

5.2.3 Shareholders Press Boards on Social, Environmental Risks

Author(s): Ernst & Young

Ernst & Young issued lately a report titled Shareholders Press Boards on Social, Environmental Risks. The report examines today's shareholders' expectations towards organizations.

<u>Key findings</u>

Shareholder resolutions that deal with sustainability issues dominated all others in 2010.

- It is estimated that in 2011 half of all shareholder resolutions will focus on social and environmental concerns.
- The number of corporate social responsibility (CSR)-related shareholder proposals brought to a vote increased from 150 in 2000 to 191 in 2010.
- Not only that, those resolutions were far more popular among shareholders voting their shares, more than doubling the support they received at the beginning of the 10-year span and going from 7.5% to 18.4%.
- Shareholder resolutions tend to attract the attention of corporate board members when they reach a threshold of 30% of shareholder support.
- And the percentage of social and environmental resolutions reaching that level increased from only 2.6% in 2005 to 26.8% in 2010.
- Increased awareness among investors and regulators of the reputational and financial risks associated with CSR and environmental sustainability places more pressure on companies to identify and manage these issues.
- This trend has truly evolved over the last decade and it is gaining more traction as reflected in the growing number of proposals voted on and the level of 'for' votes cast this season.

- Financial and reputational risks tied to climate change and sustainability are driving institutional investors to propose more, and more specific, targeted environmental and social shareholder resolutions.
- Increasingly, these link social and environmental issues to traditional governance issues like compensation and board member qualifications.
- In light of the report findings, Ernst & Young executives suggested several actions for board members to take regarding such resolutions:
    - better disclosure regarding social/environmental issues and better dialogue with shareholders about them (thorough and sound sustainability reporting will help);
    - tying director skills to stakeholder concerns, including risk management in social and environmental areas, and making shareholders aware of how director skillsets fit with corporate strategy;
    - consider the possibility of nontraditional performance metrics, including those that focus on environmental/sustainability issues, to help align compensation with risk.

Source: Governance Research Digest, May 2011 (Vol. 2, No. 1)

5.2.4 Who Should Control a Corporation? Toward a Contingency Stakeholder Model for Allocating Ownership Rights

Author(s): A. Zattoni

The article contributes to an understanding of evidence that a number of companies allocate ownership rights to stakeholders different from shareholders, despite the fact that the law attributes these rights to the equity holders. A contingency model is developed that sheds light on why companies, despite pressures from the law, vary in their allocation of ownership rights.

Key findings

The model is based on the assumption that corporations increase their chance to survive and prosper if the stakeholders supplying "critical contributions" receive the ownership rights.

- According to the model, "critical" contributions involve:
  - contractual problems due to specific investments, long-term relationships, and low measurability;
  - the assumption of the uncertainty resting on the company;
  - and the supply of scarce and valuable resources.
- The model is dynamic because it also provides a basis for understanding why the allocation of ownership rights changes with time.
- Finally, the article presents the strategies companies can use to realize an efficient distribution of ownership rights among their stakeholders.

Source: Governance Research Digest, October 2011 (Vol. 2, No. 6)

5.2.5 Equity and Expectancy Considerations in Stakeholder Action

Author(s): S. Hayibor

In this article, the author uses two motivation theories—equity theory and expectancy theory—to address the general research question, "What are the conditions under which stakeholders will take action against an organization?" Doing so allows for a more explicit elaboration of an interest-based approach to understanding stakeholder action.

Key findings

An "interest-based" view of stakeholder action—a view that stakeholders act against organizations to safeguard or promote their own interests— underlies much research in stakeholder theory.

- Applying the theories, the author develops propositions concerning the conditions that are likely to precipitate stakeholder sanctions directed at a focal organization and develops a basic framework for understanding when such stakeholder action is likely.
- Finally, the author discusses the theoretical and practical implications of this work.

Source: Governance Research Digest, May 2012 (Vol. 3, No. 5)

5.2.6 Stakeholder Pressure as Determinants of CSR Strategic Choice: Why do Firms Choose Symbolic versus Substantive Self-Regulatory Codes of Conduct

Author(s): L. A. Perez-Batres, J. P. Doh, V. V. Miller and M. J. Pisani

To encourage corporations to contribute positively to the environment in which they operate, voluntary selfregulatory codes (SRC) have been enacted and refined over the past 15 years. Two of the most prominent are the United Nations Global Compact and the Global Reporting Initiative.

Key findings

In this paper explores the impact of different stakeholders' pressures on the selection of strategic choices to join SRCs.

- The results show that corporations react differently to different sets of stakeholder pressures and that the SRC selection depends on the type and intensiveness of the stakeholder pressures as well as the resources at hand to respond to those pressures.
- Authors' contribution offers a more specific and finely variegated analysis of firm-stakeholder interactions.

Source: Governance Research Digest, October 2012 (Vol. 3, No. 10)

5.2.7 Stakeholder Forces of Socially Responsible Supply Chain Management Orientation

Author(s): H. Park-Poaps, K. Rees.

This study investigates the influence of stakeholder forces on socially responsible supply chain orientations in the apparel and footwear sector. The authors focus on labour management issues, and identify the primary stakeholders as consumers, regulators, industry and the media. A total of 209 mail survey responses from sourcing managers of US apparel and footwear companies were analysed.

Key findings

Regulation was not found to have a significant impact on company actions related to labour management as part of socially responsible supply chain management.

- This may reflect the current lack of control, coverage and uniformity of labour regulations designed to promote ethical labour management.
- Inclusion of labour standards in trade regulations has resulted in disputes and disagreements among countries due to different economic conditions and trade competition.
- The current lack of widely supported and applicable regulations means that NGO action to raise and uphold labour management standards is on the rise.
- The use of voluntary codes has also been suggested. While these have been criticized for having limited impact on actual labour conditions, they still remain primary forces of change.
- The authors suggest that media and industry pressure may have been more influential than customer pressure in motivating companies to proactively work with suppliers to improve labour conditions in their supply chains.
- Industry peer pressure had a significant effect on company actions on labour management issues at various points in the supply chain.
- Partnership approaches to labour issues were more apparent among companies dealing with more foreign suppliers.
- Firm size was found to have no significant relationship with the likelihood of socially responsible labour management practices at the firm.

Source: Social Research Digest, December 2009 (Vol. 1, No. 12)

5.2.8 The Market Reaction to Corporate Governance Regulation

Author(s): D. F. Larcker, G. Ormazabal and D. J. Taylor

The paper investigates the market reaction to recent legislative and regulatory actions pertaining to corporate governance. The managerial power view of governance suggests that executive pay, the existing process of proxy access, and various governance provisions [e.g., staggered boards and Chief Executive Officer (CEO)-chairman duality] are associated with managerial rent extraction.

Key findings

This perspective predicts that broad government actions that reduce executive pay, increase proxy access, and ban such governance provisions are value-enhancing.

- In contrast, another view of governance suggests that observed governance choices are the result of value-maximizing contracts between shareholders and management.
- This perspective predicts that broad government actions that regulate such governance choices are value destroying.
- Consistent with the latter view, authors find that the abnormal returns to recent events relating to corporate governance regulations are, on average, decreasing in CEO pay, decreasing in the number of large blockholders, decreasing in the ease by which small institutional investors can access the proxy process, and decreasing in the presence of a staggered board.

Source: Governance Research Digest, August 2011 (Vol. 2, No. 4)

5.2.9 The Emergence, Variation and Evolution of Corporate Social Responsibility in the Public Sphere, 1980-2004: The Exposure of Firms to Public Debate

Author(s): S. Y. Lee and C. E. Carroll

The study examines the emergence of corporate social responsibility (CSR) as a public issue over 25 years using a content analysis of two national newspapers and seven regional, geographically dispersed newspapers in the U.S. This study examined newspaper editorials, letters to the editor, op-ed columns, news analyses, and guest columns for three aspects: media attention, media prominence, and media valence.

Key findings

Results showed an increase in the number of opinion pieces covering CSR issues over the 25-year period.

- The prominence of each of the four CSR dimensions varied over time.
- Each of the four CSR dimensions had its moment of media prominence when it was more important than the other dimensions.

- The most prevalent valence of the opinion pieces was negative; the volume of negative pieces increased over the 25 years, whereas the number of opinions with positive, neutral, and mixed tones showed little change over time.
- The study concludes by tracing the implications of the role of the news media for business ethics research.

Source: CSR Research Digest, November 2011 (Vol. 3, No. 11)

5.2.10   Going Green: Market Reaction to CSR Newswire Releases

Author(s): P. A. Griffin and Y. Sun (University of California)

The study used archives of the Corporate Social Responsibility Newswire to identify climate change-related press releases issued between 2000 and 2010. The researchers tracked the stock changes of the companies from two days before a press release was issued to two days after.

Key findings

Companies that voluntarily issue press releases disclosing their carbon emission information see their stock prices rise significantly in the following days.

- For the 172 companies identified as making voluntary disclosures, average stock prices increased just under a half percent in the fiveday span around the disclosures.
- To test their findings, the researchers compared stock movements of these companies to those of similar firms that did not disclose carbon emission information during the same time periods.
- The companies that did not disclose climate change information did not see a statistically significant increase in values, and their prices actually tended to fall.
- The researchers also analyzed the stock changes for smaller firms that disclosed carbon emission information.
- These firms saw an even greater effect on their stock values, with prices increasing 2.32%.
- Small firms are not followed as closely by analysts, and investors know less about them, so the release of climate change information would have a more pronounced effect.

- The study looked at voluntary disclosures only, so the authors said they could not determine if mandatory disclosures by all such companies would have yielded similar increases.

Source: Environmental Research Digest, February 2012 (Vol. 3, No. 2)

5.3   Stakeholder Management and Engagement

5.3.1   Stakeholder Engagement Report

Author(s): Brunswick Insight

Brunswick Insight, the opinion research practice of Brunswick Group, a corporate communications consultancy, conducted an online survey of 130 European senior communication professionals to understand their views and practices in the area of stakeholder engagement. The Future of Stakeholder Engagement' report summarized the views of senior European communicators from companies, associations, government organizations, NGOs and other organizations.

Key findings

Senior communicators across Europe (82%) consider stakeholder engagement to be important to their organization's success, with 55% saying it is 'extremely important'.

- The scope and scale of stakeholder engagement activities are expected to increase dramatically in the next five years, with a sizable increase in the percentage who say engagement will be important to their organization's success (90%) and nearly as many saying their organizations will be doing more engagement in the future (82%).
- Lack of understanding is the biggest internal obstacle to creating engagement programs.
- At most organizations, stakeholder engagement tends to be ad hoc (79%) rather than strategic and just three in ten (29%) use specific KPIs to measure the success of their organization's engagement.
- Currently, communicators are much more likely to engage with traditional (e.g. employees, suppliers, business partners,

customers/members) rather than nontraditional (e.g. NGOs, consumer groups, special interest groups, activist groups) stakeholders.

- Communicators acknowledge that engagement with non-traditional stakeholders carries sizable risks, the biggest of which is the possibility of not meeting expectations (60%).

- Two in three communicators (68%) feel overwhelmed by the amount of time and resources required to engage properly.

Source: Governance Research Digest, May 2013 (Vol. 4, No. 5)

5.3.2 Short-Run Impact and Long-Run Consequences of Stakeholder Management

Author(s): R. Garcia-Castro

The article provides empirical evidence of the negative effects of stakeholder management in shareholders' value in the short run and the positive effects over the long run. The study us using a longitudinal database of 658 U.S. firms.

Key findings

The stakeholder view of the firm has been justified under instrumental and normative bases.

- Given the difficulties of anticipating the instrumental long-term financial effects of short-run decisions affecting the different stakeholders, the authors' findings support the view of the normative basis for stakeholder theory based on ethics, norms, and heuristic criteria as a way to solve conflicts among the claims of different stakeholders.

Source: Social Research Digest, September 2011 (Vol. 2, No. 5)

5.3.3 Perceptions on the Demand Side and Realities on the Supply Side: A Study of the South African Table Grape Export Industry

Author(s): C. Müller, W.J.V. Vermeulen, P. Glasbergen.

This article reports on the mechanisms of business-to-business regulation as governance approach in agricultural supply chains. The empirical data informing this study was gathered via open interviews with a variety of stakeholders in the South African table grape export industry supply chain.

Key findings

To a large extent, producers accept their corporate social responsibility and carry the costs involved. This relates not only to auditing costs but also capital costs involved in establishing the necessary infrastructure to comply with market criteria and government policy.

- The large majority of producers provide more benefits to workers than required. However, a small percentage of producers still do not comply with standards and regulation.
- Across the participating grape farms in this study, on average, permanent employees are paid 19-23% more than the required minimum wage, while the wages of seasonal workers are 10-12% higher than the legal level. Female workers earn 1.6-3.2% less than male colleagues.
- More than 85% of producers pay incentives or bonuses to employees. These are often linked to productivity or the general profitability of the harvest.
- Over 90% or producers provide their permanent employees with basic services such as housing, water and electricity.
- The requirements of business standards as determined by dialogue between stakeholders in the northern hemisphere are mostly met.
- The findings suggest that supply chain actors other than producers do not contribute to the uplift of the social circumstances of workers.
- This provision of benefits can, potentially, be a competitive advantage to South African producers, giving them a relative front runner's position compared with suppliers from other developing countries such as Chile or China.
- From a northern hemisphere perspective, NGO involvement in supply chains is successful in addressing sustainability concerns as perceived by northern civil society. Counterparts in the southern hemisphere do not have as much influence in the process.
- Since reputation is one of the motivational factors for CSR, it should be emphasized in markets that increasingly focus on sustainability.

Source: Governance Research Digest, November 2009 (Vol. 1, No. 11)

5.3.4 An Overview of Multi-Stakeholder and Industry Activities to Achieve Conflict-Free Minerals

Author(s): Responsible Sourcing Network

Responsible Sourcing Network released a white paper for companies and for investors expecting corporations in their portfolios to live up to their ethical responsibilities. 'An Overview of Multi-Stakeholder and Industry Activities to Achieve Conflict-Free Minerals' aims to educate investors and assist companies in implementing responsible, sustainable and conflict-free practices with regards to sourcing minerals and supporting initiatives in central Africa's Great Lakes region (GLR).

Key findings

- The ICT industry has been noticeably active in addressing conflict mineral sourcing with companies incorporating the OECD Due Diligence Guidance into their supply chain management systems.
- Leading ICT companies such as Intel, Hewlett-Packard, Motorola Solutions and Apple are committed to finding solutions and developing programs contributing to smelter auditing, traceability and development projects.
- Advanced Micro Devices (AMD), Apple and Panasonic are notable for surveying their suppliers, and Intel has committed to making a conflict-free product.
- One member of the automotive industry has begun to make progress and is driving the industry to do more through the Automotive Industry Action Group (AIAG). Ford Motor
- Company has taken major steps to develop traceability systems and is active in multistakeholder groups and legislative efforts.
- The aerospace/defence industry has not been very active regarding conflict minerals with the exception of General Electric Company. Boeing Company and Lockheed Martin Corporation are participating in the OECD Guidance implementation pilot.
- The food packaging, medical device, retail, apparel and footwear, tooling, and toy industries have made little to no progress.

Source: Governance Research Digest, November 2013 (Vol. 4, No. 11)

5.3.5 Collaborating With Customer Communities: Lessons From the Lego Group

Author(s): MIT Sloan Management Review

Between 2003 and 2011, authors engaged in a multisite research program to examine
community development and user innovation among adult fans of Lego and to learn about Lego's experiences and practices in working with external communities. Authors participated in eight conventions in North America, Denmark and Germany, also observed adult users at smaller and locally arranged events; in addition conducted 25 in-depth interviews and several informal interviews with members of the community.

Key findings

By tapping into the knowledge and enthusiasm of thousands of longtime users of its products, Lego has been able to enhance its product offerings — without increasing long-term fixed costs.

- Companies need to open lines of communication through programs that users of the products see as valid.
- Collaboration with customers is most effective when companies provide several platforms for interaction.
- Since the company and users may have different interests, companies need to develop clear guidelines for considering user input.
- Based on its experiences working with the user community, Lego has developed a set of principles that summarize what it has learned about collaborating and interacting with knowledgeable users.
- Be clear about rules and expectations. Lego learned that it had to be more specific about its expectations upfront, including when its projects would begin and end.
- Ensure a win-win. Lego management learned, as studies of innovators have found, that the intrinsic rewards associated with designing and building products are frequently more motivating than financial rewards. Recognizing this, Lego has tended to pay outside collaborators with a combination of experience, access and Lego products. However, users who participate in long-term projects or who provide services

that are more like "work" are given a choice: they can receive free products or a more conventional stipend.

- Recognize that outsiders aren't insiders. Lego employees involved with the user community learned early in the process that while participants were indeed committed to the Lego brand and the Lego brick, they were also attracted to the sense of community they experienced with other adult fans. User communities are not just extensions of the company — they are independent entities.
- Don't expect one size to fit all. Lego also learned early on that different users prefer different modes of communication, and different types of innovations call for different environments. As a result, Lego relies on many different collaboration platforms.

Source: Social Research Digest, April 2012 (Vol. 3, No. 4)

5.3.6 Crowdsourcing and Social Engagement Study

Author(s): Weber Shandwick

Weber Shandwick partnered with KRC Research to examine top executives at Fortune 2000 companies who have responsibility for philanthropic, social responsibility or community outreach. It was interviewed more than 200 corporate executives to determine the value of crowdsourcing and social engagement for corporate social responsibility (CSR) efforts.

Key findings

Forty-four percent said they have used crowdsourcing – asking customers to provide ideas and help in decision-making.

- Among those executives, an overwhelming 95% reported that it was valuable to their organization's CSR programming.
- When asked why crowdsourcing is so valuable for CSR, executives said it:
  - Surfaces new perspectives and diverse opinions (36%)
  - Builds engagement and relationships with key audiences (25%)
  - Invites clients and customers from nontraditional sources to contribute ideas and opinions (22%)
  - Brings new energy into the process of generating ideas and content (16%)

- Among executives who haven't experimented with crowdsourcing, 55% view it favorably and 43% believe it could be valuable for future CSR efforts.
- The survey also explored how executives communicate about their companies' CSR efforts.
- Seventy-two percent said they have used social media and 59% believe it has had a positive impact on their communications with consumers.
- Interestingly, those executives consider Facebook most valuable (67%), followed by blogs (60%), LinkedIn (58%), Twitter (46%) and FourSquare (44%).
- Overall, they said the value of social media is to:
  - Create opportunities for companies to reach broad and diverse audiences (38%)
  - Allow companies to connect directly with consumers in low-cost, efficient ways (29%)
  - Enable companies to engage specific constituencies with greater ease (11%)

Source: CSR Research Digest, February 2011 (Vol. 3, No. 2)

5.3.7   Cause Trend: Can Voting Campaigns Win?

Author(s): Cone

The report covers one of the most popular techniques for consumer engagement in the cause space – voting campaigns, in which companies let consumers choose how they will invest their philanthropic dollars. In report Cone discusses if the voting campaigns are sustainable and covers the different approches.

<u>Key findings</u>

Consumer voting campaigns are a novel way to engage consumers, and they can be a powerful way to make a cause program more tangible on the local level.

- There are various approaches for voting campaigns:
  - open-sourced: company sets minimal, if any, limits on which charitable organizations may qualify, allowing consumers to

nominate any charity that appeals to them, large or small, in a range of issue areas;

o partnership-based: company asks consumers to select among a short-list of pre-approved organizations, typically their existing nonprofit partners; the company will often divide the total grant among the organizations based on percent of votes received;

o outcome-focused: company builds voting around a specific issue area aligned with the company's cause focus. It provides a short-list of organizations within that focus area from which consumers can choose or allows consumers to nominate a particular type of organization (e.g., school, historic monument) that fits the social goals of the program.

- Although voting campaigns are most effective when they are focused and tied to an organization's strategic partnerships and social goals, the open-sourcing approach dominates the landscape.

- Most notable is Pepsi Refresh, whose grassroots rallying cry and significant investment make it one of the most talked about cause campaigns in recent memory.

- Open-sourced campaigns stand out because they are a bit radical, they tend to be ongoing efforts and they are backed by significant marketing investments.

- Unfocused voting campaigns are not sustainable ways to engage stakeholders and achieve long-term brand equity or social outcomes when used as a stand-alone strategy.

- Most (61%) would rather buy from a company that makes its own long-term commitment to a focused issue than from one that allows them to choose which causes the company will support this month or this year (39%).

Source: Social Research Digest, July 2011 (Vol. 2, No. 3)

5.3.8   The 2014 GreenBiz NGO Report

Author(s): The GreenBiz Intelligence Panel

The GreenBiz Intelligence Panel asked sustainability executives from large corporations to rate and rank 30 leading NGOs. The way large corporations view the different NGOs is reflected in four category profiles: (1) Trusted Partners – Corporate-friendly, highly credible, long-term partners with easy-to-find public success stories; (2) Useful Resources – Highly credible organizations known for creating helpful frameworks and services for corporate partners; (3) Brand Challenged – Credible, but not influential, organizations; (4) The Uninvited – Less broadly known groups, or those viewed more as critics than partners.

<u>Key findings</u>

Three NGOs stand at the top of the list when it comes to corporate partnerships. In no particular order, those are The Nature Conservancy (TNC), World Wildlife Fund (WWF) and the Environmental Defense Fund (EDF).

- All three of these organizations are engaged in very public, solutions-oriented partnerships with major corporations. They seek to leverage the scale of their corporate partners to make a significant impact on issues important to their organization.

- The NGOs classified as useful resources are highly credible organizations best known for creating helpful frameworks and services for corporate partners. Examples of the resources we are describing include:

- Ceres created a Roadmap for Sustainability which details 20 specific expectations for corporate performance, broadly divided into four areas of activity: governance, stakeholder engagement, disclosure and performance.

- World Resources Institute may be best known for its partnership with the World Business Council for Sustainable Development to develop the Greenhouse Gas Protocol (GHG Protocol), the most widely used international accounting tool for government and business leaders to understand, quantify and manage greenhouse gas emissions.

- BSR (formerly Business for Social Responsibility) launched the HERproject in 2007, linking multinational companies and their factories to local NGOs to create sustainable workplace programs that increase women's health awareness. BSR has more than a dozen other multi-company partnerships and working groups in place.

- Perhaps the most vexing category contained NGOs that provide sound and mostly scientifically based resources, but which nonetheless lack influence. These are the Brand Challenged. Greenbiz asked about NGOs where corporations had no interactions.

- Nearly a third had no interaction with the Trust for Public Lands (35%), Union of Concerned Scientists (34%) or the National Audubon Society (32%).

- However, both the Trust for Public Lands and Audubon were rated in the top half of effective organizations.

- Many of the Brand Challenged groups offer important insights for corporate sustainability leaders. It may be time for them to invest a little of their supporters' donations in a marketing program to expand their influence and forward their causes.

- The final group of NGOs, the Uninvited, is comprised of those that are even less broadly known or which have chosen to focus primarily on name-and-shame actions rather than on developing working partnerships with companies.

- On its website, the Dogwood Alliance states that marketplace campaigns are a key factor in its work. But our panelists ranked them as the least influential and only slightly more credible than Earth First, a self-organizing group with no obvious funding and a vague (but slightly threatening) mission.

- Of the Uninvited, only Rainforest Action Network made it into the top half of effective organizations. This more than likely reflects its effective and aggressive campaigns against large brands — as well as its partnership with those brands with which it reaches settlements.

Source: CSR Research Digest, March 2014 (Vol. 6, No. 3)

5.3.9 Creating New Models: Innovative Public-Private Partnerships for Inclusive Development in Latin America

Author(s): World Economic Forum

World Economic Forum's Global Agenda Council on Latin America launched a report that provides 15 case studies highlighting the ways in which innovative collaboration between governments and private actors has improved the quality of public goods and services or contributed to sustainable development. The report, Creating New Models: Innovative Public-Private Partnerships for Inclusive Development in Latin America, offers key recommendations to policy-makers on how to create an enabling environment for such partnerships and the case studies cover a broad set of thematic areas, including education, health, sustainable development, climate change, access to and use of information and communication technologies, post-disaster prevention and reconstruction, and gender equality.

Key findings

Successful partnerships between the public and private sectors are needed to strengthen economic development and innovation in Latin America.

- A key component of an effective partnership lies in the financial sustainability. The nature of the financing framework needs to be set from the beginning of the collaboration as to reduce the dependency on a single actor and to ensure the continuity of the work. For example, the Digital Health Project of the Federation of Internal Medicine (FEMI) in Uruguay showcases economic and financial sustainability as its funds are divided between the contributions of its institutions as well as 3% of the amount paid by the national health fund to health service providers.

- In the current context of a shifting paradigm, the role of the state remains vital in designing, fostering and implementing social covenants, regulatory frameworks, incentives, policies and innovative partnerships with the private sector and civil society actors to encourage progress in society, the economy and the productive sector within a rights-based approach. To forge a new social contract facilitating the exercise of citizenship in all its dimensions, the state must encourage the transformational agenda through a combination of coherent economic and productive development policies and provide for an inclusive social safety net. It must also work towards universal employment with full rights, universal social protection and capacity building.

- In the case of the private sector, businesses have become more interested in pushing for greater involvement in solving social problems both in industrialized and (increasingly) in emerging countries, thereby going beyond traditional corporate social responsibility to touch on issues such as poverty, inequality, fair trade or the environment, which are progressively becoming part of their corporate values Engage with your stakeholders: Know who your key stakeholders are and what they think

- More importantly, the business case through which the private sector seeks to position itself among more vulnerable sectors of society by providing them with goods and services and to address issues of environmental sustainability is quickly gaining acceptance as a new source of value creation.

- Corporate and philanthropic foundations help bridge the gap between the corporate world and the fight against poverty at the national or community levels. Today, financial flows from private philanthropy to the developing world outweigh the monetary contributions of all governments combined.

- Over the past decade, NGOs and organized local communities from civil society have become very significant stakeholders in the analysis and debate of issues related to sustainable development, the environment and the rights of the most vulnerable sectors of society. These actors have progressively become more informed, organised and relevant in raising public interest and in formulating and implementing concrete initiatives addressing economic, social and cultural rights-based issues in sectors as diverse as education, health, food security, the rights of indigenous populations and young people, access to water, and the impact of extractive industries

Source: CSR Research Digest, April 2014 (Vol. 6, No. 4)

5.3.10 Changing the game: communication and sustainability in the mining industry

Author(s): Brunswick and the International Finance Corporation (IFC)

Brunswick and the International Finance Corporation (IFC) coauthored a report that explores several emerging themes that are shaping how companies organize, manage and execute effective stakeholder communications. The insights in the report, "Changing the game: communication and sustainability in the mining industry", are drawn from conversations with industry leaders and practitioners as well as the first-hand experience of IFC and Brunswick Group advising on a variety of situations from new mine development to mergers and acquisitions.

Key findings

Trends towards resource nationalism and greater environmental and social expectations mean that maintaining a social license to operate is more directly linked to value perceived by host communities/countries.

- The mining industry has been embracing the call for greater transparency.
- Where practiced, regular disclosure of key decisions, performance metrics and contributions to local and national economies has garnered company trust with stakeholders.
- Almost universally, executives talked about the need to invest more in their internal communications activities – effectively engaging with employees and business partners to convey information and build a common culture.
- There was clear recognition that these internal stakeholders often receive insufficient communication.
- While the majority of companies preferred to keep their external and internal communications functions separate (employee communications was most often a human resources department responsibility), a few companies have begun to merge internal and external communications functions

Source: Governance Research Digest, December 2013 (Vol. 4, No. 12)

5.3.11 A Framework for Dialogue on National Market Participation and Competitiveness

Author(s): WBCSD

The World Business Council for Sustainable Development (WBCSD) has developed the National Market Participation Framework. The new tool is to help open up dialogue between business and government on supplier competitiveness.

Key findings

Competitiveness is key to enabling local firms' participation in the value chains of large inward investments and to local economic development.

- Investing companies and host governments often have shared interests in enhancing local firms' capabilities and competitiveness.
- The tool presents the case that these shared interests are best realized through working to improve the competitiveness of local firms rather than through mandatory requirements ('local content rules').
- While such mandatory requirements can boost local firm participation in the short term, substantial evidence suggests these measures can be counterproductive and often impose significant costs on consumers and investing firms, increase project risk, reduce competition and innovation, and discourage investment.
- The tool can be used across a broad range of sectors, geographies and scales of investment.
- It will be particularly useful in circumstances where investing companies have opportunities to engage with governments, government agencies or other key stakeholders on the parameters to maximize the developmental benefits of large investments.

Source: Governance Research Digest, March 2012 (Vol. 3, No. 3)

5.4 Credibility and Trust

5.4.1 Foundations of Organizational Trust: What Matters to Different Stakeholders?

Author(s): M. Pirson and D. Malhotra

The study aims to develop a framework that distinguishes between organizational stakeholders along two dimensions: depth of the relationship (deep or shallow) and locus (internal or external). The authors test the predictions of the framework using original survey data from 1,298 respondents across four stakeholder groups from four different organizations.

Key findings

Prior research on organizational trust has not rigorously examined the context specificity of trust nor distinguished between the potentially varying dimensions along which different stakeholders base their trust.

- As a result, dominant conceptualizations of organizational trust are overly generalized.
- Building on existing research on organizational trust and stakeholder theory, it is introduced a more nuanced perspective on the nature of organizational trust.
- The framework identifies which of six dimensions of trustworthiness (benevolence, integrity, managerial competence, technical competence, transparency, and identification) will be relevant to which stakeholder type.
- The results reveal that the relevant dimensions of trustworthiness vary systematically across different stakeholder types and provide strong support for the validity of the depth and locus dimensions.

Source: Governance Research Digest, August 2011 (Vol. 2, No. 4)

5.4.2   Do Credible Firms Perform Better in Emerging Markets? Evidence From China

Author(s): R. Zhang, Z. Rezaee

This article examines whether corporate credibility is related to company performance using Economic Observer's rating of corporate credibility in China. The 50 highest and 51 lowest ranked firms in the 2004 Economic Observer Research Institute's corporate credibility index (CCI) formed the total sample of 101 companies.

Key findings

A significant positive relationship exists between firm credibility and performance in China.

- In general, the evidence is consistent with stakeholder theory: stakeholders, other than investors and management, play an important role in financial policy and constitute a vital link between corporate strategy and corporate finance.
- Firm with a reputation for high credibility may find that they have more low-cost implicit claims than other firms, thus exhibiting higher financial performance.
- The credibility issues faced by firms – low earnings quality and poor corporate governance – significantly impair performance, as well as

board effectiveness and governance.

- The authors suggest that building corporate credibility is the key to the success of future reforms aiming to improve market efficiency and investor protection in China.

- Firms operating in China and seeking competitive advantages in global markets may consider strengthening their credibility and reputation to ensure sustainability of performance.

Source: CSR Research Digest, January 2010 (Vol. 2, No. 1)

5.4.3 The Recovery of Trust: Case Studies of Organisational Failures and Trust Repair

Author(s): IBE

A new report by the IBE explores how organisations have dealt with crises of trust and the processes they have undergone to rebuild their reputations internally and externally. Taken from interviews with those involved and media reports at the time, this publication shares insights into the process of organisational trust repair and asserts the case for a commitment to ethical business practice.

Key findings

Real case studies of how trust has been lost, and regained, for six international organisations.

- The six organisations included in the report are:
  - o Siemens: Accused of systemic bribery in 2006, the German engineering giant has overhauled its structures, leadership, processes and culture.
  - o Mattel: Faced with a series of toy recalls in 2007, the firm's exemplary response has drawn widespread praise, and minimised reputation damage.
  - o Toyota: By contrast, Toyota's initial response to its own product recall crisis in 2009-10 was widely criticised. However, its subsequent programme of thorough reforms has attempted to recover its lost reputation.
  - o BAE Systems: Beset with persistent allegations of corruption and bribery in arms deals, the company has undergone a major

programme of cultural, structural and procedural transformation in pursuit of a more ethical reputation.

o The BBC: The Corporation's phone-in scandals in 2007-08 led to a comprehensive review of its operations, and a series of innovative reforms, but implementation has not been easy, or necessarily welcome.

o Severn Trent: Found guilty of distorting performance data for the industry regulator Ofwat and fined a total of £38m, Severn Trent had, within two years, been voted Utility of the Year by its peers, in part due to its innovative and impressive recovery efforts.

Source: Governance Research Digest, February 2012 (Vol. 3, No. 2)

5.4.4   Trust Barometer

Author(s): Edelman

Edelman has released a midyear update on its Trust Barometer, as a result of the continuing global recession, bank bailouts, nationalizations and bankruptcies. This forms an update to the January 2009 Trust Barometer, in which trust in business was at the lowest level recorded in a decade of Edelman tracking. For this report, 1,675 individuals in six countries (the US, UK, France, Germany, India and China) were surveyed.

Key findings

Trust in business has stabilized and is recovering significantly in the US and France, following a devastating loss of trust in the private sector. Trust remains high in India and China.

- The twelve point increase in trust in the US includes the addition of a younger sample of 25-34 year olds.
- In the United States alone, trust in business among the younger age group was up by 26 points in six months; their trust in government was up 24 points.
- Trust in business and trust in government are now moving synchronously, unlike previous years where they tended to move in opposing directions.
- The expectation today is for these two institutions to work collaboratively to tackle economic and societal challenges. Yet 55% of

respondents say business hasn't done enough to cooperate with government to solve the global economic crisis.

- Companies that have repaid bailout or loan money to the government, reduced CEO and executive pay, or fired non-performing management teams are more trusted by eight out of 10 informed publics.

- However business still has work to do: Only 6% in six countries describe the reputation of large global businesses as "excellent" and 52% say companies haven't managed business operations well enough to ensure they survive the global economic crisis.

- Technology has historically ranked high in the Edelman Trust Barometer and continues to be highly trusted.

- In response to a question about what actions build trust, 89% of informed publics said they would trust companies that drive better innovation by investing in research and development.

- In addition to investors ranking third in the list of stakeholders whose interests CEOs should heed, profitability and performance falls behind employee well-being, transparent and honest business practices, and frequent communication in the list of factors that could build trust in a company.

- Informed publics place great importance on business's commitment to finding solutions for global issues like global warming, energy costs, and access to affordable healthcare but say business has not done enough to create solutions for these causes (71%, 70%, and 64%, respectively).

- India and China are the most positive about business. At 75%, India recorded the highest level of trust in business of any of the six countries surveyed. China followed with 60% saying they trust business to do what is right.

- In China and India, 96% and 81% of informed publics, respectively, say their country is headed in the right direction, compared with 47% of Americans and Germans, 37% of British, and 31% of French.

- In another marked contrast to the West, nearly seven out of 10 informed publics in India and China rate the reputation of large multinational corporations as good or excellent, compared with 30% of Americans, 29% of Germans, 24% of French, and 13% of British.

Source: CSR Research Digest, September 2009 (Vol. 1, No. 9)

5.4.5   Trust Barometer Study

Author(s): Edelman

The annual Trust Barometer surveys informed publics around the world, including Australia, on the state of trust in various issues, ideas and institutions. This year's results point to the importance of aligning the business' profit motive with the needs of society.

Key findings

Demand for authority and accountability has set new expectations for corporate leadership and pushing company's messages through multiple voices and channels is critical in order to overcome an evolving media landscape and deepening skepticism.

- Trust in government and business has reached heights similar to that before the global financial crisis.
- While governments in Australia faced major criticism last year, the 2011 Edelman Trust Barometer found more than half (52%) of Australia's opinion influencers trust government to do what is right.
- This represents an increase of 11%age points since 2010, bringing trust in government back to 2009 benchmark levels.
- Ensuring ethical behaviour is vital for our companies as transparency and honesty topped the list of corporate reputation attributes that Australians value.
- Transparent and honest business practices (64%) are as important as quality products (63%).
- Price also matters: Australians are looking for companies to price brands fairly and competitively (55%), an important attribute for reputation in 2011, up 17%age points since 2010.
- The Trust Barometer found a flight to qualified spokespeople, with academics/experts (69%) and technical experts within a company (67%) seen as most credible.
- By contrast, a "person like me," has dropped by 10%age points since 2009, down to 31%.

Source: CSR Research Digest, March 2011 (Vol. 3, No. 3)

5.4.6 Reputation and Corporate Social Responsibility Aberrations, Trends and Hypocrisy: Reactions to Firm Choices in the Stock Option Backdating Scandal

Author(s): J. J. Janney and S. Gove

Drawing on strategic corporate social responsibility (CSR) and reputation theory, the paper examines the market reaction to firm disclosures of involvement in the US stock option backdating scandal. Authors examine how a firm's prior signals regarding ethical behaviour and values, as demonstrated through CSR initiatives, may both ameliorate and exacerbate market reactions.

Key findings

CSR initiatives may buffer a firm against general wrong-doing but expose it to greater scrutiny and sanction for related wrong-doing.

- The results show that firms with enhanced overall reputations for CSR are partially buffered from scandal revelations.
- However, authors find that when firms possess an enhanced reputation for CSR associated with corporate governance, violations pertaining specifically to governance are viewed as hypocritical and more harshly sanctioned.
- Also authors find lower and negative market reactions for firms that delay but self-disclose their involvement in the scandal.
- The study extends the emergent, related literatures on strategic CSR and reputation management, and documents dynamics in the relationship between corporate social and financial performance.

Source: CSR Research Digest, November 2011 (Vol. 3, No. 11)

5.4.7 The Company behind the Brand: In Reputation We Trust

Author(s): Weber Shandwick

A report by Weber Shandwick looks into how corporate reputation impacts brand preference today and to what extent. Between October and November 2011, company polled both senior executives and consumers from the United States, United Kingdom, China and Brazil to determine their opinions on the issue.

Key findings

CEO and company reputation are inextricably linked and, together drive a firm's market value.

- While 40% of consumers hold large corporations in lower regard than a few years ago, their respect in small businesses has grown.
- At the same time 50% of all consumers surveyed lost respect for corporate leaders, particularly in the United States and UK.
- Approximately 66% of consumers and 84% of executives hold a moderate or strong belief that perceptions of the CEO impact views of the company as a whole.
- The survey results indicate greater interdependence between CEO and company reputation in emerging markets where consumers place company leaders and their communications in higher regard.
- A majority of consumer respondents (69%) say they frequently or regularly discuss how they feel about a product they bought.
- Not surprisingly these conversations hold major sway in perception of reputation and future purchase behavior.
- Word-of-mouth remains the leading source of influence when it comes to opinion of a company (88%), whether the genesis is online or offline.
- A subset (83%) cited online reviews as very or somewhat influential on consumer opinion about companies.
- Advertising (56%) lagged pointing to more limited impact of traditional image-building campaigns.
- Consumers (70%) said they will avoid buying a product if they don't like the company that makes it.
- They now consider themselves rightful investors in the companies they choose to support.
- Consumers (67%) increasingly check product labels to see who the company is behind the product.
- They want to know where their money is going and who they are supporting when buying their goods.
- Consumers get annoyed (61%) when they can't identify the parent company of the brand being considered.
- People want to know who makes the product, the values they embody and how well they treat employees.

- Respondents (56%) hesitate to buy products if they can't tell who makes them.

Source: CSR Research Digest, July 2012 (Vol. 4, No. 7)

5.4.8 The Advertising Effects of Corporate Social Responsibility and Brand Equity: Evidence from Life Insurance Industry in Taiwan

Author(s): K-T. Hsu

This study investigates the persuasive advertising and informative advertising effects of CSR initiatives on corporate reputation and brand equity. It is based on the evidence from the life insurance industry in Taiwan.

Key findings

Policyholders' perceptions concerning the CSR initiatives of life insurance companies have positive effects on customer satisfaction, corporate reputation, and brand equity.

- The advertising effects of the CSR initiatives on corporate reputation are only informative.
- The impacts of CSR initiatives on brand equity include informative advertising and persuasive advertising effects.
- This study contributes the literature by explicit defining the advertising effects of CSR initiatives.
- The obtained results in this research first identify the informative advertising effects and persuasive advertising effects of CSR initiatives.

Source: CSR Research Digest, October 2012 (Vol. 4, No. 10)

5.4.9 Most Criticised Companies 2008 Ranking

Author(s): Ecofact

Barclays, E.ON and Wal-Mart all make the list in a new report of the most criticized companies in 2008. Zurich-based reputational risk consultant Ecofact has released its report of the most criticised global companies in 2008. The report is based on media coverage of companies' environmental and social performance from multiple sources.

Key findings

The most controversial company in 2008 was Shijiazhuang Sanlu Group Holding Co – the Chinese company that became embroiled in a major scandal involving contamination of milk powder with melamine.

Top five most controversial companies				
Emerging Markets	**North America**	**Financial Sector**	**Utilities**	**Overall**
Shijia-zhuang Sanlu Group Holding Co. Ltd.	Wal-Mart Stores	Barclays PLC	E.ON AG	Shijia-zhuang Sanlu Group Holding Co. Ltd.
China Petroleum and Chemical Corp.	Baxter International	Citigroup Inc.	Endesa AG	China Petroleum and Chemical Corp.
Samsung Group	Monsanto	Société Générale	Areva AG	Samsung Group
China National Petroleum Corporation	Chevron Corp.	Bank of America Corp.	Electricité de France	Siemens AG
Inner Mongolia Yili Industrial Group Co.	Exxon Mobil	Deutsche Bank	Duke Energy Corp	Arcelor-Mittal

- Out of all financial institutions, Barclays attracted the most criticism in 2008 on environmental and social grounds. In particular, Barclays came under fire for investing in the weapons and coal industry, and for paying out large bonuses during the current financial crisis.
- E.ON was ranked most controversial utility, after being targetted by environmentalists over its coal-fired power plants, particularly its Kingsnorth power station in the UK.
- Wal-Mart Stores topped the list of North American companies, over accusations of labour violations and poor conditions at factories in

Bangladesh and China. It also has several large lawsuits pending against it for social discrimination.

Top three issues for each group				
Emerging Markets	*North America*	*Financial Sector*	*Utilities*	*Overall*
Human rights violations and corporate complicity	Impacts on ecosystems/ landscapes	Impacts on ecosystems/ landscapes	Impacts on ecosystems/ landscapes	Human rights abuses and corporate complicity
Supply chains	Supply chains	Impacts on communities	Impacts on communities	Corruption, bribery, extortion, money laundering
Impacts on ecosystems/ landscapes	Impacts on communities	Global pollution (incl. Climate change)	Global pollution (incl. Climate change)	Impacts on communities

Source: Governance Research Digest, January 2009 (Vol. 1, No. 1)

5.4.10 Public Trust in Business

Author(s): Edelman Trust Barometer

The 2009 Edelman Trust Barometer is the 10th edition of the firm's annual trust and credibility survey. It was launched in partnership with the Financial Times on 27th January 2009 in London. The survey sampled 4475 consumers in 20 countries aged between 25 and 64.

Key findings

Nearly two-thirds of informed publics (62%) trust corporations less than they did a year ago. When respondents in the United States were asked about trust in business in general, only 38% said they trust business to do what is right - a 20% plunge since last year - and only 17% said they trust information from a company's CEO.

- Both of the above are lower levels of trust than those Edelman measured in the wakes of Enron, the dot-com bust, and September 11th.
- Indian and Chinese consumers have retained the most trust in companies over the last year.
- Trust in banks plummeted in the US, from 69% in 2008 to 36% in 2009. Conversely, in China, trust in banks rose from 72% to 84%, and in Brazil from 52% to 59%.
- 77% of respondents said they refused to buy products or services from a company they distrusted.
- 72% of those surveyed criticized a distrusted company to a friend or colleague.
- By a 3:1 margin respondents say that government should intervene to regulate industry or nationalize companies to restore public trust.
- In the major Western European economies of the U.K., France, and Germany, three-quarters of respondents say that government should step in to prevent future financial crises (73%, 75%, and 74%, respectively).
- In the United States, not even half (49%) say that the free market should be allowed to function independently.
- Trust in business magazines and stock or industry analyst reports—last year's leaders—is down from 57% to 44% and from 56% to 47%, respectively.
- Only 29% and 27% view information as credible when coming from a CEO or government official, respectively, declining from 36% and 32% last year.

Source: Governance Research Digest, February 2009 (Vol. 1, No. 2)

5.4.11 Contextual Factors Surrounding Reputation Damage With Potential Implications for Reputation Repair

Author(s): M. Rhee & M.E. Valdez

This paper examines the contextual factors surrounding reputation damage and their potential implications for reputation repair. The authors propose a model that examines how the organization's age, the diversity of market segments served by the organization, and third parties influence a firm's perceived capability to cope with a reputation-damaging event. They also consider the effect of external visibility of the event, which, in turn, can determine the difficulty of the firm's reputation repairing activities.

<u>Key findings</u>

Reputation is one of the most important ways firms can compete for economic resources and differentiate themselves from others in uncertain environments.

- A higher-weighted proportion of positive to negative reputation dimensions increases stakeholders' perceptions of an organization's capability to repair its reputation and makes reputation repair easier.
- The greater the relevance of a damaging event to a firm's positive dimensions, the greater the external visibility of the event and, thus, the more difficult it is for the organization to repair its reputation.
- A firm's age increases the external visibility of a reputation damaging event, which, in turn, makes reputation repair more difficult.
- The diversity of market segments served by a firm decreases stakeholders' confidence in the firm's capability to repair its reputation and, thus, makes reputation repair more difficult.
- The diversity of market segments served by a firm increases the external visibility of reputation damaging events and, thus, makes reputation repair more difficult.
- The more prevalent and severe watchdog agencies' negative reactions (e.g., scrutiny and punishments) are to a firm's reputation damaging events, the more visible the events are to stakeholders and, thus, the more difficult it is for the organization to repair its reputation.
- The more prestigious the media outlet reporting a firm's reputation-damaging events, the more visible the events are to the public and, thus, the more difficult it is for the organization to repair its reputation.
- Endorsers' persistent support of a firm after its reputation damaging event increases stakeholders' perceptions of the firm's capability to repair its reputation, thus making reputation repair easier.

Source: Governance Research Digest, February 2009 (Vol. 1, No. 2)

5.4.12 Financial Trust Index

Author(s): University of Chicago Booth School of Business/Kellogg School of Management

To study how recent events have undermined Americans' trust in the stock markets and institutions in general, the University of Chicago Booth School of Business and the Kellogg School of Management have launched a Financial Trust Index. The Financial Trust Index is a measure of the confidence Americans have in the private investment institutions. It is calculated quarterly on a sample of 1,000 American adults.

Key findings

Of those surveyed, only 19% of Americans trust the financial system. The greatest level of trust is for banks (29%), with the lowest for large corporations (10%).

- There has been a slight increase in trust toward the stock market, from 11% in December 2008 to 13% in March 2009.
- There has been a substantial decrease in trust toward banks, from 34% in December 2008 versus 29% in March 2009, and in large corporations, from 12% to 10% over the same time period.
- Government intervention still makes the majority of Americans less confident in investing in financial markets (67%). However, this is a big change from 80% who felt less confident in December 2008.
- 25% of respondents who identified themselves as Democrats feel more confident in investing in the stock market after the government intervention, compared to only 12% in December.
- 12% of independents feel the same way, as compared to 9% three months ago.
- The fraction of Republicans who are less confident in investing in the stock market following the recent government interventions has dropped from 82% in December to 76% in March.
- More respondents (41%) in March 2009 said they were very angry with the current economic situation versus 38% in December 2008.

Source: Governance Research Digest, April 2009 (Vol. 1, No. 4)

5.4.13 Trust in Business Barometer

Author(s): Edelman

The 2009 Edelman Trust Barometer is the firm's tenth annual study of global trust and credibility. The 2009 Barometer surveyed 4475 college educated, upper income respondents in 20 countries.

<u>Key findings</u>

Nearly two-thirds of respondents (62%) say they trust corporations less today than they did a year ago.

- In the United States, home to some of the largest corporate collapses, trust in business collapsed as well, dropping 20% over the course of one year.
- With only 38% of informed publics in the United States trusting business today, levels are the lowest they have been in the Barometer's tracking history - even lower than in the wake of Enron and the dot-com bust.
- For US businesses, this downturn marks a stark reversal from the steady rise in trust of the last five years and a new parity with Western Europe, which historically shows the lowest trust levels in business among all nations surveyed.
- Over the past seven years of Barometer research, trust in business among Europeans has been gauged as relatively stable, with overall trust scores in the 30%-to-40% range.
- This year, trust in business dropped in Italy, Spain, and Ireland.
- The social model economies of the Netherlands and Sweden are the exceptions to the rule, as both recorded a slight increase of trust in business.
- The West's skepticism about business stands in contrast to Asia Pacific and Latin America, where trust in business remains strong.
- In emerging economies, even where trust fell, it remained much higher than levels recorded throughout much of the rest of the world.
- Significantly, in China, the trust in business score rose from 54% last year to 71% this year, and in Brazil it rose from 61% to 69%.
- Overall trust levels were high in Japan, India, and Indonesia, a country new to this year's Barometer.

- The incongruity may well be attributed to the fact that people in emerging economies traditionally credit business with having introduced an improved standard of living.
- However, this trust may be short-lived. The survey shows that 79% of Japanese, 56% of Chinese, and 49% of Indian informed publics say they now have growing concerns about business.
- Data from the 2008 Barometer suggested that younger respondents (25-34) tended to display greater trust in business than their older counterpart. However, in the 2009 Barometer this trust has vanished and levels more closely mirror those of older groups.
- Large drops in trust in business among the younger group occurred in France (52% to 32%), the United States (60% to 32%), and South Korea (52% to 32%), reflecting the overall lower levels of trust in business in these established economies.
- Around the world, technology remains the single most trusted industry sector, with 76% of respondents telling us that they trust this sector to do what is right, followed by biotechnology and life sciences.
- The least trusted industries are media and insurance companies; just 40% of respondents trust insurance companies - a five-point decline from the year before.
- In the United States, virtually no major industry was spared the erosion of informed publics' trust.
- Trust in banks was nearly cut in half - falling from 69% to 36% - while the automotive industry experienced a 27-point plunge.
- Viewed together, the UK, France and Germany demonstrated a similar drop in major industries, with banks (41% to 27%), energy (44% to 39%), and media companies (35% to 28%) all taking a hit.
- Yet in several emerging economies, the industries that are suffering in the West, such as banking and automotive, remain trusted or have made gains over the past year.
- Trust in banks rose by 7 points in Brazil; trust in media companies rose by 10 points in India.
- In China, trust in banks, automotive, energy, and media all increased in the last year.

Source: Governance Research Digest, April 2009 (Vol. 1, No. 4)

5.4.14 World's Most Reputable Companies

Author(s): The Reputation Institute

The Global Reputation Pulse 2009 is the fourth annual study of the reputations of the world's largest companies. Over 70,000 online interviews with the general public in 32 countries on six continents were conducted in January and February 2009. More than 190,000 ratings were used to create reliable measures of the corporate reputation of more than 1,300 companies.

Key findings

Corporate trust is higher in emerging markets and lower in industrialised markets.

- Proportionally, the largest companies in Brazil, Russia, India and China enjoy a stronger emotional connection with consumers than the largest companies in the industrialised world.
- The most influential dimension on reputation is product/services, followed by governance and citizenship.
- In 2009, governance takes over from citizenship as the second most important driver, and other reputation dimensions are increasingly becoming more important.
- In the 2009 ranking, a group 0f 17 companies stand out with excellent reputations indicated by scores of 80 or above.
- In this year's ranking, there is a 60 point difference between the companies at the top of the table and those at the bottom.
- Corporate India has the best reputed companies. Of the 27 Indian companies ranked among the 600 largest in the world, almost 90% received scores above the global mean. Five rank in the Top 50.
- Of the 289 companies from the US, Japan, the UK, France and Germany, 45% have reputations that rank below the global average.
- Only 34% of the 142 companies from Brazil, Russia, India and China have below-average reputations, with Chinese companies dragging down the BRIC average substantially.

Rank	Company	Country	Score
1	Ferrero	Italy	85.17

2	Ikea	Sweden	83.98
3	Johnson & Johnson	US	83.58
4	Petrobras	Brazil	82.37
5	Sadia	Brazil	82.06
6	Nintendo	Japan	81.63
7	Christian Dior	France	81.37
8	Kraft Foods	US	81.09
9	Mercadona	Spain	80.99
10	Singapore Airlines	Singapore	80.97
11	Tata	India	80.89
12	UPS	US	80.84
13	General Mills	US	80.80
14	El Corte Inglés	Spain	80.80
15	Matsushita Electric Ind.	Japan	80.31
16	FedEx	US	80.30
17	Grupo Bimbo	Mexico	80.22
18	Honda Motor	Japan	79.86
19	Whirlpool	US	79.86
20	Votorantim	Brazil	79.59

Source: Governance Research Digest, May 2009 (Vol. 1, No. 5)

5.4.15 Country Reputation Report

Author(s): Reputation Institute

The Reputation Institute has released the 2009 version of its Country Rep report, which offers details of countries' individual reputations and illustrates key reputation drivers. The CountryRep project was conducted in 33 countries. More than 22,000 consumers representing both the G8 countries and emerging markets took part.

Key findings

Countries with strong reputations are more likely to attract both foreign direct investment, a highly skilled workforce and tourists. A positive country reputation also supports the companies operating in that country.

- CountryRep 2009 indicates that public perception is most influenced by a country's physical beauty, lifestyle, possibilities for enjoyment and global community involvement, which combined account for more than 40% of a country's reputation.
- This makes it critical for countries worldwide to communicate how they offer a wide array of appealing lifestyle options.

Top Five Country Rankings By Reputation Theme					
	1	2	3	4	5
Business Environment	Switzer-land	Sweden	Canada	Australia	Finland
Brands & Innovation	Japan	Switzer-land	Germany	Sweden	USA
Technology	Japan	Germany	Sweden	Switzer-land	USA
Products & Services	Switzer-land	Japan	Germany	Sweden	Canada
Physical Beauty	Canada	Australia	Switzer-land	Ireland	Norway
Enjoyment	Italy	Australia	Spain	Canada	Switzer-land
Lifestyle	Australia	Canada	Switzer-land	Sweden	Spain
Culture	Italy	France	UK	Germany	Sweden
Contribution to Global Community	Sweden	Canada	Switzer-land	Norway	Finland
Effective Government	Switzer-land	Sweden	Canada	Norway	Finland
Social Welfare	Sweden	Switzer-land	Norway	Canada	Finland

- Having a broad reputation platform reduces risk. Countries build their reputations on different platforms, but all platforms should communicate strength across a number of dimensions. A diverse image reduces reputation risk and provides a stronger platform for support.

- According to respondents from the G8 countries, Canada is the most desirable country to work in, followed by Switzerland, Australia, Sweden and Norway.
- The same respondents considered Switzerland the best country to invest in, followed by Sweden, Canada, Australia and Norway.

Source: Governance Research Digest, December 2009 (Vol. 1, No. 12)

5.4.16   The Structure in Trust in China and the US

Author(s): Ho-Kong Chan, Kit-Chun Joanna Lam and Pak-Wai Liu

The article investigates the structure of trust in China and compares it with the U.S., using the 2000 and 2005 waves of the World Value Survey (WVS). The study analyzes two dimensions of trust – trust in people and trust in major companies.

Key findings

It is found that the level of trust has remained stable in China within the 5-year period.

- On the other hand, trust in major companies has declined dramatically in U.S. while trust in people has increased slightly.
- The structure of trust in companies is different from trust in people.
- For both countries, individuals with higher education tend to have a higher level of trust.
- Individuals who are divorced tend to have lower trust in people.
- Individuals who think that other people are fair are more likely to trust in people.
- Preference for competition has a positive effect on trust in major companies.
- But, some differences between the two countries are observed.
- Perception of fairness does not affect trust in major companies in China, while it has a positive effect in U.S. in year 2006.
- Preference for equality has a negative effect on trust in major companies in U.S. but no significant effect in China.
- The pattern of trust and its changes over time may reflect differences in market conditions in the two economies.

Source: Governance Research Digest, June 2011 (Vol. 2, No. 2)

5.4.17 Building and Restoring Organisational Trust

Author(s): IBE

The IBE report Building and Restoring Organisational Trust demonstrates why organisations need to know how trust is won, developed and sustained, and what to do when that trust is threatened or has broken down. Combining academic research on the 'science' of trust, lessons from corporate interviews and prominent case studies of trust failures and trust repair, this report illustrates good and poor practice in repairing internal trust after an organisational failure.

Key findings

BP, The BBC, Severn Trent, Siemens, Goldman Sachs, Mattel Toys – just some of the organisations that have faced crises in recent years which damaged their reputation, affected their share prices, and threatened their sustainability.

- Living up to principles of trustworthy conduct is a formidable challenge for business.
- Getting it wrong can damage stakeholders' trust, including that of employees, and undermine reputation and share price, and threaten sustainability.
- Organisations that aspire to be known for taking ethics seriously will need to be trustworthy and foster trustworthiness in the workplace.
- A strong reputation for trustworthiness underpins organisational resilience and authenticity.
- Such a reputation can provide sustainable competitive advantage because it enables the organisation to attract and retain top talent, establish valuable business partnerships and retain a loyal customer base.
- It is possible to recover and even enhance an organisation's trustworthiness after a crisis.
- However, it typically requires a decisive system-wide set of reforms aimed at preventing a reoccurrence of the failure, as well as demonstrating positive displays of renewed trustworthy behaviour throughout the process.
- There are 4 stages to this:

- o immediate response: the organisation needs to stabilise the situation, reassure staff and show that it is competent;
- o diagnosis: there needs to be a thorough and systematic investigation process to establish why the failure occurred;
- o reforming interventions: at this stage the organisation needs to tackle not only the direct causes of the crisis but also the contributory factors that allowed it to happen;
- o evaluation: an evaluation is valuable to monitor progress and to maintain focus on the reforms, and the importance of the organisation's reputation for trustworthiness.

Source: Governance Research Digest, July 2011 (Vol. 2, No. 3)

5.4.18 Building a Corporate Reputation of Integrity

Author(s): Ethics Resource Center

The Fellows of the Ethics Resource Center (ERC) have assembled insights from brand management and public relations gurus to produce a guide on how to establish, develop, and protect a corporation's reputation of being an honest broker in the marketplace. The guide will help executives maneuver through the increasingly complicated landscape on the path to "Building a Corporate Reputation of Integrity."

Key findings

Now more than ever, consumers consider a company's reputation when shopping for goods and services.

- As with a new service or product, the odds of success are generally better when based on an empirical foundation about audiences and how they think.
- Establishing a benchmark of stakeholders' existing perceptions provides a valuable starting point for developing communications goals and strategies.
- Knowing what employees think is invaluable.
- Line workers tend to know where problems exist, and they also understand a company's strengths from firsthand experience.
- Employees can be a company's best advocate if they feel good about where they work and have confidence in its commitment to integrity.

- One way to do that is to by understanding colleagues' responsibilities and the challenges they face.
- Pushing into new skill areas is another way to break down needless distinctions between internal functions.
- For example, ethics officers can be trained to act as company spokespeople in appropriate circumstances and also how to communicate most effectively to external and internal audiences alike.
- Communications staff can be trained to understand the ethics and compliance department's programmatic activities and the basic concepts of how people can uphold corporate values.
- Communications experts tell us reputation can be enhanced when CEOs and other senior executives are also effective and aggressive external advocates.
- Identifying senior leaders with the right skills to become effective messengers is a way to burnish reputation and also build a company's internal culture.
- Reputation building may require a change in the way key audiences think and achieving that goal is not likely to happen by itself.
- Working together, the ethics and compliance team and the communications function can identify schemas that need to change and develop strategies for changing them.

Source: Governance Research Digest, January 2012 (Vol. 3, No. 1)

5.4.19 Consumer Trust Study

Author(s): BBMG

A new study from US branding and marketing group, BBMG, highlights a widespread 'green trust gap' between companies and consumers. The report combines ethnographic research in two US markets (conducted in January and February 2009) with a national survey of 2,000 adults (conducted October 26 – November 6, 2008).

Key findings

Nearly one in four US consumers say they have "no way of knowing" if a product is green or actually does what it claims.

- 77% of Americans agree that they "can make a positive difference by purchasing products from socially or environmentally responsible companies," and they are actively seeking information to verify green claims.

- Nearly 30% of respondents turn to consumer reports for verification, followed by 28% who look for certification seals or labels and 27% who read the list of ingredients on products.

- Consumers are least likely to look to statements on product packaging (11%) and company advertising (5%).

- Other key findings indicate that consumers are interested in buying green despite a tough economy with nearly 70% reporting that it is important to purchase products with social and environmental benefits.

- More than half are willing to pay more for green products.

- When asked unaided which companies come to mind as the most socially or environmentally responsible companies, 7% of Americans named Wal-Mart, followed by Johnson & Johnson (6%), Procter & Gamble (4%), GE (4%) and Whole Foods (3%).

- Wal-Mart also topped the list of the least responsible companies (9%), along with Exxon Mobile (9%), GM (3%) and Ford (3%), Shell (2%) and McDonald's (2%).

- 41% of Americans could not name a single company that they consider the most socially and environmentally responsible.

- Consumers will reward or punish companies based on their corporate practices. Seven in ten consumers (71%) agree that they "avoid purchasing from companies whose practices they disagree with" and approximately half tell others to shop (55%) or drop (48%) products based on a company's social and environmental practices.

- Price (66% - very important) and quality (64%) top consumers' list of most important product attributes, followed by good for your health (55%) and made in the USA (49%).

- Green benefits have increased in importance since last year - including energy efficiency (47% very important in 2008, 41% in 2007), locally grown or made nearby (32% in 2008, 26% in 2007), all natural (31% in 2008, 24% in 2007), made from recycled materials (29% in 2008, 22% in 2007) and USDA organic (22% in 2008, 17% in 2007).

Source: Social Research Digest, May 2009 (Vol. 1, No. 5)

5.4.20 Reputation at Risk – ACE European Risk Briefing

Author(s): ACE Group

ACE' published its latest report in its series of EMEA Risk Briefings examining new and emerging risks. The report, Reputation at Risk, explores the views of business executives across EMEA on the subject of reputational risk and offers 'top ten tips' for managing reputational risk.

Key findings

92% of companies believe that reputational risk is the most challenging category of risk to manage.

- While 81% of companies in the survey see reputation as their most significant asset, most of them admit that they struggle to protect it and identifies a number of key reasons why companies in the region often find reputational risk challenging to manage:
- 77% of companies find it difficult to quantify the financial impact of reputational risk on their business, making it harder to measure than traditional, more tangible risks.
- 68% of companies believe information and advice about how to manage reputational risk is hard to find, compounding the sense of uncertainty and confusion about how best to manage it.
- 66% of companies feel inadequately covered for reputational risk from an insurance perspective.
- 56% of companies say social media has greatly exacerbated the potential for reputational risk to affect their business.
- Companies need a clear framework for managing reputational risk. Effective management of 'traditional risks' will help avoid reputational events, and management teams need to put in place a culture and instil a risk appetite across the company that will reduce the potential for crises to emerge in the first place. In addition, taking a multi-disciplinary approach that involves the CEO, PR specialists and other business leaders will also help to build the broader perspective that is necessary for identifying and managing less obvious reputational risks.
- Companies should work harder at measuring how their reputation is perceived. Understanding perceptions of key stakeholders, their interplay and their impact on corporate reputation, is essential for

tracking and managing reputational risk effectively. Companies must ensure that they are collecting an "outside-in" perspective to complement their own internal perspective.

- Companies should sharpen up their crisis management plans to keep pace with today's faster-moving world. Our research suggests that many companies may be over-confident in their abilities to respond to a crisis. Regular review and testing – including the incorporation of social media scenarios – will allow a faster response when disaster strikes.

- The insurance market can do more to help companies manage reputational risk. This includes the provision of more holistic solutions that include crisis response assistance. It also includes helping companies to take a 'reputational lens' to more traditional risks to evaluate the reputational consequences in each case.

Source: CSR Research Digest, May 2014 (Vol. 6, No. 5)

5.4.21 America's 100 Most Trustworthy Companies

Author(s): GMI Ratings

Forbes released the 2014 list of the America's 100 Most Trustworthy Companies, based on data from proprietary ratings provider and investment advisor GMI Ratings. The list includes publicly-traded North American companies of all sizes and industries except one: financial companies, more specifically, banks and insurance companies.

<u>Key findings</u>

The companies that make this list garnered the 100 highest scores for trustworthy behavior over the four quarters of the previous fiscal year.

- The company with the strongest AGR—"Aggressive Accounting and Governance Risk," the final composite by which companies on the list are scored—is Casey's General Stores, a mid cap Iowa-based chain of convenience stores and gas stations that achieved an AGR of 99 out of a possible 100.

- Houston-based Oceaneering International holds the best AGR, 93, among large cap companies, while mechanical products operation Altra

Industrial Motion Corp., with an AGR of 97, holds the best score among small cap companies.

- GMI's ranking is sorted into large cap companies with market caps of $5 billion or higher, mid cap companies with market caps of $1 to $5 billion, and small cap companies with market caps of $25 million to $1 billion. Only four companies have appeared on the list three times in the previous seven years.
- Many of the companies on this ranking are new this year or have only appeared in one or two of these lists over the past seven years.
- Companies that don't appear on the list aren't necessarily engaged in wrongdoing–these are merely the 100 with the most sterling reputations this year.

Source: CSR Research Digest, June 2014 (Vol. 6, No. 6)

5.4.22 2014 Global RepTrak® 100: The World's Most Reputable Companies

Author(s): Reputation Institute

Reputation Institute, a consulting firm based in New York and Copenhagen, surveyed 60,000 people in 15 countries in January and February 2014 and asked them a series of questions about whether they trusted, respected, had good feelings about and admired the reputation of companies known around the world. The Global RepTrak® 100 study measures the reputation of the 100 most highly regarded companies covering more than 75% of the global GDP, including: Australia, Brazil, Canada, China, France, Germany, India, Italy, Japan, Mexico, Russia, South Korea, Spain, UK, and US.

Key findings

The Walt Disney Company and Google have the best corporate reputations in the world with consumers.

- Rolex rated no. 1 for products and services
- Apple considered the most innovative company
- Google considered the best place to work
- BMW rated no. 1 for governance
- The Walt Disney Company considered the best corporate citizen
- Google rated no. 1 for its leadership

- Google rated no. 1 for its financial performance
- Amazon has the best reputation in North America
- Sony has the best reputation in Europe
- Google has the best reputation in Latin America
- Rolex has the best reputation in Asia

Source: CSR Research Digest, June 2014 (Vol. 6, No. 6)

5.4.23 The Most Controversial Companies of 2013

Author(s): RepRisk

RepRisk released their analysis of documented negative incidents, criticism and controversies related to the 10 firms that received the highest Reputational Risk Index (RRI) in 2013. The report, 'The Most Controversial Companies of 2013' captured information from a wide range of third-party sources including online and print media, NGOs, government agencies, blogs and more.

<u>Key findings</u>

The 10 most controversial companies of 2013 are headquartered around the world and stem from a range of industries including banking, pharmaceutical and retail. The issues for which they were criticized spanned the spectrum of ESG issues including poor labor conditions, anti-competition breaches, human rights violations as well as fraud, bribery, and money laundering.

- The 10 Most Controversial Companies of 2013 were:
  - International Federation of Association Football (FIFA)
  - Punta Fa SL (Mango)
  - Comigel SAS
  - HSBC Holdings PLC
  - Findus Group Ltd
  - Fonterra Co-operative Group Ltd
  - GlaxoSmithKline PLC
  - BNP Paribas SA
  - ICAP PLC
  - Samsung Group.

- The 10 most controversial companies of 2013 are headquartered around the world and stem from a range of industries including banking, pharmaceutical and retail. The issues for which they were criticized spanned the spectrum of ESG issues including poor labor conditions, anti-competition breaches, human rights violations as well as fraud, bribery, and money laundering.

- The Federation Internationale de Football Association (FIFA) topped the list. FIFA was treated as a company according to RepRisk methodology. In Qatar the conditions of migrant workers has been likened to forced labor during the construction of the 2022 World Cup facilities. In the summer of 2013, FIFA came under fire in relation to the deaths of approximately 40 Nepalese workers under "suspicious circumstances". The association has also experienced issues with corruption regarding the selection of Qatar, while in Brazil there have been a myriad of social issues as locals have been affected by the 2014 World Cup preparations.

- Retailer Punta Fa, otherwise known as Mango, suffered a blow to its reputation after the fatal factory collapse of Rana Plaza in Bangladesh.

- Food and beverage companies Comigel and Findus made the list due to their involvement in the horse meat scandal, while HSBC and ICAP's reputations suffered after investigations into their role in the manipulation of interbank offered lending rates and foreign exchange rates.

- HSBC and BNP Paribas were also highlighted for issues related to money laundering, fraud and for financing controversial projects with negative environmental and social impacts.

- Dairy company Fonterra has suffered repeatedly due to allegations of contaminated products, while GlaxoSmithKline was a target of criticism because of health issues associated with its medications as well as drug trials in developing countries, market manipulation and bribery.

- Finally, poor working conditions at Samsung's factories and in its supply chain have left the company exposed to numerous health and safety issues with workers suffering severe injuries and illnesses, resulting in death in some cases.

Source: Governance Research Digest, April 2014 (Vol. 5, No. 4)

5.4.24   2014 Trust Barometer

Author(s): Edelman

Edelman published their 14th annual exploration of trust. The 2014 Edelman Trust Barometer resulted from having surveyed 33,000 people (27,000 General Public and 6,000 Informed Public respondents) in 27 markets around the world on their trust in institutions, credible sources/channels and specific issues and perceptions impacting trust in business and government.

Key findings

Public trust in governments around the world trails far behind trust in business. Moreover, the 'trust gap' has increased markedly in the 2014 findings compared to 2013 – now a 14-point gap – and, indeed, overall compared to five years ago when the financial crisis was starting to bite.

- While this gap illustrates a global average, where people's trust in governments varies within each of the 27 countries in which Edelman conducted its research for the 2014 survey, it's small comfort as the gap is driven by a decline of trust in government and not an increase in trust in business, with the gap at 20 points or greater in nearly half of the countries surveyed.
- Business is now expected to play a much bigger role around the debate and design of regulation as 79% of those surveyed believe government should not be working alone when setting policy.
- A majority of respondents (84%) believe that business can pursue its self-interest while doing good work for society.
- There is call for more regulation in several industries including financial services (53%), energy (51%) and food and beverage (48%). Regionally, the study found that 66% want more regulation of the financial services industry in Germany, 73% of people in the UK want more regulation of the energy business, while in China, 84% desire stronger regulation of the food industry.
- Trust in CEOs has plateaued, and while they have recovered from a low of 31% in 2009 to 43% this year they still rank seventh out of eight, sitting only above government official (36%), as most credible spokesperson (and Edelman believes that CEOs must become "chief

engagement officers" to educate the public about the economic, societal, political and environmental context in which their business operates).

- Academics (67%) and technical experts (66%), a "person like yourself" (62%) and employees (52%) continue to be far more trusted. CEOs can build trust in themselves and their companies by communicating clearly and transparently (82%), telling the truth regardless of how unpopular it is (81%) and engaging regularly with employees (80%).
- Globally, family-owned (71%) and small- and medium-sized businesses (68%) are more trusted than big business (61%)

Source: Governance Research Digest, April 2014 (Vol. 5, No. 4)

5.4.25 Most Controversial Companies of 2012

Author(s): RepRisk

RepRisk released a report that analyses news on thousands of companies across the globe in relation to their environmental, social and corporate governance (ESG) risks, the information being taken from a wide range of sources including newspapers, news sites, NGO and governmental sites, blogs and social media. The 'Most Controversial Companies of 2012' report analyzes documented controversies, both fact and allegation, related to the 10 firms that received the highest Peak RepRisk Index in 2012.

<u>Key findings</u>

The 10 most controversial companies of 2012 were headquartered in different countries in Europe and Asia as well as the US, stemmed from a range of industries including telecommunications, pharmaceutical, media, banking and mining, and spanned the spectrum of ESG issues.

- Notably, poor labor conditions and human rights violations as well as bribery, fraud and money laundering, were the main issues criticized.
- Two of the top-ranking firms were included in the report due to specific incidents at their facilities in the second half of the year: a fatal fire at Tazreen Fashions' factory in Bangladesh; and violent clashes between police and 3,000 striking workers at Lonmin's Marikana mine in South Africa that led to 34 deaths and many more injuries.
- Corporate governance scandals that erupted in 2011 and continued to plague the companies in 2012 saw two further companies make the list:

Olympus for its alleged decade-long accounting fraud; and News Corp for the hacking and bribery scandal in the UK.

- HSBC and ING Bank made the top 10 due to accusations of inadequate controls to counter money laundering; the former also for its alleged role in the Libor manipulation.
- Also on the list, Samsung faced a number of investigations and lawsuits in 2012 for reported anti-competitive practices in the past as well as poor conditions at supplier factories.
- Wyeth was accused of fraudulently misrepresenting its drugs and neglecting to outline risks to the public and shareholders.
- TeliaSonera came under fire for alleged corruption and aiding oppressive regimes, while Reebok was also linked to labor breaches within its supply chain and to a fraud scandal in India.

Source: Governance Research Digest, June 2013 (Vol. 4, No. 6)

VI.   FAIR OPERATING PRACTICES

6.1. Corruption and Bribery

6.1.1   A Four Country Study of the Associations Between Bribery and Unethical Actions

Author(s): R.A. Bernardi, M.B. Witek, M.R. Melton

The purpose of this study is to test the premise that that small deviations from ethical behavior lead to even larger deviations from ethical behavior. This study examines the association between a person's willingness to bribe a police officer to avoid being issued a speeding ticket with their views on inappropriate behavior of corporate executives. The sample of 528 participants comes from Colombia (90), Ecuador (70), South Africa (131) and the United States (237).

<u>Key findings</u>

The study finds that accepting small ethical deviations affects attitudes towards larger ethical problems.

- Ethical perceptions and attitudes vary by country and across cultures, and ethical behaviour reflects the values and beliefs of each individual culture.
- In addition, what is considered 'right' and 'wrong' in business practice has significant variation between cultures.
- The participants from all four countries believed it was more acceptable to bribe a police officer to get out of a speeding ticket (i.e., a small deviation) than for three of the questionnaire scenarios: selling a defective product, overstating a repair bill, and bribing board members (i.e., larger ethical deviations).
- Participants from all countries thought that charging the cost of a spouse's trip was more acceptable than bribing a police officer to get out of a speeding ticket.

- When individuals under-report (or over-report) activities that are deemed to be socially undesirable (or desirable), social desirability response bias (SDRB) occurs. For example, respondents who had a higher propensity to respond in a socially desirable manner (i.e., less honestly when answering questions) reported a lower level of cheating behaviour.

- Respondents from Columbia, Ecuador and South Africa perceived bribery of a police officer to be less acceptable than those from the US. There was no significant difference in the responses between genders.

- An individual's attitude towards bribing a police officer was related to their attitude towards bribing corporate board members. There was little difference between genders.

Source: Governance Research Digest, February 2009 (Vol. 1, No. 2)

6.1.2   Corruption and Complicity Report

Author(s): Global Witness

A report released by Global Witness has alleged that many of the world's largest banks are complicit in facilitating the movement of illegally acquired funds from corrupt regimes. The report suggests that such actions are "facilitating corruption and state looting, which deny these countries the chance to lift themselves out of poverty and leave them dependent on aid."

Key findings

Despite the existence of a raft of anti-money laundering laws which oblige banks to undertake due diligence, this due diligence is not being undertaken.

- Six of the banks mentioned in this report – Banco Santander, Barclays, Citigroup, Deutsche Bank, HSBC and Societé Générale – are among the eleven members of the Wolfsberg Group, which has developed a set of voluntary principles to help banks fulfil their antimony laundering requirements.

- HSBC and Banco Santander hid behind bank secrecy laws in Luxembourg and Spain to avoid revealing the owners of accounts they held which received suspicious transfers of millions of dollars of Equatorial Guinea's oil money.

- Citibank, through correspondent banking relationships, enabled Charles Taylor, the expresident of Liberia now on trial for war crimes, to use the global banking system to earn revenues from timber sales, which were fuelling his war effort as well as being diverted into his personal bank account.
- Deutsche Bank was the banker for the late President Niyazov of Turkmenistan, whose regime was notorious for human rights abuses, repression and impoverishment of the population.
- Deutsche Bank held the central bank accounts for gas-rich Turkmenistan for 15 years, despite the fact that the money was being kept out of the national budget and was effectively under the personal control of Niyazov.
- Bank of East Asia, Hong Kong's third largest bank, and offshore companies in Hong Kong and the UK Overseas Territory of Anguilla helped funnel Republic of Congo's oil money into an account controlled by the president's son, Denis Christel Sassou Nguesso, which he used to pay his personal credit card bills.
- Huge oil-backed loans from large consortia of banks to Angola's state-owned oil company Sonangol helped to fuel corruption and support a system of parallel financing, beyond public scrutiny, which provided opportunities for cash to be diverted to the shadow state and into private pockets.
- The report makes a number of recommendations including a tightening of anti-money laundering laws backed up by proactive government enforcement. Banks should also change their policies and tighten due diligence practices.

Source: Governance Research Digest, March 2009 (Vol. 1, No. 3)

6.1.3 Supply Chain Corruption Reports

Author(s): Ethical Corporation Institute

Two new briefings from the Ethical Corporation Institute find that China's traditional business culture contributes to the ongoing problem of corruption in the country. However, government regulation and attention by corporations to supply chains help mitigate corruption.

Key findings

Corruption in China takes a range of forms, from small cases of bribery to avoid bureaucratic requirements to bribes in order to secure major business contracts.

- Multinational corporations operating in the inland provinces are more likely to encounter examples of protectionism and other forms of corruption, as well as issues related to intellectual property protection.
- Anti-corruption initiatives are increasingly effective in China's coastal provinces, where foreign investment has been concentrated.
- Most executives interviewed for the ECU briefing believe that legal steps are being taken to address the issue of corruption in China, but many of them express concern that China's traditional business culture could make enforcement of anti-corruption laws difficult.
- The global economic crisis has not spared the Chinese economy, where exports decreased 17.5% and imports fell 43.1% during the yearlong period ending in January 2009.
- Some executives surveyed fear that economic pressures will increase the tendency to resort to corruption in China.
- During this difficult economic climate, corruption in China will continue to persist according to geographical variations, with anticorruption efforts taking hold much more readily in the coastal provinces.
- The briefings encourage multinational corporations with supply chains in China to develop programs that implement compliance codes and evaluate partners based on ethical and compliance criteria.

Source: Governance Research Digest, April 2009 (Vol. 1, No. 4)

6.1.4   Corporations As A Crucial Ally Against Corruption

Author(s): R. Calderón, J.L. Álvarez-Arce, S. Mayoral.

This paper examines the role that corporations can play in anticorruption efforts. The study uses cross-country data from three databases: the Bribe Payers Index (BPI), the Corruption Perception Index (CPI) and Doing Business.

Key findings

While companies in most countries have improved domestic transparency, corporations still tend to lack integrity when operating abroad.

Countries with the biggest change in behaviour*		
Region	*Best*	*Worst*
Africa	Singapore	Mexico
New Independent States	Singapore	Saudi Arabia
Low Income Countries	Singapore	Brazil
Middle East	Sweden	Mexico
Asia-Pacific	Hong Kong	Russia
Europe	Singapore	Mexico
OECD	Singapore	Mexico
America	Singapore	Russia

*The country whose behaviour is best/worst when its companies operate internationally.

- There is a considerable propensity for companies of all nationalities to bribe when operating abroad.
- Even the best-performing nation – Switzerland (7.81) – is far from the highest possible score of 10.
- Businesses from developing and in-transition countries, such as China, Russia, or South Korea, are increasingly putting effort in improving transparency and integrity.
- Pro-bribery investment climate conditions in host countries are not related to the payments of bribes by multinational companies when these corporations operate abroad.
- The global average of BPI ratings has improved from 5.7 in 1999 to 6.4 in 2006.

Source: Governance Research Digest, May 2009 (Vol. 1, No. 5)

6.1.5   Countering Bribery Principles

Author(s): Transparency International

Transparency International (TI) has released the second edition of its Business Principles for Countering Bribery. These provide a framework for companies that enable them to develop comprehensive anti-bribery policies and programmes. The principles cover business practices in relation to bribery, political contributions, charitable contributions and sponsorships, facilitation payments (these are small unofficial payments made to secure or expedite certain acts) as well as gifts, hospitality and expenses.

Key findings

The Business Principles are: that the enterprise shall prohibit bribery in any form, whether direct or indirect; and the enterprise shall commit to implementing a programme to counteract bribery.

- The whole of an enterprise's anti-bribery efforts including values, code of conduct, detailed policies and procedures, risk management, internal and external communication, training and guidance, internal controls, oversight, monitoring and assurance.
- The Business Principles are based on a Board commitment to fundamental values of integrity, transparency and accountability.
- Enterprises should aim to create and maintain a trust-based and inclusive internal culture in which bribery is not tolerated.
- Developing a programme for countering bribery should take into consideration the following factors:
  - An enterprise should develop a Programme that clearly and in reasonable detail, articulates values, policies and procedures to be used to prevent bribery from occurring in all activities under its effective control.
  - The Programme should be tailored to reflect an enterprise's particular business circumstances and culture, taking into account such potential risk factors as size, business sector, nature of the business and locations of operation.
  - The Programme should be consistent with all laws relevant to countering bribery in all the jurisdictions in which the enterprise transacts its business.
  - The enterprise should develop the Programme in consultation with employees, trade unions or other employee representative bodies.
  - The enterprise should ensure that it is informed of all internal and external matters material to the effective development and implementation of the Programme, and, in particular, emerging

best practices including engagement with relevant interested parties.

Source: Governance Research Digest, June 2009 (Vol. 1, No. 6)

6.1.6   Anti-Corruption and Ethical Compliance Report

Author(s): Ethical Corporation

Ethical Corporation has released a report which aims to address the complexities of corporate ethics and compliance for multinational businesses that operate in Russia. It incorporates a special focus on anti-corruption.

Key findings

Corruption in Russia affects all types and sizes of organisations, public and private, local and foreign, and it appears to be on the increase.

- This increase exists both in terms of the level of corruption and of its cost to companies. The general public does not approve of corruption, but people do not see how it can be eradicated.
- New anti-corruption laws were introduced in early 2009 and these have been welcomed by both business and the public sector.
- Leading foreign companies active in Russia are all operating according to codes of conduct that generally have clear policies on compliance issues such as bribery, gifts and the use of suppliers and agents.
- These companies run training programmes on these issues for employees so that they know how to act when they encounter unethical activity.
- The research indicates that high-profile Russian companies are following the lead established by their foreign counterparts with regard to corporate codes of conduct, ethics and compliance.
- Increased exposure to a western-style compliance culture has influenced the Russian business environment so that it now presents a very different picture to that of the 1990s.
- However, for smaller companies, it is more difficult to avoid bribery and extortion, and in some instances accepting a certain level of corruption may appear to be the only effective way to sustain business operations.

- The report highlights the costs to foreign companies of ensuring compliance with local laws and regulations.
- The process of obtaining permits and licences and of ensuring that offices and premises meet the requirements in areas such as fire and health and safety, can take a great deal of time and money. In addition, these situations typically provide officials with opportunities for bribes and favours.
- From the company's perspective, it is essential to have a clear zero-tolerance policy in place, as once bribes are condoned, then the company culture is irrevocably compromised.

Source: Governance Research Digest, July 2009 (Vol. 1, No. 7)

6.1.7 Why Firms Engage in Corruption: A Top Management Perspective

Author(s): J.D. Collins, K. Uhlenbruck, P. Rodriguez

This study builds upon the top management literature to predict and test antecedents to firms' engagement in corruption. The authors use data from a survey of 341 executives in India, representing a wide range of industries. Participants took part in semistructured interviews in 2003.

Key findings

Top managers' personal relationships are significant predictors of engagement in corruption and, more particularly, these relationships promote a greater willingness to ignore legal proscription regarding corruption.

- Membership of political parties and support for political activities promote a willingness to engage in corruption.
- Familial ties to government officials may lead top managers to be more willing to engage in illegal corrupt transactions because they receive favourable opportunities and terms, or because they are more confident that their transactions will be effective and secreted.
- Firms with the government as a customer were found not to be more involved in government corruption.

- The authors thus conclude that it is the personal ties of executives, not the organizational relationship between supplier and the government as buyer, that create opportunity for engagement in corruption.
- When a practice is widely seen as the ways things are done, even harsh sanctions may fail to change behaviours.
- Managers' perception of corruption as taken for granted may lead them to believe that these acts are less likely to be discovered or punished.
- Managers' beliefs about the harmfulness of corruption did not significantly affect their willingness to engage in these illegal behaviours.
- Despite the costs and risks of engaging in corruption, managers may justify corrupt acts on economic grounds related to performance or because of beliefs about the importance of engaging in corruption.
- This misalignment between normative beliefs regarding corruption and the nature of opportunity structures in which the firm is embedded also contributes to organizations ignoring legal proscriptions of corruption.
- Industry norms significantly affect the likelihood of managers' engagement in these illegal transactions. This result likely is generated by a combination of opportunities to engage in corruption in some industries as well as differences in normative pressures across industries.
- This finding suggests that the variance in corruption within and across industries proceeds in part from managers' beliefs and industry or professional associations, placing them as central actors in determining the incidence of these illegal transactions.

Source: Governance Research Digest, July 2009 (Vol. 1, No. 7)

6.1.8   Anti-Corruption as Strategic CSR Report

Author(s): FSG Social Impact Advisor/The Ethics Resource Center The Merck Company Foundation

This report presents a critical assessment of corporate anti-corruption efforts in the developing world and offers a guide for corporations to move beyond traditional ethics and compliance activities to strategic anti-corruption efforts. The report is based on interviews with multinational corporations, as well as leading ethics and anticorruption experts and stakeholders.

Key findings

The report uncovers several examples of proactive, external efforts to take a radically different approach to anti-corruption efforts.

- Google is working with African governments to increase communications and transparency through online tools, GE is influencing Chinese anti-bribery governance regulations, and Merck has a program to fund anticorruption NGOs in several markets.
- The report recommends four complementary approaches which would help corporations become leaders in fighting corruption:
  o Ensure compliance. Corporations should continue to invest significantly in ethics and compliance programs to maintain or increase their level of integrity throughout all divisions and countries.
  o Strengthen collective action. Efforts need to shift from broad-based, diffuse declarations to more outcome-oriented pacts that can create effective incentives for members to change behaviour.
  o Engage demand-side forces. While the typical focus of corporate anti-corruption work is on the "supply side" of corruption (the private sector), corporations should expand their efforts to influence the "demand side" (the public sector).
  o Leverage corporate assets. Corporations possess unique and powerful strengths in the fight against corruption, including communications power from the corporate brand, economic leverage, technical expertise, and cash resources for grantmaking.

Source: Governance Research Digest, July 2009 (Vol. 1, No. 7)

6.1.9 Bribery: Australian Managers' Experiences and Responses When Operating in International Markets

Author(s): K.L. Pedigo, V. Marshall

This article explores the findings from a qualitative research study that examines critical ethical dilemmas confronting Australian managers in their international business operations and their responses to those dilemmas. The findings in this study are drawn from face-to-face interviews with Australian business managers who were asked to talk about experienced ethical dilemmas. Seventy senior Australian managers operating internationally in the mining, textile, and information technology industries took part.

Key findings

The key dilemmas that confronted Australian managers included: bribery, breach of contract, abuse of human rights, and loss of confidentiality.

- These ethical dilemmas affected all three industry groups investigated and emerged as the main generic issues associated with crosscultural ethical problems when Australian managers operated overseas.
- While there was a diversity of countries referred to by respondents in this study, reference was made predominantly to Australia's regional trading partners in the Pacific Ocean and Indian Ocean Rims.
- Bribery was the largest and main category to emerge, with all three industry groups investigated reporting that bribery was the most predominant ethical issue experienced in their international operations.
- The main emphasis was on requests or expectations for rewards such as payments of money, the predominant request, as well as other informal rewards including entertainment (wining and dining), gifts (including small cultural tokens to expensive products), prostitution (requests for call girls), and junkets (free travel to Australia).
- Many respondents cited a large number of incidents where some form of payment was required in order to be eligible to negotiate business dealings or progress with tenders.
- There were many who reported bribery as being sanitized by organizations, through the appointment of agents and subsequent distancing of managers from direct personal involvement in the process.
- A number of respondents from all three industry groups made reference to facilitation payments where additional money was paid to ease or expedite a process, rather than influence the tendering or negotiation process of contracts.

- Most of the incidents provided by the respondents from the three industry groups referred to incidents of large-scale bribes that were important in influencing decisions relating to awarding business contracts.
- The expectation or demand of officials or those in positions of power to be entertained was another ethical issue associated with bribery or inappropriate influences.
- Similarly gift giving was also identified as unacceptable across all three industries. Similar to monetary bribes, there was an expectation for gifts to be provided to facilitate business negotiations and trade.
- In all aspects of bribery, respondents were confronted with the dilemma of choosing either the provision of informal rewards or losing business. This was one of the greatest dilemmas for respondents from all the three industry groups.
- Respondents stated they were constantly faced with deciding whose standards should be applied.
- To be successful, respondents were often confronted with situations that required them to violate their own cultural values and norms.
- Organizational commitment or corporate values generated a strong resistance to what many of the respondents viewed as unethical conduct.
- In addition, personal values, and judgments regarding what is considered right and wrong resulted in many respondents providing strong views and feelings about how they thought businesses should or should not operate.
- Some respondents felt that the only way to be successful is to observe the host countries cultural norms and disregard their own values and ethical positions.
- Others relied on industry-specific arbitrators to intervene others relied on establish guidelines, codes or rules to establish a basis for international trade in relation to right and wrong practices.
- Some respondents discussed relationship building as their approach when responding to ethical dilemmas in international markets. The relationship approach was often closely associated with related terms, such as trust, honesty, respect, and integrity by respondents.

- Respondents viewed the development of mutual trust among people from different cultural backgrounds as part of establishing a successful relationship. Indeed, trust and relationship building were seen as essential in avoiding ethical conflicts across the three industry groups.

Source: Governance Research Digest, July 2009 (Vol. 1, No. 7)

6.1.10 Determinants of Bribery in Asian Firms: Evidence From The World Business Environment Survey

Author(s): X. Wu

The research reported in this paper used World Business Environment Survey data to examine some distinct characteristics of bribery in Asian firms and to empirically test a number of hypotheses on determinants of bribery. The surveys were carried out over a period of roughly 18 months between the end of 1998 and the middle of 2000. Data were collected mostly through personal interviews conducted at the managerial level, and 10,032 enterprises from 83 countries participated in the survey.

Key findings

Although most Asian firms consider corruption among the major obstacles for business development, a substantial percentage of these firms are engaged in bribery activities on a regular basis.

- The corporate sector, often portrayed as the victim of corruption, is an important source of rampant corruption problems in Asia.
- In most countries a majority of firms have engaged in bribery activities, and in some countries almost all firms are involved in one way or another.
- These bribery practices are highly institutionalized, as there appears to be little uncertainty regarding the amount of bribes expected to be paid as well as the delivery of services in exchange for bribe payments.
- It is also clear that corporate bribe-payers are not always the innocent prey that they are made out to be, for many firms are active and willing parties in corrupt transactions.
- Firm size, identity of controlling stakeholders, integrity of court systems, licensing requirements, transparency of interpretation of laws and regulations, efficiency of government services, and level of taxes

are all shown to be important factors in firms' propensity to bribe and in incidence of bribery.

- Market competition may drive up the level bribery activities, and contrary to the "ability to pay" hypothesis, high-growth firms would pay a relatively lower proportion of revenue in bribes than would firms with slower growth.
- The results consistently show that conformity with international accounting standards and practices may not directly contribute to the reduction of bribery at the firm level.

Source: Governance Research Digest, August 2009 (Vol. 1, No. 8)

6.1.11 Relationship-Oriented Cultures, Corruption and International Marketing Success

Author(s): J.D. Chandler; J.L. Graham.

This study explores the general problems associated with marketing across international markets and focuses specifically on the role of corruption in deterring international marketing success. Data from three exporting countries (France, Japan and the US) are used to provide empirical findings.

Key findings

French and Japanese exporters, unlike their American counterparts, appear to be deterred by corruption in international markets.

- Bribery and intellectual property piracy were deemed to pose the most significant threats.
- Black markets and disease were of relatively little concern.
- For French exporters, relative violence levels also appeared to be important.
- Corruption is broadly insignificant in determining market attractiveness for Americans. This may be explained, at least in part, by the thirty-year existence of the US Foreign Corrupt Practices Act.
- In contrast, France and Japan have only recently joined the OECD and UN anti-bribery conventions. As a result, executives in those countries may be, temporarily, more reluctant to trade with corrupt nations.

- The apparent lack of concern about intellectual property piracy expressed by Americans in the study may be explained by their use of alternative business strategies.
- Physical distance hampers marketing success and attractiveness for marketers from all three countries.
- Air travel, the internet and other communications advances are ameliorating physical distances but temporal distance remains a significant barrier to trade between countries.
- Crossing time zones appears to limit marketing success, which results in a strong preference for north-south trade or at least trade with close neighbours.
- For French exporters, cultural distance also limits marketing success in international markets.
- The contrary is true for Japanese exporters, who have close trade relations with a number of countries with very different cultural traits and values (e.g. Kenya, Indonesia, Thailand).

Source: Governance Research Digest, September 2009 (Vol. 1, No. 9)

6.1.12 Corruption and Transparency in Africa

Author(s): US Chamber of Commerce

A new report from the US Chamber of Commerce examines the extent to which African countries are creating investment-friendly environments, and the extent to which this is attracting interest from US businesses. Top management decision makers from thirty leading multinational companies participated in the research. The majority were from US Fortune 100 companies. A wide range of business sectors were represented by the sample.

Key findings

US companies in some sectors, particularly technology, now regard Africa as the last frontier for growth. At the same time, US corporations do not lack investment choices and rarely consider African nations.

- The survey revealed five factors that influence US corporations' decisions to invest in Africa:

o   Rule of law - A strong consensus exists among the respondents that the rule of law does not prevail to the degree required to make Africa an attractive investment destination. This applies to corporate, societal, and criminal law.

o   Attraction – Africa does not offer a sufficiently large middle class of consumers or show consistent economic growth that could promise a future market. Most African countries are small and have poor markets, and there are barriers to regional markets - such as taxes and the freedom of movement of people and goods. However, Africa does offer enormous natural resources and that is an attraction.

o   Risks versus rewards - US corporations look at "risk adjusted ROI" when considering Africa as an investment destination. Given the currently perceived risks in Africa, the rewards have to be very high to make it worthwhile to invest. Presently, US corporations say that there are very few visible promises of high future returns to justify significant interest in investing.

o   Supportive business framework – Transportation and communications infrastructure, trained or trainable human resources, and equitable trade and employment practices are essential elements to support corporate investment. Currently, these elements are insufficient.

o   A welcoming environment – In order for US companies to employ locals, African countries must do a better job of providing education and health services to the potential workforce. By making it easy for companies to set up and do business, African countries will show a willingness to encourage FDI. Respondents also highlighted three impediments to American investment in Africa:

o   Difficult business case – Planning for investment in Africa is fraught with uncertainty because the risks seem too high and the returns too inconclusive to merit significant capital allocation. Executives find that any investment in Africa needs a lot of hard selling within a corporation—the push-back is that it is too much trouble for an unreliable promise of return.

o   Corruption and uncertainty – The main problems concerning investment in Africa relate to corruption and the apparent lack of political will to curb it. US businesses believe that these practices handicap those who will not or cannot "play the game" by these rules. In addition, returns are not reasonably ensured or sustainable because costs can often escalate for reasons unrelated to business operations and the rules can change unexpectedly. This means that the time and resources already invested could be lost.

o   Opportunity cost – Executives do not yet believe that they are at a competitive disadvantage because they are not investing in African countries. With no competitive traction, there is no sense of an opportunity being missed. Furthermore, since Africa is not selling itself overtly by asking for investment, the continent does not attract enough attention amidst competition for investment from other developing countries or regions. The only exceptions to this are China and India.

Source: Governance Research Digest, September 2009 (Vol. 1, No. 9)

6.1.13   Global Corruption Report: Climate Change

Author(s): Transparency International

The Global Corruption Report is the first comprehensive publication of its kind to explore the corruption risks related to tackling climate change. From international policy-making to national level mitigation and adaptation strategies and with a special focus on the forestry sector, the GCR draws on the expertise of more than 50 experts and practitioners from the anti-corruption movement and the climate change field.

Key findings

Important decisions on climate change are taken in many institutional settings – more than the spotlight on some high-profile international meetings would suggest.

*   The attention and record attendance that a few key climate policy processes enjoy make it easy to overlook persistent disparities in influence, even in these settings.
*   The lobbying landscape is diversifying, and the associated risk of undue influence is higher than ever.
*   A robust system for the measuring, reporting and verification (MRV) of emissions is crucial to transparency, and ultimately to the success of mitigation strategies.

- As a critical mechanism for mitigation, carbon markets need safeguards to reduce the risk of corruption, as well as to ensure their sustainability and capacity to reduce greenhouse gas emissions.
- The path to a green economy should create opportunity for developing countries by addressing governance concerns directly; the risk if it does not is that global inequalities will be sustained and deepened.
- Strengthening citizen participation is essential to adaptation governance, as adaptation will take place in countries with high corruption risks.
- Strengthening coordination, mutual accountability and operational transparency in the governance of adaptation funds is essential to building the trust needed for sustainable climate change policy.

Source: Governance Research Digest, May 2011 (Vol. 2, No. 1)

6.1.14 Strategic Response to Perceived Corruption in an Emerging Market: Lessons from MNEs in China

Author(s): Yadong Luo

This study addresses how MNE subunits strategically respond to perceived corruption in the business segment of a foreign emerging market wherein they invest and operate. Author's analysis suggests that an MNE subunit's investment commitment decreases, and its export market orientation increases, with perceived escalated corruption in the specific business segment.

Key findings

Success in foreign emerging markets is increasingly critical to the global market leadership for many multinational enterprises (MNEs).

- However, corruption in emerging markets is pervasive and rampant.
- Though perceived corruption in an industrial setting (sectorial corruption) has a stronger effect on the subunit's market orientation, changes in perceived corruption over time (longitudinal corruption) exert a greater influence on investment commitment.
- To individual subunits, the strength of these strategic responses to corruption is heightened by their ethical awareness but weakened by their indigenous dependence.

Source: Governance Research Digest, June 2011 (Vol. 2, No. 2)

6.1.15 Principles for an Anti-Corruption Programme under the UK Bribery Act 2010

Author(s): IBE

The Institute of Business Ethics (IBE) has launched the publication of Principles for an Anti-Corruption Programme under the UK Bribery Act 2010 for the Energy and Extractives Sector. The Principles have been developed by a group of leading energy and mining companies and draw on their considerable experience of managing potential bribery and corruption.

<u>Key findings</u>

The Principles represent a sharing of best practice and are intended to provide assistance to organisations operating in these areas on the key issues to consider as they seek to prevent bribery in their organisations.

- The key Principles are based on those that the contributor companies employ in their own businesses.
- It is anticipated that the Principles will be used as a helpful reference to assist organisations to develop or enhance their own policies and procedures.
- The Principles may also be of benefit to companies in other sectors who are considering policies and procedures to help prevent bribery in their own organisations.

Source: Governance Research Digest, July 2011 (Vol. 2, No. 3)

6.1.16 Fluidity of Regulation-CSR Nexus: The Multinational Corporate Corruption Example

Author(s): O. Osuji

The article demonstrates that ethical CSR highlights the role of regulation, and a principal stance is that regulation is neither incompatible nor irreconcilable with ethical CSR. The article argues that cognizance of the intrinsic moral justification of 'pure' CSR is required for delineating the scope of CSR as well as for clarifying the desirability and extent of its regulation.

Key findings

The study argues that the dynamic history and visage of multinational corporate corruption illuminates the fluidity of the regulation–CSR relationship.

- The current and widening backlash against transnational corporate corruption is, arguably, a demonstration of the position that regulation and CSR are not mutually exclusive and absolute concepts.
- This article submits that recognition and application of this 'ethical' and 'instrumental' CSR distinction is fundamental to the development of CSR and resolution of connected questions of regulation.

Source: Governance Research Digest, September 2011 (Vol. 2, No. 5)

6.1.17 Government Intervention, Perceived Benefits, and Bribery of Firms in Transitional China

Author(s): Y. Gao

This article examines whether government intervention causes bribery (or corruption) as rentseeking theory suggested. In addition it examines whether a firm's perceived benefit partially mediates the relationship between government intervention and its bribing behavior, as rational choice/behavior theory suggested, and other firms' bribing behavior moderates the relationship between government intervention and a firm's perceived benefit.

Key findings

Government intervention causes bribery/corruption indeed, but it exerts its effect on bribery/corruption through the firm's perceived benefit.

- In other words, a firm's perceived benefit fully mediates the relationship between government intervention and its bribing behavior.
- It also finds that other firms' bribery positively moderates the relationship between government intervention and a given firm's bribery.

- This study partly proves that firms are rational actors.
- Potential benefit encourages them to practice bribery.
- Besides, this research also supports the rentseeking view of bribery/corruption, which argues that government intervention is a source of bribery/corruption.
- However, study has also identified that only those government interventions that will create "rent" can cause bribery/corruption.

Source: Governance Research Digest, December 2011 (Vol. 2, No. 8)

6.1.18 To Pay or Not to Pay? Dynamic Transparency and the Fight Against the Mafia's Extortionists

Author(s): A. Vaccaro

The article presents the results of the longitudinal study of Addiopizzo, a successful anti-bribery organization founded in Sicily in 2004. It analyzes how this organization has used information disclosure as a strategy to fight adverse environmental conditions and the immoral activities of the Sicilian Mafia.

Key findings

This article extends the business ethics and corporate social responsibility literature by showing how multi-level strategic information disclosure processes can help gain organizational legitimacy in adverse social environments and successfully fight against social resistance to change, low levels of moral imagination and attacks from criminal organizations.

- This article provides an additional contribution to the literature by linking the three research streams on corporate transparency, the fight against corruption, and organizational legitimacy.
- The results of this research also contribute to the special issue of the EBEN AC 2010, "Which values for which organizations", since it provides a unique example of an organization capable of spreading the values of social justice and honesty in a difficult social environment plagued by Mafia.

Source: Governance Research Digest, February 2012 (Vol. 3, No. 2)

6.1.19 Corruption Perceptions Index 2012

Author(s): Transparency International

Transparency International published its latest Corruption Perceptions Index, highlighting the levels of corruption all over the world. The Index is based on expert assessments and data from 13 surveys from independent institutions, covering issues such as access to information, bribery of public officials, kickbacks in public procurement, and the enforcement of anti-corruption laws.

Key findings

Two thirds of the 176 countries ranked in the 2012 index score below 50.

- The lowest scored country in Europe, however, is troubled Greece - ranked down 14 places to number 36.
- Syria too, presently in the middle of civil war, is down 15 places to number 144, making it one of the most corrupt countries on earth.
- Egypt, presently in the middle of demonstrations, is down six places to 118 out of 174 countries ranked by the index.
- Afghanistan, North Korea and Somalia share last place with a score of only eight out of 100 for transparency.
- At the top are some of the world's most stable countries - New Zealand, Denmark and Finland are number one.

Source: Governance Research Digest, December 2012 (Vol. 3, No. 12)

6.1.20 Anti-Bribery & Corruption Benchmarking Report

Author(s): Kroll

Kroll released a report that gives compliance officers a view into the antibribery and corruption threats they face and share resources for creating a risk-based compliance program. The findings give compliance officers a view into the anti-bribery and corruption threats they face and share resources for creating a risk-based compliance program.

Key findings

Larger corporations based in the United States took anti-corruption programs more seriously than their smaller counterparts based elsewhere.

- 47% of all respondents said they conduct no anti-corruption training with their third parties; of those who do train their third parties on anti-corruption, only 30% believe their efforts are effective.
- 20% of corporations based outside the United States do not conduct anti-corruption training with their own employees.
- 18% of respondents said they either have an anti-corruption policy but don't require employees to read it, or don't have an anticorruption policy at all.

Source: Governance Research Digest, July 2013 (Vol. 4, No. 7)

6.1.21 Business, Corruption and Crime in the western Balkans

Author(s): United Nations Office on Drugs and Crime (UNODC) and the European Commission (EC)

The United Nations Office on Drugs and Crime (UNODC) and the European Commission (EC) jointly released a study that offers a comprehensive assessment of corruption as experienced by businesses in the western Balkans, based on interviews with more than 12,700 companies. By identifying areas of vulnerability, the survey 'Business, Corruption and Crime in the western Balkans: The impact of bribery and other crime on private enterprise' aims to support governments in the region to implement the United Nations Convention against Corruption and work effectively with the private sector to develop and put into action anti-corruption strategies and measures.

<u>Key findings</u>

The percentage of businesses experiencing bribery over a 12-month period is high in Serbia (17 per cent) and Albania (15.7 per cent), while more bribes are paid by businesses in Croatia (8.8 bribes per year) and in Kosovo* (7.7 bribes per year). The most expensive bribes are paid in Kosovo (average 1,787 EUR per bribe) and Serbia (average 935 EUR per bribe).

- At the regional level, over one-third (35.7 per cent) of bribes to public officials are paid in cash, at a hefty average of 880 EUR per bribe. Food and drink (33.6 per cent) are the next most popular form of payment, followed by other goods in exchange for a "favour" (21 per cent).

- The frequency and prevalence of bribery are substantially higher among small businesses than larger ones, as well as among those companies in which foreign capital has been invested (16.6 per cent) than among those with no foreign capital.
- The building and construction is the sector most seriously affected, with 12.2 per cent of respondents confirming that they had paid a bribe to a public official. This is followed by businesses in the wholesale and retail trade sector (10.3 per cent), transportation and storage (9.9 per cent), manufacturing, electricity, gas, and water supply (9.2 per cent) and accommodation and food services (9 per cent).
- The largest shares of bribes are paid to local public officials (municipal or provincial officers) and to officials in tax and customs administration, suggesting that bribery is commonly used for tax evasion, which could have a negative impact on public finances.
- Corruption, together with crime, places a considerable burden on the economic development of the region. 5.9 per cent of businesses decided not to make a major investment in the 12 months prior to the survey due to fear of having to pay bribes, while 9.1 per cent decided not to make a major investment due to fear of crime.
- The most common purpose for paying bribes is to "speed up business-related procedures" (40.3 per cent of all bribes), with businesses citing "better treatment" (14.1 per cent) and "making the finalization of a procedure possible" (12.7 per cent) as other reasons.

Source: Governance Research Digest, October 2013 (Vol. 4, No. 10)

6.1.22 Global Corruption Barometer

Author(s): Transparency International

Transparency International released a report that addresses people's direct experiences with bribery and details their views on corruption in the main institutions in their countries and it also provides insights into people's willingness to stop corruption. The Global Corruption Barometer 2013 draws on a survey of more than 114,000 respondents in 107 countries.

<u>Key findings</u>

Bribery is widespread.

- Overall, more than one in four people (27 per cent) report having paid a bribe in the last 12 months when interacting with key public institutions and services.
- Public institutions entrusted to protect people suffer the worst levels of bribery.
- Among the eight services evaluated, the police and the judiciary are seen as the two most briberyprone.
- An estimated 31 per cent of people who came into contact with the police report having paid a bribe.
- For those interacting with the judiciary, the share is 24 per cent.
- Governments are not thought to be doing enough to hold the corrupt to account.
- The majority of people around the world believe that their government is ineffective at fighting corruption and corruption in their country is getting worse.
- Around the world, political parties, the driving force of democracies, are perceived to be the most corrupt institution.
- Personal connections are seen as corrupting the public administration.
- People surveyed regard corruption in their country as more than just paying bribes: almost two out of three people believe that personal contacts and relationships help to get things done in the public sector in their country.
- Powerful groups rather than the public good are judged to be driving government actions.
- More than one in two people (54 per cent) think their government is largely or entirely run by groups acting in their own interests rather than for the benefit of the citizens.
- Nearly 9 in 10 surveyed say they would act against corruption.
- The majority of people said that they would be willing to speak up and report an incident of corruption. Two-thirds of those asked to pay a bribe say they refused.

Source: Governance Research Digest, November 2013 (Vol. 4, No. 11)

6.1.23 2013 Corruption Perceptions Index

Author(s): Transparency International

Transparency International has released its 2013 indicator of corruption worldwide, compiled from a combination of surveys and assessments of 'the abuse of entrusted power for private gain'. The Corruption Perceptions Index (CPI) ranks 177 countries and territories based on how corrupt their administrative and political institutions are perceived to be on a scale from 0 (highly corrupt) and a 100 (very clean).

Key findings

- Denmark, New Zealand, Finland, and Sweden are list as the four least corrupt countries while the U.S. came in 19th.
- Syria, in the midst of a brutal civil war, dropped eight points in the last year as government officials profit from the food crisis.
- Libya, in the midst of post-revolutionary turmoil, dropped six points to surpass Iraq in official corruption.

Source: Governance Research Digest, December 2013 (Vol. 4, No. 12)

6.1.24 The Shareholder-Manager Relationship and Its Impact on the Likelihood of Firm Bribery

Author(s): D. Ramdani and A. van Witteloostuijn

The article examines the impact on firm bribery of two corporate governance devices heavily studied in corporate governance research—i.e., separation of ownership and control, and equity share of the largest shareholder. In addition, it investigates the impact of the principal–owner's gender on firm bribery.

Key findings

From agency theory, authors predict that firms with the owner also acting as a manager (owner–manager) are more likely to engage in bribery compared to their counterparts with separation of ownership and control.

- Using a rich dataset of the World Bank Enterprise Surveys of 2002–2005, authors find that the equity share of the largest shareholder is negatively and male principal–owner is positively associated with the likelihood of firm bribery.
- Furthermore, they reveal that owner–manager is more likely to bribe when the principal–owner is male rather than female.

- Authors also observe that the effect of owner– manager is smaller as the equity share of the largest shareholder increases.

Source: Governance Research Digest, July 2012 (Vol. 3, No. 7)

6.1.25 Office of Anticorruption and Integrity Annual Report

Author(s): Asian Development Bank (ADB)

The Asian Development Bank published the annual report of its Office of Anticorruption and Integrity that highlights achievements made on case screening and investigations, project procurement-related reviews, and learning and development. In 2013, OAI received 250 complaints, surpassing the previous record of 240 received in 2012 and it converted 92 complaints into investigations and processed sanctions imposed on 30 individuals and 31 firms.

Key findings

Fraud related to work experience, qualifications, and technical and financial capacities of consulting firms or consultants continues to be the most common type of integrity violation reported to OAI.

- ADB continued to use sanctions as a remedial measure to protect the integrity of ADB-financed, supported, and administered activities. In justified circumstances, ADB also utilized temporary sanctions to manage integrity and reputational risks arising from continued involvement with firms and individuals that are the subject of an OAI investigation.
- In collaboration with ADB operations departments, OAI has continued to roll out targeted project procurement–related reviews (PPRRs). In 2013, OAI conducted seven new PPRRs and issued three reports for PPRRs conducted in 2012. Summarized findings from PPRRs conducted since 2003 have been injected into OAI's training and awareness-raising initiatives.
- In 2013, as ADB increased its commitment to private sector development and private sector operations and as part of Strategy 2020, OAI's due diligence advisory function saw a dramatic uptake. In its second full year of carrying out its additional mandate of providing independent advice on integrity due diligence (IDD) and anti-money-

laundering and combating the financing of terrorism (AML/CFT) risks, requests for advice from OAI increased from 15 in 2012 to 253 in 2013.

- OAI has continued to expand its awareness-raising activities to proactively inform staff , civil society, and the private sector about the negative impacts of fraud and corruption. Staff training emphasizes the role and responsibility of ADB staff in implementing ADB's Anticorruption Policy. OAI also actively encourages staff to be discerning and to undertake due diligence and conflict of interest checks as effective preventive measures against corruption and to mitigate integrity risks.

Source: Governance Research Digest, March 2014 (Vol. 5, No. 3)

6.1.26 Exporting Corruption: Progress Report 2014: Assessing enforcement of the OECD Convention on Combating Foreign Bribery

Author(s): Transparency International

Transparency International published its tenth annual progress report on OECD Anti-Bribery Convention enforcement. Exporting Corruption Progress Report 2014: Assessing Enforcement of the OECD Convention on Combating Foreign Bribery evaluates the strength of government measures taken to enforce the Convention.

Key findings

The fundamental goal of creating a corruption-free level playing field for global trade is still far from being achieved: 22 Countries with little or no enforcement and 8 Countries with only limited enforcement.

- Active Enforcement - 4 countries with 23.1% of world exports: US, Germany, UK, Switzerland
- Limited Enforcement - 8 countries with 7.6% of world exports: France, Sweden, Norway, Hungary, South Africa, Argentina, Portugal, New Zealand
- Moderate Enforcement - 5 countries with 8.3% of world exports: Italy, Canada, Australia, Austria, Finland
- Little or No Enforcement – 22 countries with 27% of world exports: Japan, Netherlands, Korea (South), Russia, Spain, Belgium, Mexico,

Brazil, Ireland, Poland, Turkey, Denmark, Czech Republic, Luxembourg, Chile, Israel, Slovak Republic, Colombia, Greece, Slovenia, Bulgaria, Estonia

Changes in enforcement level 2013 – 2014:

- 2 Countries have improved: Canada and New Zealand
- 2 Countries have regressed: Bulgaria and Denmark
- Canada has moved from the Limited category to Moderate and New Zealand from Little or No Enforcement to the Limited category. It is promising that New Zealand, which has never prosecuted any foreign bribery case before, started its formal investigations into foreign bribery cases. During the last four years Australia and Canada have launched a number of new investigations and moved them forward to court proceedings. Both countries have introduced major legislative reforms in the field, which taken together with the investigations provide a good basis for their anti-foreign bribery drive.
- In Finland the foreign bribery investigations and prosecutions of the last four years show that the country could become an active enforcer if inadequacies in the legal framework that prevent adequate sanctioning were remedied. Austria, which is also a moderate enforcer, is increasing its efforts.
- Austria and New Zealand were taken off the regular follow-up process on money laundering laws and practice by the Financial Action Task Force, which is a positive indication regarding their ability to step up investigations of money laundering used for foreign bribery. Italy, another moderate enforcer, adopted an anti-corruption law at the end of 2012 and an anti-corruption plan in 2013. These provide a basis for better enforcement, but the key problem of inadequate statutes of limitation still needs to be solved.
- Norway and Sweden are in the position to move into the Moderate category from the Limited category if the ongoing investigations turn into prosecutions. Of the world's major exporters (having a two per cent or more share of world exports), five have little or no enforcement – Japan, Russia, Spain, South Korea and Netherlands – while France shows limited enforcement activity.

Source: Governance Research Digest, October 2014 (Vol. 5, No. 10)

6.1.27 2014 Anti-Bribery and Corruption Benchmarking Report

Author(s): Kroll and Compliance Week

Kroll and Compliance Week authored a report that captures the experiences of nearly 200 senior-level executives working in ethics, compliance or anti-corruption across diverse geographies and industries. For the first time, this year the Anti-Bribery and Corruption Benchmarking Report also asked compliance officers exactly what types of misconduct qualify as "corruption" that they are responsible for addressing.

Key findings

Compliance departments still struggle to understand and tame several key corruption risks.

- Compliance officers' understanding of how their anti-corruption programs should work is fairly widespread; one can certainly say many "standard" anti-corruption compliance practices have emerged and been adopted.
- Large U.S. corporations lead the way in anti-corruption programs and worry more about bribery risks, while smaller and overseas businesses trail behind.
- Third parties continue to vex compliance officers; in 2014, the percentage of respondents who said they don't train their third parties on anti-corruption actually went up.
- Due diligence at the beginning of a business relationship is strong, but monitoring anti- corruption efforts on a continuing basis is weak.
- 44% said the CCO is only responsible for breach disclosure after a privacy breach of some kind, and 31% said the CCO plays no role in cyber security or breach disclosure at all.
- To understand the CCO's delicate position today, we must consider all these circumstances together — that even while several elements of an effective compliance program still pose problems for many CCOs (risk assessments, third parties, monitoring), the types of risks their programs must address are proliferating (money laundering, bid-rigging, data security)

Source: Governance Research Digest, November 2014 (Vol. 5, No. 11)

6.2   Illicit Financial Flows and Money-Laundering

6.2.1   Money Laundering Report

Author(s): Transparency International

A new report by Transparency International assesses the UK financial systems' effectiveness on combating money laundering. It also offers recommendations on how due diligence mechanisms and regulation can be improved.

Key findings

Globally, approximately US$40bn is taken by corrupt leaders or Politically Exposed Persons (PEPs) from state ministries as well as through bribes. The majority of this is moved to overseas financial institutions.

- About US$24.5bn or £15bn is laundered through the UK each year. Money launderers find it easier to mingle their dirty funds in a large financial centre like London.
- Because of its key international connections, its position as a leading international financial centre and its links with many of the world's offshore centres, the UK should be prepared to take a lead in implementing anti-money laundering (AML) standards and in assisting victim countries to recover stolen assets and the proceeds of corruption.
- Particular challenges arise in respect of some of the UK Overseas Territories (OTs) that are offshore financial centres. They are constitutionally not part of the UK and in some of them, the Governor-General is accountable for financial services.
- All the OTs have implemented AML regimes. However, some of the smaller OTs have very limited regulatory and law enforcement capacity making it difficult to address money laundering (ML) risks effectively. This vulnerability has serious implications for the UK's reputation.
- Recent allegations of fraud and corruption in the Turks and Caicos Islands have underlined the need for urgent action to mitigate risks.
- The prevention of money laundering depends crucially on the diligence of reporting institutions in knowing their customers, especially PEPs.

- PEPs are defined broadly in the UK as persons (and their immediate family members and close associates) who are, or at any time in the preceding year have been, entrusted with prominent public functions by a state other than the UK.
- The majority of PEPs are legitimate customers. It is the activities of a minority of corrupt PEPs that are of concern to reporting institutions and UK law enforcement.
- Corrupt PEPs often hide behind complex structures, with anonymous trusts and companies, including offshore trusts and shell companies.
- Reporting institutions should be satisfied that a PEP is legally entitled under his or her domestic laws to establish a business relationship in the UK, and should know any limits on that business relationship.
- Increased transparency and stronger regulation in financial markets will have a positive impact on AML efforts, particularly in relation to tax havens and those financial centres that refuse to cooperate in the exchange of tax and other information relevant to regulatory, law enforcement and AML investigations.
- The creation of the UK's Asset Recovery Office creates some opportunities for enhanced engagement with developing countries.

Source: Governance Research Digest, August 2009 (Vol. 1, No. 8)

6.2.2   Illicit Financial Flows from Developing Countries

Author(s): Global Financial Integrity

In the third update of its original report, Global Financial Integrity estimates illicit financial flows from the developing world. The report presents four different methodologies for estimating illicit financial flows from developing countries, including the methodology used in Global Financial Integrity's previous research.

<u>Key findings</u>

From 2001 to 2010, developing countries lost US$5.86 trillion to illicit outflows.

- The developing world lost US$859 billion in illicit outflows in 2010, an increase of 11% over 2009. The capital outflows stem from crime, corruption, tax evasion, and other illicit activity.

- Conservatively estimated, illicit financial flows have increased in every region of developing countries. Real growth of illicit flows by regions over study period is as follows: Africa 23.8%, Middle East and North Africa (MENA) 26.3%, developing Europe 3.6%, Asia 7.8%, and Western Hemisphere 2.7%.
- Top 10 countries with the highest measured cumulative illicit financial outflows between 2001 and 2010 were: 1. China: US$2.74 trillion, 2. Mexico: US$476 billion, 3. Malaysia: US$285 billon. 4. Saudi Arabia: US$210 billion, 5. Russia: US$152 billion, 6. Philippines: US$138 billion, 7. Nigeria: US$129 billion, 8. India: US$123 billion, 9. Indonesia: US$109 billion and 10. United Arab Emirates: US$107 billion

Source: Governance Research Digest, December 2012 (Vol. 3, No. 12)

6.2.3   Illicit Enrichment Report

Author(s): Stolen Asset Recovery (StAR), a joint initiative by World Bank and UN Office on Drugs and Crime (UNDOC)

Stolen Asset Recovery (StAR), a joint initiative by World Bank and UN Office on Drugs and Crime (UNDOC) published a study that analyzes how the criminalization of illicit enrichment works and sheds light on its contributions to the fight against corruption and the recovery of stolen assets. "On the Take: Criminalizing Illicit Enrichment to Fight Corruption" aims to assist jurisdictions that are considering adopting particular illicit enrichment provisions by highlighting key questions that might arise during implementation, including how states define and enforce the offense.

<u>Key findings</u>

44 juridisctions have criminalized illicit enrichment, most of them in developing countries.

- However, only a limited number of these jurisdictions regularly investigate or prosecute the offense.
- Several elements of the illicit enrichment offense are common to the jurisdictions that prosecute it. Those elements are persons of interest, period of interest, significant increase in assets, intent, and absence of justification.

- One critical issue subject to ongoing debate relates to the compatibility of illicit enrichment with human rights principles and related concerns regarding the perceived reversals of the burden of proof.
- Apart from substantive aspects of the offense, research conducted for this study revealed that the design and implementation of government structures are critical to ensure full respect of Article 2 of the International Covenant on Civil and Political Rights (ICCPR).
- The status and existence of legislative, administrative and judicial measures for the implementation of these rights must be considered from the point of view of the elimination of corruption.
- Of particular relevance is whether institutions involved in the investigation, prosecution, and adjudication of illicit enrichment are properly monitored, accountable, resourced and trained so that they are in a position to implement the obligations taken under the ICCPR and to pursue corrupt money effectively and fairly.
- Any illicit enrichment should be tailored to suit the particular needs and concerns of the country, specifically with regard to legislative, administrative and judicial measures, including the role and limits of the prosecution.
- In all jurisdictions reviewed, the illicit enrichment law addresses the recovery of the assets illicitly acquired.
- However, there remains an absence of solid statistical data with which to establish whether such laws have actually contributed to the recovery of assets.

Source: Governance Research Digest, July 2013 (Vol. 4, No. 7)

6.2.4   Illicit Trade – an Irish and global challenge

Author(s): Grant Thornton

Grant Thornton issued a report focused on the challenges currently facing both the Irish and international community across areas of intellectual property crime, cybercrime, money laundering and retail. The report puts forth a number of key recommendations to help address these challenges and to help policy-makers and businesses to better understand the international issue of illicit trade and support informed decision-making.

Key findings

The scale of illicit trade operations globally is enormous. It results in significant financial losses to the international and domestic communities and businesses. It supports organised crime and affects the overall wellbeing of the global population.

- Average cost of a databreach for a business is €3m in the US
- An estimated €5.4bn laundered in Ireland 2012
- IP intensive industries create 90% of EU exports
- Costs of Cybercrime €241bn to the global economy
- Costs of Cybercrime €630mto the Irish economy
- 7 out of 10 consumers believe illicit trade supports organised crime
- 23% of consumers in Ireland knowingly purchase illicit tobacco
- 64% of consumers believe stricter fines and harsher laws will help to diminish illicit trade
- 23% of employment in Ireland is in IP intensive industries
- €390m cost of illicit tobacco to the Irish economy
- Loss to the economy due to fuel laundering up to €466m in Ireland
- Cost of IP crime up to 7% of global GDP
- Up to 5% of global GDP laundered

Source: Governance Research Digest, April 2014 (Vol. 5, No. 4)

6.2.5   Global Surveillance of Dirty Money

Author(s): The Center on Law and Globalization

The Center on Law and Globalization released a report which questions the effectiveness of the global fight against worldwide money laundering and the financing of terrorism. Co-authors, Professors Terence Halliday, Michael Levi, and Peter Reuter believe the 'Global Surveillance of Dirty Money' report can strengthen systems for fighting money laundering and the financing of terrorism, while helping policy-makers recognize the potential costs and harms of financial surveillance and enforcement.

Key findings

The international regulation and surveillance of dirty money is at a crossroads. Assessing national compliance with global standards has been problematic.

- The fight against money laundering is costly. A full-scale system consumes extensive government resources in participating countries and makes heavy demands on the private sector.
- Major international banks in the UK, US and Europe have admitted to massive violations of money laundering controls over long periods, indicating that highly developed anti-money laundering systems have not worked well in countries whose economies are systemically important to international financial markets.
- The methods and scope of global surveillance of financial transactions by individuals, companies and non-profits are also engendering public debate.
- It will take years to test whether objectives are met and investments in financial regulation yield a net positive return.
- No credible scientific evidence has yet been presented that there is a direct relationship between installation of effective AML/CFT regimes and the IMF mandates to produce domestic and international financial stability.

Source: Governance Research Digest, August 2014 (Vol. 5, No. 8)

6.2.6   Illicit Financial Flows from Developing Countries

Author(s): OECD

OECD issued a publication that identifies the main areas of weakness and potential areas for action to combat money-laundering, tax evasion, foreign bribery, and to identify, freeze and return stolen assets. The report, Illicit Financial Flows from Developing Countries also looks at the role of development agencies and identifies some opportunities for a scaled-up role for development agencies.

Key findings

In OECD countries, the sanctions for foreign bribery offences are increasing. While peer reviews confirm that OECD countries are taking a harder stance against corruption, around half of OECD countries have yet to see a single prosecution.

- Some countries have loopholes for bribe payers in their legal frameworks, including overly narrow definitions or short statutes of limitations; other countries impose impractical burdens of proof, or let strategic considerations influence whether or not to pursue a bribery case.

- To mitigate these challenges, potent mechanisms to uncover bribery and prosecute bribe payers are needed, including penalties that will constitute a tangible deterrent. Effective protection for whistle-blowers is also essential.

- Twenty-seven out of 34 OECD countries store or require insufficient beneficial ownership information for legal persons, and no country is fully compliant with the beneficial ownership recommendations for legal arrangements.

- Since 2000, OECD countries have signed roughly 1 300 bilateral exchange of information agreements with developing countries.

- As of 2012, 221 individuals and 90 companies have been sanctioned for foreign bribery, yet around half of all OECD countries have yet to see a single prosecution.

- Between 2010 and 2012, OECD countries have returned USD 147 million and frozen almost USD 1.4 billion of stolen assets.

Source: Governance Research Digest, August 2014 (Vol. 5, No. 8)

6.2.7 Staying on Side: How to Stop Match-Fixing

Author(s): Transparency International (TI), the Association of European Professional Football Leagues (EPFL) and the German Football League (DFL)

The anti-corruption organisation Transparency International (TI), the Association of European Professional Football Leagues (EPFL) and the German Football League (DFL) teamed up to fight match-fixing in football. The project partners issued a report named 'Staying on Side: How to Stop Match-Fixing', which aims to identify the key risk factors associated with match-fixing and make recommendations on how to prevent it.

Key findings

The growth of the global betting market and the potential gains from gambling and money laundering associated with betting have made football a target for organised crime.

- This puts players, officials and all those involved with football at risk.
- The emergence of match-fixing as a serious threat to the integrity of football has prompted responses from both inside and outside the sport.
- Education and prevention have been identified as key measures in the fight against match-fixing.
- A key learning from the project is that whistleblower systems are critical to support those who want to report match-fixing approaches or need advice of how to handle difficult situations. Leagues in Germany, Austria and Scotland have already implemented such systems and other leagues such as the Italian Serie B have committed to establish them.

Source: Governance Research Digest, September 2014 (Vol. 5, No. 9)

6.2.8   Anti-money laundering annual report 2013/14

Author(s): Financial Conduct Authority (FCA)

UK's Financial Conduct Authority (FCA) published its second Anti-Money Laundering Annual Report. This report sets out policy developments in the last year, findings and outcomes from FCA's recent specialist supervisory work and their new anti-money laundering (AML) supervision strategy.

Key findings

In 2013/14, the FCA:

- Imposed more than £425m in regulatory penalties;
- Took action against 34 firms and 28 individuals;
- Published 56 final notices;
- Secured five criminal convictions;
- Authorised 1,046 firms
- Did not refuse any applications for authorisation or variations of permission;
- Cancelled the permission to conduct regulatory business of 28 firms;
- Cancelled the registrations of 32 payments services firms for basic failings;
- Completed and published 15 thematic reviews on a range of topics;

- Intervened early in 21 cases where a risk to consumers was identified, four of which involved anti-money laundering in banks;
- Issued 295 consumer warnings – half relating to suspected boiler schemes;
- Received 1,040 whistleblowing cases;
- Had 49,405 firms registered for consumer credit interim permission on 1st April 2014;
- Received 748 FOI requests.

Source: Governance Research Digest, September 2014 (Vol. 5, No. 9)

6.2.9   Illicit tobacco in Australia

Author(s): KPMG

British American Tobacco Australia, Imperial Tobacco Australia Limited and Philip Morris Limited commissioned KPMG LLP to conduct an independent report to estimate the size of the consumption of illicit tobacco in Australia. The purpose of the 'Illicit tobacco in Australia' report is: 1. To provide an overview of the nature and dynamics of the legal and illicit tobacco markets in Australia of the legal and illicit tobacco markets in Australia, and 2. To provide an independent estimate of the size of the illicit tobacco market in Australia.

Key findings

Illegal tobacco use in Australia is continuing to grow and around one in every seven cigarettes consumed is illegal.

- Illegal tobacco use in the last 12 months has increased from 13.5% to 14.3% of total consumption.
- 2.5 million kilograms of tobacco, or 3.1 billion cigarettes, or more than 156 million packs of 20 were sold on the black market in one year. Had that tobacco been sold legally, the Australian Government would have received an additional $1.2 billion in tobacco excise.
- Instead of paying tax to the Australian Government, criminal gangs are profiting from this illegal tobacco trade at the expense of Australian taxpayers and law-abiding retailers.
- While legal tobacco sales have declined slightly, total consumption of tobacco has remained stable due to increases in illicit consumption.

- The mix in the tobacco black market has changed since 2012.
- More branded illegal cigarette packs are being smuggled into Australia than ever before. Contraband cigarettes are now the largest component of the black market.
- The illegal tobacco trade is up from 13.5% to 14.3% of total consumption in the 12 months to June 2014.
- The Australian Government and taxpayers are losing $1.2 billion in unpaid excise annually.
- Contraband cigarette consumption (imported to Australia without excise paid) is growing.
- A pack of 20 cigarettes is up to 7 times more expensive in Australia than South Korea.

Source: Governance Research Digest, November 2014 (Vol. 5, No. 11)

6.2.10 Brazil: Capital Flight, Illicit Flows, and Macroeconomic Crises, 1960-2012

Author(s): Global Financial Integrity

Global Financial Integrity released its fifth country case study on illicit flows. Brazil: Capital Flight, Illicit Flows, and Macroeconomic Crises, 1960-2012 uses the largest Structural and Behavioral Equations Model developed by Dr. Kar to analyze the drivers and dynamics of Brazil's illicit flows.

Key findings

More than US$400 billion flowed illegally out of Brazil between 1960 and 2012—draining domestic resources, driving the underground economy, exacerbating inequality, and facilitating crime and corruption.

- The Brazilian economy lost at least US$401.6 billion in illicit financial outflows from 1960 to 2012.
- These outflows represent the proceeds of crime, corruption, and tax evasion, and have serious negative consequences for Brazil.
- Outflows were found to drain resources from the Brazilian economy, to drive the underground economy, and to exacerbate inequality.
- Furthermore, the report found that illicit outflows are growing. Annual average illicit outflows increased from US$310 million in the 1960s to

US$14.7 billion in the first decade of the twenty first century before jumping to US$33.7 billion over the last three years of the study, 2010-2012. On average, Brazil's illicit outflows are equivalent to 1.5% of the country's official GDP.

- Trade misinvoicing is the major conduit of illicit financial flows from Brazil. The report reveals that the vast majority of Brazil's illicit outflows—92.7%, or US$372.3 billion of the US$401.6 billion in total outflows—were channeled through the misinvoicing of trade transactions. The remaining US$29.4 billion in the illicit outflows detected by GFI occurred via hot money outflows, such as unrecorded wire transfers.

Source: Governance Research Digest, December 2014 (Vol. 5, No. 12)

6.2.11 Global Anti-Money Laundering Survey 2014

Author(s): KPMG

KPMG conducted a survey whose overarching aims of included: • Identifying emerging trends, opportunities and threats; • Capturing industry perceptions on regulation, cost, and effectiveness; and • Benchmarking anti-money laundering (AML) efforts in the financial services industry. The Global Anti-Money Laundering Survey 2014 compares firms' AML programs and looks at emerging areas of risk, such as Trade Finance and Tax Evasion, as well as AML trends within the Insurance and Asset Management sectors.

Key findings

88% of respondents stated that the Board of Directors takes an active interest in AML issues; this is an increase of 26% from our 2011 result.

- Significantly, 98% of respondents confirmed that AML issues are discussed formally at the Board, with the majority stating that this was done on a quarterly or as required basis.
- 84% said money laundering is considered a high risk area within their business risk assessment, further emphasizing how seriously senior management deems failures to meet the regulatory requirements.

- 75% of respondents stated that the same AML policies and procedures are applied to all branches and subsidiaries, demonstrating that senior management is taking a more global approach to AML compliance.
- The cost of AML compliance has increased since our the previous KPMG survey and shows no signs of slowing down in the near future.
- Accurate cost forecasting is vital for members of senior management to make informed decisions, but it remains a key area of weakness

Source: Governance Research Digest, December 2014 (Vol. 5, No. 12)

6.3   Fraud and Economic Crime

6.3.1   Fraud, Enforcement Action, and the Role of Corporate Governance: Evidence From China

Author(s): C. Jia, S. Ding, Y. Li, Z. Wu.

This paper examines enforcement action against fraud in China's emerging markets by focusing on the agents that impose and the role played by supervisory boards. The authors focus on enforcement since 2000 and include a total of 362 observations of fraud in their analysis.

Key findings

Of the 362 observed fraud cases, 47.5% of the firms were punished by the China Securities Regulatory Commission (CSRC) and the remainder by one of the two stock exchanges.

- Both supervisory boards and standard corporate boards play critical governance roles in firms that commit fraud.
- A higher percentage of those firms guilty of fraud have board chairs who are the same as their CEO.
- The company profitability of the fraudulent firms, as measured by return on assets, is significantly lower than that of non-fraudulent firms. They also tend to have more tradable shares.
- Fraudulent firms with supervisory boards that meet more frequently are more likely to receive enforcement sanctions from the CSRC, which are more severe than those imposed by the stock exchanges.

- However, this may represent reverse causality; that is, a more severe punishment may cause supervisory boards to meet more frequently.
- One additional member on a supervisory board increases the probability of receiving sanctions from the CSRC by 27%. The higher agency costs in these firms may be a source of more severe fraud.
- No formal professional ethical codes for supervisory boards have been established or implemented in China. It is therefore difficult to measure the effectiveness and diligence of those boards.

Source: Governance Research Digest, November 2009 (Vol. 1, No. 11)

6.3.2   Secrecy Jurisdictions and Tax Avoidance

Author(s): imug

In this position paper, German research consultancy, imug, draw upon the issue of "secrecy jurisdictions and tax evasion" in line with expertise and research provided by internationally regarded governmental and non-governmental organizations. In this regard, the authors have selected a group of organizations as main focal points for their approach towards the topic: OECD, IMF, Financial Action Task Force, At-tac, Tax Justice Network and Global Financial Integrity.

Key findings

Tax avoidance and tax evasion are conceived of as being global challenges with significant financial and social impacts.

- Whereas tax evasion is a crime and therewith illegal, tax avoidance is not a criminal offence as it involves the abusive exploitation of gaps and loopholes in domestic and international tax law.
- Here, multinational companies (MNCs) capitalize on the possibility to shift profits from country to country, often to or via tax havens, with the intention of reducing the tax they pay on some or all of their profits.
- The issue of secrecy jurisdictions, tax honesty and tax avoidance implies numerous challenges and opportunities, as well as a clear business case for including tax as a corporate responsibility issue.
- The harmful consequences stemming from the existence of tax havens are manifold and can be clustered along the lines of three key themes:
  - Loss in tax revenue

- o Jeopardizing financial market and economic stability
- o Enabling criminal activities

Source: Governance Research Digest, May 2012 (Vol. 3, No. 5)

6.3.3 Global Fraud Report

Author(s): Kroll & Economist Intelligence Unit

Kroll commissioned the Economist Intelligence Unit to conduct a survey on fraud and its effect on business during 2012. Global Fraud Report covers 10 industries with 50 respondents from each, including: Financial Services; Professional Services; Retail, Wholesale & Distribution; Technology Media & Telecoms; Healthcare, Pharmaceuticals & Biotechnology; Travel, Leisure & Transportation; Consumer Goods; Construction, Engineering and Infrastructure; Natural Resources; and Manufacturing.

Key findings

67% of all fraud cases are committed by insiders, up from 60% last year and 55% in 2010.

- Information theft remains the second most common fraud, hitting 21% of companies in the last year.
- Thirty percent of respondents say they are most vulnerable to information theft, and the same number cite IT complexity as the leading cause of increased exposure.
- Surprisingly, it is employees, rather than hackers, who are more to blame for the loss of information. Where there has been a loss, 35% of the time the issue is employee malfeasance, more than twice the rate at which external hackers are to blame (17%).
- Concern about fraud is dropping faster than fraud itself. Concerns about all frauds declined considerably this year with the two most common frauds, information theft, loss or attack and theft of physical assets or stock, registering some of the greatest decreases.
- Many companies have become overconfident about their vulnerability to fraud, which likely increases their risks.
- Companies that lose the most to fraud are those that are less likely to have fraud controls in place.

Source: Governance Research Digest, May 2013 (Vol. 4, No. 5)

6.3.4   Online Fraud Report

Author(s): CyberSource

CyberSource conducted an online fraud survey of U.S. and Canadian online merchants. "2013 Online Fraud Report – Online Payment Fraud Trends, Merchant Practices, and Benchmarks" is the 14th annual survey addressing the detection, prevention and management of online payment fraud.

Key findings

In 2012, companies lost $3.5 billion to online fraud, which accounts for an average of 0.9% of total online revenue, similar to 2010 levels.

*   Using 2012 industry market projections on eCommerce sales in North America, CyberSource estimates that total revenue loss translates to approximately $3.5 billion. Because the size of the overall market has grown, the revenue loss equates to $100,000,000 more versus 2011.
*   With international sales comprising 14% of overall orders (and even more so for the largest companies), fraud management mitigation strategies will need to be closely monitored and scrutinized.
*   77% of survey participants indicated that both fraud staffing levels and budgets would remain the same or lower.

Source: Governance Research Digest, May 2013 (Vol. 4, No. 5)

6.3.5   US Fraudulent Financial Reporting Analysis

Author(s): Center for Audit Quality, Mark S. Beasley (North Carolina State University), Joseph V. Carcello (University of Tennessee), Dana R. Hermanson (Kennesaw State University) and Terry L. Neal (University of Tennessee)

Center for Audit Quality commissioned a study which examines U.S. Securities and Exchange Commission (SEC) sanctions against auditors over the period 1998–2010 that are related to instances of alleged fraudulent financial reporting by U.S. publicly traded companies. "An Analysis of Alleged Auditor Deficiencies in SEC Fraud Investigations: 1998–2010" highlights insights for the audit profession related to eightyseven instances of alleged auditor deficiencies.

<u>Key findings</u>

The top five areas cited by the SEC are: 1. Failure to gather sufficient competent audit evidence (73% of the cases), 2. failure to exercise due professional care (67%), 3. insufficient level of professional skepticism (60%), 4. failure to obtain adequate evidence related to management representations (54%) and 5. failure to express an appropriate audit opinion (47%).

- Some of the deficiencies cited suggest a failure on the part of the auditor to discharge responsibilities with competence and diligence to the best of the auditor's ability, including the performance of procedures generally expected to be performed in an audit.
- Some of the cases highlight challenges in maintaining appropriate levels of professional skepticism that affect the auditor's mindset.
- While auditing standards have been risk-based for a number of years, more recent developments in the risk management arena, including the emerging discipline of enterprise risk management, are revealing a number of complexities associated with any risk identification.
- In some cases, the auditor failed to adjust audit procedures to gather sufficient competent evidence in light of risks identified and documented by the audit team

Source: Governance Research Digest, July 2013 (Vol. 4, No. 7)

6.3.6 Asia-Pacific Fraud Survey

Author(s): Ernst & Young, Asia Risk

Ernst & Young commissioned Asia Risk to conduct a survey designed to elicit the views of staff with responsibility for tackling fraud, bribery and compliance matters at multinational corporations, domestic companies and stateowned enterprises across sectors including Oil & Gas, Financial Services, Technology, Private Equity, Retail, Hospitality, and Mining & Minerals. The Asia-Pacific Fraud Survey polled 681 executives, senior managers and working level employees from March to May 2013 across the Asia-Pacific area comprises Australia, China, Indonesia, Malaysia, New Zealand, Singapore, South Korea and Vietnam.

<u>Key findings</u>

Weak systems and controls are exposing companies in Asia-Pacific to significant risks as internal controls and compliance programs are not implemented as thoroughly as they should be.

- The slower growth environment is putting management under pressure to take short cuts.
- Fraudulent practices are on the rise, and there is a disconnect between the policies that are in place and how they are applied in practice.
- Overall, one in five respondents considers bribery and corruption to be widespread in their home countries.
- Whereas if we isolate the rapid growth markets, where growth is relatively high but systems and procedures are typically less developed — such as China, Indonesia, Malaysia and Vietnam — the figure is closer to one in two.
- In Australia 75% of respondents do not appear to operate a whistleblowing programs.
- In China 34% still believe that company management is likely to take shortcuts when economic conditions are tough.
- In Indonesia 36% of respondents say it is a commonplace to use bribes to win contracts in their industry.

Source: Governance Research Digest, December 2013 (Vol. 4, No. 12)

6.3.7 Navigating today's complex business risks Europe, Middle East, India and Africa Fraud Survey 2013

Author(s): Ernst & Young

Ernst & Young produced a report that highlights the views of employees of large companies regarding fraud, bribery and corruption. 'Navigating today's complex business risks Europe, Middle East, India and Africa Fraud Survey 2013' research report is based on 3,459 interviews in 36 countries.

<u>Key findings</u>

One in five employees are aware of financial manipulation in their own company.

- This awareness increases to over a quarter of respondents in rapid-growth markets but decreases greatly when looking solely at the Swiss market with only 1 in 10 employees are aware of unethical conduct occurring in their companies.
- At board and senior manager level, 42% of those asked said that sales or costs had been manipulated at their company, while 57% believe bribery and corruption are widespread in their country.
- 38% of all respondents believe companies within their jurisdiction overstate their financial performance. Almost half the respondents in rapid-growth markets agree that companies in their countries often misrepresent financial performance, compared with 29% of those with headquarters in Western Europe while only 16% of Swiss respondents perceive that financial manipulation is prevalent in Switzerland.
- Risks of misreporting are compounded by an unethical business environment. While only 10% of Swiss respondents believe that bribery and corruption are widespread in their country, an alarming 57% for all respondents believe that bribery and corruption happens frequently in business in their countries.
- This number rises even further to 67% in rapid-growth markets. The proportion dropped however, to 26% (7% in Switzerland) who feel it is common to use bribery to win contracts in their own sector.

Source: Governance Research Digest, January 2014 (Vol. 5, No. 1)

6.3.8 Growing Beyond: A Place for Integrity 12th Global Fraud Survey

Author(s): EY

EY undertook the 12th Global Fraud Survey in order to understand views on fraud, bribery, and corruption risk and how organizations are mitigating them. EY interviewed over 1,700 chief financial officers and heads of legal, compliance and internal audit from 43 countries, to get their views of fraud, bribery and corruption risk and how their organizations are mitigating them.

Key findings

39% of respondents reported that bribery or corrupt practices occur frequently in their countries.

- In Brazil, 84% responded that corruption was widespread.
- 24% stated bribery and corrupt practices have increased because of the economic downturn.
- 15% of respondents are increasingly willing to make cash payments (up 6% from the last survey) in order to survive an economic downturn.
- 42% of respondents had no training on anti-bribery/anti-corruption (ABAC) policies.
- 81% stated ABAC policies and codes of conduct are in place, but nearly half tell us that they do not believe people have been penalized for breaching ABAC policies.
- 75% stated they use external auditors to monitor ABAC compliance.
- 33% use regular reviews by external law firms or specialist consultants.
- 27% believe planned investments by their company in new markets will open them up to new risks.
- 59% use the list of approved suppliers to manage and monitor relationships with third parties.
- 45% of respondents identified audit rights or regular audits of the third party as a process in place to monitor the relationship.
- 77% of US respondents report that pre-acquisition due diligence is always performed. This compares to a global figure of only 43%. Reports also indicate many are cutting back on pre-acquisition due diligence, especially in China.
- 15% of CFO's are willing to make cash payments to win business.
- 34% of CFO's are willing to entertain to retain/win business.
- 39% stated the company and the third party have joint liability for the actions of the third party.
- 52% of respondents think the board needs a more detailed understanding of the business if it is to be an effective safeguard against fraud or corrupt practices.
- 36% of respondents from Africa think regulators and law enforcement do not appear willing to prosecute cases of bribery and corruption.
- 90% of respondents from Brazil believe there should be more supervision by regulators and government in the future to try to reduce risk of fraud, bribery, and corruption.

- In Eastern Europe, only 14% of respondents think that national regulators were willing and effective in securing convictions. Of those who think the authorities were not willing to prosecute, 48% feel that this is due to bribery and corruption being too widespread.
- 70% of respondents from India think that bribery and corruption are widespread in the country and 72% believe that management is likely to cut corners to meet targets.
- 54% of respondents from India believe it is okay to entertain to win/retain business.

Source: Governance Research Digest, February 2014 (Vol. 5, No. 2)

6.3.9   Global Economic Crime Survey 2014

Author(s): PwC US

PwC US released a survey that details companies' changing costs from and perceptions of economic crime, particularly cybercrime. The 2014 Global Economic Crime Survey was completed by 5,128 respondents from 95 countries between August and October 2013.

Key findings

Economic crime is a persistent threat to business and business processes— 37% of respondents reported economic crime.

- The schemes used may vary, but the global threat remains— Respondents from 79 territories reported experiencing economic crime.
- Economic crimes of a "systemic" nature, such as bribery and corruption, money laundering, Cybercrime reports continue to rise. It is the fourth-most reported type of crime in this year's survey. However, cybercrime is not just a technology problem. It is a business strategy problem.
- Over the 14 years we have been conducting our Global Economic Crime Survey, the effectiveness of internal controls in detecting economic crime has improved. Respondents to this year's survey report 55% of instances were uncovered by internal controls, be they preventative or detective—up from 50% in 2011.
- The most damaging forms of economic crime exploit the tension between two equally fundamental business goals—profit and

compliance. Organisations with operations in high risk markets were twice as likely to report being asked to pay a bribe.

- Economic crime follows megatrends—such as the movement of wealth from the West to the South and East and the increasing use of technology platforms for all types of business processes.

- There was a relative increase of 13% in reported incidences of bribery and corruption since our last survey; the 17th Annual CEO survey reveals that more than half of CEOs are concerned about bribery and corruption.

Source: Governance Research Digest, March 2014 (Vol. 5, No. 3)

6.3.10 The Mobile Payments and Fraud Survey

Author(s): Kount, Inc., The Fraud Practice LLC, and CardNotPresent.com

Kount, Inc., The Fraud Practice LLC, and CardNotPresent.com conducted a survey focused entirely on fraud and the mobile channel, with nearly 2000 participants across the globe. Conducted from November 2013 to January 2014, The Mobile Payments and Fraud Survey included merchants, service providers, acquirers, card associations and issuers.

Key findings

While the mobile channel grows in importance and revenue for merchants, so does their fear of fraudulent attacks and the realization that combating that risk requires specialized tools.

- The mobile channel accounts for 20% of their business, double that of last year

- 66% of merchants surveyed now actively support mobile – up by 30% year to year

- Merchants that offer a mobile app for online shopping more than doubled from 21% to 54%, while nearly half of merchants now offer a dedicated mobile website

- 32% percent see mobile as riskier than standard e-commerce – up from 24% last year

- Merchants that believe standard eCommerce fraud processes are enough for managing mobile channel risk fell from 37 to 26% since the inaugural survey

- 32% say fraud prevention specific to mobile is increasingly necessary – nearly double the sentiment of last year's responses.

Source: Governance Research Digest, March 2014 (Vol. 5, No. 3)

6.3.11 Economic Impact of Trade Secret Theft: A framework for companies to safeguard trade secrets and mitigate potential threats

Author(s): The Center for Responsible Enterprise And Trade (CREATe.org), PricewaterhouseCoopers LLP (PwC)

The Center for Responsible Enterprise And Trade (CREATe.org) has collaborated with PricewaterhouseCoopers LLP (PwC) to assess the economic impact of trade secret theft. Their effort has culminated in a report that focuses on four issues that are critical to understanding trade secret theft and how to improve companies' ability to protect their most valuable information: an estimate of trade secret theft across advanced industrial economies; a threat assessment focusing on what threat actors are most active in targeting trade secrets; an original framework for companies to assess the value of their own trade secrets; and a look forward 10-15 years in the future to consider what forces and drivers may make trade secrets more or less secure.

Key findings

Estimates of trade secret theft range from one to three percent of the Gross Domestic Product ("GDP") of the United States and other advanced industrial economies.

- The national level estimate of trade secret theft is important as a guide to policy creation, industry awareness and advocacy, but is less relevant to individual companies.
- A company-level approach to estimating losses attributable to trade secret theft will drive more reliable national level results, but companies can do more than serve as the subjects of anecdotes.
- Increasing company-level awareness of the internal and external threat environment facilitates enhanced protection of trade secrets, an improvement in the quality of the national level estimate of trade secret theft over time, and the potential for a long-term reduction in losses.

- Modeling future scenarios highlights the drivers influencing trends in trade secret theft and provides insights that enable companies to create long-term strategies to protect trade secrets.
- Management will be better able to formulate and implement new strategies to safeguard investments and mitigate threat if armed with a greater understanding of current and future trends, threat actors seeking to engage in illicit activity, companies' own trade secret portfolios and organizational vulnerabilities.
- The challenge of trade secret theft is too large for any one government, company or organization to deal with alone—only a collective focus on this issue will help improve innovators' ability to secure their most critical information and intellectual property.
- This cooperative effort will be strongly aided by the investment of individual companies' time and resources to help to establish they know who threatens their own interests and how to measure the value of their own trade secrets.
- Replication of this sort of increased self-awareness across entire sectors would produce a detailed understanding of the collective threats and challenges,
- and the thorough extent of the value of trade secrets.
- Private sector companies—and other targets of trade secret theft—should approach this issue with a sense of urgency. Threat actors show no signs of slowing their attacks on trade secrets, and each new advance in technology brings new potential vulnerabilities with it.

Source: Governance Research Digest, June 2014 (Vol. 5, No. 6)

6.3.12 2014 Report to the Nations on Occupational Fraud & Abuse

Author(s): Association of Certified Fraud Examiners' (ACFE)

The Association of Certified Fraud Examiners' (ACFE) released its annual report detailing the current trends and findings in the areas of fraud detection and prevention. The 2014 Report to the Nations on Occupational Fraud & Abuse contains an analysis of 1,483 cases of occupational fraud that occurred in more than 100 countries.

Key findings

The typical organization loses 5% of revenues each year to fraud. If applied to the 2013 estimated Gross World Product, this translates to a potential projected global fraud loss of nearly $3.7 trillion.

- The median loss caused by the frauds in the study was $145,000. Additionally, 22% of the cases involved losses of at least $1 million.
- The median duration — the amount of time from when the fraud commenced until it was detected — for the fraud cases reported was 18 months.
- Occupational frauds can be classified into three primary categories: asset misappropriations, corruption and financial statement fraud. Of these, asset misappropriations are the most common, occurring in 85% of the cases in the study, as well as the least costly, causing a median loss of $130,000. In contrast, only 9% of cases involved financial statement fraud, but those cases had the greatest financial impact, with a median loss of $1 million.
- Corruption schemes fell in the middle in terms of both frequency (37% of cases) and median loss ($200,000).
- Tips are consistently and by far the most common detection method. Over 40% of all cases were detected by a tip — more than twice the rate of any other detection method. Employees accounted for nearly half of all tips that led to the discovery of fraud.

Source: Governance Research Digest, July 2014 (Vol. 5, No. 7)

6.3.13 Hiding in Plain Sight: Trade Misinvoicing and the Impact of Revenue Loss in Ghana, Kenya, Mozambique, Tanzania, and Uganda: 2002-2011

Author(s): Global Financial Integrity

Global Financial Integrity published a study that explores the economic and the policy side of the issue of trade misinvoicing using case studies of Ghana, Kenya, Mozambique, Tanzania, and Uganda. The study, Hiding in Plain Sight: Trade Misinvoicing and the Impact of Revenue Loss in Ghana, Kenya, Mozambique, Tanzania, and Uganda: 2002-2011, measured and analyzed the breakdown of each country's trade misinvoicing figure by under-invoicing and over-invoicing for exports and for imports.

Key findings

The fraudulent over- and under-invoicing of trade is hampering economic growth and costing these developing governments billions of U.S. dollars in lost revenue.

- Between 2002 and 2011, US$60.8 billion moved illegally into or out of Ghana, Kenya, Mozambique, Tanzania, and Uganda using trade misinvoicing.
- The potential average annual tax loss from trade misinvoicing amounted to roughly 12.7% of Uganda's total government revenue over the years 2002-2011, followed by Ghana (11.0%), Mozambique (10.4%), Kenya (8.3%), and Tanzania (7.4%).
- Policies to combat trade misinvoicing:
- Governments should significantly boost their customs enforcement, by equipping and training officers to better detect intentional misinvoicing of trade transactions;
- Trade transactions involving tax haven jurisdictions should be treated with the highest level of scrutiny by customs, tax, and law enforcement officials;
- Government authorities should create central, public registries of meaningful beneficial ownership information for all companies formed in their country to combat the abuse of anonymous shell companies;
- Financial regulators should require that all banks in their country know the true beneficial owner of any account opened in their financial institution;
- Ghana, Kenya, Mozambique, Tanzania, and Uganda should actively participate in the worldwide movement towards the automatic exchange of tax information as endorsed by the G20 and the OECD;
- Kenya and Uganda should follow the lead of Ghana, Mozambique, and Tanzania in joining and complying with the Extractives Industry Transparency Initiative (EITI); and
- Government authorities should adopt and fully implement all of the Financial Action Task Force's anti-money laundering recommendations.

Source: Governance Research Digest, November 2014 (Vol. 5, No. 11)

6.4 Responsible Political Involvement

6.4.1 2013 CPA-Zicklin Index of Corporate Political Accountability and Disclosure

Author(s): Carol and Lawrence Zicklin Center for Business Ethics Research and the Center for Political Accountability

The Carol and Lawrence Zicklin Center for Business Ethics Research and the Center for Political Accountability published a report that analyses how the largest U.S. public companies – the top 200 companies in the S&P 500 Index – are navigating political spending. The CPA-Zicklin Index looks at the companies' policies and practices for disclosing, decision-making and managing the risks associated with their political spending.

Key findings

Between 2012 and 2013, many leading American companies have expanded political spending disclosure and accountability, reflecting a sustained national shifting toward more comprehensive disclosure that further establishes political disclosure as a mainstream corporate practice.

- The number of companies receiving top-tier ratings for political disclosure and accountability increased dramatically. New companies advancing into the top tier reflect a continuing change in mainstream corporate attitude.
- Almost 70% of companies in the top echelons of the S&P 500 are now disclosing political spending made directly to candidates, parties and committees.
- Almost one out of every two companies in the top echelons of the S&P 500 has opened up about payments made to trade associations.
- Corporations have increased their disclosure of payments to nonprofit 501(c)(4) groups. These groups, often labeled "dark money" conduits when they make independent expenditures without disclosing donors, have increased significantly in number and magnitude.

Source: Governance Research Digest, October 2013 (Vol. 4, No. 10)

6.4.2   Influencing Climate Change Policy: The Effect of Shareholder Pressure and Firm

Author(s): C. E. Clark and E. P. Crawford

Environmental Performance Building on the corporate political strategy literature, the authors evaluate how firms choose to influence the climate change policies when faced with pressure from shareholders and activists. The authors triangulate firms' choice of corporate political activity (CPA) with their environmental performance to draw out whether performance affects the firm's choice of engagement level in CPA.

Key findings

The authors find that firms in the S&P 500 use a form of constituency-building (CB) more often than a financial-incentive (FI) tactic and that environmental performance moderates this choice.

- To date, there is little research connecting corporate political activity and climate change policies and performance.
- This research is intended to contribute to this literature gap.

Source: Governance Research Digest, February 2012 (Vol. 3, No. 2)

6.4.3   Bang for Their Buck: How Seven-Figure Donations from Clayton Williams Energy Are Driving the NRA to Turn its Back on Sportsmen

Author(s): Corporate Accountability International and the Gun Truth Project

Corporate Accountability International and the Gun Truth Project issued a report that exposes Clayton Williams' ties to the National Rifle Association and detail how the energy giant may be driving the NRA's ever-deadly agenda. The report, Bang for Their Buck: How Seven-Figure Donations from Clayton Williams Energy Are Driving the NRA to Turn its Back on Sportsmen, makes clear the full extent of the company's donations is unknown but may be as high as $5 million since 2010.

Key findings

Williams has not only given hundreds of thousands of dollars of his own money to support conservative political candidates and committees. Remarkably, he has also used the public corporation he manages – CWEI – to funnel millions of dollars to the NRA.

- In sum, CWEI has given at least $2 million to the NRA, making it the largest non-firearm industry contributor to the NRA. It appears that CWEI has given more money to the NRA in recent years than any other public corporation.
- The contributions from CWEI and those from oil and gas interests appear to have influenced the NRA's legislative priorities.
- For example, the NRA has backed legislation to enable road-building on federally-controlled lands – legislation that would benefit the energy industry, but would be detrimental to one of its core constituencies: hunters and sportsmen.
- The confluence of unusually large financial support from CWEI and lobbying activity on the roadbuilding legislation by the NRA point to one of two potentially disconcerting conclusions: either a public corporation is using shareholders dollars to pursue a personal political crusade on behalf of its CEO, or the NRA is promoting legislation that benefits a major corporate contributor to the detriment of its grassroots members.
- CWEI shareholders, which include public pension funds around the country, should be made aware of this political relationship with the NRA and compel the corporation to sever its political relationship with the NRA by divesting from CWEI.
- Meanwhile, the five million members claimed by the NRA12 should call on their leaders to stop promoting policies in their name for a quick payout from large corporations.

Source: CSR Research Digest, May 2014 (Vol. 6, No. 5)

6.4.4   Federal Transfer Report – Fortune 100 Companies

Author(s): Open the Books

A new venture called Open the Books released a report on how the US federal budget is spent. The report, Federal Transfer Report – Fortune 100

Companies, reveals how much the top Fortune 100 companies received from the government in the form of tax breaks, grants, loans and subsidies– what some have called "corporate welfare."

Key findings

$1.22838 trillion in The Federal Transfer™ spending (FY2000-2012) flowed to Fortune 100 companies – an average of $12.2 billion per corporation.

- 1.73%, or $21.277 billion, flowed to the Fortune 100 in the form of grants, direct payments, loans, farm susidies or insurance payments. The Fortune 100 each collected an average total of $212.77 million of federal dollars outside of contracts and should not be underestimated.
- The Federal Transfer™ into the Fortune 100 doubled during the eight years of the Bush Administration (FY2000- $59.820 billion; FY2008- $118.511 billion), but has been roughly flat during the first four years under the Obama administration (FY2009- $123.46 billion; FY2012- $124.055 billion).
- The Top Five Fortune 100 in Contracts: 1. Lockheed Martin ($392.039 billion), 2. Boeing ($269.623 billion) 3. General Dynamics ($170.469 billion), 4. United Technologies ($73.248 billion), 5. General Electric ($35.875 billion).
- Plains All American Pipeline was the only company in Fortune 100 receiving ZERO federal monies: searches for its subsidiaries and acquisitions also zeroed.
- General Electric received $35.8 billion- an amount equal to 7X more than the $5 billion GE 2010 profit.
- Legacy construction contractors at Walmart received $13 million in Small Business Administration "surety bond" subsidies.
- Ten Fortune 100 corporations rolled out their national distribution networks by subdividing their businesses to glean $250 million in Small Business Association taxpayer subsidized loans.

Source: CSR Research Digest, May 2014 (Vol. 6, No. 5)

6.4.5   The Myth of Corporate Disclosure Exposed

Author(s): Citizens for Responsibility and Ethics in Washington (CREW)

Citizens for Responsibility and Ethics in Washington (CREW) released a report exposing the failure of major corporations to keep their promises on political spending disclosure. The document, "The Myth of Corporate Disclosure Exposed" CREW compared political spending reports from 60 companies to contributions disclosed on tax forms filed by section 527 political organizations such as the Democratic and Republican governors' associations and found significant discrepancies for more than one-third of the companies.

Key findings

For 25 of the 60 companies included in the study, CREW found significant discrepancies between companies' reports and the 527 organizations' disclosures.

- 527 organizations reported contributions from 20 companies that had not disclosed those contributions at all.
- The significant discrepancies in political spending for the 25 companies totaled more than $3.1 million between 2011 and 2013.
- Among the companies included were:
- Microsoft, whose reports omitted nearly $1 million in political contributions to 527 organizations from 2011–2013;
- Pfizer, whose reports had approximately $395,000 in discrepancies between what the company voluntarily disclosed and what 527 organizations reported in contributions; and
- Prudential, whose reports differed from contributions disclosed by 527 organizations by approximately $211,000.

Source: Governance Research Digest, July 2014 (Vol. 5, No. 7)

6.4.6 Money in Politics with a Gender Lens

Author(s): The National Council for Research on Women, in collaboration with the Center for American Women and Politics at Rutgers University's Eagleton Institute of Politics and the Center for Responsive Politics

The National Council for Research on Women, in collaboration with the Center for American Women and Politics at Rutgers University's Eagleton Institute of Politics and the Center for Responsive Politics issued a report that compares data from the 2008, 2010, and 2012 federal election campaigns offering a "before and after" snapshot of the monetary environment of campaigns for men and women, but also establishing a strong baseline of analysis for future explorations. "Money in Politics with a Gender Lens" is the first attempt to explore the effects of the Citizens United decision by looking specifically at how women fared as candidates and acted as donors in elections held after the U.S. Supreme Court decision in 2010.

Key findings

Women remain significantly underrepresented among campaign "mega-donors," including top overall donors and top donors to Super PACs.

- Male donors outnumber and outspend female donors in reported political giving ($200 and over). Though the gender gap in political giving is significant at every level of giving, men make up an even greater proportion of donors at the highest levels (above $95,000).
- More men than women donate to outside groups. This gender gap closed slightly from 2010 to 2012, as overall outside group donations increased dramatically
- In both 2010 and 2012, men focused a greater proportion of their political giving on outside groups (versus individual candidates, party committees, and other political entities) than did women.
- Candidate gender was not a significant predictor of outside spending for or against congressional candidates in 2010 or 2012 independent of other factors, but there is limited evidence showing that gender does interact with variables like candidate status (incumbent, challenger, open seat) and party to influence the amount of Super PAC money spent in support of a particular candidate.
- It does not appear from these initial analyses that greater Super PAC spending will disparately reach men or women candidates, but further research is necessary after additional electoral cycles and with deeper analysis of the spending data and effects (beyond total and proportional spending).
- Women candidates appear more likely than men to support and participate in statewide public financing systems at the state legislative level, suggesting that public financing may be a particular incentive for

women running for office. However, analyses of candidate and representation data do not show strong effects of public financing on women's candidate emergence or representation.

- Men and women are equally opposed to increased campaign spending, particularly by outside organizations, based on recent public opinion polls

Source: Governance Research Digest, August 2014 (Vol. 5, No. 8)

6.4.7   Polluting Our Democracy and Our Environment: Dirty Fuels Money in Politics

Author(s): Oil Change International and the Sierra Club

Oil Change International and the Sierra Club published a report that demonstrates the enormous amount of campaign finance contributions pouring into US Congress by the fossil fuel industry. The report, Polluting Our Democracy and Our Environment: Dirty Fuels Money in Politics, asks the question: What if fighting dirty money in our elections was the key to fighting dirty fuels in our economy?

<u>Key findings</u>

The return polluters are getting on political investments — in the form of billions in corporate tax handouts — exceed 5,000%, demonstrating that Congress remains the best 'investment' possible for the coal, oil and gas industries.

- The oil and gas industries are among the worst offenders that spent $347 million on lobbying and campaign contributions and in return netted a handsome $20 billion in federal subsidies.
- Most of these came in the form of accounting gimmicks that help hide corporate profits and obscure tax breaks that help cover drilling and refining costs. Because of loopholes like these, the actual taxes paid by most big energy companies fall well below the top corporate rate of 35%.
- Solid majorities of Americans support action on climate change, investment in renewable energy and a repeal of fossil fuel subsidies. And yet, Congress is arguably in its most rabidly anti-environment phase in US history, voting repeatedly to block action on climate

change, cut support for renewable energy and hobble enforcement of clean air and water provisions.

Source: Governance Research Digest, August 2014 (Vol. 5, No. 8)

6.4.8 Silencing Science: How Citizens United and Fossil Fuel Campaign Cash Has Silenced Public Debate on Climate Change

Author(s): Common Cause

Common Cause issued a report that explores how political spending by fossil fuel corporations and related dark money groups have silenced US elected officials on the issue of climate change, almost as if the issue doesn't exist. The report, Silencing Science: How Citizens United and Fossil Fuel Campaign Cash Has Silenced Public Debate on Climate Change highlights that fossil fuel money pumped in the US political system remains the most significant threat to not only action on climate change, but even getting members of US Congress talk about the issue.

Key findings

The silencing of debate on climate change legislation – and the deep-pocket attacks on climate science itself – should serve as a loud warning about how powerful special interests and unlimited political spending can distort American democracy.

- While the problem of undue influence has been with the US citizens for a long time, the Supreme Court's recent radical decisions have unleased the power of big money in ways unseen for a century.
- in January 2010, just seven months after the U.S. House passed cap-and-trade legislation, the U.S. Supreme Court issued a ruling in Citizens United vs. FEC that took the lid off corporate and dark money political spending altogether by striking down the longstanding ban on corporate political spending and holding that independent expenditures will not corrupt politics.
- This new era of unbridled political spending comes at a steep price for the US nation and future generations.

- As the amount of special interest money spent to influence U.S. elections, and as global temperatures continue to rise, both the American democracy and our planet are at risk.

Source: Governance Research Digest, September 2014 (Vol. 5, No. 9)

6.4.9 The 2014 CPA-Zicklin Index of Corporate Political Disclosure and Accountability

Author(s): The Center for Political Accountability and the Zicklin Center for Business Ethics at the Wharton School

The Center for Political Accountability and the Zicklin Center for Business Ethics at the Wharton School released their fourth installment of the annual ranking of top publicly-held companies based on their voluntary political spending disclosure. The 2014 CPA-Zicklin Index of Corporate Political Disclosure and Accountability has this year expanded its scope from the top 200 to the top 300 companies on the S&P 500.

Key findings

Between 2013 and 2014, many leading American companies have expanded political spending disclosure and accountability.

- Noble Energy, Inc. and CSX Corp. both received a record high overall score of 97.1 points out of a possible 100 in the 2014 CPA-Zicklin Index of Corporate Political Disclosure and Accountability.
- With this sustained national shifting toward more comprehensive disclosure, more leading companies are establishing political disclosure as a mainstream corporate practice.
- Voluntary disclosure is making inroads among even those public companies that have not been engaged by shareholders to disclose.
- Among the top 300 companies in the S&P 500, 20 received top-five rankings for political disclosure and accountability.
- Increasing corporate acceptance of political disclosure and accountability spans industrial sectors.
- The top-ranked corporate sectors for political disclosure and accountability in 2014 are Utilities, Health Care,and Materials.

- Sixty-one percent of companies in the top echelons of the S&P 500 are now disclosing political spending made directly to candidates, parties and committees
- Almost half of companies in the top echelons of the S&P 500 have opened up about payments made to trade associations.

Source: Governance Research Digest, October 2014 (Vol. 5, No. 10)

6.4.10 Election Spending 2014: 9 Toss-Up Senate Races

Author(s): The Brennan Center for Justice

The Brennan Center for Justice issued an analysis that examines outside spending in 2014's nine most competitive U.S. Senate races, the outcomes of which will likely determine which party controls the Senate for the next two years. The Election Spending 2014: 9 Toss-Up Senate Races report describes the realities created by Citizens United by examining the races where it is likely to have the biggest impact in 2014: competitive races for the U.S. Senate.

Key findings

Dark-money groups that hide some or all of their donors accounted for $88.6 million, or 56%, of nonparty outside spending.

- In the seven races for which we have data on both candidate and non-candidate spending, dark money amounted to 24% of all spending.
- Our analysis does not include tens of millions of dollars spent on ads that are not required to be reported to the FEC, all of which is dark money, meaning the true portion of outside spending is higher.
- Outside spending in favor of Republicans is much more likely to be dark money, (80% of nonparty outside expenditures), than pro-Democrat spending (32% of which comes from dark-money groups).
- Single-candidate outside groups are active in every state in our sample, and they accounted for approximately half of nonparty spending in Alaska and Kentucky, as well as 30% in Georgia.
- There is more single-candidate group spending on the Republican side, at $20 million. Pro-Democrat candidate-specific groups spent $8.3 million. There is reason to believe the partisan difference is due to the fundraising success of Senate Majority PAC, a Democrat-aligned group

and the biggest non-candidate spender in our sample. Senate Majority has apparently attracted donors who might otherwise have given to Democratic single-candidate groups.

- Single-candidate groups that are also dark-money groups are a new phenomenon in this election. In our sample, six of the eight highest-spending candidate-specific groups hide some or all of their donors, including the top candidate-specific spender overall.

- Single-candidate groups depend heavily on money from double-dipping donors — individuals who have given up to the legal limit in direct contributions to the favored candidate's campaign. All but one of these groups got the great majority of their individual donations from maxed-out campaign donors.

- At least 76 donors gave money to single-candidate groups in addition to giving the maximum amount to either the favored candidate's primary or general campaign.

- Single-candidate groups also accept sizable contributions from corporations and unions, which are completely prohibited from giving directly to candidates. Some groups got all their revenue from these entities.

Source: Governance Research Digest, November 2014 (Vol. 5, No. 11)

6.5 Promoting Social Responsibility in the Value Chain

6.5.1 Responsible Supply Chain Ranking

Author(s): AMR Research

AMR Research has released it ranking of the responsible supply chain Top 25 for 2009. The annual Top 25 ranking identifies those Fortune 500 companies that best demonstrate leadership in innovatively serving customers.

Key findings

Rank	Company	Rank	Company
1	Apple	14	Nike

2	Dell	15	Tesco
3	Procter & Gamble	16	Walt Disney
4	IBM	17	Hewlett-Packard
5	Cisco Systems	18	Texas Instruments
6	Nokia	19	Lockheed Martin
7	Wal-Mart Stores	20	Colgate-Palmolive
8	Samsung Electronics	21	Best Buy
9	PepsiCo	22	Unilever
10	Toyota Motor	23	Publix Super Markets
11	Schlumberger	24	Sony Ericsson
12	Johnson & Johnson	25	Intel
13	The Coca-Cola Company		

Source: CSR Research Digest, July 2009 (Vol. 1, No. 7)

6.5.2 Codes of Conduct in Supply Chains Study

Author(s): L. Preuss.

This article examines corporate codes of conduct that stipulate CSR criteria for suppliers. Examining the ethical sourcing policies adopted by FTSE 100 companies, the authors draw out which environmental, social and economic issues large corporations perceive to be important in the management of their supply chains.

Key findings

Adopting an ethical sourcing code is not the only approach to addressing CSR challenges in purchasing and supply. Most sample companies have a range of other tools in place to address this aspect of CSR, such as general codes of conduct that guide whole company behaviour.

- Some companies, such as Shell, insert CSR clauses into supplier contracts. These can include health, safety and environmental criteria.
- Irrespective of such additional tools, a large number of companies – at least 44% of the FTSE 100 constituent companies – have adopted an ethical sourcing code.
- These codes achieve quite a comprehensive coverage of the CSR terrain, and tend to fall into one of three groups: employment conditions for

supplier employees; environmental protection in supplier plants; and economic issues affecting supplier firms.

- Working conditions for supplier employees have received by far the most attention to date, suggesting that FTSE 100 companies see employment issues as the greatest CSR challenge in their supply chains. In contrast, economic issues are only mentioned in isolated cases.

- Environmental issues occupy a middle position with some requirements frequently included, while most of the more concrete stipulations appear in a minority of codes only.

- The Base Code of the Ethical Trading Initiative appears to be a particularly influential model for FTSE 100 companies, although at the same time it is subject to a degree of adaptation.

- The public pressure model of CSR is noticeable in the prevalence of ethical sourcing codes among retailers and, correspondingly, their complete absence in hospitality or construction firms.

- At the intra-sectoral level, the mining industry shows evidence of how host country effects influence the range of CSR tools employed.

Source: Governance Research Digest, September 2009 (Vol. 1, No. 9)

6.5.3 Public Versus Private Sector Procurement Ethics and Strategy: What Each Sector can Learn from the Other

Author(s): T. G. Hawkins, M. J. Gravier and E. H. Powley

The purpose of the research is to explore differences between the for-profit and not-for-profit sectors on two critical aspects of business-to-business procurement: ethics and strategy. Using survey data from a sample of 328 procurement professionals in the for-profit and not-for-profit sectors, key differences are explored.

Key findings

Findings suggest that buyers in the for-profit sector are more likely to behave opportunistically.

- Conversely, the buyers' leaders in the not-forprofit sector behave more opportunistically and are more willing to turn a blind eye to their subordinate buyers' opportunistic behaviors.

- In addition, key differences in procurement strategy are unveiled suggesting that not-for-profit procurement practices have some room for improvement.
- Based on the findings, theoretical and managerial implications are drawn, and a future research agenda is proposed.

Source: Governance Research Digest, November 2011 (Vol. 2, No. 7)

6.5.4 When does Ethical Code Enforcement Matter in the Inter-Organisational Context? The Moderating Role of Switching Costs

Author(s): S. R. Colwell, M, J. Zyphur and M. Schminke

The paper draws on side-bet theory to hypothesize how switching costs influence the importance of a supplier's enforcement of ethical codes in predicting a buyer's continuance commitment to a supplier. Authors empirically test their model with data from 158 purchasing managers across three manufacturing industries.

Key findings

Results confirm the connection between ethical code enforcement and continuance commitment.

- However findings suggest that a supplier's enforcement of ethical codes matter less when switching suppliers is perceived as too costly.

Source: Governance Research Digest, November 2011 (Vol. 2, No. 7)

6.5.5 Procurement Report

Author(s): Eurosif

The Eurosif Procurement report examines trends and factors used in assessing responsible corporate supply chains by investors. It provides an overview of sustainability challenges and opportunities in global procurement and supply chain management.

Key findings

Responsible supply chain management is seen as a significant factor in reducing business risk and improving the attractiveness of an investment.

- A responsible supply chain takes into account environmental and social issues to reduce the risk of expensive business disruption.
- A robust supply chain audit includes:
  - an assessment of the extent of outsourcing and locations of suppliers;
  - corporate policies and standards;
  - effective monitoring procedures;
  - capacity building along the supply chain;
  - active collaboration with competitors and stakeholders;
  - clear product labeling.
- The report is mainly concerned with the textile and technology sectors though the the impact of responsible supply chain management, especially regarding environmental issues, is cross-sector.

Source: Governance Research Digest, June 2012 (Vol. 3, No. 6)

6.5.6 Corporate Perceptions of the Business Case for Supplier Diversity: How Socially Responsible Purchasing Can 'Pay'

Author(s): I. Worthington

This paper reports on a cross-national study of large purchasing organisations (LPOs) that had introduced, or were in the process of introducing, purchasing initiatives aimed at ethnic minority businesses (EMBs). The research investigates how LPOs portray the benefits of this form of socially responsible purchasing and highlights a number of contextual factors that appear to have shaped business case rationales. Businesses from the UK and US are used as case studies. Semi-structured interviews with procurement and supplier development specialists form the basis of the findings.

<u>Key findings</u>

Purchasing programmes targeted at ethnic minority businesses have the potential to provide a number of organizational benefits.

- These benefits form the 'business case' for supplier diversity and include:
  - Improved organisational performance. This includes reductions in total costs; access to markets that may have their own prerequisites

for dealing with certain countries; reduction of reliance on existing suppliers; and greater ability to embed the company in local markets or communities.

o Building stakeholder relationships. Many of the improvements in organizational performance arise, at least in part, from the capacity of an organization to enhance its stakeholder relationships via its supplier diversity programme.

- The ability of LPOs to do this is tied up with the knowledge and reputation they can derive from having a more diverse supply base.

- By engaging with ethnic minority suppliers, organizations not only tend to gain a better insight into the needs and expectations of ethnic consumers, but they can also create a reservoir of goodwill and trust within (and beyond) the minority community.

o Contributing to strategic objectives. For private, public and voluntary sector bodies committed to CSR, supplier diversity offers an opportunity to demonstrate their CSR credentials via the procurement process, while simultaneously leveraging the performance and stakeholder bene ts discussed above.

o For some commercial organisations, a supplier diversity programme is perceived as a way of achieving market development and expansion, by providing access to a previously untapped group of consumers and/or government contracts and more generally by contributing to local economic development and growth.

o Responding to a changing external context.

- A supplier diversity programme can be seen as addressing the problem of 'fit' between the organisational's internal environment (its resources, capabilities, structures) and its external context.

- As the ethnic population grows in size and in uence, and as social, political and legal imperatives point in the direction of greater equality of treatment for individuals, groups and organisations, corporate bodies will face increased pressures to examine their internal practices, processes and procedures, including their procurement policies.

Source: Social Research Digest, September 2009 (Vol. 1, No. 9)

6.5.7 Good Practices for Complying With Licensors' Social and Environmental Requirements: A Practical Guide for Licensees

Author(s): BSR / LIMA

The guide serves as a starting point for licensee executives and professionals to understand how they can meet licensors' requirements related to social and environmental compliance. It also provides guidance on how licensees can improve working conditions within their direct and contract manufacturing operations and supply chains.

Key findings

The primary audience for this guide includes licensees and their suppliers, subcontractors, and agents, and others involved in the production of licensed products.

- It contains more than 30 valuable tips and resources to help licensees and their suppliers:
  o understand licensors' general expectations related to human rights and labor practices, occupational health and safety, environmental compliance, and governance and anti-corruption;
  o integrate social and environmental compliance practices into their business relationships with suppliers, identify and understand compliance risks, and disclose factory information to licensors;
  o work with suppliers to address noncompliance issues and create corrective plans.

Source: Governance Research Digest, December 2011 (Vol. 2, No. 8)

6.5.8 Supply Chain PR and Risk Study

Author(s): Warwick Business School / University of Bath School of Management

The study by researchers from the U.K.'s Warwick Business School and University of Bath School of Management examined the motives of supply chain sustainability efforts. The paper reviewed 25 years' worth of academic and industry research.

<u>Key findings</u>

Most companies' efforts to improve their supply chain sustainability is focused on managing risk and public relations, not on actual improvements to the environment or worker safety.

- Instead of instituting preventative policies, companies use expensive and ineffective actions against suppliers after disruptions have already occurred.
- Many companies today talk about developing 'sustainable' supply chains, but they're actually talking about managing risk and preventing public relations crises.
- The result of their after-the-fact approach is that, in the end, nobody wins.
- Recent examples of companies that have failed to manage such issues include Mattel and Apple.
- Apple faced renewed criticism in 2011 for both possible environmental indiscretions and a lack of transparency in its supply chain.
- A few years earlier, in 2007, Mattel was forced to recall $100 million worth of product when one supplier used lead-contaminated paint on the company's toys.
- Whereas the best companies in this field think about their supply chains as opportunities for competitive advantage, and collaborate with suppliers to monitor progress and help them improve.
- The study advocates a baseline of minimum supply chain practices that all companies should embrace, based on four actions: establishing a code of conduct, obtaining thirdparty certification, selecting suppliers and monitoring suppliers.

Source: CSR Research Digest, April 2011 (Vol. 3, No. 4)

6.5.9   Best Corporate Citizens in Government Contracting

Author(s): Corporate Responsibility

The second annual Best Corporate Citizens in Government Contracting List is designed to encourage government to take transparency and responsibility data into account when making buying decisions. The magazine uses publicly-available data from Russell 1000 companies, collected and analyzed by leading ESG investor data firm IW Financial, and then identifies the overlap with the top 100 government contractors for FY2010.

Key findings

IBM, Accenture, HP, Merck, Dell, Boeing and McKesson have all held their positions among the most responsible government contractors.

- The overall disclosure performance of government contractors that are the most transparent about their corporate responsibility practices improved by some 5% over last year.
- At the same time, three-year average returns to shareholders of these firms outpaced the S&P average by .65%age points, or 32%.
- This proves that "transparency pays".
- The Top-10 companies in the rank:
  - IBM Corp.
  - Accenture plc
  - Hewlett-Packard Co.
  - Merck & Co. Inc.
  - Dell Inc.
  - United Parcel Services Inc.
  - Verizon Communications
  - Boeing Co.
  - AT&T Inc.
  - McKesson Corporation

Source: Governance Research Digest, July 2011 (Vol. 2, No. 3)

6.5.10 Codes of Conduct in Supply Chains Study

Author(s): L. Preuss.

This article examines corporate codes of conduct that stipulate CSR criteria for suppliers. Examining the ethical sourcing policies adopted by FTSE 100 companies, the authors draw out which environmental, social and economic issues large corporations perceive to be important in the management of their supply chains.

Key findings

Adopting an ethical sourcing code is not the only approach to addressing CSR challenges in purchasing and supply. Most sample companies have a range of other tools in place to address this aspect of CSR, such as general codes of conduct that guide whole company behaviour.

- Some companies, such as Shell, insert CSR clauses into supplier contracts. These can include health, safety and environmental criteria.
- Irrespective of such additional tools, a large number of companies – at least 44% of the FTSE 100 constituent companies – have adopted an ethical sourcing code.
- These codes achieve quite a comprehensive coverage of the CSR terrain, and tend to fall into one of three groups: employment conditions for supplier employees; environmental protection in supplier plants; and economic issues affecting supplier firms.
- Working conditions for supplier employees have received by far the most attention to date, suggesting that FTSE 100 companies see employment issues as the greatest CSR challenge in their supply chains. In contrast, economic issues are only mentioned in isolated cases.
- Environmental issues occupy a middle position with some requirements frequently included, while most of the more concrete stipulations appear in a minority of codes only.
- The Base Code of the Ethical Trading Initiative appears to be a particularly influential model for FTSE 100 companies, although at the same time it is subject to a degree of adaptation.
- The public pressure model of CSR is noticeable in the prevalence of ethical sourcing codes among retailers and, correspondingly, their complete absence in hospitality or construction firms.
- At the intra-sectoral level, the mining industry shows evidence of how host country effects influence the range of CSR tools employed.
- CSR risks turning into a competitive disadvantage for Western firms as it imposes additional costs that their developing or newly industrialized countries do not (yet) share.

Source: Governance Research Digest, September 2009 (Vol. 1, No. 9)

6.5.11 Public Versus Private Sector Procurement Ethics and Strategy: What Each Sector can Learn from the Other

Author(s): T. G. Hawkins, M. J. Gravier and E. H. Powley

The purpose of the research is to explore differences between the for-profit and not-for-profit sectors on two critical aspects of business-to-business procurement: ethics and strategy. Using survey data from a sample of 328 procurement professionals in the for-profit and not-for-profit sectors, key differences are explored.

Key findings

Findings suggest that buyers in the for-profit sector are more likely to behave opportunistically.

- Conversely, the buyers' leaders in the not-forprofit sector behave more opportunistically and are more willing to turn a blind eye to their subordinate buyers' opportunistic behaviors.
- In addition, key differences in procurement strategy are unveiled suggesting that not-for-profit procurement practices have some room for improvement.
- Based on the findings, theoretical and managerial implications are drawn, and a future research agenda is proposed.

Source: Governance Research Digest, November 2011 (Vol. 2, No. 7)

6.5.12 When does Ethical Code Enforcement Matter in the Inter-Organisational Context?

Author(s): S. R. Colwell, M, J. Zyphur and M. Schminke

The paper draws on side-bet theory to hypothesize how switching costs influence the importance of a supplier's enforcement of ethical codes in predicting a buyer's continuance commitment to a supplier. Authors empirically test their model with data from 158 purchasing managers across three manufacturing industries.

Key findings

- Results confirm the connection between ethical code enforcement and continuance commitment.
- However findings suggest that a supplier's enforcement of ethical codes matter less when switching suppliers is perceived as too costly.

Source: Governance Research Digest, November 2011 (Vol. 2, No. 7)

6.5.13 Procurement Report

Author(s): Eurosif

The Eurosif Procurement report examines trends and factors used in assessing responsible corporate supply chains by investors. It provides an overview of sustainability challenges and opportunities in global procurement and supply chain management.

Key findings

Responsible supply chain management is seen as a significant factor in reducing business risk and improving the attractiveness of an investment opportunity.

- A responsible supply chain takes into account environmental and social issues to reduce the risk of expensive business disruption.
- A robust supply chain audit includes:
  o an assessment of the extent of outsourcing and locations of suppliers;
  o corporate policies and standards;
  o effective monitoring procedures;
  o capacity building along the supply chain;
  o active collaboration with competitors and stakeholders;
  o clear product labeling.
- The report is mainly concerned with the textile and technology sectors though the impact of responsible supply chain management, especially regarding environmental issues, is cross-sector.

Source: Governance Research Digest, June 2012 (Vol. 3, No. 6)

6.5.14 Corporate Perceptions of the Business Case for Supplier Diversity: How Socially Responsible Purchasing Can 'Pay'

Author(s): I. Worthington

This paper reports on a cross-national study of large purchasing organisations (LPOs) that had introduced, or were in the process of introducing, purchasing initiatives aimed at ethnic minority businesses (EMBs). The research investigates how LPOs portray the benefits of this form of socially responsible purchasing and highlights a number of contextual factors that appear to have shaped business case rationales. Businesses from the UK and US are used as case studies. Semi-structured interviews with procurement and supplier development specialists form the basis of the findings.

<u>Key findings</u>

Purchasing programmes targeted at ethnic minority businesses have the potential to provide a number of organizational benefits. These benefits form the 'business case' for supplier diversity and include:

- Improved organisational performance. This includes reductions in total costs; access to markets that may have their own prerequisites for dealing with certain countries; reduction of reliance on existing suppliers; and greater ability to embed the company in local markets or communities.
- Building stakeholder relationships. Many of the improvements in organizational performance arise, at least in part, from the capacity of an organization to enhance its stakeholder relationships via its supplier diversity programme.
  - The ability of LPOs to do this is tied up with the knowledge and reputation they can derive from having a more diverse supply base.
  - By engaging with ethnic minority suppliers, organizations not only tend to gain a better insight into the needs and expectations of ethnic consumers, but they can also create a reservoir of goodwill and trust within (and beyond) the minority community.
- Contributing to strategic objectives. For private, public and voluntary sector bodies committed to CSR, supplier diversity offers an opportunity to demonstrate their CSR credentials via the procurement process, while simultaneously leveraging the performance and stakeholder bene ts discussed above.
- For some commercial organisations, a supplier diversity programme is perceived as a way of achieving market development and expansion, by providing access to a previously untapped group of consumers and/or government contracts and more generally by contributing to local economic development and growth.
- Responding to a changing external context.

- o A supplier diversity programme can be seen as addressing the problem of 'fit' between the organisational's internal environment (its resources, capabilities, structures) and its external context.
- o As the ethnic population grows in size and in uence, and as social, political and legal imperatives point in the direction of greater equality of treatment for individuals, groups and organisations, corporate bodies will face increased pressures to examine their internal practices, processes and procedures.

Source: Social Research Digest, September 2009 (Vol. 1, No. 9)

6.5.15 Good Practices for Complying With Licensors' Social and Environmental Requirements: A Practical Guide for Licensees

Author(s): BSR / LIMA

The guide serves as a starting point for licensee executives and professionals to understand how they can meet licensors' requirements related to social and environmental compliance. It also provides guidance on how licensees can improve working conditions within their direct and contract manufacturing operations and supply chains.

Key findings

The primary audience for this guide includes licensees and their suppliers, subcontractors, and agents, and others involved in the production of licensed products.

- It contains more than 30 valuable tips and resources to help licensees and their suppliers:
  - o understand licensors' general expectations related to human rights and labor practices, occupational health and safety, environmental compliance, and governance and anti-corruption;
  - o integrate social and environmental compliance practices into their business relationships with suppliers, identify and understand compliance risks, and disclose factory information to licensors;
  - o work with suppliers to address noncompliance issues and create corrective plans.

Source: Governance Research Digest, December 2011 (Vol. 2, No. 8)

6.5.16 Supply Chain PR and Risk Study

Author(s): Warwick Business School / University of Bath School of Management

The study by researchers from the U.K.'s Warwick Business School and University of Bath School of Management examined the motives of supply chain sustainability efforts. The paper reviewed 25 years' worth of academic and industry research.

Key findings

Most companies' efforts to improve their supply chain sustainability is focused on managing risk and public relations, not on actual improvements to the environment or worker safety.

- Instead of instituting preventative policies, companies use expensive and ineffective actions against suppliers after disruptions have already occurred.
- Many companies today talk about developing 'sustainable' supply chains, but they're actually talking about managing risk and preventing public relations crises.
- The result of their after-the-fact approach is that, in the end, nobody wins.
- Recent examples of companies that have failed to manage such issues include Mattel and Apple.
- Apple faced renewed criticism in 2011 for both possible environmental indiscretions and a lack of transparency in its supply chain.
- A few years earlier, in 2007, Mattel was forced to recall $100 million worth of product when one supplier used lead-contaminated paint on the company's toys.
- Whereas the best companies in this field think about their supply chains as opportunities for competitive advantage, and collaborate with suppliers to monitor progress and help them improve.
- The study advocates a baseline of minimum supply chain practices that all companies should embrace, based on four actions: establishing a code of conduct, obtaining thirdparty certification, selecting suppliers and monitoring suppliers.

Source: CSR Research Digest, April 2011 (Vol. 3, No. 4)

List of Organisations

ACCA (the Association of Chartered Certified Accountants)
Accenture
AccountAbility
ACCSR
ACE Group
ACGA
Acona
Adam Friedman Associates
Albert Luthuli Centre for Responsible Leadership
Aldersgate Group
American Society of Quality
American Sustainable Business Council
AMR Research
Article 13
ASEAN Capital Markets Forum
Ashridge Business School and IBLF
Asian Development Bank (ADB)
Association of Certified Fraud Examiners' (ACFE)
Association of Chartered Certified Accountants (ACCA)
Association of European Professional Football Leagues (EPFL)
Australian Centre for Corporate Social Responsibility (ACCSR)
B Lab
Baker & McKenzie

Baltic Institute of Corporate Governance
Barclays
BBMG
Beverage Industry Environmental Roundtable (BIER)
Black Sun
Bloomberg LP
Blue and Green Tomorrow
Boston College Center for Corporate Citizenship
Boston Consulting Group
BRANDfog
BRASS
BrownFlynn
Brunswick Insight
BSR
Business in the Community
Carbon Disclosure Project
CardNotPresent.com
Carol and Lawrence Zicklin
Center for Business Ethics Research
CECP
Center for American Progress
Center for American Women and Politics
Center for Audit Quality
Center for Corporate Citizenship
Center for Political Accountability
Center for Responsive Politics
Centre for Corporate Governance in Africa

Ceres
Christian Aid
Citi Foundation
Citizens for Responsibility and
Ethics in Washington (CREW)
Claremont McKenna College's
Roberts Environmental Center
Climate Policy Initiative
Common Cause
Compliance Week
Cone
Conference Board
Corporate Accountability
International
Corporate Citizenship
Corporate Knights Capital
Corporate Register
Corporate Responsibility
Corporate Responsibility
Magazine
Corporate Responsibility Office
CorporateRegister.com
Covalence
CR Magazine
CSR Network
CyberSource
Danish Ministry of Foreign Affairs
David and Lucile Packard
Foundation
DB Climate Change Advisors
(DBCCA)
Deloitte
Deloitte Touche Tohmatsu
Duke University
Ecofact
Economist Intelligence Unit (EIU)
Edelman

EIRIS
EKO Asset Management Partners
Emerging Markets Disclosure
Project (EMDP)
Environment Agency
Environmental Defense Fund
Environmental Investment
Organisation
Ernst & Young LLP
ESG screens
Ethical Corporation Institute
Ethical Markets
Ethics Resource Center
Ethisphere Institute
Euromed Management School
European Academy of Business in
Society (EABIS)
European Business Ethics Forum
European Commission (EC)
European Parliament
European Sustainable Investment
Forum (EUROSIF)
Fair Jewelry Action
Federal Trade Commission
Federal University of Ceará,
Brazil
Financial Conduct Authority
(FCA)
Forum for Sustainable and
Responsible Investment
Foundation for Financial Service
Professionals
Founder
FSG Social Impact Advisor
Fundacao Brasileira para o
Desenvolvimento Sustentavel
(FBDS)

G&A Institute

German Football League (DFL)

German Ministry of Economic Cooperation and Development (BMZ)

Global Compact LEAD

Global Corporate Governance Forum

Global Corporate Governance Forum

Global Financial Integrity

Global Impact Investing Network

Global Investor Coalition,

Global Reporting Initiative

Global Reporting Initiative (GRI)

Global Sustainable Investment Alliance

Global Witness

GlobeScan and SustainAbility

GMI Ratings

Gordon and Betty Moore Foundation

Governance and Accountability Institute

Governance Metrics International

Grant Thornton

Grayling

Green Growth Action Alliance Initiative & Accenture

Greenpeace

Gun Truth Project

Harvard University

Heart and Mind Strategies

ICCSR

IFC Global Governance Forum

IIRC

imug

Institute of Business Ethics

Institutional Shareholder Services' (ISS)

International Centre for Journalists

International Finance Corporation (IFC)

International Integrated Reporting Committee

International Integrated Reporting Council (IIRC)

Investor Responsibility Research Institute (IRRCI)

JPMorgan Chase

Kellogg School of Management

Kennesaw State University

Keystone Accountability

Korean CSR Research Services

Kount

KPMG

Kroll

Leeds University

Lifeworth Consulting

LIMA

LRN Knowledge Service Provider

Maala

Main Street Alliance

Maplecroft

MaRS Centre for Impact Investing

Mercer

Methodologie

Ministry of Statistics and Programme Implementation Government of India

MIT Sloan Management Review

MSCI

Nasdaq

National Statistical Organization
NAVEX Global
North Carolina State University
Northern Trust (NTRS)
OECD
Oil Change International
Open the Books
Oxfam
Pacific Institute
PE International
Portfolio 21 Investments
PricewaterhouseCoopers LLP
(PwC)
Principles for Responsible
Investment (PRI)
Purpose Capital
Radley Yeldar
RepRisk
Reputation Institute
Responsible Research Singapore
Responsible Sourcing Network
Rutgers University's Eagleton
Institute of Politics and the
S-Network
SABMiller
SAI Global
Security and Exchange Board of
India (SEBI)
Shell Foundation
Sierra Club
Small Business Majority
SMI
Stolen Asset Recovery (StAR)
SustainAbility
Sustainability Advisory Group
Sustainable Investments Institute
(Si2)

Sustainable Life Media
The Asian Development Bank
(ADB)
The Black Sun
The Brennan Center for Justice
The Center for Political
Accountability
The Center for Responsible
Enterprise And Trade
(CREATe.org)
The Center on Law and
Globalization
The CEO Water Mandate
The Chartered Institute of
Management Accountants (CIMA)
The Co-operative
The Conference Board
The Ethics Resource Center
The Ethics Resource Center The
Merck Company Foundation
The Ethisphere Institute
The Fraud Practice LLC
The GreenBiz Intelligence Panel
The Institute of Directors in
Southern Africa
The National Council for
Research on Women
The Nature Conservancy
The Network, Inc., and BDO
Consulting
The Reputation Institute
The Shared Value Initiative and
FSG
The SMI-Wizness Social Media
Sustainability Index 2012
The State Securities Commission
of Vietnam

The Taskforce on Social Impact Investment

The Toniic Institute—in collaboration with Duke University

Thomson Reuters

Thought Arbitrage Research Institute (TARI)

Transparency International

UKSIF

UN Global Compact

UN Office on Drugs and Crime (UNDOC)

UNDP

UNEP FI

UNGC / Accenture

United Nations Environment Programme (UNEP)

United Nations Office on Drugs and Crime (UNODC)

United Nations Principles for Responsible Investment (UNPRI)

University of Bath School of Management

University of California

University of Chicago Booth School of Business

University of Pretoria

University of Stellenbosch Business School

University of Tennessee

US Chamber of Commerce

US SIF Foundation

US Sustainable Accounting Standards Board (SASB)

Useful Social Media

Volans

Warwick Business School

WBCSD

Weber Shandwick

Wharton School

World Bank

World Economic Forum

World Growth

World Justice Project

World Resources Institute

WWF

Zicklin Center for Business Ethics

List of Authors

A-M. Schneider	C-A. Tetrault Sirsly	D. Sigurthorsson
A. Oravecz	C. G. Mitchell	D. Wood
A. Acevedo	C. Baan	D.-J. Lee
A. Amran	C. Caldwell	D.H. Schepers
A. Ardichvili	C. E. Carroll	Dana R. Hermanson
A. Gyzman	C. E. Clark	E. Bajo
A. Kolk	C. Fieseler	E. Cornachione
A. Lämsä	C. Garcés-Ayerbe	E. H. Powley
A. Martynov	C. H. Kim	E. Higgins
A. Millington	C. J. Resick	E. Lugli
A. Russo	C. Jia	E. P. Crawford
A. Singhapakdi	C. Lattemann	E. T. Vieira Jr.
A. Spiller	C. Müller	F. Farache
A. Vaccaro	C. Nigrisoli	F. Ahammad
A. Van Rossem	C. Peng	Sobhani
A. Van Witteloostuijn	C. R. Bateman	F. Albersmeier
	C.-J. Suh	F. Azmat
A. W. H. Chan	C.J. Rees	F. Damanpour
A. Zattoni	C.J. Resick	F. Küskü
A.B. Brik	D. A. Lamond	F. Magnusson
B. Burnes	D. Arenas	F. Perrini
B. Fasterling	D. F. Larcker	G. Ligeti
B. Kowske	D. Hillier	G. K. Henning
B. M'Zali	D. Hollingworth	G. Miazhevich
B. Neville	D. J. Taylor	G. Moore
B. Petracci	D. Jamali	G. Ormazabal
B. Rettab	D. Jondle	G. S. Martin
B. W. van de Ven	D. Malhotra	G. Svensson
B.K. Burton	D. Pearlman	G. Wood
Barbara R. Bartkus	D. Ramdani	G. Wood

G.F. Maggio

G.S. Martin

H-J.Ahn

H. Lafferty

H. Runhaar

H. Jo

H. K. Kwan

H. Leroy

H. Park-Poaps

H. Schulze

H. Sheth

H. van Dijk

H. Y. Cheung

Ho-Kong Chan

I. Alon

I. Barreda-Tarrazona

I. Worthington

J. Cohen

J. Azevedo-Pereira

J. C. Matallín-Sáez

J. Chen

J. D. Mahadeo

J. Fitzgerald

J. Gibbon

J. J. Graafland

J. J. Janney

J. Kujala

J. Li and T. Thakadipuram

J. Marta

J. Nilsson

J. P. Doh

J. Paauw

J. Sandström

J. Siddiqui

J. Singh

J. Woiceshyn

J.D. Chandler

J.D. Collins

J.E. Schroeder

J.F. Jaramillo

J.J. Wu

J.L. Álvarez-Arce

J.L. Graham

J.L. Murillo-Luna

J.L.Borgerson

J.M. de Sousa Filho

J.M. Lozano

J.P. Katz

J.P. Mulki

J.Y.J. Shi

José Luis Fernández Sánchez

Joseph V. Carcello

K-T. Hsu

K. Lamertz

K. Udayasankar

K. Amaeshi

K. G. Jin

K. Mellahi

K. Penttilä

K. Rees.

K. S. Grover

K. Uhlenbruck

K. Ye

K.L. Pedigo

K.M. Babiak

Kit-Chun Joanna Lam

L. Holder-Webb

L. Nath

L. A. Floyd

L. A. Perez-Batres

L. Alpkan

L. Preuss

L.S.O. Wandeley

Ladislao Luna Sotorrío

M-D. P. Lee

M-F. Turcotte

M. A. Harjoto

M. A. Keating

M. A. LaRocca

M. A. Trujillo

M. Barnett

M. Bigelli

M. Callaghan

M. Callaghan

M. Dickson

M. E. Palanski

M. Eckman

M. Elçi

M. Escudero Magnusson

M. Fetscherin

M. Fleck

M. Fox

M. G. S. Atakan

M. Goldsby

M. Gonzalez

M. J. Gravier

M. J. Pisani

M. J. Zyphur

M. Jun

M. Keeney

M. Meckel

M. Mueller

M. Pirson

M. R. Balaguer-Franch

M. Rhee
M. Rojas
M. S. Schwartz
M. Schminke
M. Statman
M. van Engen
M. Vilanova
M. W. Dickson
M.A. Keating
M.A. Naeem
M.B. Witek
M.E. Valdez
M.L-L. Lam
M.R. Melton
M.W. Dickson
Marcelle Colares
Oliveira
Mark S. Beasley
Myron Glassman
N. Forster
N. Kobeissi
N. Nohria
Nick Johnson
O. Osuji
P. A. Griffin
P. Broberg
P. Glasbergen
P. Gugler
P. Long
P. Maclagan
P. Merrigan
P. Perego
P. R. Woods
P. Rivera-Torres
P. Rodriguez
P. Schreck
P. Ziek

P.A. Marquez
P.Bouvain.
Pak-Wai Liu
R. Lucian
R. A. Bernardi
R. Ameer
R. Atkins
R. Barkemeyer
R. Cacioppe
R. Calderón
R. Drozdenko
R. Garcia-Castro
R. Holzgrefe
R. Khurana
R. Mitra
R. Othman
R. Samaratunge
R. Slack
R. T. By
R. Welford
R. Zhang
R. Zhang
R. Zhang
R.Bampton
R.H. Montgomery
R.L. Laud
R.L. Sims
R.T. Peterson
S. Brammer
S. Burnaz
S. Chen
S. DeLoughy
S. Ding
S. Du
S. Gove
S. Harris
S. Hayibor

S. Helin
S. Li
S. Mayoral
S. Özen
S. R. Colwell
S. R. Valentine
S. Scott
S. Seuring
S. Valentine
S. Y. Lee
S.O. Collin
T. Hill
T. G. Hawkins
T. Ozkaracalar
T. Simons
T. Soobaroyen
T. Tagesson
Terry L. Neal
U. Garay
U. Kocollari
V. Blank
V. Gomes de Santos
V. Marshall
V. Oogarah-
Hanuman
V. V. Miller
W. Tan
W. Y. Oh
W.B Locander
W.J.V. Vermeulen
X. Luo
X. Wu
Y-L. Cheung
Y. Fassin
Y. Gao
Y. I. Topcu
Y. K. Chang

Y. Kim

Y. Li

Y. Shin

Y. Sun

Y. Sun

Y. Zainuddin

Yadong Luo

Z. Rezaee

Z. Rezaee

Z. Wu

Z. Zhang

About the Editors

Wayne Visser

Dr Wayne Visser is Director of the think tank Kaleidoscope Futures, Founder of CSR International and Vice President of Sustainability Services for Omnex Inc. Wayne is also Chair of Sustainable Business at the Gordon Institute of Business Science in South Africa, Adjunct Professor of Sustainable Development at Deakin Business School in Australia and Senior Associate at the University of Cambridge Programme for Sustainability Leadership in the UK. Wayne is the author of twenty one books and has been listed as one of the Top 100 Thought Leaders in Trustworthy Business Behavior. Before getting his PhD in Corporate Social Responsibility (Nottingham University, UK), Wayne was Director of Sustainability Services for KPMG and Strategy Analyst for Cap Gemini in South Africa. His work has taken him to 70 countries in the last 20 years. Wayne lives in Cambridge, UK, and enjoys art, nature, writing poetry and travel. Much of his writing and art is on www.waynevisser.com.

Ileana Magureanu

Ileana is currently the research director for CSR International. She began her career as a researcher at the Romanian Institute of Soil Science and Environment Protection before working as an environmental journalist for Green Report, the first magazine in Romania dedicated to environmental issues. In 2010 she became an environmental assessor for the Green Revolution Association, an urban ecology NGO. Ileana has successful prepared applications for community projects that aim to promote a low-carbon economy and was also a key expert in the Green Business Index project, the barometer of corporate environmental responsibility in Romania. She is a certified CSR 2.0 assessor and advisor, currently managing Green Citadel, her own environmental NGO, which aspires to catalyse the transformation of resource-dependent human settlements into self-sufficient and nature-harmonious green citadels. She also speaks five foreign languages: English, French, Spanish, Portuguese and German.

Karina Yadav

Karina Yadav is a corporate sustainability and responsibility (CSR) professional focusing on sustainability agenda in Asia and Europe. Her main research area comprises of the state of CSR in India, including the role of the government to institutionalise CSR. Besides her research interest, Karina is managing India Business & Biodiversity Initaitive (IBBI), hosted by the Confederation of Indian Industry (CII). IBBI is a multi-stakeholder national platform for dialogue, sharing and learning on conservation amd sustainable use of biodiversity. Karina is Founder of an advisory firm CSRway. Prior she has served as Managing Director of the think-tank CSR International. She holds MSc in CSR from Nottingham University Business School's (UK) International Centre for Corporate Social Responsibility (ICCSR). Additionally, she has been a scholar at Blekinge Institute of Techology (Sweden) in strategic sustainable development.